HOMEWRECKERS

ALSO BY AARON GLANTZ

The War Comes Home: Washington's Battle Against America's Veterans

Winter Soldier: Iraq and Afghanistan—Eyewitness Accounts of the Occupations

How America Lost Iraq

HOMEWRECKERS

How a Gang of Wall Street Kingpins, Hedge Fund
Magnates, Crooked Banks, and Vulture Capitalists
Suckered Millions out of Their Homes and
Demolished the American Dream

AARON GLANTZ

CUSTOM
HOUSE

HarperCollins books may be purchased for educational, business, or sales promotional use. For information, please email the Special Markets Department at SPsales@harpercollins.com.

FIRST EDITION

Designed by Bonni Leon-Berman

Library of Congress Cataloging-in-Publication Data has been applied for.

ISBN 978-0-06-286953-1

19 20 21 22 23 LSC 10 9 8 7 6 5 4 3 2 1

For Jacob Mai and Louis Van
May you live the American Dream . . .

CONTENTS

THE AMERICAN DREAM

I AM ONE OF THE lucky ones. I profited off the housing bust. I leveraged the Great Recession to live the American Dream.

In May 2009, with the housing market in free fall, I bought a foreclosure. I scrounged money saved living in a nonprofit housing complex near the University of California at Berkeley, where I'd gone to school, and, with help from my parents, my wife's parents, and my grandmother, cobbled together a down payment on a two-bedroom house.

The house isn't much. It's boxy, a thousand square feet, up a hill on the southern edge of San Francisco, but from my favorite chair in the living room, I can see the Pacific Ocean. Like millions of other Americans, my home is now my primary source of wealth. It's my hope for retirement and my backup plan for financing my children's college education. Eight years after I bought it, my mortgage payments are lower than what many of my friends and colleagues pay to rent their apartments. In the morality play of recession and recovery, my experience shows the good guys can win, and the profiteers sometimes lose.

Before I bought it, the home had fallen into foreclosure, subject to a scheme hatched by three Filipino American women who flipped San Francisco real estate between one another, artificially driving up the purchase price. The first woman bought the house for $547,000 in 2003, quickly defaulted on the new mortgage, and then unloaded the house for the generous sum of $663,000. The seller repaid what was owed to the bank, but since the resale price had been much more than what she paid, the result was a huge profit. Given that banks pay the full amount of the purchase price to the seller, those earnings came out of the loans issued to the second buyer.

That was in 2004. The trio did the same thing again for $825,000 in 2007, just before the crash of 2008–09. Each time, property records show, the women put down almost no money. Credit flowed free and easy, and nobody from any of the banks appeared to ask any questions. Through this system, the women were able to clear more than $100,000 in profit each time they sold.

Besides this hustle, the women divided up the home, splitting the kitchen in two with cheap Sheetrock to create an extra bedroom. They rented the house out to undergrads from nearby San Francisco State University, who doubled up in rooms (and painted the living room a fluorescent-lime green). But the $2,500 the speculators collected each month in rent did not come close to covering their monthly mortgage payments, which—thanks to the ballooning purchase prices and ever-larger amounts of debt— came to nearly $4,000, excluding property tax and insurance. Again they defaulted on their mortgage. Previously, that might simply have been the cue to pull the same six-figure trick as before, but here the three women ran out of luck. When property values collapsed in the bust, the speculators were left without access to easy credit, and their small real estate empire crumbled. In April 2008, when they lost the house to foreclosure, the mortgage on the house was $44,000 greater than it was when they'd taken it out the year before. Nevertheless, in less than five years they had managed to pocket hundreds of thousands of dollars from banks that did not care if the loans they were making were in any way responsible.

"People were doing things they never should have been doing," our agent, Menelva Boyd, said when we told her about the scheme. Menelva, a sixty-eight-year-old African American divorcée from Tyler, Texas, was also a neighbor of ours in the nonprofit housing complex. She'd spent weeks driving us to open homes in her silver Nissan Ultima before locating this foreclosure—which was discounted on account of its confusing tenant situation.

My wife, Ngoc, and I hadn't been looking for a home on top of this hill. I wanted to live closer to the shops and streetcar line that ran down Ocean Avenue—from City College of San Francisco, to the tony neighborhood of West Portal, and then into a tunnel that sped commuters downtown each morning.

And yet, when I saw the house, I felt like we had won the lottery. A third-generation San Franciscan who has never felt at home anywhere else, I had previously given up the possibility of raising my own children in the city of my birth. Successive waves of gentrification had driven real estate prices far beyond the modest means of working journalists, and the housing bubble had made things worse. Now, thanks to the bust, a home had miraculously fallen into my price range. If I could pull this off, we would have the peace of mind that came with our own piece of land. We would know that if we worked hard and made our mortgage payments, we could never be evicted. Secure in the locked-in payments of a fixed-rate mortgage, we'd be able to breathe easy with the knowledge that there would be no landlord to skimp on repairs, jack up the rent, or try to force us out in favor of wealthier tenants.

Still, there were complications. I worried that if we did buy the house, we wouldn't be able to move in. The garage was full of junk hoarded by one of the women, a thin, forty-four-year-old with hip, rectangular eyeglasses, who—together with another one of the three speculators—had sold the home at a hefty profit in 2007, when all appeared fine in the housing market. Now she was claiming to be a tenant, creating a sticky legal situation that drove away other prospective buyers. But we needed to move. Ngoc was pregnant with our first child, and though we had rearranged our apartment to fit a crib in our bedroom, we knew we would soon need more space than our affordable-housing unit could provide.

Our families urged us to be aggressive. Ngoc had come to the United States as a refugee in 1975, the result of the courageous actions of her father, a lieutenant in the South Vietnamese navy. On April 30, the day Saigon fell to the Communist North Vietnamese, he loaded his family onto a boat and steered it to an American base in the Philippines. After the US government flew them to a resettlement camp in Arkansas, her family made a series of brief moves—first to the cold of western Michigan, where they were sponsored by a Christian family; then to not-much-warmer upstate New York, where they reunited with other members of the Nguyen clan—before settling in Southern California.

Ngoc's parents toiled for decades as factory workers in the aerospace industry. Her father, a swing-shift machinist, logged hundreds of hours of overtime, while her mother labored six days a week making brake parts on an assembly line. But like millions of other immigrants, their path to the American Dream also had a lot to do with savvy real estate investments. In 1979, just four years after they arrived in the States, the two pooled together their life savings—much of which they had carried out by hand in the form of gold bars as they fled Vietnam—and bought a small single-story bungalow near LA's Griffith Park for $24,000 in cash. By 1987, the home had already increased in value. So, they went to Bank of America and took out a $30,000 home equity loan to

finance the purchase of a Minimart and a small apartment building in the San Fernando Valley. Two more apartment buildings
followed. While the women who speculated on our house were
in it for the quick flip, Ngoc's family invested for the long haul.
They never stopped working their blue-collar jobs, and dedicated
their nights and weekends to maintaining the buildings themselves. They made money month after month charging rent on the
apartments. Eventually they sold them, using the profits to buy a
Laundromat and then a small medical building on Ball Street in
Anaheim—a stone's throw from Disneyland. As property values
increased, their wealth grew, their future secure.

"Buy property," was one of her father's favorite sayings. After
the crash, it seemed to begin every conversation. "You want to
find something in a neighborhood that's up and coming—not one
that's hot right now. You'll end up paying too much." Failing to
buy during the downturn, when the nation's housing market was
having a 50-percent-off sale, was simply not an option.

Ngoc's parents offered—or rather insisted—on helping us with
the down payment. "Think of your family. Think of your future,"
her father said. During visits to their Los Angeles–area home,
we spent hours looking at online real estate listings together. He
could talk of little else.

My own parents' story was less dramatic but offered the same
message. I was raised in San Francisco, the son of a nurse and a
college professor whose smartest financial decision had been to
buy a three-bedroom house two blocks from Golden Gate Park
in 1975. According to family lore, my paternal grandfather, who
lived in Toledo, Ohio, couldn't believe the $75,000 purchase
price and ranted that my parents had been fleeced. But with the
passage of years, the home proved to be a bargain. By the time
Ngoc and I began looking for a house after the bubble burst, my

parents' mortgage was all paid off. They, too, were able and eager to help.

So, on May 23, 2009, I walked six blocks to the credit union where I'd banked since I graduated from high school in 1995, and applied for a loan. The loan officer, Richard Ruiz, looked at our tax returns, the money we'd saved living in an affordable-housing complex, and the help we expected to get from our family. "Let me see what I can do," he said. A half hour later, he came back with a letter we could show to the sellers' real estate agent. We would become homeowners.

THREE MONTHS AFTER we bought the house, we negotiated the women's exit. After consulting a lawyer, I gave them three months' free rent—during which time they continued to pocket $2,500 a month from the San Francisco State students—after which they promised to deliver the building vacant.

When we moved in, everything was gone, including some of the things they were supposed to leave behind—a refrigerator, stove, and washer-drier—but we didn't make an issue of it, as the Obama administration was helping us remodel. The Internal Revenue Service sent a check for $8,000; technically a tax credit for first-time home buyers. We used the money to hire a family friend to paint the exterior, demolish the Sheetrock wall that divided the kitchen, restore scuffed hardwood flooring, and build a deck off a second-floor bedroom that provided access to the backyard. We were able to take a stimulus tax credit for that, too, for energy efficiency, because when adding the deck, we replaced old, leaky windows with an insulated sliding door.

This, of course, was how the stimulus was supposed to work. Many economists argued that these tax credits did little to help the recovery because they rewarded relatively privileged people—like me—who probably would have bought anyway. But knowing we would get an $8,000 stimulus check put us over the top in our debate over whether to buy the foreclosure. Once we purchased the house, it gave us money to put people to work.

It was a story visible all around our southwest San Francisco neighborhood. Soon after we finished our reconstruction, an elderly Chinese immigrant bought the crumbling home next door. He moved in with his grown son, a union member who delivered room service at one of the downtown hotels. They proceeded to fix it up, planting cherry blossom trees and African amaryllis in a backyard that had been overgrown with weeds. Through our son's day care, we met another recently arrived family: a community college instructor married to an urban gardener who ran a nonprofit that restored native plants. They, too, had combined frugal savings practices with family help to achieve the American Dream.

During this period, contractors' trucks were so ubiquitous in my neighborhood that I naively assumed the housing crisis allowed many young people like me to become homeowners. But as a business reporter writing for the *New York Times*, I came to see how rare my experience was.

Most of the people foreclosed on during the crisis were not scam artists but hardworking victims of a down economy, or decent people taken in by aggressive salesmen hawking predatory mortgage products. Big banks, which had received a multitrillion-dollar taxpayer bailout, did little to help struggling borrowers. In March 2010 the US Treasury Department estimated that six million home loans were at least sixty days delinquent, but the government reported that only 230,801 Americans had renegotiated their loans with the help of the Making Home Affordable program,[1] the part of the bank bailout that was supposed to help homeowners stave off foreclosure.

Getting assistance was hard for everyone, but institutional racism meant that African American and Latino borrowers, who banks had consistently given worse terms to during the boom, found it especially hard to access government programs designed to help during the bust. In surveys, housing counselors reported that as they dealt with the bureaucratic hell of recalcitrant banks' mortgage modification programs, their black and brown clients were far more likely to be told that the lender had lost their documents or that their applications were incomplete. The result was that while a majority of people who lost their homes were white, people of color were disproportionately impacted. As of June 2010 the nonprofit Center for Responsible Lending estimated that 11 percent of African American and 17 percent of Latino homeowners had already lost their homes or were "at imminent risk of foreclosure"—compared with 7 percent of whites.[2]

The story of Theodros Shawl was typical. Until October 2011, the forty-year-old chiropractor had owned a three-bedroom, two-bathroom bungalow in West Oakland, a hardscrabble neighborhood with streets lined with dilapidated homes that had long been a center of African American political organizing on the West Coast. In 1966, it gave birth to the Black Panther Party. Shawl bought the house for $335,000 in 2004, his first since emigrating from Ethiopia in 1990. In the intervening seven years, he'd rebuilt its foundation and replaced its aging plumbing and electrical systems. "I liked the fact that it was an older home that I could repair and paint and fix there on the weekends," he told me. "I was always at Home Depot. I was living the American Dream."

Shawl paid for that maintenance by taking out loans against the value of his property, which, on paper, at least, increased over time. Gradually, the amount he owed went up rather than down, and his payments increased. This wasn't a problem for Shawl, who made a good living. But in the fall of 2011, after he was sidelined with a wrist injury, he fell behind on his payments and lost the home to foreclosure. At the time, Shawl owed about $400,000. If Bank of America "had been willing to reduce my balance to three hundred thousand, I would have been able to afford to keep it," he told me. But the bank—which had been saved by a $45 billion taxpayer bailout[3]—wasn't willing to pass that relief on to him.

INDEED, MOST OF the beneficiaries of the foreclosure crisis were not first-time home buyers who secured a thirty-year fixed mortgage with family support. Instead, they were a new breed of corporate landlord that bought up entire neighborhoods and held the homes in shell companies, with the true identities of their owner unknown to most of the new tenants. In Oakland, for example, a nonprofit organization called the Urban Strategies Council found that between January 2007 and October 2011, more than 40 percent of the 10,508 homes that went into foreclosure in the hard-hit city had been purchased by real estate investors—usually with cash.[4]

After Bank of America took Theodros Shawl's bungalow, it sold it to a shell company called REO Homes 2 LLC, which purchased 171 foreclosures in Oakland after the bust.[5] The sale price? Just half the balance Shawl was seeking in mediation: $152,000.

Two months later, the company put the home back on the market as a rental, describing it as a "gorgeous remodeled Craftsman-style house" with a converted basement, a large deck, and a backyard. This turn of events confounded economic expectations. Rents were already high. On paper, at least, all the economic incentives favored homeownership. For example, Shawl's old home was listed for a daunting $2,595 a month—a price that would allow the new, corporate owner to repay the entire cost of the purchase in less than five years. Most of the other homes in the limited liability company's portfolio were being rented out at similarly high prices. Public records showed that, on average, the company paid $139,000 per home—meaning that if families had bought these houses with traditional thirty-year mortgages, they would have ended up paying about $600 a month, not counting taxes and insurance. By buying at the bottom, they—like me—would also have insulated themselves from rising rents, keeping down costs as the economy recovered. With each monthly payment, they would have been paying down the principal, building equity, and generating wealth to pass on to the next generation. Instead, all that wealth would go to the shell company's investors.

THE RISE OF these corporate landlords drove a generational transfer of wealth from hundreds of thousands of individual homeowners to a handful of well-heeled bankers and titans of private equity. But wasn't this just the way of the market? If someone wanted to buy one of those $139,000 homes, he or she just needed to get there first, before REO Homes or whichever LLC was trying to scoop up the local housing stock. The problem was that the system was rigged in favor of the speculators. In fact, as the years passed and the economy recovered and jobs returned, banks still refused to lend to individuals and families, and the nation's homeownership rate continued to fall, until, in 2016, eight years after the crash, it hit its lowest level in more than fifty years. Like the wave of foreclosures themselves, this credit desert particularly harmed people of color, with the homeownership gap between blacks and whites opening wider than it was during the Jim Crow era, when discrimination was legal and encouraged by the government.

These developments had sweeping implications. In America, the average homeowner boasts a net worth that is a hundred times greater than that of a renter: $200,000 for homeowners compared with $2,000 for renters, according to the US Census Bureau.[6]

This is not because homeowners make a hundred times more money than renters. (Homeowners take home about twice as much every month, according to the government.) Rather, it is because owning a home represents the only way for most middle-class families to save money. Researchers at the nonpartisan Brookings Institution found the average middle-class household spends nearly 80 percent of its income on just five essentials: housing, food, clothing, health care, and transportation. In other words, most of a family's money is gone before they can even think about going to the movies or sending their children to college.[7] The news gives us daily updates on the Dow Jones Industrial Average, but figures from the US Census Bureau tell us this is largely irrelevant to most Americans' savings plans. Indeed, only 20 percent of American families own stocks or mutual funds, and the average household has about $4,000 in the bank.

So, month after month, most of a family's income disappears. Clothing is worn until it is discarded. Food is eaten. Health care dollars disappear into the accounts of insurance companies and hospital chains. Gas money is burned up by a car that, if purchased, loses value the moment it is driven off the lot. Only housing, representing 35 cents of every dollar spent by the average middle-income family, has the chance to retain, or even increase, in value. Every month, when a homeowner makes a mortgage payment, she basically makes two payments. The first is a tax-deductible check to the bank that covers the interest, and the other is to herself, in the form of additional equity in her home.

By buying up large numbers of homes during the bust, real estate magnates removed properties from the market and stole this opportunity from millions of Americans. These speculators were part of a great but inglorious US tradition. In every generation, there are people who hold their money, waiting for a crisis, so they can pounce and profit off the pain of others, often creating financial dynasties that last generations. Their organized disaster profiteering has been with us since at least the Civil War. The Panic of 1873, a multiyear economic collapse spawned by inflation and rampant speculation by railroad tycoons, allowed John D. Rockefeller, founder of the Standard Oil Company, to buy out his competitors and corner the oil market, while industrialists Henry Clay Frick and Andrew Carnegie gobbled up large sections of Pittsburgh and its nearby mining assets and launched US Steel. President John F. Kennedy's father, Joseph Kennedy, famously shorted the stocks of America's largest corporations after the 1929 stock market crash and then used the Great Depression to amass an empire's worth of real estate, liquor companies, and movie studios.

The very phrase "American Dream" comes from this dark period, coined in 1931 by Pulitzer Prize–winning historian James Truslow Adams in an immodestly titled book, *The Epic of America*. An early selection of the Book of the Month club, it was a runaway best seller. What made the country unique, Adams argued, was opportunity. America, he proclaimed, was not like the Old World of Europe, where vast sums of wealth passed from kings, queens, and lords as a result of their noble birth. It was a place where success was based on hard work. "The American dream," he wrote, is a "dream of being able to grow to the fullest development as a man or woman, unhampered by barriers which had slowly been erected in older civilizations, presented by social orders which had developed for the benefit of classes rather than for the simple human being of any and every class."[8]

To some extent, that may seem like a call for unfettered capitalism and free markets, but Adams was a New Dealer who believed the government should intervene to make sure everyone had the chance to live the American Dream. "The project is discouraging today, but not hopeless," he wrote, as leaders "are beginning to realize that, because a man is born with a particular knack for gathering in vast aggregates of money and power for himself, he may not on that account be the wisest leader to follow nor the best fitted to propound on a sane philosophy of life."[9]

This vision of the American Dream wasn't against capitalism or moneymaking per se, but it was against amassing money simply for money's sake. It was in favor of a certain type of moral capitalism, where people worked hard not only to make money but also to help their families and their communities. For Adams, the stakes in curtailing the power of gluttonous billionaires were high. Allowing them to effectively own the country would be "the failure of self-government, the failure of the common man to rise to full stature, the failure of all that the American Dream has held of hope and promise for mankind."[10]

FROM OUR EARLIEST days in school, most of us are taught that the United States has always been a nation of homeowners and that homeownership is central to the American way of life. But the reality is that until President Franklin Delano Roosevelt launched his New Deal during the Great Depression, the franchise of ownership in America was overwhelmingly rural. Slavery and its legacy meant that very few African Americans owned homes, but nor did the vast majority of city-dwelling whites. For the first 150 years of our republic, the federal government didn't help city dwellers buy homes. It simply encouraged them to move. In 1862 President Abraham Lincoln signed the first of several Homestead Acts, this one granting up to 160 acres of land to settlers who farmed it for five years. "Go West, young man, and grow up with the country," the influential New York newspaper publisher Horace Greeley wrote in 1865.[11] Still decades later, homeownership remained scarce not only in a major metropolis such as New York City but also in small towns and frontier cities such as Omaha and Saint Louis, where the homeownership rates in 1890 were 26 percent and 21 percent, respectively.[12]

That year, the frontier "closed" with the displacement of Native Americans from large sections from Oklahoma, the last time the federal government would hand large amounts of land to white settlers by expropriating it from American Indians. The era of western expansion was over. The industrial revolution was pushing an increasing number of Americans to cities, as the United States was no longer an agrarian society. Three-fifths of Americans lived in homes that were not on farms, and, the Census Bureau found, 63 percent of them rented.[13]

Homeownership was available only to the rich, and the inability for most Americans to buy their own home was at the heart of the wealth gap. It wasn't just that wages were low; there was also almost no way for working people to finance a major purchase. Bankers such as the emerging John Pierpont "J. P." Morgan didn't make home loans that allowed working-class Americans to acquire property. Instead, their focus was large and industrial: they financed railroad barons, the builders of steel mills, and other tycoons of the Gilded Age. The mortgages that did exist were usually offered by builders and life insurance companies, but they were decidedly short term—usually no longer than five years— during which time many borrowers paid interest but very little, if any, principal. At the conclusion of the loan's truncated term, the borrower would be required to come up with the entire amount, then called a "bullet" payment. If the borrower couldn't manage that (and most usually couldn't), he could refinance into a new loan, also short term and including a bullet payment provision. Property values usually went up over time, and banks could always take the house if the borrower couldn't refinance. Still, the requirement to put down half the purchase price and repay the rest so quickly put homeownership out of reach. Hardworking families had no choice but to crowd into buildings that lacked proper plumbing and frequently caught fire. "Dirt and resolution reign in the wide hall-way, and danger lurks on the stairs," muckraking journalist Jacob Riis wrote in his 1890 opus on New York City tenements, *How the Other Half Lives*:

> The arched gateway leads no longer to a shady bower on the banks of the rushing stream, inviting day dreams with its gentle repose, but to a dank and nameless alley, shut in by high brick walls, cheerless as the lives of those they shelter. The wolf knocks loudly at the gate in the troubled dreams that come to this alley, echoes of the day's cares. A horde of dirty children play about the dripping hydrant, the only thing that thinks enough to make the most of it: it is the best it can do. These are the children of tenements, the growing generation of the slums; this is their home.[14]

The tenements' residents, Riis wrote, were hardworking families: Irish bricklayers, Italian produce vendors, and owners of Chinese laundries. "New York's wage-earners have no other place to live, more is the pity. They are truly poor for having no better homes; waxing poorer in purse as the exorbitant rents keep rising."[15]

Riis's work sparked outrage, leading to the creation of modern building codes and health and safety standards. However, neither Riis nor other prominent progressives of his day made the argument that these industrious Americans should be given a path to homeownership, so they could build wealth and pass it on the next generation. Instead, Riis offered this: "The tenement has come to stay and must itself be the solution of the problem with which it confronts us. This is the fact from which we cannot get away, however we may deplore it."[16] At the time, 1.5 million people lived in Manhattan, two-thirds of them in tenements.[17] The homeownership rate there was 6 percent.[18]

As even more Americans moved to the cities, the nation's homeownership rate declined further. Their incomes devoted to landlords instead of to mortgages, working Americans had no means to save, and wealth became increasingly concentrated. The federal government paid little attention—that is, until the 1917 Russian Revolution led politicians to worry. Income inequality in the United States had become so severe that comparisons between working Americans and the elites and Russian peasants and the tsar did not seem far off to many. When, in 1917, the US Socialist Party leader Eugene V. Debs declared "class war is our war and our only war" and opposed America's entry into World War I on the grounds that its proponents were "lined up side by side with the vultures of Wall Street . . . with Morgan, Rockefeller, Schwab [Charles M. Schwab, the steel magnate] and company,"[19] it resonated because those families had amassed vast fortunes, while the vast majority of Americans had almost nothing. According to researchers at UC Berkeley, the richest 1/10th of 1 percent of America's families held a greater share of the country's wealth in 1917 than the bottom 90 percent combined. (The Berkeley researchers found that in today's dollars, rich families were worth $65 million, on average, more than four thousand times the equivalent of the average of $17,000 held by the overwhelming majority of Americans. As I'll explain, the wealth gap narrowed over the ensuing decades, but the researchers found that most Americans began losing ground in 1986, and when the housing bust hit, the wealth gap exploded. By 2012, the top 1/10th of 1 percent again owned as much as the overwhelming balance of the American people.)[20]

President Woodrow Wilson argued that increasing homeownership was key to preventing Communism in the United States. People who owned property, the former Princeton University president reasoned, would be invested in the capitalist system. But Wilson did little that actually made it easier for families to buy homes. Instead, he pushed public relations over policy. In 1917 the US Department of Labor launched an Own-Your-Own-Home campaign, handing out "We Own Our Own Home" buttons to schoolchildren and distributing pamphlets saying it was a "patriotic duty" to cease renting.[21] Such impossibly aspirational trinkets were as far as the federal government was willing to go.

The effort continued in the 1920s under Herbert Hoover, who, as commerce secretary, headed up the quasigovernmental Better Homes in America organization, which likewise carried out a public relations campaign to promote homeownership. Problem was, there was still no way for working-class people to get loans without a bullet payment at the end of five years.

"The finance of home building especially for second mortgages, is the most backward segment of our whole credit system," Hoover, now president, fumed at a 1931 national planning Conference on Home Building and Homeownership. "It is easier to borrow eighty-five percent on an automobile and repay it on the installment plan than to buy a home on that basis—and generally the house requires a higher interest rate."[22] But despite his rhetoric, Hoover, like Wilson before him, did little to force the banking industry to help Americans buy homes. And as the Great Depression deepened following the 1929 stock market crash, his relief efforts focused on subsidizing financial institutions rather than tottering homeowners. Instead, in a move eerily repeated eighty years later after the 2008 housing bust, Hoover created a new government agency to pump money into banks, propping them up, with the idea that it would eventually trickle down to working-class families.

That did not transpire. In its first two years, the Hoover program received forty thousand applications from individual borrowers for direct loans. *Three* were approved.[23] Progressives, and some Democrats, called it a "millionaires' dole." And as with the Great Recession, activists argued that the banks' failure to lend to individual home buyers was holding back the entire economic recovery. "Millions of families would jump at the chance if homeownership were really put within their reach," the housing reformer Edith Elmer Wood wrote in 1930. "The building trades would go to work again, other industries would follow in their wake, and the present era of depression would be over."[24] But it would take a new president to help the country realize the dream.

IN US HISTORY, few policies have brought us closer to a universal American Dream than the New Deal. Though, as we'll discuss later, its appalling racism barred millions of African Americans from purchasing their own places to live—powering a racial wealth gap that would span the century—the impact of its housing programs was dramatic. Thanks to Franklin D. Roosevelt's sweeping plan, the US economy emerged from the Great Depression fundamentally changed—not only richer than when it began but also more economically equal, as white working-class families were empowered to own their own homes and control their own destinies.

By 1945, the year World War II ended—shortly after FDR's sudden death three months into his unprecedented fourth term in the White House—an astounding 50 percent of city-dwelling Americans owned homes. That figure rose to 54 percent in 1950 and surpassed 60 percent in 1960, by which time thirty-two million US families owned their own homes—twice as many as in 1940.[25] The postwar boom was a golden age in terms of prosperity and income equality. At the center of it was the way Franklin Roosevelt's New Deal made homeownership an integral part of the middle class. By the year 2000, more than two-thirds of Americans owned their own homes.[26]

This book is about the latest group of vulture capitalists, who were smart enough to pull their money out of the mortgage market before the Great Recession and then canny enough to jump back into the market in a stunning—and highly profitable—reversal. Throughout it, you'll meet businessmen (yes, all of them are men) who made billions betting big after the bust, often with the help of the government. Years later, they presented themselves as daring risk takers who saved the United States from economic disaster. But the truth is they took advantage of a rigged system, buying so low that they risked comparatively little, especially when we, the taxpayers, agreed to pick up their losses.

I call these magnates Homewreckers because of the way they caused and then profited off a historic decline in US homeownership. Though the ultimate owner of Theodros Shawl's home was a young speculator from Southern California, many of the biggest players turned out to be close friends and associates of Donald Trump, and, in many ways, their moves during the Great Recession mirrored those of Donald's father, Fred, who built the family fortune by buying foreclosures on the cheap during the Great Depression. It should not be a surprise, then, that Donald Trump cheered for a housing bust during the boom that preceded it. "I sort of hope that happens," he said in a taped conversation for students at his Trump University real estate seminar program in 2006. "People like me would go in and buy like crazy."[27]

Not for the first time, Donald was all bluster. His money stayed in golf courses and casinos, and one company, Trump Entertainment Resorts, declared bankruptcy in 2009.[28] It was his friends and sometime business partners who would buy homes and trade them on Wall Street. The Homewreckers had a lot in common with the future president. Like Trump, many were real estate moguls with Hollywood connections who regularly traded in their wives for younger models. And most of them maintained a residence in a small patch of Manhattan not far from his signature building, Trump Tower, which rises fifty-eight floors above Fifth Avenue in Midtown Manhattan—although, of course, that was only one of their many homes. Now, ensconced in power following Trump's election, these capitalists are creating new financial products that threaten to make the wealth transfers of the bust permanent. This book is that story.

THE HOMEWRECKERS

A CAST OF CHARACTERS

Thomas J. Barrack Jr., founder and CEO, Colony Capital; contrarian investor; chairman of President Donald Trump's inaugural committee

James Christopher "J. C." Flowers, managing director and CEO, J. C. Flowers & Co.; private equity investor specializing in financial services

John Paulson, founder, Paulson and Co., and hedge fund manager whose firm made $15 billion betting against the US mortgage market

Jamie Dimon, chairman and CEO, JPMorgan Chase, America's biggest bank by assets

Sean Hannity, Fox News personality, real estate investor

Jared Kushner, real estate investor, senior advisor to his father-in-law, President Donald J. Trump

Steven T. Mnuchin, US Treasury secretary; former chairman and CEO, OneWest Bank

Joseph Otting, US comptroller of the currency; former CEO, OneWest Bank

Wilbur L. Ross Jr., US secretary of commerce; founder, WL Ross & Co.; bankruptcy expert; buyer of BankUnited

Stephen A. Schwarzman, chairman and CEO, the Blackstone Group; buyer of BankUnited; investor in Invitation Homes

George Soros, Hungarian American investor who once "broke the Bank of England"

John Thain, former chairman and CEO, CIT Group; buyer of OneWest Bank

Donald Trump, president of the United States

Fred Trump, home builder, father of the president of the United States

HOMEWRECKERS

PART I

FINANCIAL FREEDOM

CHAPTER 1

THE SALESMAN

RICHARD HICKERSON WAS SEVENTY-NINE YEARS old, dying of cancer, with a lesion the size of a tennis ball that was slowly taking over his liver.

Dick, as everyone called him, had been a garrulous man. Generously overweight and given to wisecracks and Hawaiian shirts, he'd spent almost his entire life in and around Los Angeles, with the exception of the four years as a navy cook after World War II and the two years he worked in Arizona when his children were young.

Dick had lived a good life, retiring at age sixty-seven from a career at the local water department, but now it was coming to an end. His doctors prescribed painkillers to make his chemotherapy easier, but it wasn't enough. He drank, hiding spent vodka bottles around the house so that his children wouldn't see them.

His seventy-seven-year-old wife, Patricia, was also sick, three years into the downward spiral of Alzheimer's disease. A former executive at a company that printed personal and business checks, she had lost the ability to comprehend simple financial transactions such as making change or paying bills. On her worst days, Patricia experienced hallucinations. "Please, please—you have to come get me," she said during a call home to her eldest daughter, Sandy Jolley, after she was hospitalized for knee replacement surgery. "They have locked me in the basement with little children who are screaming."

When Patricia returned home from the hospital, she was docile, submissive, childlike. She stopped tending to the rose bushes she'd planted alongside the row of fruit trees in their backyard. She had enjoyed computer games such as Solitaire but stopped playing them because she could no longer do the math required to play cards.

The dementia was hard for Sandy to take. A fiercely independent woman, with straight black hair and intense brown eyes, Sandy had, at age fifty-three, moved back home to take care of her parents. She loved them, but the role did not come naturally.

Sandy had left home at nineteen for an ill-fated marriage to an airline pilot, divorced, and then raised their daughter, Kristin, as a single mother, spending much of the 1980s selling computer hardware up and down the West Coast. She was driven; the sort of woman who has an opinion about everything—a trait she tried to balance by rigorously practicing meditation and yoga.

Now, with Kristin grown, Sandy did her parents' shopping, paid their bills, and did their laundry—all while working as an event planner for an organization that sponsored networking luncheons for professional women at hotels and conference centers in downtown Los Angeles and Beverly Hills. However, her job allowed her to work from home much of the time.

Enfeebled by their illnesses, the Hickersons did what a lot of old people do as the end nears: they watched TV in the living room for hours. Dick would sit in his favorite chair, with his golden retriever, Travis, in his lap; Patricia, on the sofa. Dick usually picked the station. He loved reruns of *The Rockford Files*, a 1970s NBC drama starring James Garner as fast-talking Southern California private detective Jim Rockford, who deployed wordplay more frequently than his unpermitted Colt revolver. Another favorite was *Hart to Hart*, an early-eighties ABC crime show starring Robert Wagner and Stefanie Powers as a wealthy couple who often find themselves working as amateur detectives.

Dick Hickerson grew up in a solidly middle-class family. His father, Percy, owned a small tool and die factory. But according to census records, Percy rented the family home, a stucco, single-story Spanish-style bungalow in West Los Angeles, where he and his homemaker wife, Ella, raised Richard and his older brother, William.

Homeownership came by way of the GI Bill. When Dick returned home from the navy in 1954, at the age of twenty-seven, he and his new wife, Patricia, used a loan backed by the Veterans Administration to buy their first home: a single-story bungalow in the far-western reaches of the still-rural San Fernando Valley. As their family grew, and the equity in their house grew along with it, they got another VA loan to buy a slightly larger home in the horse-pasture suburb of Chatsworth. Finally, in 1980, they used a fixed-rate VA loan to buy the two-story home in neighboring Thousand Oaks, where they would live for more than twenty years.

The house lacked a swimming pool but was otherwise the very definition of the suburban Southern California domicile many Americans dream of. It was simple but spacious, painted white with decorative black shutters. There was a lemon tree, a hydrangea bush, and a wooden bench on the front lawn, and a two-car garage where Dick installed a workbench and they parked a late-model Oldsmobile sedan.

They lived on Benson Way, a side street just north of Highway 101, slightly up a hill. From their second-floor bedroom in the back, which faced north, Patricia and Dick could see for miles, past the future home of the Ronald Reagan Presidential Library, to the mountains behind, while a smaller front bedroom boasted a panoramic view of the Santa Monica Mountains.

They had so many memories there. The Hickersons built a deck, and for years, on the Fourth of July, they invited the entire family—their four daughters, one son, and eventually seven grandchildren, along with many of their friends and neighbors—over for a barbecue that ended with fireworks. As he grilled, Dick would crack jokes that, at least to him, never got old. One favorite: he'd yell for Patricia to get something out of "the icebox" just so he could hear her respond, in frustration, "We don't have an icebox; it's a refrigerator."

Now, such hosting duties beyond them, Dick and Patricia stared at the screen. Not only the same shows, but the same commercials played over and over again. The pitchmen were James Garner and Robert Wagner.

The two actors were selling reverse mortgages, a financial product available to Americans sixty-two and older that allows them to pull money out of their home. They are, as the name suggests, the reverse of a traditional mortgage. Rather than lending an amount of money that must be paid back gradually over time, with interest, the reverse mortgage company allows a senior citizen to borrow cash against their house and never asks for it back. Instead, the lender makes money by charging interest and fees each month and folds those charges into the principal. As time goes on, the balance grows larger, often far outstripping the amount of money the homeowner actually receives. When the elderly borrower dies, the loan comes due. At that point, the reverse mortgage lender is required to offer the house to the heirs—for either the size of the loan or 95 percent of the home's appraised value, whichever is smaller. The loans can grow so big that foreclosure is common, with the bank taking the house.

The Hickersons didn't need money. They weren't hurting for cash. Late in life, they had a $300,000 investment portfolio and received $2,600 a month in Social Security. They still owed $120,000 on the house, thanks to a series of refinances over the years, but they weren't underwater. They had about $400,000 in equity in their home, and their mortgage payments were well within their means—just $600 a month—which they paid using the interest from their savings.

Still, Dick was worried about his wife. How would she fare once he was gone? He'd asked his daughter Sandy to research what veterans' benefits might be available to her as a surviving spouse. Since Patricia had already been diagnosed with Alzheimer's disease, a preexisting condition, long-term-care insurance would not be available.

Garner represented the biggest reverse mortgage lender, Financial Freedom Senior Funding. The former Jim Rockford was an old man now, with a raspy voice and a grey, receding hairline. He wore a blue sweater vest and stared into the camera on an empty set with a digital image of the red, white, and blue logo of Financial Freedom Senior Funding waving like an American flag behind him. It was a soft sell, using the same sort of folksy straight talk Garner's characters used on TV. "I'd like to talk to you about something you should know. It's called a reverse mortgage," Garner said. "It's a safe, easy way to get tax-free money.

"Now, I've got to tell you I was reluctant to talk about reverse mortgages because, like a lot of folks, I didn't understand the facts," he added. "But as I learned more, I realized that this is something that many senior homeowners can benefit from. I sure think you should at least look into it."

Dick reached for the phone and called the number on his screen. A few days later, a packet came in the mail, and soon a salesman arrived at their door.

THE SALESMAN, LESLIE Barnhart, lived over the hill in Simi Valley, about ten miles away. He was new to reverse mortgages, having been trained at a seminar in Orange County the previous December. It was easy. There was no license or exam required to sell reverse mortgages. He was paid 100 percent on commission: $1,300 per transaction for loans based on preset appointments and $2,500 for cold calls. A veteran salesman in his midfifties, he also held a valid California real estate license and sold long-term-care insurance. The more he sold, the more money he made. On the other hand, if he failed to sell, he made no money, so while James Garner's television pitch was soft, Les Barnhart's was significantly harder.

His first visit to the Hickerson home was on Friday, March 11, 2005. The weather was sunny and mild, the high 66 degrees. Barnhart came with his standard presentation: a nineteen-slide red, white, and blue PowerPoint deck illustrated with stars and piles of cash, with text punctuated by exclamation points.

"With a Reverse Mortgage, you don't have to make monthly payments," one of the first slides read. "Instead, a Reverse Mortgage pays you!" Said another: "You can continue to live in the comfort of your own home and enjoy its full appreciation while receiving monthly tax-free cash advances and long-term financial security."

Barnhart's contract was with Pacific Reverse Mortgage, a San Diego company that sold loans to Financial Freedom the same day it made them. So, the salesman wasn't the only player whose interest lay solely in selling. His employer was also essentially a sales outfit. If Barnhart did his job and got the Hickersons to sign, Pacific Reverse Mortgage would never have to pay a cent—that would be the responsibility of Financial Freedom. The way the system worked, it wouldn't matter to Barnhart or his employer if anything went wrong after they originated the mortgage. By then, they would be long gone.

In his presentation, Barnhart downplayed the possibility that the bank might, in theory, take the Hickersons' home. The house would remain in their name until they both died, he said, and, at that point, their heirs would have the choice of keeping the home or selling it. There it was, in PowerPoint:

"How safe are Reverse Mortgages? They are totally safe. It is impossible to fall behind on payments because there are none to make."

"So, you ask, 'What's the catch?'" the final slide read. *"None."* The government, in the form of the Federal Housing Administration, "has designed this so there are no catches."

That Sunday, two days after his initial visit to the Hickersons' home, Barnhart was back. Dick and Patricia invited him to stay for lunch. He returned again later in the month and brought Patricia flowers. Each time Les visited, Sandy was out—either working or running errands for the household—and her parents never told her about the salesman's visits. She had no idea a reverse mortgage was even under consideration; she was primarily concerned with their health.

Then, on May 12, 2005, a day after Sandy took her father to the hospital, where he was placed under general anesthesia for a liver operation, Barnhart returned to oversee the signing of the loan documents.

Dick was home, recovering, when Barnhart arrived. The salesman came at 3:30 in the afternoon and waited 45 minutes for a notary to show up. Then the four of them went through the stack of documents and disclosures page by page. Under the terms of the reverse mortgage, the Hickersons' existing $120,000 home loan would be paid off, and $85,000 would be wired into their savings account.

That $85,000 would be all the money they'd get. Then the interest would start accruing, and the amount they owed would grow. Their reverse mortgage was an adjustable-rate product: the interest started at 4.8 percent but could go as high as 14.8 percent depending on market conditions. There were also fees—$17,443 to start—and more as the years went by. They also couldn't move, the documents said. If they both left the property, they were breaking the terms of deal, and the lender could take it in foreclosure.

Patricia and Dick initialed the disclosures and signed their names on the ninth and tenth pages of the loan document. Even in her frail state, Patricia exhibited exquisite penmanship; Dick's signatures were illegible.

Their businesses concluded, Leslie Barnhart packed up his material and drove off. It wasn't until a few days later that Sandy learned about the loan, when her father told her over breakfast. "I found a way to take care of your mother," he said. "I got a reverse mortgage." She didn't follow up, though, because in the same conversation, just a moment before, Dick had given Sandy a piece of bad news: he would be heading back to the hospital for another surgery. Despite chemotherapy, his baseball-sized tumor, which he referred to as a "spot" on his liver, was still growing. "The conversation was completely around his surgery and what that was going to entail," Sandy said later. Dick also suffered from severe heart disease and had already undergone many surgeries. "For some reason, this one scared me," she recalled. "It really worried me."

Her father's heart gave out during the operation. Sandy learned of his death at work. That day, June 21, 2005, she had started a new job: working the predawn shift behind the deli counter at Vons, a Southern California supermarket chain. The pay was terrible, but the shop was union, and the job offered health insurance, something she didn't get through her contract job as an event planner. It had been five years since Sandy moved home to take care of her parents, but at age fifty-seven, she also needed to take care of herself.

As fate would have it, Sandy worked for Vons only that one day—and not even a full shift. At five thirty in the morning, her sister Julie called Sandy on her cell phone to let her know the bad news.

Sandy left work immediately. She drove home to find her mother hysterical and inconsolable. Patricia said the hospital had called and asked what she wanted to do with her husband's body. She didn't understand why this would be. "Mom was very upset and mad at my dad for leaving her," Sandy said. "Over the next year, Mom said over and again how mad she was that Dad had left her. She just couldn't comprehend that he had died."

Six months after Dick's death, Les Barnhart sent Patricia a holiday card urging her to buy Juice Plus+, a supplement that purported to be "the most researched nutritional product in the world." In an accompanying letter, he claimed that the pills, which packed the "nutritional intensity of 17 fresh fruits and vegetables," had helped him beat colon cancer. "Dear Pat," the letter began: "This morning I realized that I needed to send you a letter because my health experience should not be kept secret! . . . As a valued client and friend, I'm extending an invitation for you to learn about something that has been of great benefit to me and my family." The letter was cribbed nearly verbatim from a DVD produced by Jack Medina, a strength and conditioning coach to many Olympic gymnasts. It was signed "Les Barnhart, Certified Senior Advisor."

WHEN THE HICKERSONS signed their reverse mortgage with Financial Freedom, they didn't know much beyond what the salesman had told them and what they'd seen in the ads on TV. They didn't know about the case of Lacy Eckhardt, whom *Washington Post* columnist Kenneth Harney wrote about in 2002. Eckhardt, a widow in Westchester County, New York, had received $58,000 in cash over a thirty-two-month period. When her home was sold a few months later, her family received a bill for $765,000.

"Sound like a nightmare? It's not. It's an actual mortgage transaction that a subsidiary of the Wall Street firm Lehman Brothers insists is legal, fair, and what the borrower requested," Harney wrote. "Welcome to the world of reverse mortgages, where poorly advised seniors—and their heirs—can lose tens of thousands of dollars almost overnight."[1]

FINANCIAL FREEDOM WAS no longer owned by Lehman Brothers when Les Barnhart got Dick and Patricia Hickerson to sign on the dotted line. Lehman had sold it the year before to IndyMac, a fast-rising thrift based down the road in Pasadena that would later become a poster child for the global financial crisis.

The reverse mortgage company was a natural fit at IndyMac, a corporate creature of the housing bubble, where the focus was on making as many loans as possible, as quickly as possible, and then making even more the following quarter. The company, which did not even exist in 2000, made an astonishing $38 billion in loans in 2004, the year it acquired Financial Freedom. That number would skyrocket by 50 percent the following year, to $60 billion. In 2006, at the apex of the housing bubble, IndyMac issued an astonishing $90 billion in mortgages.[2]

While some viewed Financial Freedom's products as usurious, IndyMac's CEO, Michael Perry, saw the potential for growth. "The acquisition of Financial Freedom makes us the largest provider of reverse mortgages in the US and illustrates our strategy of growing market share through niche products that complement our core competency as a single-family mortgage lender," he said in announcing the purchase. In addition, Perry had found a new market to tap. "With the maturing baby boom generation and the appreciation of home prices, the reverse mortgage market has the potential for very healthy growth in the years to come."[3]

Financial Freedom's reverse mortgage business took off. According to IndyMac's securities filings, it made $893 million in reverse mortgage loans in the second half of 2004, $2.9 billion in 2005, and more than $5 billion in 2006.[4] Its CEO said it controlled more than half of all reverse mortgages in America. By 2008, it had a portfolio of 160,000 reverse mortgage loans valued at $20 billion.[5] The financial press treated Perry like a boy wonder. In one profile, he was pictured behind his desk with a goofy smile, his shoes on his desk with the soles of his wing tips facing the camera, giving a double thumbs-up.[6] His final five-year contract, signed in September 2006, primarily rewarded Perry for growing the company. Although his base salary was $1.2 million a year, he could earn close to $9 million if he hit certain growth targets, encouraging him to sell, sell, sell. It didn't matter how. It didn't matter to whom.

The company's board, like the rest of the financial sector, saw nothing wrong with such incentives. "In addition to achieving stellar financial performance, Mike Perry conducts himself with the highest levels of ethics," IndyMac board member John Seymour, a former US senator from California, said as he announced the contract.[7]

But IndyMac's specular growth was a house of cards. Its focus on sales, which was replicated throughout the lending industry, was the foundation not for middle-class prosperity but for economic disaster.

LIKE MOST BANKS during the boom, IndyMac didn't keep most of the loans it originated. It bundled them into what were known as mortgage-backed securities, which were then sold off to investors. This meant that, institutionally, the bank didn't really care if the loans it originated were good or bad, or even whether they would be paid back—that would be an issue for those who purchased the bundles.

All of this upended the historical calculus of banking that we learn in elementary school: where banks made money by charging borrowers interest, which in the case of homeowners was paid back month after month as part of his or her mortgage payment. A $100,000, thirty-year fixed-rate mortgage lent out at 5 percent would generate $92,000 in interest over the life of the loan, or nearly double the amount lent. Working families got to own their own patch of land, and banks made money—so long as both behaved responsibly and neither got greedy. Many banks were community institutions where loan officers knew their customers. At IndyMac, that virtuous circle was broken. All the interest charged on the home loan was being captured by the distant owners of mortgage-backed securities. Banks such as IndyMac had essentially become salesmen, reliant on fees they charged for each mortgage at the moment of origination and sale to the securities market. The investors who bought those securities were told they were buying bundles of loans that would generate steady returns over time, but, institutionally, the IndyMac salesmen didn't really care. The more mortgages they sold, the more money they made, plain and simple.

Given that the old model made a lot of financial sense—after all, banks were able to dependably double their money over time—it might seem odd that IndyMac would want to sell these loans to someone else. But returns that accrued over decades were of no interest to Perry and his supporters. What mattered were profits right now. Others could worry about the fate of the homeowners.

Think about the 1946 Frank Capra holiday classic *It's a Wonderful Life* and how it might have been different had it been made about IndyMac. The film stars Jimmy Stewart as George Bailey, whose family-owned savings institution is coveted by the villainous Mr. Potter (Lionel Barrymore), a much wealthier man who sits on the bank's board of directors. Early in the film, the Jimmy Stewart character tears into Mr. Potter for criticizing a home loan Bailey made to his friend, taxi driver Ernie Bishop, whom Potter dismisses as "discontented lazy rabble."

Bailey tells Potter and the bank's other board members that the townsfolk in Bedford Falls work hard and deserve to own their own homes. Yes, he says, he has "all the papers" proving that the borrower has the means to repay the loans. But for him, being a banker wasn't primarily about making money. Lending money to potential homeowners was also a fundamentally moral endeavor. "Doesn't it make them better citizens? Doesn't it make them better customers?" he asks rhetorically. "Just remember this, Mr. Potter, that this rabble you're talking about, they do most of the working and paying and living and dying in this community. Well, is it too much for them to work and live and die in a couple of decent rooms and a bath?"[8]

At IndyMac, however, Bailey would have given an entirely different speech. He would have told Mr. Potter that the company's loan to Ernie Bishop wasn't a long-term bet on the health of a community but a short-term way to make a quick buck. In this twenty-first-century version of the film, Bailey might have bragged that he'd charged the taxi driver hefty origination fees, and that approving the loan had helped him exceed his sales targets. He would have told Mr. Potter that the loan, like the rest of the mortgages he'd issued in Bedford Falls, were already off the bank's books, sold in bulk to someone else—perhaps a foreign billionaire or a teachers' pension fund in California. But it didn't really matter who, he would tell Mr. Potter, because George Bailey and the bank were making money on fees. One can only imagine that Mr. Potter, obsessed with profits to the exclusion of all else, would have quickly agreed that young Bailey was on to something good.

That's how IndyMac operated. Along with reverse mortgages, one of the bank's specialties was the Alt-A mortgage, nicknamed "liar loans" and "ninja loans" (no income, no job, no assets) by critics, because many borrowers lied about their income, and the bank didn't check. The point was to make the loan. Period.

Adjustable-rate mortgages, which often included hefty balloon payments, where borrowers were required to pay off most or all of the loan at once, represented three-quarters of the loans IndyMac made between 2004 and 2006.[9] Another specialty was loans with no down payment, where the home buyer would simultaneously take out two loans from IndyMac, one for 80 percent and another for the remaining 20 percent.

More than a third of IndyMac's loans were interest only, meaning the borrower was allowed to make a "minimum payment" covering only a portion of the interest on a mortgage. Like a high-interest credit card, the amount of money the borrower owed would grow larger each month, so even as the mortgage holder made payments, the house would not be paid off. If the taxi driver in *It's a Wonderful Life* had received this loan, he would never have been able to own his home free and clear. At IndyMac, salesmen told borrowers that this was no problem. After all, they could always refinance into a new loan later—because the value of their property was sure to go up.

An investor in Bedford Falls would quickly know if the houses George Bailey built were worth more than their mortgage, but the international investors who snapped up tranches of IndyMac's mortgage-backed securities frequently knew nothing about the assets or even the basic economics of the US mortgage market. (*Tranche* is a French word meaning "slice.") "The whole securitization process depended on the greater fool theory—that there were fools who could be sold the toxic mortgages and the dangerous pieces of paper that were based on them," Nobel Prize–winning economist Joseph Stiglitz explained in his 2010 book *Freefall: America's Free Markets, and the Sinking of the World Economy.* "Globalization had opened up a whole world of fools."[10]

FARAWAY BUYERS THOUGHT they were making a good investment on IndyMac's mortgage-backed securities, because the institutions who were supposed to vet them for quality told them they were likely to make money when the bonds were paid back with interest. But the bond rating agencies, which were supposed to provide a check on IndyMac's lending by inspecting its mortgage-backed securities, blindly gave their stamp of approval to bundles of junk. In April 2006, for example, one of the leading rating agencies, Moody's, examined a $374 million package of IndyMac's Alt-A mortgages— liar loans—and rated the entire bundle AAA,[11] "judged to be the highest quality, with minimal risk."[12] Like the rest of the industry, the incentives for these rating agencies were all wrong. The bond raters were paid by fees from banks. If Moody's and the others downgraded IndyMac's securities, they could have lost business.

All of that was great for Michael Perry—until suddenly it wasn't. Borrowers began suing IndyMac, claiming they were tricked into predatory financial products they did not want or, even more seriously, that their loan documents had been falsified. According to one shareholder lawsuit filed in March 2007, a former fraud investigator at the thrift said employees had taken to calling poorly documented loans "Disneyland loans"—a reference to a mortgage issued to a Magic Kingdom cashier whose application claimed an income of $90,000 a year, "a proposition that, on its face, belies logic and common sense." Another witness in the case, a former vice president at the bank, said that Perry and other top managers focused on increasing loan volume "at all costs," and put pressure on subordinates to disregard company policies and simply "push loans through." A third ex-employee quoted in the suit claimed that Perry told him "business guys rule . . . fuck you compliance guys." It was "production and nothing else," he said.[13]

IndyMac contested the complaints brought by its borrowers

and shareholders and dismissed employees' statements as a mish-mash of hearsay and speculation, "long on words and short on substance" and "full of meaningless filler." But the writing was on the wall. With real estate prices slipping, the company could no longer sell its mortgage-backed securities and was forced to hold on to its bad loans. IndyMac turned a $343 million profit in 2006 but lost $509 million in the final three months of 2007 alone.[14]

Though the company told shareholders it was poised to return to profitability, officials in Washington had finally begun to take notice. At a March 2008 meeting of federal banking regulators, Sheila Bair, the chair of the Federal Deposit Insurance Corporation (FDIC), the government agency that backs up consumer deposits, shared an internal staff analysis predicting that IndyMac would fail by the end of the year. It crashed even faster, before anyone was punished.[15]

CHAPTER 2

A SQUANDERED OPPORTUNITY

THE FACTORS THAT LED TO IndyMac's demise were endemic in the mortgage market. Across the industry, the thirty-year fixed mortgage with a solid down payment had become more the exception than the rule. The subprime and Alt-A categories together composed more than 40 percent of the loans issued at the peak of the bubble in 2006. Loans requiring limited documentation had expanded from 27 percent of the mortgages issued in 2001 to 44 percent in 2006. The share of homes purchased with 100 percent financing skyrocketed, from one out of every thirty in 2003 to one in three in 2006.[1]

As the bubble burst and foreclosures multiplied, policy makers and academics began to scramble for solutions—and a number of them turned to the Great Depression, the only other time in American history to see such a spectacular collapse in the housing market.

"Ah, yes: interest-only loans, balloon payments, the assumption of rising house prices, and firm belief in the easy availability of the next 'refi.' This may sound familiar," Alex Pollock, a fellow at the conservative American Enterprise Institute wrote in December 2007, when the housing market had softened but hadn't yet begun to crash. The parallels he envisioned were terrifying:

> Then came massive defaults, falling prices, and a debt deflation's downward spiral: mortgage defaults, tightening credit, reduced demand for houses, foreclosures, falling house prices, greater defaults, failure of lenders, even less credit further reduced demand, more foreclosures, foreclosed properties creating greater supply for sale, further falling prices, more defaults, failure of more lenders, no credit, further falling prices, and the resulting "frozen" markets.[2]

To prevent a second Great Depression, Pollock, the former CEO of the Federal Home Loan Bank of Chicago, suggested that Congress relaunch Franklin Delano Roosevelt's fix: the Home Owners' Loan Corporation (HOLC), a government-run company that bought bad loans off banks for pennies on the dollar. The government bank was able to pay just pennies because the banks had no other options. If they hadn't taken the government's cash, they would have ended up with nothing. Having bought the loans cheaply, the HOLC then issued new, long-term mortgages back to the original homeowner at low interest rates.

The HOLC was part of a new promise promulgated by the thirty-second president. On April 13, 1933, barely a month into his administration, FDR sent Congress a letter demanding a radical change: "a declaration of national policy" that homeownership needed to be preserved "as a guarantee of social and economic stability."[3] Funded with $200 million of taxpayers' money and authorized to raise $2 billion more in the bond market,[4] the HOLC saved more than a million families from foreclosure.[5] It helped refinance one in five mortgages in urban America[6] and relegated short-term loans that required 50 percent down to the dustbin of history. The impact it had on homeownership was revolutionary for the country's white majority; African American and many immigrant groups were denied access. The new law institutionalized the 20 percent down payment and created the sort of long-term, fixed-interest-rate home loans we think of as normal today. Also, importantly to Pollock, because most consumers paid their HOLC loan back with interest, it returned a modest profit to the taxpayers.

For Roosevelt, the HOLC was only the beginning. In 1934 he induced Congress to pass the National Housing Act. It created the Federal Housing Administration, which insured loans by private institutions to middle-income families who wanted to repair their homes or build new ones. Like the HOLC, the FHA insisted on long-term, low-down-payment mortgages that allowed the borrower to pay off a little bit of the principal every month. In 1938 the Roosevelt administration created the company that would eventually become the Federal National Mortgage Association, better known as Fannie Mae, to buy and hold home loans made by banks until they were paid back. In this way, the government became the de facto lender on millions of bank loans—with the banks simply collecting homeowners' monthly mortgage payments and passing them on to Fannie Mae. The idea was to make it easier for banks to make loans and create opportunities for middle-class homeownership. If anything went wrong, Fannie Mae would be on the hook. But foreclosures were rare. Fannie Mae behaved responsibly because it held the loans on its books—rather than bundling them into mortgage-backed securities, cutting them into tranches, and selling them on the bond market, as occurred later. The basic connection between lender and repayment was maintained. Homeownership blossomed, and the government made money.

In speeches, Roosevelt linked the fight for homeownership with the fight against Fascism. "A nation of home owners, of people who own a real share in their own land, is unconquerable," he told the Savings and Loan League in November 1942, as war raged across Europe, North Africa, and the Pacific.[7] The final piece of the New Deal, the American Servicemen's Readjustment Act, better known as the GI Bill, made sure that those who fought for their country would have economic security when they got home. It created low-interest loans, with no down payment, for service members returning from World War II.

The impact of the New Deal's housing program resonated for decades, creating a fundamentally more equal society, since working Americans who were able to save could finally buy a home and build wealth—so long as they were white. The country became more prosperous—including the banking sector, which thrived because borrowers, who had poured their life savings into their homes, almost always paid their loan back. In 1953, for example, the nation's foreclosure rate was 0.04 percent, meaning just 1 out of every 2,500 borrowers defaulted.[8] Now, thanks to the aggressive tactics of lenders such as IndyMac, all that progress was at risk.

THE FIRST BIG investment bank to fall was the eighty-five-year-old powerhouse Bear Stearns Companies, which collapsed in March 2008 under the weight of its suddenly worthless mortgage-backed securities. Sensing further disaster was on the horizon, leading academics came forward with proposals to have the government intervene, much as it did during the Great Depression, in ways that both helped homeowners and concentrated losses on the companies that threatened to destroy the economy with their aggressive sales tactics. They offered good ideas that, while horrifically expensive at first glance, would have proved much more effective and less costly than the bailouts lawmakers ultimately approved.

Harvard University economist Martin Feldstein, who once chaired Ronald Reagan's Council of Economic Advisers, presented a plan to replace 20 percent of each homeowners' mortgage with a low-interest loan from the government.[9] Howell Jackson, a Harvard law professor who specialized in the mortgage market, argued that the government should help struggling borrowers stay in their homes by using eminent domain, the government's right to seize, and pay for private property for a public purpose, to take the mortgage-backed securities that had liens against the homes. Since these debt bundles were now worth less than they were on paper, the government could then use its ownership of the securities to make new, more affordable loans to consumers, much as the Home Owners' Loan Corporation had done decades earlier.[10]

"There were a series of meetings of the Democratic leadership on economic policy, and they would invite outsiders," said Princeton economist Alan Blinder, who under Bill Clinton, served as vice chairman of the Federal Reserve, charged with overseeing banks and setting monetary policy. Blinder was among those who told the lawmakers they should create a modern HOLC. He spelled out his argument in a *New York Times* op-ed. Although contemporary mortgage finance was vastly more complicated than in the 1930s, that only made government intervention more necessary. "In the 1930s, banks knew all of their customers, and borrowers knew their banks," he wrote. "Today most mortgages are securitized and sold to buyers who do not know the original borrowers. Then mortgage pools are sliced, diced, and tranched into complex derivative instruments that no one understands—and that are owned by banks and funds all over the world." Such complexity, he argued, "bolsters the case for government intervention rather than undermining it. After all, how do you renegotiate terms of a mortgage when the borrower and the lender don't even know each other's names? This is one reason so few delinquent mortgage loans have been renegotiated to date."[11]

Despite the fact that his position recalled that of the most popular Democratic president in history, FDR, Blinder's presentation to the Democratic leaders didn't go well. "I was laughed out of court," he told me. "The ideas didn't even get far enough for them to be lobbied against." The economist said Democratic politicians were worried about cost. "They didn't understand the difference between lending money and spending money," he explained. The politicians also didn't understand the size of the foreclosure tsunami that was coming. Blinder had proposed allowing the new HOLC to lend between $200 billion and $400 billion, far less than what the same politicians would approve a few months later in the $700 billion bank bailout. That bailout, however, primarily shoveled taxpayer money at banks and bondholders rather than at homeowners themselves. It meant that, unlike in the Great Depression, when the amount of money that homeowners owed on their mortgages was cut by the government-created corporation to be in line with the home's true value, modern-day homeowners were forced to pay off the full amount of debt they'd incurred or face foreclosure.

Bankers and lawmakers talked about the "moral hazard" in rescuing struggling homeowners who had made poor decisions, as they watched generations' worth of middle-class wealth be washed away. "I often muse," he'd write later, "about how much better things might have been had Congress revived the HOLC back in 2008 when the foreclosure problem was much smaller than it subsequently, and predictably, became."[12] But not everyone was disappointed—quite the opposite.

CHAPTER 3

A RUN ON THE BANK

INDYMAC'S COLLAPSE WAS SPECTACULAR, A frantic run on the bank—the kind of financial crisis that was not supposed to happen in America anymore. The scene evoked the grainy black-and-white images of the Great Depression, only this time the pictures were in color.

Insiders already knew about the bank's problems, of course, thanks to the lawsuits and IndyMac's securities filings, but the public remained largely in the dark until June 26, 2008. That's when Charles Schumer of New York, the third most powerful Democrat in the US Senate, released a public letter expressing dismay about government regulators' inability to confront "serious problems" at the thrift. "I am concerned that IndyMac's financial deterioration poses significant risks to both taxpayers and borrowers," Schumer wrote. The bank "could face a failure if prescriptive measures are not taken quickly."[1] Critics would later argue that it was Schumer who sparked the run. The senator retorted he was simply pointing out the obvious. "The regulator was asleep at the switch," he said at a press conference. "The administration is doing what they always do, blaming the fire on the person who called 911."[2]

In any case, news of the bank's troubles swept through Southern California, as local television newscasters stoked the panic with live stand-ups across six lanes of traffic. Throngs of customers pushed, shoved, and screamed in front of the six-story headquarters in Pasadena, trying to pull their deposits. If IndyMac's coffers had been eroded by piecemeal reimbursements for its sins, now they were suctioned without interruption. Customers withdrew increasing amounts of money as the days went on—$97.5 million on Monday, July 7; $185 million on Tuesday, July 8; $209 million on Wednesday, July 9.[3]

Faced with these mounting withdrawals, the Federal Deposit Insurance Corporation dispatched a team from Washington to close the bank. It was led by the FDIC's chief operating officer, John Bovenzi, a heavyset man with a wisp of hair combed over to cover an increasingly bald head. Bovenzi flew out to Burbank, using his personal credit card to buy his airplane ticket, rental car, and hotel room at the local Hilton. Dozens of other FDIC employees had done the same thing, booking their own travel out of Washington and their own accommodations in Southern California. The idea was to keep news of IndyMac's closure secret, to prevent public panic. It didn't work—especially after some customers went online and found their accounts frozen. As word leaked out, the panic snowballed. On July 11, 2008, the day the FDIC team came for IndyMac, depositors withdrew $250 million.

That day, Bovenzi and his associates arrived at IndyMac's headquarters early in the morning, and by the afternoon they rode the elevator up to the top floor and walked into an executive conference room. In a carefully staged but oddly private event, with a serene view of the San Gabriel Mountains out the conference room window providing a sharp contrast to the mania below, John Bovenzi looked Michael Perry in the eye and relieved him of his duties. Now the government owned the bank, which, on paper, at least, had $32 billion in assets.[4] Most of those "assets," however, amounted to bad loans that might never be repaid.

INDYMAC FAILED TWO months before the collapse of Lehman Brothers, before Congress passed the bank bailout, before the true scale of the financial crisis was known. Unemployment was still relatively low at 5.7 percent[5] and the Dow Jones Industrial Average hovered above 11,100.

Despite all of IndyMac's drama, outside of Southern California, the news was treated as an afterthought by politicians and the news media. On the presidential campaign trail that day, neither party's presumptive candidate, Republican John McCain and Democrat Barack Obama, spoke about the bank's collapse or even the US economy. The *New York Times* ran its story about IndyMac's failure on page five of the business section.[6]

It wouldn't be long, though, before the public woke up to the broader implications of IndyMac's collapse. As with larger banks that would fail later, such as Washington Mutual and Wachovia, the public would learn that IndyMac's business model was based on selling bundles of loans to investors in the form of mortgage-backed securities. But there was one key difference between IndyMac and its larger rivals: IndyMac collapsed before the government could save it. This meant that the government, in the form of the FDIC, now owned the bank.

The new owners of IndyMac announced they would reopen the bank the following Monday. They called big national media outlets and asked them to project a message of tranquility and composure. Predictability, that request raised eyebrows. "The federal government wants to calm customers' jittery nerves and convince them that it's business as usual," CBS News correspondent Bill Whitaker intoned at dawn, shortly before the bank reopened. "But as they say, that remains to be seen."[7]

Seen it was: by then, the crowds had exploded, twisting around the block as they had the previous week. Outside, government bankers in black suits stood in 90-degree heat, trying to keep order, distributing bottled water to combat the oppressive humidity, and telling customers to head home. One woman in the long line fainted and was taken to the hospital by paramedics. Yet despite the admonishment, the customers stayed, leaving only after they secured cashier's checks for $100,000—the maximum amount insured by the government—which they clutched in their hands as they walked back to their cars. "People were hysterical," Bovenzi told me years later.

The FDIC's chief operating officer stood for the cameras, giving one interview after another, and then circulated through the crowd. "We told them this bank is now owned by the federal government; nothing is safer in the world," he recalled. "This one woman just looked at me and said, 'Can you assure me the government will be here tomorrow?' What do you say to that?"

In the days to come, the bedlam would subside. The FDIC set up tents with folding chairs outside of IndyMac's thirty-three branches, and handed out numbers to customers, which made the withdrawals more orderly. Heart-wrenching stories began to play out in the press—ten thousand depositors had more than $100,000 in IndyMac, and they weren't necessarily rich. There was the mother of a soldier killed in Afghanistan, who'd put her son's life insurance check in an account there; the policeman who had just sold his home and deposited the proceeds; and the office manager who had $180,000 from her grandfather earmarked for a down payment on a house. Small businesses lost money set aside for payroll—and there were many, many retirees who had placed their life savings in the bank, thinking it was safe.

Consumers demanded help, and, in the days and weeks that followed, the FDIC hosted community meetings to extend a helping hand. But the law was the law: the government could provide no more than $100,000 to depositors at failed banks. The chairwoman of the FDIC, Sheila Bair, offered no apologies. Indy-Mac was the largest bank taken over by the government since the Great Depression. It was her job to safeguard not only the consumer but also the health of the banking system and the taxpayer. "It is incumbent on people to know the FDIC deposit limits and stay below them," she wrote later.[8]

THE FDIC NEVER wanted to run IndyMac, and the government certainly never hoped to run it for long. The ideal chain of events, which is common during less stressful economic times, is that the agency shutters a bank under one ownership on a Friday evening and reopens it under a new one on Monday morning. Whenever possible, the failed bank is subsumed by another financial institution with experience and staff in the region. The quick sale benefits the government because the assets of the failed bank stay off the government's books. The consumer barely notices the difference.

This was possible because banks rarely failed, and those that did tended to be of the smaller, community variety. The case of Miami Valley Bank was typical. On October 4, 2007, the government announced simultaneously that it had closed the Ohio bank, which had $87 million in assets, and that its branches would be open the next day. The only difference was that the offices would now be outposts of the Citizens Banking Company of nearby

Sandusky. The government estimated its losses at $3 million.[9] The public barely noticed. But the IndyMac situation was nothing like this. First, IndyMac was huge, with billions of dollars of bad loans. It could not easily be subsumed into some other regional bank, and, in any case, its assets were so toxic that no other bank wanted to buy them.

"IndyMac had very few true customers in the traditional sense. It was everything a bank shouldn't be," Bovenzi told me. Though it had $18 billion in deposits, IndyMac's only true customers were the investment banks that bought its mortgage-backed securities. When housing prices dropped, the investment banks wouldn't buy the securities. IndyMac could no longer off-load its risky loans. The bank started hemorrhaging money, failing even faster than the government expected.

The FDIC would eventually sue Perry for negligence, accusing him of "rolling the dice" on risky mortgages.[10] It sought $600 million but settled for just 2 percent of that, or $12 million, including a $1 million personal payment from Perry and an agreement that banished the former executive from banking for life. No one went to jail.[11]

But that settlement wouldn't come until four years later and, furthermore, suing Perry didn't help the government out of its immediate problem: with no Home Owners' Loan Corporation to buy mortgages off IndyMac and negotiate homeowners into less usurious loans, the FDIC faced a replay of bank failures that hearkened back to an earlier era. It was now the owner of a giant failed bank, and it was desperate to find a buyer.

"We had to beat the bushes," Sheila Bair told me. "Very few people had any money then, and the last thing most of them wanted to do was buy a failed bank." But if most of American business wanted nothing to do with a financial institution crippled by the housing bust, there was a handful of businessmen who saw opportunity.

ON THE DAY of IndyMac's collapse, Steve Mnuchin stood in his office in Midtown Manhattan, watching the bedlam on the financial news channel CNBC.[12] A thin man with a square face, receding hairline and trademark designer black plastic-rim glasses, the hedge fund manager had never run a commercial bank.

"We need to figure out how to buy it," he reportedly told a colleague. Mnuchin said that IndyMac's failure reminded him not of the Great Depression, when the government intervened to help homeowners, but of the savings and loan failures of the late 1980s and early 1990s, when a small group of private equity giants bought a mountain of toxic assets off the government for pennies on the dollar and then flipped them to other investors. Because the government sold so cheap, they were able to walk away with billions.

"I've seen this game before," Mnuchin declared.[13]

IT WAS AS if Steve Mnuchin had been bred for this moment. Born December 21, 1962, to philanthropist Elaine Terner Cooper and Robert Mnuchin, a Goldman Sachs partner on the firm's management committee, Steve had practically been raised on Wall Street, destined to live a life of luxury on Park Avenue while spending weekends in the Hamptons. He grew up in the rarified world of ultrawealthy New Yorkers. His grandfather, attorney Leon Mnuchin, cofounded a yacht club.[14] His parents sent him to the exclusive Riverdale Country School, its gorgeous campus set upon thirty flowing acres nestled between the Hudson River and

Van Cortland Park at the Westchester County line. There young Steve swam in what would later be called the Mnuchin Family Pool. In high school, when most of the kids from Manhattan rode the bus up to the Bronx, Steve drove a red Porsche to class. Even then, classmates said, the future hedge fund manager had a reputation as a hard charger. He was determined to win every game of tennis and argued with his teachers when he didn't like a grade.

After Riverdale, Steve attended his father's alma matter, Yale University. He lived off campus in the former Taft Hotel. His roommates included Salem Chalabi, nephew of Iraqi exile leader Ahmed Chalabi, and Edward Lampert, who would later become a billionaire investor, known for buying distressed companies, including Kmart and Sears, and stripping them of their assets.

In college, Mnuchin worked on the *Yale Daily News*, not as a journalist but as publisher. Back in those days, before the advent of on-campus start-up accelerators that propel undergrads into a career of moneymaking, the paper offered a rare opportunity for Mnuchin to showcase his business acumen. His roommate, Eddie, was the general manager. Journalists who worked on the paper in those years said the business and editorial sides were almost completely separate and usually came from different social classes. Editor Bennett Voyles, who graduated in 1985, the same year as Mnuchin, remembers the publishing team as "a sleek crew in Lacoste shirts who would glide in and out of the *News* building."[15]

The paper's editor in chief, Anndee Hochman, recalls, "The majority of us were public-school educated and saw ourselves as scrappy defenders of the underdog, truth tellers, and people who were skeptical of enshrined power. The people on the business side were the opposite of that." Hochman, who went on to become a writer on family and community, said she frequently tangled with her publisher over monetary issues, such as the number of pages per issue. But Mnuchin never interfered with the content—or even expressed an opinion about it. On a campus frequently inflamed by politics, he did not project any particular ideology. "I don't think we ever went to lunch together," she reflected. "Our interactions were almost exclusively in the *Yale Daily News* building." The only evidence of Mnuchin in the paper's archives, beyond the publisher credit in the staff box, are ads recruiting staff for the business side of the paper. "Interested in Business? Money? Call Steve Mnuchin," reads one ad from 1982.[16]

FOR MNUCHIN, THERE had never been much question about what to do next. His father had gone to Yale and then to Goldman Sachs, where he'd worked his way up the totem pole for twenty-two years. Steve's older brother, Alan, had also attended Yale, graduating a year earlier, and likewise went to Goldman. So, in September 1985, after a summer internship at rival Salomon Brothers, Steve joined Goldman, too.

It was the height of the Reagan era, with Wall Street constellated with wild parties, leveraged buyouts, hostile takeovers, and insider trading scandals, encapsulated by the Gordon Gekko line in director Oliver Stone's 1987 film *Wall Street*: "Greed . . . is good." Steve found a home in Goldman's mortgage department, working under the tutelage of cigar-smoking partner Michael Mortara, who, in addition to his business acumen, gained notoriety as an early Wall Street helicopter commuter, making two to three round trips a week from his home in Litchfield, Connecticut. "It's very convenient," he said of the forty-five-minute flight. "I could do it every night, except the demands of my business are such that I end up having to go out to dinner in New York a few times a week."[17]

Mortara was only thirty-eight when he and Mnuchin started working together, but he was already a legend. As a young man at Salomon Brothers in the 1970s, Mortara and his partner Lewis Ranieri had been instrumental in creating mortgage-backed securities, pioneering a practice far more complicated than the traditional way banks had turned a profit. Before that, lenders made money by accepting deposits from individuals and businesses, keeping the money safe, and lending it out at higher interest than they paid to depositors.

Mortara and Ranieri are credited with making it commonplace to bundle home mortgages as financial instruments. Mortara was an evangelist for the "product," which he grew as dramatically, and expansively, as he could. In 1985, for example, the investment banker formed a syndicate and partnered with Freddie Mac on a program to sell $100 million worth of American mortgages on the international market. It was the first time that the government-chartered mortgage company, established in 1970, allowed mortgages to be traded overseas.[18] For Mortara, this was great news—a way to profit off the emerging market of debt trading. But for consumers, it was just the latest indication that the connection between homeowners and their lenders was being severed.

That same year, Mortara helped American companies finance commercial real estate in the United States with money from the international bond market.[19] This meant more money pumped into financing for urban office towers and suburban shopping malls, with the investors on the hook for those deals spread around the world, totally disconnected from the relative merits and feasibility of the projects themselves—which proved to be a cause of the collapse of the savings and loan industry at the end of the decade. Mortara also expanded debt-backed securities beyond home loans to create similar products that covered other types of consumer spending.

The financial press fawned over these developments. When Mortara developed a tradeable financial product to cover car loans, the newspaper *American Banker* called it "a breakthrough"[20] because investors could now buy the underlying debt of an auto loan without taking on the servicing rights—in other words, the process of actually collecting on the debt or seizing the car if the borrower defaulted.

Mortara and other supporters of these mortgage-backed securities said they helped make loans more available because the banks that sold them into the secondary market received new cash to lend out again. What was good for Wall Street, they explained, was good for everyone.

OF COURSE, THE beneficiaries of this system were, first and foremost, investment bankers like Michael Mortara and Steve Mnuchin. The more securities that were created, the more money they made. But despite their fervent enthusiasm, the growth of these balls of debt was slower than they would have liked. They needed a change in the law to really get things going.

That came in 1986. The year after Mnuchin joined Mortara at Goldman, President Reagan signed an overhaul of the American tax system containing a provision allowing bond traders who bought and sold mortgage-backed securities to cut what had been large, single bundles into tranches. Rating agencies graded tranches from the most secure to the most risky. The highest rated—and safest—tranches fetched the highest prices and got paid first if the borrowers defaulted and the security failed. The lower rated ones were the cheapest and got paid last. A trader could buy as little, or as much, of a particular mortgage-backed security as he liked. With tranching, the market exploded—from $150 billion in 1986, to an astonishing $9 trillion in 2010.[21]

It was thus that investment bankers turned home mortgages—something so simple and essential to American family wealth—into a financial instrument to be bought, sold, and traded. It was the system of buying and selling loans that, exacerbated by the 1986 overhaul, would eventually crash the global economy. Steve Mnuchin was there from the beginning.

CHAPTER 4

LIFE ON PARK AVENUE

FOR A TIME, IT LOOKED as though Steve Mnuchin might stay at Goldman Sachs until retirement, just like his father, who spent thirty-three years at the firm before departing in 1991 to open an art gallery on the Upper East Side.[1]

On paper, it certainly seemed like he was following in his father's footsteps. Steve steadily ascended the Goldman ladder, and in 1994 he made partner and was appointed head of the mortgage securities department. By 1999, he was a member of the firm's executive committee.

But a life at Goldman was not to be. "There's a never-ending politics that rages at these firms regardless of where you are in the pecking order," said journalist William D. Cohan, author of the 2001 book *Money and Power: How Goldman Sachs Came to Rule the World*, which serves as the definitive history of the investment bank. Cohan told me that Steve Mnuchin never made his mark at Goldman Sachs; he never did a deal or made a trade that forced his colleagues and competitors to stand up and take notice. In fact, Cohan doesn't mention him once in his 672-page tome. "Nobody would have said that Steve Mnuchin was someone that I needed to talk to," the author explained. "His father, yes. His father was Goldman royalty, but Steve, absolutely not."

Then, in November 2000, Michael Mortara died of a brain aneurism in his home in Connecticut. It took everyone by surprise. Stunned, like all who knew him, Steve Mnuchin announced Mortara's passing to the world.[2] He was just fifty-one years old.

Mortara had been more than a friend and exemplar to Steve Mnuchin. He was also his "rabbi"—in the parlance of Wall Street, someone who protected him at bonus time, who made sure he got promoted, and who helped him navigate the politics of the firm. In each of his promotions over the years, Mnuchin had followed in Mortara's footsteps, stepping up into his mentor's old job as he was promoted. Now Mortara was dead. There was a power vacuum, but with his protectors gone, Mnuchin wasn't in the position to fill it.

"We're talking about alpha male land, where it's not enough for you to succeed. Other people have to fail," Cohan says. "If you understand that concept, then you understand Wall Street and you understand why Steve Mnuchin had to leave Goldman."

After seventeen years at Goldman, Mnuchin left with an estimated $46 million of company stock and $12.6 million in compensation that he received in the months prior to his departure.[3] He was thirty-nine years old, and, aside from a single summer internship, Goldman was the only place he'd worked since college graduation. But Steve Mnuchin was too young to retire. It was time for him to go out on his own.

IT DIDN'T HAPPEN right away. There would be a couple of interim steps, but each of them helped Mnuchin come into his own, building relationships that allowed him to make his big play, scooping up the remains of IndyMac after the housing market crashed in 2008.

His first stop was ESL Investments, a hedge fund run by his old Yale roommate Eddie Lampert. Like Mnuchin, Lampert had majored in economics and gone from Yale to Goldman, but he'd left after just three years to form his own firm. Also, like Mnuchin, Lampert had spent his early years in comfort, in a wealthy enclave in Roslyn, Long Island. But that changed when Lampert was fourteen and his father died of a heart attack at age forty-seven, throwing the family into financial crisis.

"That was the end of camp or going away to Europe like other children," Lampert's mother, Dolores, told the *Wall Street Journal* in 1991.[4] (Her assumption about European travel is telling.) Though Lampert's father had been a lawyer, he left his family with almost no savings. His stay-at-home mom was forced to give up her regular tennis games and ladies' lunches and get a job as a department store clerk. Eddie chipped in, too, working in warehouses after school, on weekends, and over the summer to help his mother and younger sister. "Eddie was very strong," his mother said, and tried "to be the man of the family."[5] Unlike Mnuchin, Lampert needed financial aid to attend Yale.

Those early struggles did not make him generous or charitable in his business dealings. Instead, he pursued investments with a chip on his shoulder. "Warm and fuzzy Edward S. Lampert is not," Geraldine Fabrikant wrote in a 2002 *New York Times* profile, shortly before Mnuchin joined the firm. "He is known as secretive, controlling, and so impatient for success and obsessed with work that some who know him say he takes little note of people unless he needs them."[6] But Lampert's personality did not matter to his investors, who eventually included media mogul David Geffen; Thomas Tisch, the son of Laurence Tisch, the CEO of CBS television networks; and Michael Dell, the founder of the Dell Computer Corporation. What mattered to them was that

ESL consistently beat the market. It had "scored an extraordinary 14-year record of value investing, with an average annual return of 24.5 percent."

When Mnuchin arrived at ESL in 2002, Lampert's big plays were AutoZone and Kmart, in which he had just bought a majority stake. The latter was bankrupt, so Lampert closed six hundred stores and laid off thousands of workers.[7] Critics said he was less interested in selling clothes and housewares than he was in pocketing huge sums of money by liquidating Kmart's valuable real estate. When the company emerged from bankruptcy the following year, Lampert put Mnuchin on its board.[8]

Mnuchin remained there for eleven years, as Kmart merged with Sears, in which Lampert also owned a controlling share. By most measures, the company's failure under his watch was spectacular. The number of Sears and Kmart stores shrank from nearly four thousand at their peak to just over a thousand when Mnuchin exited. More than two hundred thousand employees lost their jobs.[9] Meantime, the pension fund for retired Sears workers was underfunded by $2.1 billion.[10] But though the company was tanking, the board, with Mnuchin on it, made sure that Eddie Lampert benefitted. The company's most valuable assets, including Lands' End, Sears Canada, and most of Sears's real estate, were sold off to another entity, the largest shareholder of which also happened to be Lampert's hedge fund.[11] Then Lampert forced the failing retailer to pay hundreds of millions of dollars in rent to his hedge fund[12]—racking up huge amounts of debt in the process.

It was Lampert's way of stripping the company. When he finally took Sears into bankruptcy in October 2018, Lampert was able to do so while holding on to the parts of the company that he liked. The workers got screwed. Sears creditors got pennies on the dollar. In April 2019 the company sued Lampert and a string of high-profile former board members, including Mnuchin, accusing them of executing a "multiyear and multifaceted scheme" to steal billions of dollars from the once-storied retailer.[13] In a statement, Lampert's hedge fund, ESL, dismissed the complaint, saying its allegations were "misleading or just flat wrong. . . . We are confident that the processes we followed for each of these transactions are unimpeachable."[14] In any case, Lampert was sitting pretty. It was typical Mnuchin.

There were lessons in this evisceration, one of which stuck with Steve Mnuchin: the two iconic retailers were failing—and might have failed anyway. Why not make a profit off of it?

THOUGH MNUCHIN STAYED on the Sears board for years, he didn't work directly for Lampert for long. Less than a year after he joined ESL, septuagenarian billionaire George Soros hired him away to start an investment fund buying risky debt.[15] Working for Soros allowed Mnuchin to develop the relationships he would use in his big bid to buy IndyMac, and also enabled him to apprentice under one of the most successful hedge fund managers of all time.

Today the Hungarian-American Soros is known mostly as a liberal philanthropist with an interest in criminal justice, democracy, and Democratic Party politics. But back then, he was legendary as the man who "broke the Bank of England" in 1992, tanking the British stock market by placing huge bets against the pound. In those years, Soros was infamous for scouting the world, looking for ways to profit off distress that others hadn't yet noticed. Some blamed his currency speculation for the 1997 Asian financial crisis that devastated economies from Indonesia to South Korea and hammered the stock markets of the United States and Japan.

Now, as the housing bubble built, Soros was looking to bet on America's debt, and he enlisted Steve Mnuchin. In a letter to staff, Mark Schwartz, Soros Fund Management's chief executive, said Mnuchin's portfolio would include "senior secured loans to noninvestment-grade companies, mezzanine loans, receivables and mortgages, subordinated securities, and distressed asset purchases"—basically all the kinds of loans that no one else wanted to buy.

But, again, Mnuchin's stint would be brief. In 2004, just a year after he arrived at Soros, he left to found his own hedge fund, Dune Capital Management, named for a spot near his weekend home in the Hamptons. (Schwartz described it as a spin-off.[16]) Finally out of the shadows of his father, Mortara, and Soros, Mnuchin was ready to make his own deals.

LOOKING BACK, IT seems that Mnuchin's transformation from quiet partner at Goldman Sachs to front man for a major private equity deal began before Michael Mortara died. In 1999, after Mnuchin divorced his first wife, photographer Kathryn McCarver, he married Heather deForest Crosby, a Manhattan socialite who traced her lineage back to the *Mayflower*. The wedding echoed the Gilded Age nuptials of a century earlier. The ceremony took place at the exclusive restaurant Cipriani Wall Street, the former home of the New York Stock Exchange, in a Greek revival hall framed by monolithic columns, with a seventy-foot ceiling and a Wedgewood dome.[17] A year later, the couple moved to a two-story, 6,400-square-foot apartment on Park Avenue, in an Art Deco monument that's often called "the world's richest apartment building." They bought it from one of

Mnuchin's aunts, garment center heir Carol Lederman, for $10.5 million.[18] Now Steve was on the map, if by address alone. 740 Park Avenue.

In his book about the building, author Michael Gross called Mnuchin's union to Crosby "the ultimate modern 740 Park merger, the dark-haired child of a self-made Jewish philanthropist had married a stunningly beautiful, blond-haired descendant of several colonial families, including that of William Floyd, a signer of the Declaration of Independence." Heather's family also included a Supreme Court justice and Francis Scott Key, author of "The Star-Spangled Banner."[19]

Thomas Tisch, Mnuchin's fellow board member at Sears, lived across the hall on the eighth floor. Billionaire private equity magnate Steve Schwarzman, the founder of the Blackstone Group, lived seven floors above them in a sprawling two-level apartment once occupied by John D. Rockefeller Jr.

By 2006, John Thain lived on the top floor. Thain, who would later become a poster boy for the financial crisis, headed up Merrill Lynch, a storied investment bank that handed out billions of dollars in executive bonuses even as it collapsed in 2008.[20] At Merrill, Thain was famous for his high-flying lifestyle, adorning his office with an $88,000 rug, a $35,000 commode, and a pair of curtains costing $28,000.[21] His $27.5 million apartment on Park Avenue was similarly opulent. On its main level, the *New York Times* reported, a private elevator landing opened up to a windowed gallery twenty-seven feet long, with a grand elliptical staircase and entry onto a west-facing terrace that looks out on Central Park.[22]

Over the years, Steve Mnuchin would do business with all of them.

STEVEN AND HEATHER had three children together. In the early years of their marriage, Heather made more news than her husband. She was featured regularly in women's magazines and the society pages: photographed chairing the Whitney Gala in a navy lace dress designed by Carolina Herrera;[23] sitting in the front row at a spring fashion show in Bryant Park with their daughter, Emma; receiving a full, two-armed embrace and kiss on the cheek from developer Donald Trump at a ball on Forty-Second Street to raise funds to feed the poor.[24] *Women's Wear Daily* featured Heather in a "clip-and-save guide to the denizens of the party pages."[25] She was always good for a quote. "I tried to buy good, versatile basics—things that I can wear forever—whether it's a tweed blazer or a velvet jacket," she said in a profile in *Harper's Bazaar.* Her everyday uniform? "Always a blazer—Dolce & Gabbana, Tuleh, and Chanel have great ones," she said, along with "a white tee, because it's so easy to accessorize with something like a chunky necklace."[26]

But if Heather was featured in fashion magazines, including *Vogue*, Mnuchin mostly kept a low profile. Still, her partying and their new address offered entrée into one of Mnuchin's new interests: the movie business. On November 18, 2005, the couple hosted an invitation-only advanced screening of the George Clooney spy vehicle *Syriana*, followed by an after-party at their Park Avenue apartment. Clooney attended, along with a who's who of film and fashion elite. "George and I are old friends," Heather told *Women's Wear Daily.* "I know he always likes for a group of intelligent people to see his films."

The entire gathering was a strange combination of exclusivity and showmanship. Though it was invitation only and held in a private home, it was also meticulously documented by the paparazzi. Photographers captured Steve Mnuchin, with a goofy grin, clad in a button-down shirt and blazer, holding a glass of wine, standing next to comedian Mike Myers. Steve and Heather are also pictured together with Clooney, actresses Patricia Clarkson and Rachel Weisz, and a variety of famous fashion designers.

Mnuchin had nothing to do with the production of *Syriana*, but two months later, in January 2006, his company Dune Entertainment invested $325 million in Fox Filmed Entertainment, an umbrella company that included 20th Century Fox and News Corp's other Fox-branded film properties. A second $325 million investment came in November 2006, with hundreds of millions more in the years that followed.[27] In financing these deals, Mnuchin relied on his Goldman connections: his partner at Dune Entertainment, Chip Seelig, had been a managing director at Goldman, charged for a time with running the investment bank's mortgage division.

Like his time as publisher of the *Yale Daily News*, story and craft were not Steve Mnuchin's priorities. He was all about the money. Dune Entertainment invested in not one or two movies at a time, but in slates of films—a structure that allowed him to simultaneously put money into nearly every motion picture produced by Fox. The first deal, in January 2006, covered twenty-eight films. The next deal, signed that November, covered sixteen more.

Over the years, this strategy would lead to some huge hits, such as *Avatar* and *The Devil Wears Prada*, but also plenty of critical and box office clunkers—like *Pathfinder*, a Viking Age action epic that the *New York Times* described as "all grunting, all goring, the witless action flick [that] has little to recommend it." The *San Francisco Chronicle* called it "downright painful to sit through."[28]

But the flops didn't faze Mnuchin. "My criteria is simple," he would tell CNBC. He wanted a "deep portfolio. Investing in any one film is always a risky proposition, but if you can invest in enough films, and create a large library of content, then long term, that content becomes more and more valuable."[29]

It could be a school newspaper or movies, a discount retailer such as Kmart or mortgages on millions of Americans' homes—it didn't matter what the business was. His interest wasn't in building companies for the long haul. The key for Steve Mnuchin in each venture was money and how to make a trade so that he could make as much as possible. Mnuchin had made a career out of pulling tarnished gems from a billionaire's bargain basement. And in IndyMac's collapse, Mnuchin saw the opportunity for a trade of a lifetime.

CHAPTER 5

THE VULTURES CIRCLE

STEVE MNUCHIN WASN'T THE ONLY vulture circling around IndyMac, hoping to swoop in and buy it for a song. Another was J. Christopher (J. C.) Flowers, a soft-spoken titan of private equity, who specialized in buying troubled financial firms, flipping them, and making enormous profits.

Thin, and with a reputation for being quiet and contemplative, the fifty-one-year-old Harvard-educated mathematician preferred playing chess by himself to the New York party scene frequented by Mnuchin and other hedge fund types. He was not known for grand public pronouncements, so it surprised many when, in June 2008, just a month before IndyMac's failure, he declared that "every single investment" in his fund would make money.[1] The bottom had dropped out. Prices would never be lower. "The Super Bowl of investment," he called it. "No time to be sitting in the bleachers."[2] Flowers didn't hide the fact that his business model was predicated on profiting off pain. "A low-life grave dancer" is how he described himself to an industry group a few months later, but one who was about to "make a fortune" off the country's economic collapse.[3]

In some ways, Flowers and Mnuchin had a lot in common. Both had interned on Wall Street while completing their studies at an Ivy League university. They both went to work for Goldman Sachs immediately after graduation. Both became partners before striking out on their own. But there was no doubting that Chris Flowers was the more successful of the two. Where Mnuchin inched up the ranks at Goldman Sachs on the strength of his name and the reputation of his father, Flowers—the son of a librarian and a career naval officer who later became an administrator at Harvard—was considered to be a bit of a genius. At Harvard, he'd graduated a semester early, magna cum laude. At Goldman, he'd become head of mergers and acquisitions—in the 1980s, during the invention of the hostile takeover—ascending to become the firm's youngest partner at age thirty-one. While Steve Mnuchin had scored some success in movies and real estate, and as a tear-down artist on Sears's board, Flowers had made billions for investors by buying a formerly state-owned Japanese bank.

And Flowers was much richer. Steve Mnuchin was likely worth slightly more than $100 million at the time, while *Forbes* magazine ranked Flowers number 605 on its billionaires list, with a personal net worth of $2 billion.[4] Mnuchin rubbed shoulders with billionaires at his prestigious Park Avenue address, but Flowers lived in a rare stand-alone mansion five blocks away on East Seventy-Fifth Street, next to Central Park. In October 2006 Flowers had made headlines by buying the twenty-thousand-square-foot French Renaissance–style home for a then-record $53 million.[5] The mansion, with fourteen-foot ceilings and an elegant grand staircase, was so large that it had been marketed as a potential home for an elite private school.

Chris Flowers had seen opportunities to profit off the housing bust coming earlier than most. In 2006 he asked one of his partners, John Oros, to look into acquiring Ameriquest, a collapsing

Orange County–based mortgage company that, as recently as the year before, had been the nation's largest originator of subprime loans. Whereas Alt-A lenders such as IndyMac were famous for making high-cost mortgages to borrowers who couldn't prove how much money they made, subprime lenders like Ameriquest took risk a step further: okaying borrowers with no documented income and a history of bad credit. As subprime lenders went, Ameriquest was big, but it was a lot smaller than IndyMac. At the time of its collapse, it held serving rights to about $45 billion in mortgages,[6] which came to just a quarter of IndyMac's $180 billion.[7] But as corporate brands went, Ameriquest was more high profile. It bought the name rights to the Texas Rangers' baseball stadium in Arlington for $75 million[8] and courted attention with a big national television advertising campaign. (The slogan: "Don't judge too quickly. We won't.") The company flew blimps over sports stadiums and sponsored a Rolling Stones concert tour as well as the 2004 Super Bowl halftime show.[9]

Ameriquest's collapse started in 2005, two years earlier than IndyMac's, in part because of a scathing investigative report in its hometown newspaper, the *Los Angeles Times*. Dozens of current and former employees told reporters Mike Hudson and E. Scott Reckard they ran a "boiler room . . . deceiving borrowers about the terms of their loans, forging documents, falsifying appraisals, and fabricating borrowers' income to qualify them for loans they couldn't afford." The loans, once made, were "juiced" with "hidden rates and fees."[10]

The comparison to a boiler room was more than happenstance. In interviews, former employees said they were forced to watch the 2000 crime drama *Boiler Room* as part of their training. A DVD was passed around among managers and employees, they said, to keep them pumped up. In the movie, a parade of Wall

Street swindlers, led by Vin Diesel and Ben Affleck, revel in their powers of anything-goes salesmanship. At Ameriquest, the paper reported, forgeries were brazen. One former loan agent said she witnessed documents being altered when she walked in on coworkers using a brightly lit Coke machine as a tracing board, copying borrowers' signatures on unsigned pieces of paper.[11] The *LA Times* coverage sparked a lawsuit that was ultimately joined by forty-nine state attorney generals, and in January 2006 the company agreed to pay $325 million to settle claims of its deceptive lending practices.[12]

Like IndyMac, Ameriquest didn't hold loans on its books but instead bundled them and sold them as mortgage-backed securities—transactions that were no longer possible now that the bank had been unmasked. In May 2006, around the time J. C. Flowers looked into purchasing Ameriquest, it shuttered all 229 of its retail offices and announced it was laying off 3,800 workers.[13]

Ultimately, Flowers decided to pass on Ameriquest. The fate of the struggling home buyers, who had been sold Ameriquest's predatory products, didn't figure prominently in his decision. It was simply that the price for the failed mortgage company was too high. The market hadn't yet reached his desired bottom. (In August 2007 Citigroup purchased the right to collect on Ameriquest's remaining mortgages for an undisclosed sum.[14]) Plus, while Ameriquest held the servicing rights to billions of dollars' worth of bad mortgages, it lacked other assets that would later make IndyMac a safer bet for a hedge fund seeking to profit off corporate failure: a network of Southern California branches that it could use to launch a new business and billions of dollars of government-insured deposits.

The FDIC's backing, in particular, meant it would be almost impossible to lose money. "The opportunity going forward is unprecedented," Oros told the *New York Times*. "It is fantastic. It is as if I had been training for this the last 40 years of my career."[15] So, in the summer of 2008, after IndyMac failed spectacularly, with long lines of frantic consumers wrapping around the block to empty their accounts, Flowers stepped forward. His firm offered to take IndyMac off the government's hands, "as is," with few conditions attached. And for doing this "favor," he would pay the government almost nothing.

The FDIC said no. Its chairwoman, Sheila Bair, was desperate to unload the bank, but she, too, had conditions.

Bair, appointed by George W. Bush, had worked previously for Senate Majority Leader Bob Dole. Despite her comment, noted earlier, that depositors should have kept the $100,000 limit in mind, the sandy-haired Republican from Kansas would emerge as a rare voice for consumers during the financial crisis. She worried that if IndyMac's owner moved to foreclose on massive numbers of people, it would turn the coming recession into an economic tailspin, harming communities. Ultimately, a recession that big would also hammer the FDIC, which would have to rescue government-insured depositors as losses mounted and more banks failed.

"We hope to keep tens of thousands of troubled borrowers in their homes and avoid the negative consequences that foreclosures can have on the broader economy," she told reporters in an August 2008 conference call. One condition for any party buying the bank would be to continue loan modification programs she'd begun after the government took it over. "Foreclosure is often a lengthy, costly, and destructive process. Avoiding foreclosure not only strengthens local neighborhoods where foreclosures are already driving down property values, it also makes good business sense."[16]

Reducing the tide of foreclosure wasn't her only concern. Bair was also wary of hedge funds like Flowers's that might be more interested in making a quick buck than in the bank's—and the economy's—long-term financial health. So, she put conditions on the sale—including one that would apply to anyone who purchased a 25 percent stake in IndyMac. Those investors would be treated as "bank holding companies," subject to regulation and regular inspection by the Federal Reserve.

Of course, that was the last thing these hedge funds wanted. They were not publicly traded companies. They operated as secretly as possible in order to get an edge. Theoretically, this meant that if a hedge fund bought 25 percent of IndyMac, the Federal Reserve could send inspectors not only into the bank itself but also to the hedge fund that purchased it, in order to limit risk for investors.

Because Flowers wanted nothing to do with such regulations, he would need partners. And that led him and Oros to Steve Mnuchin, their old colleague at Goldman Sachs. Mnuchin didn't have the money to buy IndyMac himself, but he was offering to put together a group—with him in charge. This way no one investor would own a big enough share to trigger the troublesome federal regulations. Flowers decided to join Mnuchin's bid, putting up enough to own *24.974* percent.

INDYMAC'S FAILURE SENT the entire banking industry scrambling, as investors wondered who would be next. Millions of bad loans issued during the boom were coming home to roost. Shares of Washington Mutual, the nation's largest savings and loan, fell 35 percent on the news of IndyMac's failure.[17] As with IndyMac, consumers began to pull their deposits from WaMu—$1.2 billion per day during the first week after IndyMac's failure. The following week was better: they averaged $750 million per day.

"Receiving daily reports about WaMu's deposit outflows made me physically ill," Bair wrote in her book *Bull by the Horns: Fighting to Save Main Street from Wall Street and Wall Street from Itself*.[18] In Washington, top FDIC staff did what they could to shore up teetering banks and ran confidential bidding processes for those that could to be saved. By Christmas, twenty more banks had failed, including Washington Mutual, which was sold to JPMorgan Chase in a transaction brokered by the government. The deal was widely considered a triumph for Sheila Bair and the FDIC. JPMorgan agreed to honor all of Washington Mutual's deposits, and the bank would reopen the very next day. After all, the last thing the FDIC wanted was to be stuck holding another toxic bank such as IndyMac. "You always want to sell a bank quickly," John Bovenzi told me, "not only for the depositors but because the market can devalue a bank more as time goes on, wondering why the government still owns it."

The government sought favorable terms for both itself and IndyMac's struggling borrowers. But the FDIC hit one roadblock after another. The agency hired Lehman Brothers to manage its sale, with the goal of unloading the bank by October, but in September Lehman Brothers went bankrupt, and its contract with the FDIC became part of the bankruptcy proceedings.

All this meant that Bovenzi was stuck running the bank, for days, then weeks, then months. He rented an apartment in Old Town Pasadena, in the middle of the city's shopping area, a few blocks from the bank. He became a cross-country commuter, flying out to Los Angeles each Monday and returning home to Washington on Friday for weekend meetings with FDIC leaders. Bovenzi's first course of action was to stop lending. He shut down IndyMac's massive retail lending group, which sold mortgages from 182 locations across the country.[19] Occasionally, the feds might issue a new mortgage, Bovenzi told me, but they had to be careful. With the housing bust in full swing, any new loans that IndyMac made would probably serve to increase the government's losses. "We knew the existing mortgages weren't worth nearly what they were on the books for, but any buyer would want to discount the new ones, too," he explained. Still, to avoid losing reliable customers who might otherwise pull their deposits, such loans were tactically distributed.

The second order of business was to turn the bank's mortgage servicing operation into a loan modification program, to stave off foreclosures and keep people in their homes. This wasn't for charity. It was designed to stem the bank's losses and save the government money. Since housing prices were depressed, and IndyMac mortgages were inflated, the feds had little to gain by forcing borrowers to make hefty balloon payments or pay hundreds of dollars a month extra in interest on adjustable-rate mortgages they couldn't afford. So, to save both the FDIC money and save the borrower's home, the terms of the loan had to change. In order to do this, employees had to find ways to get the monthly mortgage payments down to 31 percent of the borrower's gross monthly income. They were told to use a "waterfall approach." First, they lowered the borrower's interest rate, then extended the number of years it could be paid off. Finally, they pushed the principal to the end of the loan period, so the bank could get its interest payments and the borrower could stave off foreclosure.

FDIC veteran Michael Krimminger headed up the program. Like Bovenzi, he became a transcontinental commuter, shuttling between Los Angeles and Washington as he tried to run Indy-Mac and keep the entire banking system above water. Every Monday, he'd arrive at IndyMac's Pasadena headquarters and write a number on a giant white board: 2,000 one week, 5,000 the next. This was the number of loan modifications IndyMac's staff would seek to make before the week was out. It was difficult work: the whole idea of mass loan modification was new, and IndyMac's loan servicing staff had to be completely retrained. Using FDIC guidelines, IndyMac staff calculated what might be affordable for a borrower and sent out letters in overnight delivery packages, which had to be signed for so they wouldn't be mistaken for junk mail. "We want you to stay in your home," the letters said at the top, accompanied by a dollar figure: the new, lower monthly payment being offered. To get the process going, the homeowner just had to sign a couple of forms and put them into a prepaid return envelope.

But there were some catches. The FDIC's plan did not allow IndyMac to reduce the principal the borrower owed, even though it was often substantially higher than the price the home could reasonably be expected to fetch. Also, recalculation was available only to a fraction of the loans in IndyMac's portfolio, since the vast majority of its 742,000 loans had been sold off to others and carved up into mortgage-backed securities. Those mortgages could not be changed without the agreement of the bondholders, who wanted to be paid in full. Because of Congress's failure to change this, the bondholders' right to collect in full would never be challenged.

Still, FDIC employees said the process (which Sheila Bair called "Mod-in-a-Box") was a simple, straightforward, and efficient way to modify a large number of at-risk mortgages in a short period of time.[20] The agency would ultimately send out 32,000 letters and help 8,500 borrowers this way—a blip in the ocean of hundreds of thousands of IndyMac homeowners in distress. Nevertheless, to this day, government officials are proud of their efforts. As it worked to sell the bank, the FDIC insisted that potential buyers continue to use the system to help struggling borrowers avoid foreclosure.[21]

ALLEN PUWALSKI HAD also been watching IndyMac—at least the sort of watching one can do from the office of a hedge fund headquartered on Madison Avenue. Puwalski was relatively new to the hedge fund world. Before coming to New York, the University of Maryland graduate had spent more than a decade in Washington working for the FDIC, rising to the position of chief of bank analysis. At the FDIC, his job had been to protect the taxpayer and the health of the American banking system. But in February 2007 he went to work for John Paulson, the hedge fund titan who was making headlines around the world with a gigantic bet against the US housing market.

The contrarian bet—conducted via a series of credit default swaps, which allowed Paulson to enter into contracts with other investors that would pay him big if the market declined—meant that Paulson & Co. made $15 billion in 2007 even as the economy faltered. *Wall Street Journal* reporter Gregory Zuckerman dubbed it "the greatest trade ever." In his book by the same name, Zuckerman noted that the firm's gain "topped the gross domestic products of Bolivia, Honduras, and Paraguay, South American nations with more than 12 million residents." Paulson's personal cut was $4 billion, or more than $10 million a day, "more than the combined earnings of J. K. Rowling, Oprah Winfrey, and Tiger Woods."[22]

By most measures, the fifty-two-year-old Paulson was set. The son of an accountant and a child psychologist, who grew up in a suburban, middle-class section of Queens, Paulson had dreamed of making a big trade since college. His "aha moment" was a lecture by leveraged buyout king Jerry Kohlberg Jr., cofounder of Kohlberg Kravis Roberts & Co. (The firm is widely associated with its $25 billion 1988 hostile takeover of RJR Nabisco, made famous by the best-selling book and film *Barbarians at the Gate*, though Kohlberg was not on hand for that deal, having resigned the year before.) According to Zuckerman, Kohlberg told Paulson's class at the Harvard Business School a story about an obscure company he'd recently flipped. Kohlberg said he'd put up just $500,000 to borrow $36 million and then flipped the company six months later, making $17 million in profit. "For Paulson, it was a life-changing experience," Zuckerman wrote, "like seeing the Beatles for the first time, one that opened his eyes to the huge paydays that could come from big investments."[23]

Now Paulson was richer than Kohlberg had ever been. His bets had propelled him from modest beginnings to a six-story townhouse on the Upper East Side.[24] He lived in the same neighborhood as hedge fund compatriots Steve Mnuchin and J. C. Flowers, but at twenty-nine thousand square feet, Paulson's neo-Georgian limestone mansion was bigger than Mnuchin's and Flowers's homes combined. It was so big, in fact, that before Paulson bought the building, it had housed a private club known for its indoor swimming pool and competitive bridge matches. And that wasn't Paulson's only home in Manhattan. He also owned an apartment downtown, in SoHo.[25] According to Zuckerman, Paulson, like Flowers, had turned his back on the Wall Street party scene. He spent most weekends at his $41 million 10.4-acre estate in the Hamptons with his wife, Jenny (his former assistant), and their two children.

Though he was a billionaire many times over, Paulson, like

many hedge fund kings, does not rest on his laurels. With the housing bust in full swing, Paulson needed a new trade. But by the time IndyMac failed in July 2008, everyone else knew mortgages were becoming worthless. So, betting against the housing market was no longer a lucrative play. Paulson turned to Puwalski, an expert on failed banks and with a deep knowledge of the FDIC's process. Shortly after joining the firm, Puwalski had made money for Paulson betting against IndyMac. The more the bank's mortgages failed and turned into foreclosures, the more money they made. Now that the entire bank had failed, Paulson wanted Puwalksi to help him make money on IndyMac on its way back up.

Puwalski said he felt bad for homeowners who were struggling with foreclosure, like the Hickersons. "It was horrible," he told me. "A lot of loans were made that never should have been made." But, fundamentally, Puwalski said, Paulson saw IndyMac's failure as an opportunity. "In the hedge fund world, cycles are good," he said, "if you're capable of at least having good judgment about where you are in the cycle. Having made so much money on the short side, we were there with funds capable of buying the bank."

Like Steve Mnuchin, who recalled windfalls conferred on profiteers of the savings and loan crisis from the comfort of his Manhattan office the day IndyMac failed, Paulson and Puwalski derived inspiration from the late 1980s. Now was their chance. "We had an idea in mind," Puwlaski said, that since the housing market was about to crash spectacularly, businesses that would normally want to buy a failed bank like IndyMac would shy away "because they themselves are having problems." And they would be able to buy the bank cheap—ideally with government support. But how to benefit exactly? Paulson told Puwalski to do some historical research—looking back not to the Great Depression, when Roosevelt intervened to help struggling homeowners, but on the most lucrative flips of the S&L era. In that deal, Texas businessman Gerald J. Ford, a self-proclaimed "chickenshit country banker" teamed up with corporate raider Ronald Perelman, the owner of the cosmetic brand Revlon, to buy and consolidate five failed savings and loans. The biggest of these was Houston-based First Gibraltar Bank.[26] (As it happens, Perelman—like Steve Mnuchin, John Thain, and Steve Schwarzman—was a resident of 740 Park Avenue. His apartment was a two-story affair once owned by Walter Chrysler, the founder of the eponymous auto company.)

As with the housing bust, the savings and loan crisis was brought on by deregulation and profligate lending. Until 1982, S&Ls were limited to accepting deposits and making home loans to families. But a new law now allowed them to engage in a host of other types of investments. Across the country, and especially in the Southwest, thrifts pumped billions of dollars into shopping malls and office parks that turned out to be white elephants. By the time Ford and Perelman acquired First Gibraltar, it had repossessed 18,000 apartments, 1,000 hotel rooms, 3,300 homes, 38,000 lots developed for houses, 5 million square feet of office space, 5 million square feet of retail space, and 38,000 acres of urban property.[27] But repossession just led to bigger losses, and the government stepped in to rescue First Gibraltar, striking a secret deal that handed it over to Perelman three days before Christmas 1988.

Under its terms, Perelman and Ford paid nothing for the thrift, but they promised to invest $315 million in First Gibraltar to keep it from failing. Perelman borrowed about half that amount from a Wall Street investment firm and put up the rest, $160 million, by tapping his Revlon fortune.[28] It was a small price to pay for the government largess that was about to fatten his wallet.

THE FEAR WAS familiar: if consumers at other banks saw First Gibraltar go down, they might suspect their bank would be next and pull their money. That panic could metastasize across the entire banking system, bringing devastation. Savvy investors understood they could leverage this fear, and few turned out to be as savvy as Perelman and Ford. The payouts from the secret First Gibraltar deal proved to be huge. Details of the deal leaked to the *Washington Post* showed that in addition to giving Perelman and Ford the bank for nothing, the government had agreed to cover Perelman's losses, promising the cosmetics magnate $10.4 billion—an incredible sum that amounted to more than the government's controversial bailout of automaker Chrysler in 1980. The payouts started with $4.8 billion to cover the unpaid balance of all the bad loans that consumers were not going to pay off. The government also pledged to pay Perelman another $4.1 billion to cover all the interest payments that First Gibraltar would not be able to collect on those loans because they had gone into default. Finally, reporter Kathleen Day wrote, the government agreed not to tax Perelman on any of those payments, saving him another $1.5 billion.[29]

That was only the beginning. While the government agreed to cover the new owners' losses on the failed thrift, any profits the bank made on new ventures launched under Ford's leadership were theirs to keep; in other words, no matter how much money he and Perelman raked in, they would never have to give back a cent of their government handout. On top of that, the feds paid

First Gibraltar's new owners a management fee to run the bank, which allowed Ford, its new chief executive, to reward himself with a then-princely salary of $1 million a year.[30]

News of the deal sparked outrage on Capitol Hill, but congressional investigations did not lead to prosecutions.

"I would almost be happier if there was a criminal conspiracy, but it appears that the government officials involved were just plain incompetent," Representative Matthew Rinaldo, a New Jersey Republican, said before Congress in 1990.[31]

But for lawmakers like Rinaldo, it was simply too late. The deal could not be revoked. Moreover, as flippers, Perelman and Ford were able to make money one more time. Just three years after they bought First Gibraltar, the corporate vultures sold off the bank piecemeal to Bank of America, Chase Manhattan Bank, and other buyers, netting $900 million more. Perelman never understood why people were upset. "Here we thought we were doing what the government wanted investors to do, and we raised our hand as the highest bidder," he told Bloomberg in 2012. "All of a sudden, we found ourselves in a real strong negative backlash."[32]

For Puwalski and Paulson, a big takeaway from the First Gibraltar deal was that they needed to strike early, just as Ford and Perelman had when the government hadn't yet formulated its response to the collapse of the savings and loan industry and many of their competitors waited on the sidelines to see what would happen next. "One of the lessons we'd learned from the previous crisis is that it is usually the first couple of deals that turn out to be the best deals," Puwalski told me.

Like his competitor J. C. Flowers, Paulson first tried to buy IndyMac on his own but quickly realized he needed partners in order for his hedge fund to continue to avoid government regulations. Also like Flowers, Paulson didn't want his firm to be treated as a bank holding company with all the regulations that came with it. And, again like Flowers, this led him to Steve Mnuchin, who was busy putting together his group to buy IndyMac.

"Steven and John go a long way back," Puwalski told me. "John knew Steven's father. It was very natural that they would work together." Just as Flowers had done, Paulson put up enough money to own 24.974 percent of the bank, a hair shy of the amount where regulations would kick in.

So it was that Steve Mnuchin became the linchpin for a deal that not only would make him and his partners even richer but also force into destitution a huge number of everyday Americans—whose homes might have fit in a corner of the doorman-serviced palaces of the men who now controlled their mortgages.

PART II

FORECLOSURE KINGS

CHAPTER 6

A MORTGAGE DISCOVERED

AFTER HER FATHER'S DEATH, SANDY Jolley became her mother's full-time caregiver, financial manager, health care advocate, and nursing attendant—the manager of all her daily activities. Previously, Sandy had handled a lot of this, but it was only after Dick passed away that she realized how much he had done for her mother. He counted her pills, made her breakfast, and perhaps most importantly, kept her company. It was only after Dick's death that Patricia started dropping random items down the toilet and wandering the streets.

Sandy planned a small memorial service at a nearby funeral home. She used $2,000 of her parents' savings to pay for her father's cremation and interment in a stone drawer in a nearby mausoleum. About three weeks later, Sandy and her sister Julie set about assessing her parents' financial affairs. On a series of weekends, Sandy left her mother in her daughter's care while she and Julie slowly went through the paperwork filed in her parents' second-floor home office.

Most of her parents' finances were exactly what Sandy had expected. There was still about $300,000 in an investment portfolio, most of it a lump sum payment her mother received upon retirement. There was also a savings account with tens of thousands of dollars in it. Together her father and mother received about $3,000 each month from the government. Now, with Dick's death, his Social Security check would end. So the size of that monthly check would be cut in half.

Then they came to the house. Sandy and her sister were aware of their parents' mortgage, which had a balance of about $120,000. They knew the mortgage came with a very manageable $600 monthly payment. Their suburban, two-story house with views of the Santa Monica Mountains was now worth more than $500,000, thanks to long-term property appreciation. For decades, the Hickersons had responsibly paid down their debt. Now the equity in their home was a big source of the family's wealth. Over the long term, Sandy thought, she could pay for her mother's Alzheimer's care by tapping this equity while at the same time keeping the home in her family's hands. Her plan was to refinance the home loan and replace it with a new one that gave her a lump sum of cash to be paid back over a decade or more. She was already getting letters and phone calls from lenders, including World Savings Bank, her parent's longtime bank, where they had their mortgage and savings account, offering her the chance to pull $100,000 out of the home. This was basically an additional loan of $100,000 to be added to the $120,000. For Sandy, this seemed ideal. It would allow her to hire help to care for her mother part-time, freeing her to go back to work and receive health insurance. The $220,000, to be paid back over fifteen years, would have meant monthly payments of about $1,600, but Sandy thought she could easily handle that with a combination of her own earnings, her mother's Social Security check, and the interest on Patricia's investment portfolio, leaving the principal untouched.

But Sandy and Julie were in for a shock. As they sifted through the drawers and file cabinets, they came across a huge stack of papers: it was the reverse mortgage their parents had signed in the waning days of their father's life.

The first thing they noticed was the size of the stack. The legal disclosures alone ran more than twenty pages. It was hard for the two sisters to believe that Dick had known what he was getting himself into. "There was just so much documentation; inches of paperwork," Julie said. A month before his death, Dick had been drinking and taking painkillers. Would he really sign an agreement that—in exchange for wiping out his affordable mortgage and a onetime payment of $81,000—would allow IndyMac to take the house after he and Patricia died? Did he really understand that his family could no longer access the equity they had worked so hard to build? Or the extent to which the agreement permitted the bank to pile on fees? Did he understand that he, Patricia, and their heirs would be liable for all the bank's "costs and expenses," including all "reasonable and customary attorneys' fees" should they ever want the house back? Or that they would be charged interest on each fee? Or that the interest would compound, month after month, until it snowballed to a price his children could never afford?

"I just don't think my parents could understand what they were signing," Julie said. Their mother certainly didn't. Patricia frequently didn't know where she was or who she was talking to. Julie had no memory problems, a college degree, and twenty years' experience as a computer programmer, and she couldn't understand it herself. It just looked like a bunch of legal jargon. She and her sister knew something had gone wrong. They didn't know how wrong, though.

THE HICKERSONS' PREDICAMENT became more obvious as Sandy tried to refinance her parents' home. One by one by one, potential lenders told her that this was now impossible; their old loan had been wiped out by the reverse mortgage. IndyMac had recorded a $479,000 lien on their house, and they could not access their equity as long as the reverse mortgage was on the books.

So, Sandy decided to get rid of the reverse mortgage. On July 21, 2005, exactly one month after her father died, she tried to pay it back. She sat in the living room of the family home with her mother, and together they dialed the 800 number help line in the information packet for Financial Freedom Senior Funding. Patricia told the man on the other end of the line, a V. Mendoza, to speak with her daughter Sandy. She had questions about the loan.

Sandy explained that her father had died. The man advised her to send his death certificate. Sandy also asked if she could pay the loan back. V. Mendoza told her that would be expensive. It wouldn't be enough for the family to pay back the $81,418.42 they received as a result of the reverse mortgage. They owed nearly three times that: $228,413.45. And it would have to be paid in one lump sum. To get rid of the reverse mortgage, they would also need to come up with the $120,000 they'd previously owed on the house, plus about $22,000 in interest and fees that had already been assessed. That was a combination of initial origination fees and mortgage insurance, which came to $17,433, plus $4,000 more in interest and fees that had accrued already over the first two months.

Sandy was livid. It wasn't a problem to pay back the $80,000 lump sum—that was sitting in the bank. Coming up with $120,000 to repay the old loan would be possible since there was her mother's investment portfolio. It would be depleted, but only temporarily, as they could always pay it back by getting a new loan from one of several companies offering them credit on normal terms. But the $22,000 in interest and fees would be lost forever.

Sandy was certain that her parents had been deceived; that they had been victims of elder abuse. Damn it, Sandy thought, she was not going to pay $22,000 to this company after it had defrauded her parents.

"Looking back, I should have just paid them, gotten the house back, and sued them after the fact," she told me years later. "But I was so mad. I didn't want Financial Freedom to get a cent." It would be a very costly miscalculation.

INSTEAD OF PAYING Financial Freedom, Sandy started to do research. When she wasn't preparing her mother's meals or helping her dress, she made phone calls to attorneys, asking if it would be possible to sue the company for elder abuse or fraud. One early contact was Jeanne Constantine-Davis, a senior attorney at the AARP, the nation's largest lobbying organization for senior citizens.

Jeanne put Sandy in touch with a host of other people in similar circumstances. Many shared virtually the same story, among them Carol Anthony, a middle-aged bookkeeper for a pesticide and fertilizer company in California's Salinas Valley, the heart of America's "Salad Bowl," which grows so much of the country's leafy greens. Carol's mother had been sold an expensive reverse mortgage that was quickly eating the equity in her home. When Carol found out about the loan five months later, she ran to her local bank, got a cashier's check, and paid off the balance, including the interest and fees. Carol, unlike many victims, kept her family's home. Then she sued, alleging elder abuse and fraud, and won a substantial but undisclosed cash settlement from Financial Freedom.

Though Sandy hadn't been successful in her fight with the

bank, she was among the most vocal. Her phone started to ring, as family after family sought her advice. At first, she consulted for free, but Sandy came to realize that she was gaining expertise and started to charge families a onetime $500 fee for guiding them through the process.

All of this took a toll, however. Someone needed to be with her mother every moment of the day. Sandy's only breaks came once a week when Julie would visit, or when Kristin would come over to sit for her grandmother. Sandy earned very little money. She still did some business consulting, but most of the household income came from her mother's Social Security check. She was forced by circumstances to give up her part-time job organizing events for professional women and did not return to Vons supermarket. Soon, she was drawing down her mother's investment portfolio. First, bit by bit for basic living expenses, then for her own doctor visits that she paid for in cash. The enormity of the stress and grief washed over her, and she cried constantly and broke out in hives. "I needed help coping," she said. On one doctor's recommendation, Sandy started going to the Theiss Institute of Health and Fitness, a private exercise and nutrition center off Highway 101 that promoted a program of "integrated life wellness" to reduce stress. The staff there helped Sandy stabilize her emotions, but the treatment drained her mother's account further, until the opportunity to pay off the reverse mortgage slipped away.

In fact, she wasn't nearly as alone as she felt. There were government programs that could have helped her keep the home. For example, because Dick Hickerson had been a war veteran, Patricia, now a military widow, qualified for a monthly "aid and attendance" check to pay for her care. That money could have gone either to Sandy as compensation or to a professional caregiver, which would have freed Sandy to go back to work. She could have had health insurance. She could have paid off the reverse mortgage.

None of that occurred to her at the time, however, as she became obsessed with fighting Financial Freedom. She hunted for an attorney, but suing a big bank for fraud was an expensive, complicated proposition. It wasn't easy to find someone within their budget who was willing to take the case. Finally, Sandy's sister Julie was introduced to a lawyer named Brice Bryan, a congregant at the same modest evangelical church she attended in neighboring Simi Valley. "I didn't know him personally, but I had heard good things about him," Julie told me. Bryan was a small-time attorney who handled mostly personal injury cases from auto accidents. "In hindsight, I don't know that we could have afforded an attorney well versed in going up against a big company like that," she said. Bryan charged them a $10,000 retainer, which Sandy and Julie paid by dipping into their savings and their mother's trust. Bryan said they wouldn't owe anything else except expenses until they won.

ON JANUARY 9, 2008, after the housing market had begun to unravel, Sandy and Julie sued IndyMac and its salesman for negligence, "constructive fraud," and "financial elder abuse." They wanted the loan canceled, their family's equity returned, and damages for pain and suffering. Then they sat and waited. Financial Freedom didn't respond. While the reverse mortgage business was still making money, the rest of IndyMac was collapsing. Months passed.

It wasn't until July 30—after the bank had failed and been taken over by the federal government—that Financial Freedom's lawyers filed court papers. They argued that Sandy's suit should be dismissed, on the grounds that Dick and Patricia Hickerson knew exactly what they were signing. Furthermore, they maintained, there was nothing illegitimate about the product they were selling.

More legal jockeying followed. Sandy monitored the news of IndyMac's failure. She read reports that Steve Mnuchin, a Goldman Sachs executive, was leading an investment group that wanted to buy the bank. "I hoped it would be different," she said.

CHAPTER 7

FORECLOSURE MACHINE

THE DEAL THAT STEVE MNUCHIN got to acquire IndyMac was so sweet that many observers wondered if he had benefitted from an extreme form of special treatment.

His group, which ultimately included not only J. C. Flowers and John Paulson but also Mnuchin's former boss George Soros and computer industry titan Michael Dell (whose money had been managed, in part, by Mnuchin's friend Eddie Lampert), received all of IndyMac's assets—its branches, real estate, deposits, and loans—by promising to pour $1.6 billion of capital into the bank. Given that IndyMac was worth more than $30 billion when it failed and was still valued at $20 billion—including $6.5 billion in deposits—at the time of sale, that seemed like a pittance.

The new owners tried to put as much distance as possible between themselves and the previous management, rebranding the bank OneWest the same day they bought it. Unlike IndyMac, which was focused on aggressively selling mortgages, OneWest, a press release read, would be a community bank with deep local roots, "focused on delivering personalized, relationship-focused banking to its customers."[1]

Mnuchin had finally made his big score. He'd put in a relatively small amount of money—$10 million, according to multiple sources—but was awarded a 10 percent stake in the bank owing to his work cobbling together the deal and the new roles he would be assuming: chairman and chief executive officer. Thus, he would be the biggest relative winner when it was eventually flipped. His partners would profit in proportion to what they put in, but he would also be paid a hefty salary to run the bank, in addition to an outsized return when it was eventually sold. Mnuchin started spending most of his time in Los Angeles, eventually buying a sprawling nine-bedroom, ten-bathroom Bel Air estate for $26.5 million.[2] His wife, Heather, stayed behind in their Park Avenue apartment.

Though the government estimated it would lose more than $10 billion on IndyMac's failure,[3] the deal was virtually guaranteed to make money for Mnuchin and his investors, as it featured a loss-sharing agreement similar to the one Ford and Perelman had gotten for First Gibraltar. Any money that Mnuchin and his colleagues made on IndyMac's old loans, they got to keep. Any money they made on new business activities they started, they got to keep. But if any part of the old IndyMac lost money, the government would pick up most of the tab.

The sweeteners didn't end there. The deal required OneWest to continue the FDIC's limited loan modification program, but it also effectively removed economic incentives that would have otherwise caused Mnuchin's group to think twice about foreclosing on homeowners. If the new IndyMac foreclosed on a property and the borrower owed more on the home than it was worth (as was usually the case), the government paid most of the difference—along with the company's legal and appraisal fees, insurance costs, and any other expense of the foreclosure.

So, if a borrower owed $300,000 on a home that thanks to the housing bust was now worth only $100,000, Mnuchin's group could foreclose and sell the home at auction for $100,000. Then it billed the government for the difference, $200,000, plus all the fees incurred. On the other hand, any profits Mnuchin's group cleared on new products and services they introduced they would be allowed to keep without ever paying back the taxpayer. It was "heads I win, tails you lose"—all on the government's dime.[4]

FDIC officials insisted those terms were necessary to get the bank off the government's books. "It was the only way we could have gotten anyone to buy the bank," the then-chairwoman, Sheila Bair, told me. The FDIC had put IndyMac up for bid, and Mnuchin's group was the only one willing to purchase it all. Goldman Sachs and a number of other investment firms were willing to take on IndyMac's toxic mortgages, which the government was promising to cover, but not the obligations that came with holding consumer deposits. Whoever bought the deposits would have to write checks to consumers if they withdrew their money. To vulture capitalists, toxic mortgages were worth more than the $6.4 billion in cash that they would have been able to invest at safe—likely lower—rates of return.[5] Only one company, US Bank, wanted IndyMac's checking accounts, savings accounts, and CDs. But the Minneapolis-based bank required the government to not only cover potential losses but also *pay it* for taking these accounts off the FDIC's hands.

As the crash dragged on, the federal agency provided nearly identical terms to other early buyers of failed banks. For example, in May 2009 the FDIC signed a loss-sharing agreement with the buyers of BankUnited, the largest lender based in Florida. Like IndyMac, BankUnited failed because of risky, profligate lending. The lead investor in that case was Wilbur Ross, a septuagenarian merchant of debt who had made a career out of manipulating bankruptcy proceedings. In 1990, for example, Ross negotiated on behalf of the creditors of Donald Trump's failed Taj Mahal Casino Resort in Atlantic City, New Jersey, which had been built with $645 million in borrowed money but failed to turn a profit. Trump was allowed to keep a controlling interest in the casino—"the eighth wonder of the world," he called it—only after he agreed to pay bondholders high-interest payments as well as give them the ability to wrest control of the board should the operations deteriorate.[6] When things didn't turn around by the following July, Trump was forced to take the casino into Chapter 11 bankruptcy. In so doing, he surrendered half his interest in the casino—although the Trump name was still attached.[7] "The Trump name is still very much an asset and a big draw to people in Atlantic City,"[8] journalist Hilary Rosenberg quoted Ross as saying in her 1992 book *The Vulture Investors: Winners and Losers of the Great American Bankruptcy Feeding Frenzy.*

The Trump deal was atypical for Ross. His usual game was to use bankruptcy proceedings to take control of a company, raid its assets, and then flip it after the fact. This usually started with buying at least one-third of a target's debt. Because the company was in distress, the debt could be purchased for pennies on the dollar. As Eileen Appelbaum and Rosemary Batt wrote in the public policy magazine *American Prospect*, "Ross would then become the largest creditor, giving him a lot of power in the bankruptcy proceedings. This positioned him to be the strongest bidder to take the company out of bankruptcy—paying for the purchase by forgiving the loans he had made to it. At the end of the day, the debt he held would be wiped out, but he would now be the biggest or only shareholder in the company." Over the years, Ross had used this strategy to buy and flip coal mines and textile factories. He was perhaps best known for buying several bankrupt steel companies and bundling them into a platform called

International Steel Group, which he flipped to the Indian-owned multinational Mittal Steel Company in 2005. According to Appelbaum and Batt, Ross made $4.5 billion, or fourteen times his investment. Along the way, he raided the workers' pension fund for exactly that amount; in other words, the money he made off the deal came from leaving employees without promised retirement savings.[9]

With Ross's purchase of BankUnited, it was the federal government rather than workers that took the hit. His group pledged to put in just $900 million for a bank with $12.8 billion in assets and $8.6 billion in deposits. The FDIC estimated its losses on BankUnited at $4.9 billion,[10] an amount that proved to be optimistic. A year and a half later, the agency upped its guess to $5.7 billion.[11] But Ross and his group made out fine. The bank turned a profit for nine consecutive years, largely on the strength of massive government subsidies. According to documents I obtained using the Freedom of Information Act, the government paid $2.7 billion to cover their losses on the old loans.[12]

Ross and Mnuchin were both looking to put in the least amount of money in return for the biggest government subsidy and the chance to flip the bank as quickly as possible. They bristled when Bair proposed adding rules around capitalization—forcing investors to infuse more cash into the banks they acquired to make sure they didn't fail again—and requirements that private equity buyers hold on to formerly failed banks for at least three years. In a letter of protest, Wilbur Ross proclaimed himself to be "dismayed" at rules that he called "unfair and unreasonable. . . . I assure you that my group will never again bid if the current policy statement is adopted in its present form. Does the FDIC really want to be stuck with hundreds of failed banks?"[13] Mnuchin wrote Bair too, using more measured language but delivering the same message.[14] Faced with what the *Wall Street Journal* dubbed a "ferocious lobbying effort by the buyout industry," the agency backed down.[15]

Within a year, Mnuchin and his investors bought two more failed banks from the FDIC: La Jolla Bank of San Diego and First Federal Bank of Los Angeles. In each case, the government sold the failed bank at a discount and then offered a loss-sharing agreement, guaranteeing to cover much of OneWest's losses when it repossessed borrowers' homes. Through these sales, Mnuchin's banking empire grew. By February 2010, OneWest had amassed eighty-one branches, $14 billion in deposits, and $27 billion in assets—almost all of it acquired from the government.[16] Over the life of the agreements, the feds would pay the new owners $1.5 billion[17]—roughly the same amount of money Mnuchin and his investors had pumped into IndyMac Bank to buy it.

Almost as soon as the IndyMac deal closed, signs emerged that OneWest's effort to keep families in their homes was, at best, haphazard. Homeowners felt like they were on a conveyer belt toward foreclosure. Though OneWest's deal with the FDIC required it to review a borrower's entire file, confirm all relevant facts, and offer a financially responsible work-around plan, most of the time, that didn't appear to happen.

An early, disturbing sign of OneWest's strategy came just three months into Mnuchin's ownership, on July 9, 2009, in the conference room of a law office surrounded by green grass and palm trees in West Palm Beach, Florida. A bank employee, Erica Johnson-Seck, had been flown to Florida to be deposed in a wrongful-foreclosure suit filed by Israel Machado, the owner of a pool-cleaning business who had fallen behind on his $400,000 mortgage. Since the property had declined in value, Machado wanted a "work-out," with the size of his loan reduced to the property's market value of $200,000. There was no way the bank would get more than that if it sold his property—meaning that, ordinarily, such a move would have made sense for everyone involved. "The whole intent was to get them to come to the negotiating table," Machado told the *Wall Street Journal*, "to get me in a fixed-rate mortgage that worked."[18]

Mnuchin had promised to turn OneWest into a community bank with a close, personal relationship with its customers, but Johnson-Seck was about as remote from most of the company's borrowers as one could get. She spent her days in a sprawling 129-acre office complex in Austin, Texas, supervising a team of about fifty employees charged with resolving delinquent loans. Her title was vice president of bankruptcy and foreclosure, and, she said, she was one of only eight people in the company authorized to give final approval for OneWest to take a home. But there were so many foreclosures that it was nearly impossible for her to give any individual case much attention. At the time of the deposition, OneWest had 77,000 homes in foreclosure, she said—or more than 10 percent of all its loans. The number kept climbing, with twelve thousand new foreclosures in June alone.[19]

Johnson-Seck told Machado's attorney, Tom Ice, that her team signed 6,000 foreclosure documents a week, and that she personally signed about 750 of them.

"How long to do you spend executing each document?" Ice asked her.

"Not more than thirty seconds," she replied. "I have changed my signature considerably. "It's just an *E* now."

"Is it true that you don't read each document before you sign it?" the attorney pressed.

"That's true," she said proudly. "Everyone's in a groove now."

What about outreach? Ice wanted to know if anyone from the bank ever went to a house to talk to the delinquent property owner. Sometimes, Johnson-Seck said, there would be a campaign where "they'll leave door knockers so that the borrowers know that we're trying to reach them," to deliver some kind of help. But in general, when a property was in foreclosure, the bank would send out an employee with specific instructions *not* to talk to the homeowner. "Go to the house, make sure it's not burnt down, make sure the grass is not ten feet high, and bring us that information if it is," she explained. "But don't knock on the door and contact the borrower." The bank didn't want to get anyone upset, Johnson-Seck added.

The process led to questionable foreclosures all over the country. In a Cleveland suburb, social worker Carla Duncan was heading out of town for a short trip when she stopped off at home to check her mail and found a note from a OneWest field inspector saying that her house was vacant and was going to be boarded up. "It wasn't vacant, I was living there," she told the *Columbus Dispatch*. "There were curtains on the windows. The radio was playing. The dog was there."

An incredulous Duncan had no idea that OneWest had already begun foreclosure proceedings on her three-bedroom home. She was even current on her payments. But OneWest refused to accept a loan modification that had been approved before Mnuchin's group bought the bank, and it wanted to substantially increase her interest rate and monthly payment, *and* add late fees. The court records would trace the foreclosure to OneWest's office in Austin, with Erica Johnson-Seck signing key documents.

Carla Duncan was able to keep her home, but only after a five-year court battle that included filing personal bankruptcy. "It got to the point that I was afraid to open my own door," she said.[20] And she was one of the lucky ones.

THIS PROCESS, OF having an employee sign hundreds of foreclosure documents a day without truly reviewing them, came to be known as robosigning. It devastated entire communities. It laid waste to the country's housing market and badly hamstrung the economic recovery. The process was widespread. It was also illegal. In February 2012 the US Justice Department, together with forty-nine states and the District of Columbia, reached what was called the National Mortgage Settlement with the nation's five largest banks. JPMorgan Chase, Bank of America, Wells Fargo, Citi, and Ally/GMAC agreed to provide $25 billion in consumer relief in exchange for the government dropping its case on illegal foreclosures.[21] But though the dollar amount looked big, the settlement was full of holes. Families who'd already lost their homes to foreclosure were due just $1,400 each in compensation.[22] As for borrowers fighting to hold on, the settlement allowed banks to claim they'd provided consumer relief while still dispossessing the house.

Take, for example, a delinquent borrower who owed $200,000 on a home that was now worth just $100,000. The solution advanced by consumer advocates—which was allowed by the settlement—was that the big banks could write down the loan balance to $100,000. This would be a win-win: the borrower could stay in his or her home, and the bank wouldn't get more than that anyway by selling the house through foreclosure. But the settlement also allowed the banks to take credit for helping consumers by facilitating short sales, where the bank allows the borrower to sell their house to someone else for less than value of the loan. Banks were also allowed to claim they'd provided that $100,000 in relief when they simply allowed the borrower to hand the deed of the home to the bank, a practice called deed in lieu of foreclosure. In both cases, the consumer avoided the stigma that came with a foreclosure on their credit report—but ended up with no money and no home. According to a 2014 report by the Urban Institute, a think tank in Washington, DC, this was the most popular form of relief offered by Bank of America, Wells Fargo, and JPMorgan Chase.[23] Clearly, all the money the banks had given to politicians and spent on lobbying was paying off.

Incredibly, OneWest ended up paying nothing at all. Though Treasury Department officials found the bank engaged in "unsafe and unsound" practices when handling mortgage loans and foreclosures, that bank employees lied in foreclosure paperwork, and that it failed to devote "adequate oversight" to its foreclosure process, the Justice Department didn't haul it into court. Instead, Mnuchin and his fellow board members from J. C. Flowers, Paulson & Co., and George Soros's fund simply agreed to an additional level of oversight.[24]

Despite the lack of action from Washington, OneWest wasn't out of the woods. Mnuchin's bank still could have faced a threat from California, where Attorney General Kamala Harris had ridden her tough talk against banks to national prominence, securing a prime speaking slot at the 2012 Democratic National Convention. On the National Mortgage Settlement, she negotiated a side deal for California that got Golden State consumers a higher dollar value of relief than those in the rest of the country. Harris also won plaudits for creating a Mortgage Fraud Strike Force "charged with protecting innocent homeowners and bringing to justice those who defraud them."[25]

The unit quickly went to work on OneWest, which had been

the focus of so many consumer complaints. After going through hundreds of loan files, on January 18, 2013, four deputy attorney generals produced a twenty-five-page memo detailing "evidence suggestive of widespread misconduct." OneWest employees, Harris's deputies said, "signed backdated and false" documents that propelled borrowers rapidly toward foreclosure. Bank staff also performed acts in the foreclosure process "without valid legal authority" and "failed to comply with requirements related to the execution, timing, and mailing of foreclosure documents."[26]

Harris's deputies recommended that their boss sue the bank—an important step, they said, because OneWest had already foreclosed on thirty-five thousand California homes. In addition, they explained, the bank's loss-share agreement with the FDIC stated clearly that Mnuchin's group could receive payments from the government only if it followed proper foreclosure practices, including the loan modification program established by the FDIC. If the state of California found that OneWest violated those rules, the payments could stop—saving not only homeowners, since the bank would have much less incentive to foreclose if it wasn't being paid when it did so, but government coffers as well.

Oddly, despite a strong recommendation from her staff, Harris never sued OneWest Bank. "Case NOT filed despite strong recommendations," reads a cover sheet atop the memo. As a result, no one at OneWest faced prosecution, and no customers got their homes back. Yet the loss-share payments from the FDIC kept coming. It was business as usual.

Six years later, Harris offered her first substantive explanation for the nonprosecution, telling her hometown paper, the *San Francisco Chronicle*, that her department's hands were tied. "We didn't have the legal ability," she argued, because federal law prevented the state from issuing subpoenas. "I am pretty certain based on what we knew that there should have been some accountability and consequence," Harris explained, but "the rules were written in favor of the banks."[27]

The twenty-five-page memo produced by Harris's staff, however, had presented a detailed plan for how Mnuchin's bank could be held to account using only publicly available loan records. While recognizing the difficulty of proceeding without a subpoena, the state prosecutors estimated their chance of success as "moderate."

"We believe that there is substantial public justice value in fully investigating OneWest's conduct through the use of civil discovery and holding it publicly accountable," they wrote.[28] Harris not only turned them down, but also her office buried the report. The only reason we know about California's investigation into OneWest today is because David Dayen of the news website The Intercept obtained a leaked copy of the memo Harris's staff wrote and published it in January 2017.[29] By then, Harris was no longer California attorney general. She was a US senator.

SANDY'S ROAD TO foreclosure began three years after she filed her lawsuit, seeking to void her parents' reverse mortgage. The suit had devolved into a seemingly never-ending series of depositions, motions, and countermotions. She paid the mounting court costs by borrowing money from her sister, spending down her savings, and pulling money out of her mother's trust. Steve Mnuchin's bank fought her every step of the way. The case still hadn't gone to trial, when a letter addressed to Patricia Hickerson arrived from the bank.

On the surface, at least, it had little to do with the ongoing court case. The letter, dated December 14, 2010, was from a debt collector at Financial Freedom Acquisition LLC, a wholly owned subsidiary of OneWest. The return address was a post office box in Austin, Texas, a few miles from the office complex where Erica Johnson-Seck had signed so many foreclosure notices. The letter informed Sandy's mother that she had violated the terms of the reverse mortgage:

"Upon the occurrence of a maturity event, including a borrower's decision to permanently leave and no longer occupy the subject property as a primary residence, the loan becomes due and payable." Because Patricia no longer lived in the home, the letter explained, she would need to present a plan to pay $300,000 within thirty days, or the bank would begin the process of taking the house. In the meantime, the letter disclosed, the bank would continue to add interest and fees to the total, so the required payment would likely be higher.

"As we notify you now that the above referenced loan is due and payable, we are hopeful that our services have been true to our mission and have enhanced your financial security and independence."

Sandy was livid. Her mother still lived in the house! How could the bank possibly believe that her mother had moved out? Yes, Sandy had disconnected the home phone number that the bank had on file. But that was just to stop the constant ringing of the telephone that came from solicitors seeking to sell all manner of products and services to her senile mother. Furthermore, Sandy had sent Financial Freedom all the necessary paperwork. "My mother, Patricia Hickerson, is not deceased and occupies the property," she wrote in response. "You sent a representative out here to verify her occupancy some months ago. I sent in your occupancy form shortly afterward and signed it for my mother, including my power of attorney to do so."

When she'd filed suit in January 2008, her attorney had told her the case would go to trial that November. "Financial Freedom had other ideas and created delay after delay until Mom died," Sandy declared. "They didn't want her to be seen in court." She demanded an apology. "I am sure you are also aware that we are in litigation with Financial Freedom regarding this loan fraudulently sold to my parents," she wrote. "How dare you send a letter right before Christmas without cause." The bank responded with a second notice, restating its demand. It wanted to be paid.

MEANTIME, SANDY WAS losing the legal battle. A key development had occurred earlier that year, in February, when the bank received a favorable ruling in the Simi Valley courtroom of Judge David Worley, a conservative jurist appointed by California's last Republican governor, Arnold Schwarzenegger. Worley dismissed charges of elder abuse and unfair competition against Financial Freedom on the grounds that Sandy had waited too long to file suit. The statute of limitations had expired, he said. The judge also dismissed charges of negligence and fraud, saying there was no "triable issue of material fact" regarding Dick and Patricia's reliance on the salesman's pitch.

Judge Worley allowed just one part of the case to go forward: the issue of Dick and Patricia's mental capacity. If their dementia was severe enough that they did not understand the loan documents they were signing, the reverse mortgage could be voided, he ruled. That was a matter that would have to be decided by a jury.

Here Sandy found some reason for optimism. The medical records for both of her parents were substantial. They showed that her mother had been seeking treatment from the UCLA Alzheimer's Disease Center for three years before she signed the reverse mortgage. In September 2004, eight months before Patricia signed on to the loan, the director of the center's neuropsychological lab wrote that the disease had advanced to a stage where Patricia did not know what day it was, had trouble identifying colors, and could not spell the word *world* backward. The family's regular physician, Dr. Peter Margolis, also testified, stating in a sworn deposition that, in his opinion, neither Patricia nor Dick was competent enough to sign a reverse mortgage. Though Dick was able to carry out daily tasks such as cooking and driving, a CT scan revealed "a diminution of brain structure." Dick was also suffering from cancer and enduring chemotherapy, conditions, Margolis said, that put strain on all parts of the body, including cognitive function. A heavyset man with a history of heart disease, Dick sometimes forgot to take Crestor, a cholesterol-lowering medication, and couldn't remember that it had been prescribed.

Why, OneWest's attorney asked, couldn't Dick understand that Financial Freedom would be "taking a security interest in property for the repayment of the loan"?

"He had trouble keeping track of his pills," Margolis replied. "If he couldn't keep track of his pills, how could he understand that?"

To combat this line of argument, the bank hired its own doctor, a forensic psychiatrist, and paid him $20,000 to review Dick's and Patricia's medical files. Dr. Dominick Addario was a professional expert witness who'd testified in more than two hundred depositions and fifty trials. A retired navy lieutenant commander with more than thirty years in practice, he sported a friendly beard that recalled Sigmund Freud. Unlike Margolis, who tended to hem and haw in the way that most people do under pressure, Addario spoke with measured authority.

Addario never had the chance to meet Dick Hickerson, and he

evaluated Patricia only once, in January 2009. The transcript of their exchange is painful to read. Patricia can't recall the city or state where they are meeting, or the name of the country she lives in. After failing to name the color of her dog, a golden retriever, Addario asks her about animals more generally. She isn't able to name an animal that flies in the sky.

"By the way, how many legs does a cow have?" Addario asks.

"Five," Patricia responds. Then, realizing she may have made a mistake, she lets out a little laugh. "I haven't ever had a cow," she says.

Based on this examination and a review of Patricia's medical record, Addario concluded that Patricia was competent to sign the reverse mortgage.

"At the time I saw her, she was still able to live at home and was socially functional, in that she could be guided by family members," Addario said in a deposition in his office in San Diego. Patricia still recognized her daughter, he stated "and acted in a socially appropriate way." For example, she "was able to sit for an hour with me without being panicked or confused or needing to leave the room or going to the window." Addario dismissed Margolis's testimony as lacking clinical rigor. "I have more than once seen doctors who are compassionate, caring about their patients, not describe as accurately the patient's actual condition years before," he explained.

As for Dick Hickerson, Addario testified that the diminution of brain structure noted in the CT scan was normal for a seventy-nine-year-old man. Moreover, he said, Dick's decision to take out the reverse mortgage came from a desire "to care for his family."

"His motivation and the desire to do these things appear to be within the realm of rational thinking," the psychiatrist stated. "He was not taking out a loan, for instance, to drive off in a Rolls-

Royce or . . . run off to Vegas or something. So, he appeared to be rational. There appeared to be no evidence that he was suffering from a delusional disorder or an impairment of the mind."

IN ADDITION TO her dementia, Patricia's physical health was deteriorating. In the summer of 2010, she was hospitalized with a colon infection that never went away. She had constant diarrhea, which Sandy had to clean up. Gaunt and increasingly frail, Patricia was no longer safe in her two-story home. She fell, sometimes down the stairs. (Sandy would call 911 and have paramedics come to lift her up.) Patricia really should have had professionals caring for her, but the family could no longer afford it. On top of that, the terms of the reverse mortgage were clear: a nursing home was not an option, because if Patricia left the house, the bank could take it.

But as Sandy fought the bank's attempts to foreclose, she realized reluctantly that it was time to say good-bye to her mom. She checked Patricia into Sarah House, a hospice facility in Santa Barbara, an hour's drive north.

Patricia was at Sarah House for ten days. Sandy spent the nights sleeping on a chair in her room. On the eleventh day, Sandy went home to check on the house, planning to come back early the next day. She got a call at five in the morning, telling her to come up; that Patricia's breathing was labored. Fifteen minutes later, another call. Her mother had passed away.

FIVE MONTHS AFTER Patricia died, the pretrial motions had concluded, and a jury was finally seated. Opening arguments commenced on September 2, 2011, in a fourth-floor courtroom at the

Hall of Justice in downtown Ventura, the county seat, part of a tan complex of concrete government buildings set off by green lawns. Like the earlier motions, which were heard by Judge David Worley, the trial was overseen by sixty-seven-year-old former litigator Henry Walsh. The judge, a Republican appointee, had a quick wit, a short temper, and a penchant for wearing bow ties. He could often be seen looking over a pair of clear reading glasses.

Sandy sat on a bench next to her attorney, Brice Bryan, and Ingrid Evans, an elder abuse lawyer from San Francisco who had joined the case pro bono. Financial Freedom was at the other table, represented by Eric T. Lamhofer, sporting a blue suit, a square jaw, and an even, white smile. Lamhofer worked for the law firm Wolfe & Wyman, and had driven up from Orange County for the trial. While Sandy had borrowed heavily from her siblings and spent a large chunk of her mother's estate on legal fees, Lamhofer's bills were being paid by the bank's insurance.

Sandy's attorney went first, arguing in his opening statement that Financial Freedom had perpetrated financial elder abuse. "It's about fraudulent concealment," he said. "It's about negligence." Lamhofer told a different tale. In an expansive opening statement that lasted more than two hours, he painted his client as Dick and Patricia's savior, providing the elderly couple with much needed cash in their final years. "Richard, although still very mentally sharp, was physically in a bad situation," Lamhofer told the jury. Sandy's father "saw fairly clearly that he was not going to be around for an extended period of time" and wanted to make sure his wife was well cared for. In Lamhofer's version, the salesman who visited the Hickersons' door wasn't a predator but a trusted financial advisor and friend.

"When this loan closed, the loan documents were signed,"

Lamhofer said, "Richard was so relieved that he had been able to get this done that he threw his arms around Les Barnhart and hugged him and thanked him for removing this burden, this worry that had been hanging over his head for years. . . . Doesn't sound like somebody who thinks they were taken advantage of." With Patricia and Dick gone, there was no way to know if this was true.

As he presented his case, Lamhofer turned the tables on Sandy, painting her as a greedy child who contributed little and was only after her parents' life savings. "When was the last time you worked before today?" he asked.

"I can't recall," she responded.

"So, as you sit here, you have no recollection as to when the last time is that you worked?"

"Right," Sandy said.

Lamhofer's questioning left Sandy no opening to describe how she'd put in far more than forty hours a week caring for her sick and dying mother—changing her diapers, picking her up when she fell, calling the paramedics when she wandered the streets late at night. "They were saying she was just in it for the money," her sister Julie told me years later. "They didn't care that she stopped her own personal life for five years and took care of my parents. She had no life because she was taking care of a person with Alzheimer's."

In all, the bank kept Sandy on the stand for six days. Lamhofer pressed her on an earlier, failed business ventures. (In 2002 she had invested in a tanning salon in North Carolina, a financial disaster that had led her to declare bankruptcy in 2004, a year before her father died.) The attorney also questioned the money Sandy spent on stress counseling as she fought Financial Freedom and cared for her mother. "It was just a whole failure of the federal process to protect people from being taken advantage of," Julie said.

THE SCOPE OF the trial proceeded narrowly per Judge Worley's earlier determination. While Sandy's attorneys again tried to argue wider issues of concealment and fraud, the case was fought in only one area: whether both Dick and Patricia lacked the mental capacity to understand the reverse mortgage. Even if only Sandy's father understood what he was signing, Judge Walsh told the jury, the loan would stand. This proved decisive. After the trial concluded, jury foreman Catherine Berning signed an sworn affidavit saying that although "a majority of the jury members thought fraud was committed" by Financial Freedom and that the bank "concealed important costs regarding the reverse mortgage . . . it would not matter and would not make a difference because Richard Hickerson wanted the reverse mortgage."

Ultimately, Lamhofer's attacks on Sandy's character were successful. On September 29, 2011, the jury sided with the bank. They found the bank's expert medical witnesses more credible than Dick's and Patricia's own doctors. According to Berning's statement, "There was discussion among the jury that Sandy Jolley influenced the declaration of Dr. Margolis, so as to make it more beneficial to her parents' case. Because most of the jury didn't like Sandy Jolley, or find her credible in her testimony, several said that they didn't want her to get her parents' house."

EVEN AFTER THE jury verdict, Sandy wouldn't give up. She appealed. And lost. She fought one foreclosure after another and won an additional year of delays, which she used to complain to the US Department of Housing and Urban Development, which regulates reverse mortgages. "I have been praying for an audit and investigation of the above loan since the day it was sold to my sick and dying parents," she wrote to an investigator in the HUD inspector general's office. "I have studied this contract word for word for years and have found Financial Freedom and now One-West Bank have not complied with or followed one Federal Law or regulation." HUD officials listened attentively, but no investigation followed. So, Sandy went to her congresswoman, whose staff got the agency to review the case. Again, the government found no wrongdoing.

SANDY FINALLY LOST her family home on a sunny Tuesday morning, April 2, 2013.

She got up early that day, dressed as if she were heading to court, and drove her thirteen-year-old BMW thirty miles up the California coast to Ventura, where the San Diego–based Cal-Western Reconveyance Corporation would be auctioning off the house on Benson Way for the benefit of Steve Mnuchin's One-West Bank.

The auction was scheduled for eleven o'clock in front of the same courthouse where she lost at trial. Sandy arrived an hour early and waited in her car, breathing deeply, clutching a large packet of paperwork. After everything she'd been through—fighting the reverse mortgage for eight years now, including five years in court—she was not going to give up just because the bank put the property on the block.

She'd printed a four-page flyer on her home inkjet printer and made dozens of copies. She planned to show every potential buyer that the property was legally troubled; that they would be in for a fight if they bought it, that they would not be able to take ownership, that they would not have clean title. "Unlawful, Unfair, and Fraudulent Business Practices & Rescission" was the heading of her handout, all in bold type. "Hickerson v. Financial Freedom, et al., Case Number 56–200800310670." Underneath, bullet pointed, were nearly fifty problems with the property, each linked to a specific court record. "Overcharging of recording fees—Exhibits 56, 57, 58," read one bullet. "Failure to disclose monthly servicing fees, see Exh. 186, 187, 223, 280," read another.

Sandy got out of her car and walked to a shady patch of cement in front of the courthouse. One by one, buyers arrived. She gave a packet to each of them. "I started handing out my flyers, saying, 'Please, please don't bid on this house. I am begging you,'" she recalled. Each prospective buyer agreed not to bid on the Benson Way house. There were other properties to purchase. Sandy started to feel relieved.

Then, just a few minutes before the auction was set to begin, another woman arrived. While other potential buyers held clipboards, notebooks, and legal pads, she set up a small, foldable desk for her laptop by the courthouse windows. Then she carried out a chair from her car and put on a Bluetooth headset. She wouldn't talk to Sandy. She wouldn't take Sandy's flyer. "We don't care about that," she snapped.

In that moment, Sandy's heart sank. The house, she knew, was finally lost. When her home was called, the woman bid on it, and so did one man. Bidding started at $315,097. It ended with the woman buying it for $330,000. She shut her laptop, packed up her portable desk, took off her headset, and drove off. Sandy's was the only home the woman bought at the courthouse that day.

Sandy didn't know who this woman represented—only that

she paid for the house with a wire transfer rather than a cashier's check. With no idea what would happen next, she walked back to her car, shut the door, and sat there crying. "I had a breakdown," she said. "I just sat in my car for an hour or two and just had a complete breakdown." Financial Freedom had destroyed her. "That how I felt. We lost the court case, and now we lost everything. I was helpless, and I thought soon I would be homeless." But eventually she composed herself. Sandy turned the key in the ignition and drove back to Thousand Oaks, to the home on Benson Way that had been in her family for thirty-five years. Her daughter was waiting for her there.

IT WAS A long night. Sandy and Kristin looked around. Between Patricia's illness and the court case, they had never really gone through Dick's and Patricia's belongings. There was all of their furniture, including Dick's favorite brown easy chair, still in the living room, where he had watched that reverse mortgage commercial featuring James Garner years earlier. "I was paralyzed," she recalled. "What was I going to pack? For what? For where? What was I going to pack in case they came into our house and started throwing things out?"

The next morning, Sandy and Kristin were still at home when they heard a driver kill the engine of a car and walk toward their front door. The visitor didn't knock or ring the doorbell, but they didn't leave right away.

The person, thirty-three-year-old Bruno Larrea, had come to post an eviction notice. He was affixing the three-day "Notice to Quit" to the front door with a piece of blue masking tape when Sandy and Kristen opened it to greet him.

Sandy took the paper and started to read. "Dear Occupant," the notice began. "I am a Field Manager for Strategic Property Management, who represents ColFin AI-CA5 LLC. ColFin AI-CA5 LLC purchased the home you occupy at a foreclosure auction. It is very important that you contact me right away."

Who was ColFin AI-CA5 LLC? Sandy didn't know. She couldn't imagine the person who would come up with such a strange name for a company—"only someone motivated entirely by greed," she thought. She read on. The letter described the accompanying eviction notice as a formality, "purely as a protective measure for the new owner." This new owner, the paper said, didn't want to kick them out—it wanted them to stay and pay rent.

"We want nothing more than to have you remain in the home as our tenant," it said. "Our mission is to help people whose lives have been impacted by the foreclosure crisis. We understand that you have been through an incredibly difficult process, and we would like to work with you toward a brighter future. Our goal is to give you a second chance to continue to call your house 'home.' Everyone deserves a second chance."

Sandy looked up from the letter and felt a mix of emotions. On one hand, there was anger. Her parents had made their mortgage payments month after month for decades, accruing hundreds of thousands of dollars of equity. And now she was being asked to pay rent on the same house, to build wealth for a nameless, faceless company represented by a property manager who'd come to her door? On the other hand, there was relief. She would not have to leave right away. She wouldn't be homeless.

How much would it cost? she wanted to know. The answer, Larrea said, was $2,400 a month. It was four times the monthly mortgage payments her parents had been making before they signed the reverse mortgage with Financial Freedom. It was also more than 30 percent higher than the going rate for rental homes in the neighborhood, which the Census Bureau put at about $1,800 a month.

Larrea told Sandy she would also have to buy renter's insurance and pay a security deposit of $800. That really got her going. A security deposit? On a home her family had lived in for thirty-five years? This new landlord had done nothing to fix up the property. Now it wanted to take her money in case *she* damaged it? It was outrageous.

But the deposit was nonnegotiable. If she wanted to stay, she would have to pay it, Larrea said. In any case, he argued, the security deposit was a formality. Everyone understood the house would look lived in when she moved out. The company wouldn't nickel-and-dime her, he promised. She would get her deposit back—no problem.

Sandy told Larrea she wanted to stay, but she tried to negotiate on the price. The next day, she sent him an email. "As we discussed yesterday, it is our intention to sign a year lease with you," she wrote. But she should have to pay less than $2,400 a month, she wrote, "due to the amount of money we have spent and continue to spend on maintenance and care of the property." She ticked off $4,800 in investments her family had recently made in the house: a new water heater, an upgrade to their sprinkler system, money for a gardener who helped them take care of the backyard orchard of eighteen fruit trees. "We want to continue to work with you in order to maintain the property in the best condition," she wrote. "Please let us know if we can meet and discuss."

Larrea said the new owner wouldn't budge on the price, but he gave them a $500 "concession" for the first three months. And, in exchange for the concession, the term of the lease was cut short. Instead of lasting for a year, it was set to expire in the fall, giving the landlord a fresh opportunity to raise the rent. That knocked the rent down to $1,900 until August, after which it would jump to the $2,400. The revised lease also would push much of the maintenance requirements off the new landlord and onto Sandy, the tenant. She would be responsible for maintaining the grounds and fixing the pipes if they backed up.

Sandy signed the lease with a thick, black-tipped pen. At the end of the document, she promised not to remove her parents' oven or dishwasher from the house; they were now property of the owner. She also acknowledged having received keys to the house, a garage door opener, and a key to the gas fireplace. She had them already, of course; it was she who had given a copy of the keys to her new landlord.

PART III

THE GREATEST THING I'VE EVER DONE

CHAPTER 8

COLFIN AI-CA5 LLC

HISTORICALLY, PROPERTY OWNERSHIP IN AMERICA has been transparent. When an average person buys a house, it's pretty easy to figure out who the owner is. The deed to the house, recorded by the county, is signed by the seller and the buyer. The deed to my house is signed by me and my wife. The address, on file with the county, is the house where we live. If we were to sell to another family, the new owner's name would be on file. If we were to buy a rental property, the deed to that building would list our names and our address.

The new owner of Sandy's family home was a different matter. ColFin AI-CA5 LLC wasn't a human, and it didn't even appear to be owned by one. It was a shell company incorporated in a law office in Delaware, but after the property was sold, the deed wasn't mailed to Delaware. Instead, the Cal-Western Reconveyance Corporation, which had sold the house on behalf of Steve Mnuchin's OneWest Bank, sent the deed to a suburban office park in Scottsdale, Arizona, across the street from Salt River Fields, the stadium where the Arizona Diamondbacks and Colorado Rockies play their spring training games. Sandy, meantime, was instructed by Bruno Larrea to either pay her rent online or mail the check, made out to "ColFin AI-CA5 LLC," to a post office box in New York City.

The company seemed to be everywhere and nowhere at once. Who was her new landlord?

AS SANDY STRUGGLED to get her bearings, government officials across America were asking similar questions. Title to millions of homes was changing hands not only from homeowners to landlords, but from human beings to faceless corporations whose actual owners could not easily be identified. This change had been under way for a while when it came to apartment complexes. In 1991 the Census Bureau had found that 92 percent of rental properties were owned by people.[1] After the savings and loan crisis, however, the government carried out a fire sale of hundreds of thousands of apartment units, selling them off in bulk for pennies on the dollar to corporate raiders such as the real estate magnate and self-proclaimed "grave dancer" Sam Zell. In the housing bust, this dynamic repeated itself, but with single-family homes. By 2015, the Census Bureau reported, the proportion of residential real estate owned by people had fallen to 74 percent. Nearly three million US homes, not to mention thirteen million apartment units, were owned by shell companies, LLCs, LLPs, or LPs (limited liability partnerships and limited partnerships, respectively). For the sake of comparison, that's about ten times as many as were owned by affordable-housing providers such as churches, charities, and nonprofit organizations.[2]

The change caught the eye of international money-laundering experts. "It reminds me of Moldova after the fall of the Soviet Union: oligarchs running wild, stashing their gains in buildings. It's a lot easier to hide your money in real estate than a bank account," said James Wright, an attorney and former Treasury Department bank examiner who now helps foreign governments combat money laundering. "Back then you'd walk down the street [in Moldova], and people would say, 'That building is a washing machine.' Everyone knew it. Today America is not that different."

Law enforcement officials were especially worried that homes were being used to launder money in high-cost cities like New York, San Francisco, Los Angeles, and Miami, where federal banking regulators flagged 30 percent of cash purchases as suspicious transactions. "Shell companies can often be formed without disclosing the individuals that ultimately own or control them," noted the Treasury Department's Financial Crimes Enforcement Network (FinCEN) in one public advisory. "Criminals abuse this anonymity to mask their identities, involvement in transactions, and origins of their wealth, hindering law enforcement efforts to identify individuals behind illicit activity." With the foreclosure crisis, all-cash transactions came to account for a quarter of all residential real estate purchases, "totaling hundreds of billions of dollars nationwide," the Treasury police said, "and are particularly exposed to abuse."[3]

But this shift to corporate ownership also had more prosaic implications. Tenants couldn't figure out who to complain to when something went wrong. Government officials didn't know who to hold responsible for code violations and neighborhood blight. First-time home buyers were denied the opportunity to buy affordable homes with bank loans because the properties had already been scooped up by shell companies.

These distant landlords remain hidden from public view, hiking the rent, ramping up evictions, all without anyone knowing their true identities. Though Treasury police now know the true owners of many of these residential properties, thanks to federal anti-money-laundering efforts, those ownership stakes are not disclosed to the public. When I filed a Freedom of Information Act request seeking information on the "beneficial owners" of LLCs, the Treasury Department refused to supply it—initially going so far as to say it could "neither confirm nor deny the existence of the materials," because the records were protected by the Bank Secrecy Act, an anti-money-laundering law passed in 1970.

Even today the owners of shell companies do come to light occasionally, but it can take a series of random events for that to happen. A rare example occurred in April 2018, when Donald Trump's then personal attorney, Michael Cohen, appeared in a Lower Manhattan courthouse after his home, office, and hotel room had been raided by the FBI. Following the raid, US District Court judge Kimba Wood needed to segregate material pertinent to the government's investigation from documents related to Cohen's other clients, who would still be protected by attorney-client privilege. In a legal filing, Cohen told the court he had worked for ten clients since 2017. To seven of them, he said, he provided "strategic advice and business consulting." The other three were Trump, Republican fund-raiser Elliott Broidy, and a third person whom he did not name.

Who was this third client? Cohen didn't want to say, but Judge Wood compelled him to reveal the person's identity. The answer elicited "an audible gasp in the courtroom," said reporter Jon Swaine, who was covering the proceedings for the newspaper the *Guardian*.

COHEN'S THIRD CLIENT was Fox News personality Sean Hannity, one of Trump's most vociferous defenders, whose nightly television show had 3.3 million viewers in addition to the enormous number of listeners to his daily radio show. An essential part of Fox's daily lineup since the network was cofounded by Republican political consultant Roger Ailes in 1996, Hannity positioned himself as an avatar for the common man—a self-styled crusader for simple American values against liberal elites so effete and alien they even waged "a war on Christmas." Hannity had himself grown up working class, the youngest of four siblings, in the suburban community of Franklin Square on New York's Long Island. His first-generation Irish American parents both worked in order to support the family. His mother, Lillian, was a stenographer and corrections officer in the county jail. His father, Hugh, worked as a family court officer. The Franklin Square home, the first one they owned, was likely purchased using the GI Bill, since Hannity's father bought it after fighting in the Pacific during World War II.[4]

Now Hannity was rich. Though he clashed as a child with the nuns at Sacred Heart Seminary, cut class in high school, and dropped out of college, he found his calling as a talk show host. He raged on air for four hours a day—three hours on his syndicated radio show and another on television. "My thoughts are the same: I'm mad," he said, summing up his approach in a *New York Times* profile.[5]

By 2008, Hannity's on-air fame had made him wealthy enough to buy a $10.5 million, ten-thousand-square foot colonial-style mansion that lay on a spit next to a yacht club in another Long Island community, Oyster Bay. Although Hannity now lived only a short drive from the suburb where he grew up, economically, he was a world apart. His family lived near former president Theodore Roosevelt's summer home at Sagamore Hill, which is now a national historic site and museum. The Hannity mansion was on the same street as pop star Billy Joel's vast waterfront estate.

As the years went on and his fan base grew, Hannity's wealth continued to increase. By 2018, *Forbes* estimated he earned $36 million annually, making him the best compensated man in cable news. "Like most media people on TV, I am overpaid," Hannity told *Us Weekly* in 2017. "I know this because of my blue-collar roots, for which I am grateful."[6]

Suddenly, with Cohen's revelation, Hannity found himself in the difficult position of being the center of the story rather than a commentator. In the courtroom, Cohen offered no explanation of his relationship with Hannity, leaving an army of reporters scratching their heads.

It wasn't long though, before Hannity offered an explanation on his daily radio show. He denied having retained Cohen as a lawyer and claimed that his dealings with the New York attorney had nothing to do with Trump or the 2016 presidential election. "My questions exclusively almost focused on real estate," he told his audience. "I said many times on my radio show, 'I hate the stock market, I prefer real estate' . . . [and] Michael knows real estate."[7]

"Real estate?" the assembled journalists wondered. How could this be? The public paper trail showed Hannity owned very little real estate aside from his Long Island home.

But for the *Guardian*'s Swaine, the Oyster Bay mansion provided a clue. After Hannity bought it, Swaine found, the home had been transferred for a time to a shell company called SPMK IV NY LLC, with an address in a suburban office park outside Atlanta. "That's odd," Swaine thought, so he went online and searched the public corporation register in Georgia for shell companies with the SPMK acronym. "A bunch of them showed up in the search, SPMK1, SPMK2, and so on," he said—twenty-eight in all. SPMK, Swaine learned, wasn't only the imprimatur of the shell companies, it was also the initials of the talk show host's two children run together—Sean Patrick Merri Kelly. Hannity's name wasn't on any of the documents in Georgia. Most of them were registered to an attorney, Christopher Reeves. Each of the LLCs tracked back to the same suburban Atlanta office park to which Hannity had no obvious connection.

"How could all of them be connected to Hannity?" Swaine wondered. Together, the SPMK LLCs owned a tremendous amount of property. When Swaine checked the property record, he found shell companies beginning with SPMK owned 870 properties across seven states. Most were apartment buildings, concentrated in and around Atlanta, but many were also in South Florida, Alabama, and other southern states. Nearly every property had been bought cheap in a rush of purchases that began in 2013.[8] Whoever controlled SPMK had seized an opportunity to make big bets profiting off the pain of the Great Recession. But much to Swaine's chagrin, none of the documents had Hannity's name on it. They all tracked back to the law office. The lawyer was the "registered agent" of the LLC. The true owner was hidden.

The reporter didn't give up. He began trolling the websites of county clerks' offices, pouring over original scans of documents, looking for one with the name Sean Hannity. He grew frustrated. Finally, Swaine found the name he was looking for. Among the most valuable properties bought by SPMK were two large apartment complexes in Georgia that had been bought in 2014 for $22.7 million. The developments were in poor communities, and the rents on one- and two-bedroom apartments started at $735 a month.[9]

Within the documents on these properties was a record of

$14.7 million in loans from the US Department of Housing and Urban Development. Unlike other records, which had been handled by lawyers, Hannity had signed his own name to this loan documents. The conservative talk show host, who railed nightly against government social programs as evidence of a "nanny state," was himself the recipient of massive government subsidies.

With this, Swaine called Christopher Reeves, and told him he would be writing a story on Hannity's ownership of all these properties. The attorney did not dispute that Hannity was the owner.[10]

After the article appeared, Hannity released a statement calling reports on his real estate holdings "a fake news attack."

"It is ironic that I am being attacked for investing my personal money in communities that badly need such investment and in which, I am sure, those attacking me have not invested their money," he said. "The LLCs are *real* companies that spend real investment money on real properties."[11]

When Swaine went down to Georgia to visit the buildings, he found tenants grappling with rising rents and an increase in evictions. At one apartment complex, the number of evictions went up by 400 percent after Hannity's LLC bought it. Protected by a web of shell companies, though, their celebrity landlord was unknown to the tenants. "None of the tenants knew Hannity was the owner," Swaine told me.

Soon the details of Hannity's real estate empire would be spelled out for all to see. The *Washington Post* dispatched its own reporters to his properties and found that among the tenants the talk show host sought to evict were a "a former corrections officer and her wife, who fell behind while awaiting a disability determination; a double amputee who had lived in an apartment with her daughter for five years but did not pay rent on time after being hospitalized; and a single mother of three whose $980 rent check was rejected because she could not come up with a $1,050 cleaning fee for a bedbug infestation."[12]

Other media used the Hannity story as a reason to address the broader impact of the rise of shell companies. "Should tenants have the right to know who they're renting from? Should cities have a right to know who owns the property? The answer is a resounding yes," Susan Pace Hamill, a law professor at the University of Alabama who has been studying LLCs since the 1980s, told the *New York Times*.[13]

The LLC was originally designed, Hamill explained to me, as a solution to the help small and midsized businesses. The first one was created in 1977 by the state of Wyoming at the behest of the Hamilton Brothers Oil Company, an independent driller based in Denver.[14] The firm owned oil rigs in Panama and was worried about political instability there, so it sought a new corporate structure that would allow it to pay lower taxes, while at the same time prevent its owners from being sued individually if the situation in Panama deteriorated. The idea was never to hide who the owner was. "No one ever thought it would be used as a tool to hide the ball when it comes to real estate," Hamill explained. By 2019, however, all fifty states required more information to obtain a library card than to incorporate a business. In every state, governments mandated the holder of a library card be the person using the card, and that the card holder apply in person and provide their name and home address. Forty-seven states required a photo ID, and nearly all of them also required a second form of identification such as a utility bill. By contrast, the non-profit Global Financial Integrity found that "no state requires any information about the person(s) who directly or indirectly own or control the company."[15]

This left Hamill, the law professor, incredulous. "It's kind of like some bandits got hold of our beloved LLC and turned it into something that it's not supposed to be."

One of those "bandits" was now the owner of Sandy Jolley's home.

CHAPTER 9

POLO PONIES AND WINE

THE "COLFIN" IN COLFIN AI-CA5 LLC stood for Colony Financial, a real estate finance company that had been created after the housing bust by Southern California billionaire Thomas J. Barrack Jr. to "acquire, originate, and manage a diversified portfolio of real estate debt instruments." More than three hundred limited liability companies incorporated in Delaware bear the "ColFin" prefix. Between 2009 and 2012, these companies purchased everything from bad debt originated by failed banks in the Midwest, to a delinquent loan on a single Arizona office tower, to a partially developed master-planned community in California, to a bundle of bad mortgage loans in Germany.[1]

But Barrack's big play was saved for the American Dream itself. By the time ColFin AI-CA5 LLC purchased Sandy's family home, his company had bought up 8,326 houses across the Sand Belt and Sunbelt: California, Arizona, Texas, Florida, Georgia.[2] As wages stagnated and the economic recovery lagged, he kept buying. By the beginning of 2016, his company owned a staggering 30,000 homes.[3]

Sandy didn't know any of this. Barrack's name wasn't on any of the court documents, legal notices, or the lease presented by the property managers who arrived at her door. I was able to connect these LLCs to him only by examining hundreds of pages of documents on file with the US Securities and Exchange Commission (SEC) and the Delaware Division of Corporations. But while Barrack didn't take the time to introduce himself to tenants or local officials, he was more than happy to crow about his purchases to investors in keynote speeches at business conferences. "It's the greatest thing I've ever done in my professional life," Barrack, then sixty-five, told a lunch crowd at a real estate conference at the University of Chicago in November 2012. Pacing the stage like a motivational speaker, he regaled the audience with stories of the "twenty-one-year-old kids with Bluetooths" that he'd sent out to county courthouses with "bags of cashier's checks." Barrack said he was providing opportunity for families like Sandy's, whose wealth had been destroyed by predatory loans and aggressive foreclosure practices. They would rent from him, he said, because they "had been humiliated by this process and were looking for options."[4]

Barrack went on to explain, "We're buying so inexpensively," and managing the houses was cheap. "I can't get a plumber to come to my house for fifteen hundred dollars, and we retrofit many of these houses for fifteen hundred total." It was easy—like managing a chain of franchise businesses. "How do you manage Wendy's? How do you manage McDonald's? How do you manage FedEx? How do you manage Kinkos?" he asked rhetorically.

"This is my investment philosophy," he told the friendly crowd. "You walk into a jungle where no one else wants to be, and you swing and you fight and you bite, and eventually, if you're successful, they're all swinging with you, and then you have to move to another jungle." At the conclusion of Barrack's keynote address, the audience of real estate investors put down their forks and gave him a rousing ovation.[5]

IN ALL THE ways that Steve Mnuchin, J. C. Flowers, and John Paulson exemplify the hedge fund managers of the Upper East Side, Tom Barrack is the consummate Southern California money man. He simply oozes Los Angeles. Tall and tan, with a shaved head and a muscular build that comes from regular time with a personal trainer, he was sufficiently fit that, in 2010, at age sixty-three, he was unafraid to be photographed shirtless on a yacht. Barrack presents himself as a Renaissance man—riding the waves and growing Bordeaux wine grapes at his horse ranch northeast of Santa Barbara, where he raises polo ponies and hosts an annual polo tournament.

"Oftentimes people say what is the connection between polo and wine?" he says softly in the promotional video for his winery, Happy Canyon Vineyard, backed by the gentle trills of a flute. "And there are several, but the most important one is stewardship. The ingredients that are involved in turning out great polo ponies and, as a consequence, great polo teams, is the same kind of commitment, dedication, and focus that's required to produce great wine."[6]

One of Barrack's favorite aphorisms is that a great businessman "befriends the bewildered." At the time his company bought Sandy's family home, he was perhaps best known as the man who'd "saved" Michael Jackson's Neverland Ranch from foreclosure. Barrack didn't know the King of Pop, but he and Jackson were neighbors in Santa Barbara County; Neverland's property line ran right up to Barrack's ranch. Another thing they had in common: Jackson's business manager at the time, Tohme Tohme, was also a former consultant to one of Barrack's companies. Jackson hadn't worked for years, when, in May 2008, a private equity firm called Fortress Investment Group, which held a loan against Neverland, was poised to take the property from the delinquent pop star. At Tohme's request, Barrack flew to Las Vegas, where Jackson was living at the time. In his book *Michael Jackson Inc.*, *Forbes* reporter Zack O'Malley Greenburg writes that Barrack agreed to buy Fortress's note for $23 million on the condition that Jackson begin performing again. "Even if it's you making an appearance on a late-night show and singing a song. Even if it's you doing one two-day appearance at a Vegas show," it would be enough, Barrack said. "Something that shows you're still Michael Jackson, that you still have that capability, that you're still coming back." Otherwise, Barrack explained, "I have the names of five bankruptcy lawyers, and I suggest you get ahold of them as fast as you can, because that's where you're going."[7]

Jackson agreed to perform, and Barrack wrote a check for the $23 million,[8] preventing Fortress from foreclosing. It wasn't an act of charity. The partnership agreement they signed gave Barrack's company the right to manage the property and increased his company's ownership stake in the ranch with every dollar it spent.

On June 25, 2009, just a year after Barrack and Jackson executed the deal, Jackson died of a drug overdose. As of this writing, Barrack was seeking to sell Neverland for $67 million,[9] three times what he originally put in. Because an LLC now owns the ranch, it's unclear how much of the property Barrack owns—possibly all of it.

IN HIS SPEECHES and interviews, Barrack doesn't present himself as a vulture capitalist. Instead, he places his success as part of the great American narrative. His grandfather, Joseph Barrack, immigrated to the United States from the Beqaa Valley of Lebanon at the turn of the twentieth century, entering the country through Ellis Island as a child. "I often tell my children," he said in one interview, that America is a special place, a country where in two generations his grandfather "can leave in the belly of cargo ship going to nowhere, and I can come back in the cabin of my own airplane."[10]

By 1910, Joseph had headed west, settling in the tiny Front Range community of Las Animas, Colorado. There, census records show, he was surrounded by an ethnic rainbow of immigrant railroad workers and coal miners. At first, Joseph lived in a rooming house with a Greek barber and a Japanese pool hall manager. He opened a bakery, and met and married Tom's grandmother, Mary, whose family hailed from Missouri. In 1915 Mary gave birth to Tom Barrack's father, Thomas J. Barrack Sr.

By the time of Tom Sr.'s birth, conditions in Las Animas had become tense. A series of deadly accidents in the coal mines, which were the main source of employment in the area, had transformed the region into a center of labor agitation. Lingering tension between the United Mine Workers of America and coal company owners erupted into the violent Colorado Coalfield War in 1913. After thousands of mine workers went on strike seeking better wages and working conditions, Colorado's governor sent in the National Guard on the side of the bosses. Habeas corpus was suspended, strikers were jailed en masse and tortured, while a demonstration of miner's wives and children was met with a cavalry charge. But the workers didn't give in, and the strike dragged on for months until April 20, 1914. On that day, nicknamed the "Ludlow Massacre" by miners, the National Guard attacked a tent colony the strikers had set up north of the mine. At least thirteen women and children were killed in the assault.[11]

Though the Census Bureau shows that Joseph was still running his bakery in Los Animas in 1920, by the end of that decade, he and his family had relocated to Los Angeles. These were boom times for LA, with the birth of Hollywood and the rapid expansion of the aviation industry. The Barrack family settled in a brand-new Spanish-style bungalow off Melrose Avenue near the La Brea Tar Pits. Building documents on file with the city of Los Angeles show that their house was nearly identical to the one that Sandy's grandparents, Percy and Ella Hickerson, lived in a few miles to the west: the typical Southern California home eventually seared into the nation's imagination through classic Hollywood movies and television shows.

LIKE PERCY AND Ella Hickerson, Joseph Barrack wasn't in LA for the glitz and glitter. He took a job as a manager at a dry goods store, and he put his son, Tom Sr., to work. Tom Sr. never went to college, but he saved money and eventually made the transition from worker to owner, building a small fortune as the proprietor of three Southern California grocery stores. In 1952 Tom Sr. and his wife, Mamie Fadel, bought a home in Culver City, on the west side of Los Angeles, south of Beverly Hills, a few miles east of the beach. There they raised two children, Tom Jr. and his sister, Carole.

"My father was an incredible man," Barrack recalled. "He lacked the financial education and discipline but was by far the smartest man I've ever known. He never lost his humility or footing, and never allowed me to lose my humility or footing."[12]

But while Barrack's father and grandfather lived the American Dream, working hard, playing by the rules, and leaving the next generation better off than the one before, Tom Jr. set off on a different course, playing by his own rules. He didn't want to be slightly better off than his father. He wanted to be rich.

This different set of values is apparent when you compare the composition of Tom Barrack's family with his father's. While Tom Sr. was married to the same woman for sixty-seven years,[13] Tom Jr. has wed three times. Each time the age gap between him and his bride was larger than before. In 2014 Tom was sixty-seven when he married his third wife, thirty-seven-year-old Rachelle Roxborough, at his 1,200-acre ranch. When they wed, the couple already had two preschool-age children together. Two years later, in 2016, she filed for divorce. To Barrack, there was likely nothing odd about this series of events, as such arrangements were typical of his social circle. Among his closest friends and frequent business partners was another billionaire with children that span generations, himself decades older than his third, much younger, wife.

TOM BARRACK'S PARENTS tried to instill conservative values in their son. They sent him to Loyola High School of Los Angeles, an all-boys Jesuit school where students wore suits and ties to class. It was 1965. The Rolling Stones and Beatles were topping the charts, but at Loyola, the students were stuck in a previous era. The short-haired editors of the school yearbook declared "leadership" to be the class theme and asked FBI Director J. Edgar Hoover to contribute the foreword.

"Never in the course of history has the youth of this Nation been faced with a future that has held such challenge," wrote Hoover, whose agents had been spying on the civil rights leader

Dr. Martin Luther King Jr. for a decade by then. "In the years to come, you who are the leaders of tomorrow will make decisions that will be a measure of your strength and ability to keep America free. Discipline, that virtue which is the wellspring of order, must be learned through self-sacrifice and devotion to duty." He added, "In such individuals, imbued with precepts which guided the founders of our Republic in the establishment of a birthright unmatched in history, will flourish the dynamic standards which are vital in leading America to new pinnacles of achievement and progress."

Barrack was a popular kid. He played football and was elected to student government. As student body secretary, he headed the dance committee, and organized a sock hop, where boys and girls were able to mix. It was "a swinging success," the yearbook said, which "immediately became as much a part of Loyola's campus life as its oldest traditions."

Barrack stayed close to home for college, studying business and playing rugby at the University of Southern California. On the rugby field, he was famously tough, entering into the season finale against Stanford University with a broken nose; by the final whistle, he also had a broken left ankle, separated shoulder, and torn right knee. The team's captain, Ed Todd, remembers Barrack as "a wild man player whose heart and crazy head made him better than his athletic talent. . . . There are certain guys who, when they get into the pitch, their eyes change to wolf eyes, and they really like contact. That's what they're there for. Tom was one of those guys."

Barrack didn't party with the team, though. After most matches, Todd and Barrack saluted their opponent and then went their separate ways. Todd, a retired lawyer who now works as a referee for USA Rugby, which officiates the sport at the high school, collegiate, and national levels, told me that off the field Barrack was jovial and kind, "like a high school teacher. He had a certain warmth that was easy to be around, to have a joke with him. He was a guy who always seemed to be laughing and happy, and that's the kind of person who seems to be a successful high school teacher." Instead, Barrack went on to earn a law degree from another private academy in Southern California, the University of San Diego. Then, after graduating from law school, his world started to broaden. His ambition became clear.

His first job after law school was at the law firm of Herbert W. Kalmbach, President Richard Nixon's personal lawyer. In 1972 the firm sent Barrack to Saudi Arabia to negotiate a contract for a construction company. He ended up the squash partner of a Saudi prince, eventually reviewing deals for the royal family itself.[14] Barrack was more than a lawyer. He was a deal maker. At one point, at the request of one client, a Texas oilman, he helped open diplomatic relations between Saudi Arabia and Haiti, which was then ruled by the despotic "president for life" Jean-Claude "Baby Doc" Duvalier.[15]

Throughout these formative years, Barrack blended into the background, rarely garnering public notice. But this changed in 1984, when a curious land deal involving Ronald Reagan's attorney general, Ed Meese, led Congress to appoint a special prosecutor and haul Barrack in to testify before the US Senate Judiciary Committee. The scandal, which resulted in lengthy congressional hearings, seems overly complicated and incredibly minor by today's standards, but it was a big deal at the time. An examination of what happened gives a glimpse of how the young Barrack operated.

Meese was a longtime associate of Reagan's, dating back to the Gipper's time as governor of California, but he was by no means a rich man. When Reagan became president in 1981 and Meese moved to Washington to work in the administration, the new counselor to the president was desperate to sell his Southern California home. The problem was that Meese couldn't find a buyer willing to pay his asking price of $300,000. So, Barrack simply gave the buyer of the house $60,000 (about $175,000 in today's money), which was then paid to Meese as part of a higher purchase price. Barrack also charged nothing—neither a finder's fee nor a commission—for arranging the deal.

Soon after, Barrack was appointed deputy undersecretary of the Interior. Democratic senators raised a fuss, claiming that he had essentially bought his high-ranking position, but the independent council found no criminal wrongdoing. The director of the Office of Government Ethics also cleared both him and Meese, saying Barrack's "primary motive" in subsidizing the sale of Meese's home "was to help his friends by bringing them into a good business venture."[16]

Documents released by the Ronald Reagan Presidential Library reveal Barrack's connection to Meese was far from his only avenue to the appointment. In October 1982 a prominent Los Angeles socialite and Republican fund-raiser, Margaret Brock, wrote to White House deputy chief of staff Michael Deaver to recommend "a relatively new friend here in California" who had bought a Bel Air home "originally owned by my parents.

"Tom Barrack has completely—and beautifully—restored the house and grounds," she said. "During and after the construction, my sister, Elizabeth Handley, and her husband, Joe, and I have enjoyed several guided tours and luncheon at the house." Brock went on to praise Barrack "as an active political contributor" to Republican causes who had already met with Meese and Helene von Damm, Reagan's special assistant for personnel. Brock suggested a meeting in Washington or at Barrack's ranch in Santa Barbara County, where he was "a neighbor of President and Mrs. Reagan.

"I would be so pleased, Mike, if you and Tom could meet," she wrote.

"Dear Margaret," Deaver replied on White House stationary. "We haven't forgotten Tom Barrack. Helene is trying to find something for him, and she should be in touch soon."[17]

BARRACK DIDN'T LAST long in Washington. By 1985, he was back in the world of real estate. It was then that Barrack met Donald Trump, who would become his close friend for the next thirty-plus years. Fittingly, their relationship began with Barrack getting the better end of a deal. That year, Barrack got Trump to overpay for the New York department store chain Alexander's. Three years later, he enticed Trump to fork over $410 million for Manhattan's landmark Plaza Hotel, right before the hotel market collapsed. (Trump subsequently lost both properties to creditors.)[18] Despite having been fleeced, Trump was gracious: "A totally brilliant guy" is how the brash New Yorker described Barrack to *BusinessWeek*.[19]

Over the next decade, Barrack would help bail out one of Trump's struggling casinos in Atlantic City[20] and buy a condo on the fourteenth floor of a Trump property on Central Park South,[21] one block from the Plaza. When Donald's father died in 1999, they sat together next to Fred Trump's casket.[22] "Trump is one of the brightest businessmen I ever met," Barrack told *USA Today* without a hint of irony. "He doesn't let emotion drive him on any decision."[23]

It was also shortly after Barrack met Trump that the Californian found his true calling. For the last thirty years, he's been one of America's most prolific "contrarian investors"—meaning that he makes money by buying assets when everyone else thinks they are garbage and then flipping them a few years later when those assets are worth many times more—especially if the government is on the hook.

His first big play came during the savings and loan crisis. Working with Texas financier Robert Bass and then-upstart investor David Bonderman, he bought up a portfolio of bad loans held by American Savings and Loan, a failed California thrift that had been taken over by the government. For taxpayers, the American Savings deal turned out to be one of the most expensive bailouts of the S&L debacle, costing at least $4.8 billion in government subsidies.[24] For Barrack and his partners, though, all those subsidies meant they couldn't lose. After buying the thrift's bad loans, they turned around and sold them back to the same investors who had owned them before the crisis, turning a $400 million profit.

But that was at the beginning of the S&L bust, and Barrack knew there would be more opportunities. "He kept saying to me, 'The government will have to take over all these loans,'" Bill Rogers, then one of Robert Bass's partners, told *Fortune* magazine in October 2005. "He said we need to be raising money to get ready for an incredible buying opportunity."

In 1990 Barrack formed Colony Capital, the first vulture fund for S&L debt. "His timing was perfect," reporter Shawn Tully wrote in the *Fortune* profile.[25] Thrifts were failing so fast and furious (by the end of the crisis, 747 savings and loans would fail) that in June 1990 the newly formed Resolution Trust Corporation began pooling the S&Ls' bad loans and foreclosed real estate and selling them in bulk, usually at a steep discount.[26] Barrack entered this market with a big splash, buying $1.1 billion in assets for just $510 million.[27] Over the next four years, he bought package after package.

"It turned out even better than American Savings had," Tully wrote. "Owners who were eager to keep their properties bought back their debt for 70 cents or so on the dollar. Any loans Barrack couldn't unload, he bundled together and sold on the public markets as mortgage-backed securities."[28] As the real estate market recovered, Barrack sold off properties to large real estate investment trusts—basically mutual funds for property speculation, which gobbled up his office buildings and shopping centers. Because he had bought the buildings off the government for a song, it was easy to make a profit.

Like the sale of First Gibraltar to Revlon magnate Ron Perelman, these deals were roundly criticized in Congress. An official history of the crisis, published in *FDIC Banking Review*, noted that by selling large pools of debt in bulk, the Resolution Trust Corporation created "a lack of competition among bidders," handing "'sweetheart deals' to large investors," and potentially hurting local real estate markets. But "such concerns were largely trumped by the desire to get assets moved" off the government's books quickly, the *Review* said.[29]

For Barrack, this was like hitting the lottery. He heaped praise on the government officials who enriched him by selling so low. "They've done an incredible job," he told *American Banker* in 1994.[30] And why not? While the nonpartisan Government Accountability Office found the Resolution Trust Corporation had lost $87.9 billion in taxpayers' money by the end of 1995,[31] *Fortune* reported that Barrack reaped a profit of $2.5 billion.[32]

Barrack appeared on the cover of that issue of *Fortune* under the headline "The World's Greatest Real Estate Investor," with an image of a gold house reflecting in his aviator sunglasses. In

October 2005 the housing market was exploding, but Barrack saw something different. The overall message of the article was simple. Tom Barrack, a businessman who had made billions of dollars off an earlier banking catastrophe, saw a housing bust coming.

"The World's Best Real Estate Investor Has Made Billions in the U.S. Market. Now He's Cashing Out," the article's subhead read. "Should You Cash Out Too?"[33] Most Americans didn't cash out. They continued to buy—in part because of the high-pressure tactics of salesmen who promised that home prices would go up forever. The housing bubble continued to build for two more years until it burst spectacularly in 2008. Millions of Americans lost their homes and their wealth. The US economy teetered on the verge of another depression. But Tom Barrack was sitting pretty. He had pulled his money well before the crash. Now he was ready to buy.

CHAPTER 10

FOR INFINITY

AFTER THE HOUSING BUST, TOM Barrack went on a buying binge. But he didn't start with housing. "You have to buy at the right point in the cycle," is one of his aphorisms. Before Barrack started scooping up residential real estate, the economy needed to hit rock bottom. "He who can sustain the most pain wins," is another Barrack adage. So, he waited, as a tsunami of foreclosures washed across America.

In 2008 the wave made landfall in the suburbs of Southern California, where IndyMac had done so much of its aggressive and predatory lending. It spread across the Sunbelt, decimating Las Vegas and Phoenix, before continuing on to wreak havoc in Atlanta and across Florida. Whole communities were devastated; entire sections of town abandoned. In Lehigh Acres, a suburb of Fort Myers, Florida, with fewer than a hundred thousand residents, banks foreclosed on more than 40 percent of the homes.[1] Sheriff's deputies there found that a hundred of the empty properties had been turned into grow houses for marijuana. Elsewhere, college students organized keg parties in vacant homes. Vandals broke in and relieved them of their air conditioners.[2]

In Moreno Valley, in Riverside County east of Los Angeles, a suburb with winding roads and cul-de-sacs lined with spacious stucco houses behind large green lawns, more than one out of every five homes would be lost to foreclosure. In one particularly horrific instance, a group of teenage boys led a girl to a foreclosed home, got her drunk, and raped her while she was unconscious. She was discovered, naked and near death, with gang graffiti scrawled on her body in red marker, by a property agent who stopped in to inspect the house.[3] Working-class families had moved to Moreno Valley to achieve both physical and financial security. Having so many empty homes presented sinister opportunities that hadn't been there before.

Barrack bided his time—which was easier now, since there were so many other deals to be had. He used Qatari money to buy the flagging film studio Miramax, founded by Harvey and Bob Weinstein. At the request of his friend Donald Trump, Barrack bailed out Trump's son-in-law Jared Kushner, buying $45 million of Kushner's debt on a Fifth Avenue office tower, saving the young man's company from foreclosure.[4] He toyed with purchasing the Los Angeles Dodgers after the club's owner, Frank McCourt Jr., filed for bankruptcy.[5] Barrack also continued to market himself to struggling celebrities, striking a deal in March 2010 with famed photographer Annie Leibovitz. Like Michael Jackson, she had found herself deep in debt and about to lose everything. As with Jackson, Barrack swooped in days before Leibovitz's foreclosure and agreed to pay off a $24 million debt. In exchange, Colony took over management of many of Leibovitz's iconic photographs, which were put up as collateral, including her 1991 *Vanity Fair* magazine cover of a naked, pregnant Demi Moore and her *Rolling Stone* cover photo of a nude John Lennon embracing his wife, Yoko Ono, taken just hours before the former Beatle was shot to death by a deranged fan outside his and Ono's Manhattan apartment building in December 1980. (Barrack also reserved the right to seize Leibovitz's two Greenwich Village townhomes and two other properties in upstate New York if she failed to pay him back.[6])

Meantime, the recession continued. By November 2010, four million Americans had lost their homes to foreclosure.[7] The unemployment rate was nearly 10 percent.[8] Still, Barrack sat on the sidelines, waiting for his moment.

That month, *New York* magazine found him at the pool at Neverland Ranch. As he held court on new ways to rescue celebrities in distress, Barrack trained with his friends actor Rob Lowe and surfer Laird Hamilton. With Hamilton's help, Barrack and Lowe would hold "twenty-pound dumbbells, sink to the bottom of the thirteen-foot deep end, explode upward to the surface, gasp for air, and repeat. Tomorrow," reporter Benjamin Wallace wrote, Hamilton and Barrack "will run on the beach, pulling railroad ties behind them."[9]

WHILE TOM BARRACK trained with Lowe and Hamilton, a second major wave of foreclosures was under way. When the tsunami made landfall in 2008, it struck primarily people who had taken out "bad loans" at shops such as IndyMac and Ameriquest. Their loans featured high interest rates, incomprehensible terms, and balloon payments. When housing prices softened, these homeowners were unable to refinance out of these predatory products and quickly faced foreclosure. Then, in 2010, a second wave hit, jeopardizing the dream of homeownership for millions of Americans who were out of work and simply needed a break. By then, more than six million people had been unemployed for more than six months, the highest number since the government began keeping records in 1948.[10] In 2011 a million more Americans would lose their homes[11]—a number that didn't include fighters such as Sandy Jolley, who created what economists called "a backlog of foreclosures" because they were almost certain to lose their homes in the future.

Through all this, the administration of Barack Obama, like George W. Bush's before him, did very little to stem the tide of foreclosures. First, as we've already discussed, Congress passed a massive bank bailout that did little to help individual borrowers. The terms of the deals the federal government brokered afterward, like the sale of IndyMac to Steve Mnuchin's group of hedge fund managers, encouraged foreclosure.

Then, as the foreclosures spiraled out of control and the number of vacant and foreclosed homes mounted, the federal government did almost nothing to prevent communities from collapsing entirely. The most significant program sponsored by the federal government to deal with the plague of blight, the Neighborhood Stabilization Program, extended grants to hard-hit communities to provide "emergency assistance to stabilize communities with high rates of abandoned and foreclosed homes." But the amount of money appropriated was laughably small.[12] A typical NSP grant went to Riverside, California, where fourteen thousand homes were lost to foreclosure.[13] The city, which was already dealing with a shrinking budget thanks to lower tax receipts brought on by job losses, higher vacancies, and declining property values, received just $6.5 million—barely enough to buy fifty homes[14] (not even 1 percent of Riverside's foreclosures), fix them up, and sell them to new families who might call them home. In many cities, foreclosures were piling up so fast, government officials told federal auditors, that by the time they fixed up one vacant home, two more on the same block would be seized by the banks.

But like the foreclosures themselves, this glut of bank-owned property was not inevitable. It was a direct result of inaction from Washington. As mentioned earlier, during the Great Depression, New Deal programs such as the Home Owners' Loan Corporation had fought valiantly to prevent foreclosure. Not only did the HOLC buy bad loans off banks for their true value and issue new, long-term mortgages that kept borrowers in their homes, but it also was extremely lenient with homeowners who had trouble making their payments. "Every possible forbearance was exercised before foreclosure was authorized," the HOLC said in its final report to Congress in 1952. In stark contrast to modern banks like Steve Mnuchin's OneWest, which put loans in foreclosure after a borrower fell sixty days behind, the HOLC usually didn't start the foreclosure process until a borrower had been delinquent for a year or more. In about a quarter of cases, the HOLC went even further, lowering homeowners' monthly payments by giving them five more years to pay off the debt and lowering their interest rate in the segregated neighborhoods where it operated.

The HOLC ended up acquiring nearly two hundred thousand properties through foreclosure. Even in those cases, however, it did what it could to help the community. The government bank kept the homes occupied and well maintained. It employed a small army of inspectors and contractors to fix those homes and rent them out until new buyers could be found. According to the HOLC's final report, "The practice of 'dumping' properties was not followed on the premise that such a policy would have weakened the market, which, in general, did not become stabilized until the effects of the defense industries in 1939 and 1940 were reflected in the national economy."

Eventually more than 90 percent of those homes were sold to families who paid for the property over time through installments.[15] The sale price was almost always extremely close to the amount of the original loan. The system left little room for speculators. Communities were stabilized, and taxpayers got their money back. The homeownership rate surged, and an era of shared prosperity blossomed for decades—especially in the white neighborhoods where the HOLC operated.

The Bush and Obama administrations could have played the same stabilizing role during the Great Recession—which, despite the pain, was in most ways far less severe than the Great Depression. Just as the Home Owners' Loan Corporation came to own hundreds of thousands of homes in the 1930s, so, too, did the federal government become a major, inadvertent landlord during the housing bust. Fannie Mae and Freddie Mac, the government-chartered mortgage companies set up by FDR and Richard Nixon, respectively, to help Americans buy homes, had enormous market power. In an era where banks had been transformed from lenders to sales agents, where they no longer held most of the mortgages they made on their own books, Fannie and Freddie were the largest, most important buyers.

This meant that when loans went bad and banks foreclosed, Uncle Sam was often stuck holding the house. By August 2011, the federal government owned 248,000 properties—nearly a third of all of the nation's repossessed and unsold homes.[16] But unlike the Home Owners' Loan Corporation generations earlier, the federal government showed no particular inclination or ability to manage the inventory or go through the time-consuming process of finding individual families who might buy the homes to live in them. Instead, the feds tried to dump them. A 2011 audit by the Government Accountability Office reported that Fannie Mae and Freddie Mac spent nearly $1 billion on maintaining properties it had assumed though foreclosure the year before. That sounds like a lot until one considers the sheer number of homes that had fallen into the government's clutches. The total per property averaged just $1,744—and 40 percent of that went to boarding up homes and carrying away junk cars and other trash.[17]

"There was always a desire for a quick fix," said housing expert Julia Gordon, who managed a team of policy analysts for the Federal Housing Finance Agency, which oversees Fannie Mae and Freddie Mac. There were many meetings, she said, "usually a bunch of bureaucrats in a room, usually with some kind of political leader representation. A lot of decisions were driven by convenience. Everybody just wanted to keep things simple, and keeping simple always means selling things to Wall Street."

In August 2011 the government moved to unload the properties. The Treasury Department, the Federal Housing Administration, and the Federal Housing Finance Agency put out a joint request for input, asking the public for the best way to dispose of all their foreclosed homes. Consumer advocates and Realtors argued that they should be sold to individuals to stabilize neighborhoods, and that banks, which had received huge taxpayer bailouts, should be forced to lend to prospective home buyers. But the government request was narrower. The government said it needed help finding the best way to sell the houses in bulk as rentals, in huge blocks valued at between $50 million and $1 billion[18]—or between about five hundred and ten thousand homes at a time.

In his comments to the agencies, Ron Phillips, the president of the National Association of Realtors, tried to change the debate. He invoked the words of the regulators' boss, President Obama, who, that same month, had taken the banks to task for accepting billions of dollars in taxpayer bailouts and providing few opportunities for families to buy housing. "We've obviously been going through a tough time over these last two and a half years," Obama told a young woman at a town hall meeting at a seed company in Atkinson, Illinois, but "companies have never been more profitable . . . it's just they're hoarding their cash; they're not investing it. A lot of banks have now recovered, but they're not lending the way they used to. Now, they need to have a slightly tighter lending criteria than they used to have, obviously, because that was the part of the reason that we had that housing bubble. But one of the things we've talked about is, can we encourage banks now to take a look at customers who are good credit risks but are being unfairly punished as a consequence of what happened overall?"[19]

Phillips argued that the federal agencies should follow through on the president's rhetoric. In disposing of hundreds of thousands of foreclosed homes on its books, he said, the feds should push banks to make loans to responsible families. Selling homes individually would "maximize recovery on the assets and minimize the impact on housing values," while "selling in bulk to large national investors at deep discounts only works to further consolidate a large section of the housing market into the hands of fewer market participants."[20]

A coalition that included the American Civil Liberties Union and the Lawyers' Committee for Civil Rights Under Law offered an alternative vision. The federal government should turn its suddenly vast inventory of foreclosed homes into affordable housing for the poor. Local governments and nonprofits should be given first refusal, and if private investors purchase the homes, they should be required to set aside a portion of the homes they bought to be rented out to the poor at affordable prices. "Communities will benefit if properties are put into the hands of responsible affordable-housing owners and managers rather than into the hands of speculators willing to pay a higher up-front dollar," they wrote in a letter to federal housing regulators. "Local housing markets will benefit if properties are taken off the market." The government's unexpected inventory of foreclosed homes offered a "once-in-a-generation opportunity" to provide affordable, suburban rentals to people of all income levels and racial backgrounds.[21]

Either of these two options—helping families buy homes so they could build wealth, or getting the homes into the hands of affordable-housing nonprofits so that those same families could save money on rent—would have helped working-class America recover from the pain of the bust. But the Obama administration didn't embrace either one. Instead, it opted once again for a rescue plan that would concentrate the wealth of many in the hands of a few.

One maxim of investing, especially relevant in real estate, is that a smart businessman buys low and sells high. The Obama administration did the opposite. In February 2012, as housing prices bottomed out at the lowest level of the Great Recession, the Federal Housing Finance Agency announced it would go through with its plan and start selling thousands of houses in bulk. There were very few conditions attached. For example, corporate bidders were supposed to show that they knew how to manage property and present a plan for community engagement. The agency's inspector would later report that these conditions were largely ignored. Sales agreements released to the public by Fannie Mae run hundreds of pages and include a broad range of financial and legal conditions but no promises that the buyer would maintain the properties, keep housing affordable, or engage with the community.

This was the moment Tom Barrack had been waiting for.

AS BARRACK SEES it, "There's one common factor" running from the savings and loan crisis of the late 1980s and early 1990s, through the Asian financial crisis of the midnineties, through the dot-com bust and collapse of the American housing market of the aughts. "Anytime the government is intervening in our business, if you buy, you will be successful."[22] Obama's dump was the best yet. This time the assets weren't abstract financial products. They were houses—brick and mortar, concrete, wood, stucco—in communities all over America. In some southwestern cities, such as Las Vegas, Phoenix, and the Inland Empire—Riverside and San Bernardino counties in Southern California—prices had dropped by more than 50 percent since their peak. The country was having a half-off sale.

It was the moment Barrack for which had been quietly planning. On August 30, 2011, just after the government had sent out its proposal for comment, he inked a deal that gave him a massive and mysterious line of credit for buying distressed assets. The transaction was facilitated by a Bermuda law firm called Appleby and never would have become public knowledge if not for a massive leak of secret international banking records five years later to the International Consortium of Investigative Journalists. The documents, dubbed the Paradise Papers, exposed the offshore interests of Queen Elizabeth II of England and more than 120 politicians around the world. Among those ensnared were Donald Trump's future US commerce secretary, Wilbur Ross, who we met earlier as the buyer of a failed Florida bank, BankUnited. In the Paradise Papers, Ross was revealed to have a stake in a shipping company co-owned by the son-in-law of President Vladimir Putin of Russia.[23]

The documents show how Barrack marshaled funds to make his purchases. In the August 2011 deal, Appleby devised a rolling credit facility (basically a line of credit) that linked Barrack's US-based investment funds with a pair of subsidiaries chartered in the Cayman Islands. Money was to flow from funds housed at one LLC incorporated in Delaware, to another LLC in the Cayman Islands. The Cayman fund would be exempted, meaning that it paid no local taxes. The money would then be sent through a web of other companies before arriving at yet another Delaware limited liability company—which, unlike the earlier Delaware LLC, was closely tied to Barrack's parent company, Colony Capital.

As they reviewed the Paradise Papers, the International Consortium of Investigative Journalists focused on allegations of money laundering. Had Tom Barrack washed his money through the Cayman Islands in order to avoid taxes? Barrack declined to talk about that. His company denied any wrongdoing.[24]

But the documents offered an insight into an even more interesting question: Where was Barrack getting his money? Who were his investors? Sometimes, as in the case of the Miramax purchase, his investors were disclosed publicly, but usually they operated in the shadows. Who, for example, had been putting up all the cash he'd used to take control of Annie Leibovitz's photo catalogue or buy single-family homes formerly owned by everyday Americans? This seemed important, because if you were a city official dealing with the proliferation of homes owned by corporations, or, like Sandy Jolley, a tenant in one of these homes, you would want to know who was buying up your town. These people putting up the money likely had only the vaguest idea of which houses were being bought—or even that Barrack was buying houses in the first place—but they were the ones collecting dividends based on the rent and hoping for a windfall down the line. The investors, the true owners of the homes Barrack's companies bought, were shielded by the opaqueness of the LLCs, but with the Paradise Papers, a window opened, if only by a crack.

The documents show which bank extended the line of credit—

Sumitomo Bank of Japan—and listed twelve investors who to-gether pledged $188 million for the purpose of buying distressed assets. The largest chunk, $75 million (enough to buy about 500 homes) came from the Korea Exchange Bank, as a trustee and on behalf of the National Pension Service, part of the South Korean government. The next largest chunk, $30 million (200 homes), came from Sanba II Investment Company, of Qatar, followed by $25 million (175 homes) from ACE American Insurance Com-pany, in Philadelphia. Other investments came in from shell com-panies in California, the Cayman Islands, and the British Virgin Islands.[25] To my knowledge, none of them has ever commented about its role in buying distressed assets after the housing bust.

BARRACK'S COMPANY INFORMED Fannie Mae that it wanted to buy the government-owned houses and eventually outbid five other firms to take control of the largest bundle: 970 prop-erties across Las Vegas, Phoenix, and Southern California. Col-ony put up $34 million, or about 20 percent of what independent appraisers—who had been in the buildings—told Fannie Mae they were worth. In exchange, Barrack got the same type of terms as the arrangement with Michael Jackson that allowed him to take control of Neverland Ranch, except this time it involved nearly a thousand single-family homes. Basically, he would now do to America what he had done to Michael Jackson.

Tenants were to pay their rent to a newly created Barrack shell company, SFR 2012-1 US West LLC, which, in turn, would chan-nel that rent to Barrack's firm, Colony Capital. Colony would start off owning only a minority share of the houses, but that would increase every month as it collected rent from its tenants. In ad-dition, Barrack's firm would be allowed to charge Fannie Mae a "management fee" of 20 percent of the total amount of rent it collected. There was no language requiring rents to be affordable or for the houses to ever return to individual homeownership.[26] Still, the government said it had accomplished its mission. The Federal Housing Finance Agency "undertook this initiative to help stabilize communities and home values hard-hit by the foreclosure crisis," the agency's acting director, Edward DeMarco, said in a statement. "We are pleased with the response from the market."[27] It's hard to imagine a deal so perfectly designed to lazily allow the government to undercut working-class Americans on behalf of a small group of billionaires, but that is exactly what happened again and again.

The details of this particular sell-off took months to iron out. Though Fannie Mae didn't finalize the deal until the end of October, Barrack didn't wait for the bulk auction to finish to start buying houses. Colony's securities filings show Barrack made its initial investment in buying single-family homes in March 2012, right after the government announced it had started its fire sale. That month, he went on Bloomberg Television, telling anchor Betty Liu that he had begun to place his bet, starting with five hundred homes.

"Obviously, the American Dream is still alive," Barrack said. "But homeowners are now in the box." The recession had taken away many families' savings, he added, and ruined their credit. So, it didn't matter that interest rates were at an all-time low or that an investor like him could afford to buy "twice the amount of housing" as a few years earlier. Regular, working Americans still wouldn't be able to buy a house.

Liu readily agreed. "Right, they're foreclosed or about to be foreclosed on," she said.

Barrack proclaimed that he had a vision to establish "a national brand of ownership for families that lost their homes." It was a new sort of American Dream, one where a family did not own its own home but would instead "live in a home as a rental."

Like his other interviews with the financial press, Barrack was never challenged on affordability or on the role such a large corporate landlord would play in widening America's ever-widening wealth gap. In their eight minutes on television together, Liu, the host, spoke twelve times. In five of them, she prompted him with only one word: "Right."

Toward the end of the interview, Liu did pose this question: "Now, how long will you keep these units as rentals?" she asked.

"Our view is that you're going to keep most of them for infinity," Barrack responded.[28]

CHAPTER 11

SON OF A LINEN STORE OWNER

THE OBAMA ADMINISTRATION'S BULK SALES gave rise to a class of landlord that had never been seen before. At the beginning of 2012, *National Real Estate Investor* magazine reported, not a single landlord owned as many as a thousand single-family homes. But just two years later, industry analysts were tracking more than a dozen vulture companies that had swooped in after the housing bust to buy thousands—removing them from individual homeownership and concentrating the wealth contained in all those properties in the hands of billionaire investors.[1]

Some of these investors, including Barry Sternlicht, the founder and CEO of Starwood Capital Group, were veterans of the savings and loan crisis. Just like Tom Barrack, they were looking for a fresh opportunity to profit off a government-backed fire sale. Others, like B. Wayne Hughes, were more traditional real estate men. Hughes was born in 1933, at the height of the Great Depression, in the small town of Gotebo, Oklahoma. Like the Joad family at the center of John Steinbeck's *The Grapes of Wrath*, his family moved west to California during the dust bowl. By 1940, they were renting a home in the San Gabriel Valley, east of Los Angeles.

Hughes was a true self-made man, determined to own property and stand on his own. He went to public high school, then studied real estate at the University of Southern California, where he graduated with a degree in business in 1957. Today he is best known as the founder of Public Storage, a company he created in 1972 with a $50,000 investment after driving down a long Texas road and noticing a self-storage warehouse loaded to capacity. In 2008 *Forbes* put his net worth at $3.6 billion.[2]

"Wayne founded Public Storage at time when the industry was run by moms and pops out of their garages," Paul Saylor, chairman of CS Capital Management, told Bloomberg. "It's kind of the same pattern." Buying "single-family homes has been dominated until very recently by small investors across the country doing it locally."[3] For Hughes, there was little difference between a single-family home and a storage locker. By 2014, his company, American Homes 4 Rent, had purchased twenty-three thousand houses.[4]

The biggest buyer of foreclosed homes was the Blackstone Group, the nation's largest private equity firm. At various points since its inception in 1985, Blackstone had paid billions to buy the television ratings company Nielsen, the soda company Orangina, and Merlin Entertainments—the owner of Madame Tussauds, Alton Towers, and the London Eye. The key to most of these transactions was debt. Blackstone was a leveraged buyout firm, which meant that it borrowed large sums of money to purchase these companies and then tried to turn around and sell them at a profit. Using debt was preferable to cash because it meant that Blackstone could buy larger companies and, if all went well, vastly increase its returns. Let's say I buy a watch for $10 and sell it to you for $11. I've put in $10 and made $1—a return of 10 percent. But say I put in just $1 of my own money and borrow the other $9. Then, when I sell it to you for the same price, $11, my return isn't 10 percent. I've doubled my dollar. Even with interest on the loan, I can come out far ahead of where I'd be if I'd used my own money.

Amid Blackstone's octopus of holdings was a real estate arm that aggressively flipped property. In November 2006, at the height of the boom, the firm smashed records by paying $38 billion to buy Equity Office Properties (EOP), a vast network of commercial real estate from New York to Miami that had been assembled by investor Sam Zell. The price was so high that Zell, known for scavenging, stripping, and selling, considered it a "Godfather offer"—one that he couldn't refuse.[5]

Many observers thought Blackstone might be making a mistake, since buying at the top of the market can be a sure way to lose money. But, in retrospect, it seems the company forecast correctly that the boom would continue for just a few months longer, meaning there would be opportunity to flip the buildings quickly, getting top dollar before the coming crash. Indeed, less than a week after it closed the deal, Blackstone was well on its way to selling half of the properties it bought from Zell.[6] The results were glorious for Blackstone and a spectacular train wreck for the people who bought from them. By 2009, David Carey and John Morris wrote in their book *King of Capital: The Remarkable Rise, Fall, and Rise Again of Steve Schwarzman and Blackstone*, the company "had left a trail of carnage across the real estate industry."[7] Among the suckers was New York real estate developer Harry Macklowe, who paid $7 billion for eight of Blackstone's office towers in Manhattan.[8] Less than a year later, he was forced to turn control of the buildings over to his lender, Deutsche Bank, in order to avoid foreclosure.[9] Blackstone's buyers in San Francisco and Chicago couldn't make their payments, either. The private equity giant was sitting pretty, though. "Because Blackstone received such extravagant offers for the EOP buildings it sold," explained Carey and Morris, "it ended up paying only half what the properties were worth in 2007, in effect earning a $3.5 billion gain."[10]

The quick profits were even more amazing when one considers what Blackstone didn't do. It didn't improve the buildings. It didn't create jobs for the people who went to work inside them (apart from a handful of moneymen involved in the trades) or articulate a vision for a stronger and vibrant urban landscape. Blackstone made money. The tycoons on the other end suffered. The public got nothing.

Heading up Blackstone was Stephen A. Schwarzman. Standing just five foot six, with a paunch and a receding grey hairline, he was nonetheless among the most flamboyant billionaires in New York. In May 2000 he paid a reported record $37 million to buy an apartment at 740 Park Avenue, the same building where Steve Mnuchin lived, but on a higher floor and for a much grander unit. Schwarzman's apartment, once home to John D. Rockefeller Jr., was three times larger than Mnuchin's, at twenty thousand square feet, with thirty-five rooms, including a foyer the size of a ballroom, his-and-hers saunas, a pine-paneled library, eleven fireplaces, and thirteen bathrooms. In 2007 the *Guardian* reported that works by Claude Monet and the American abstract artist Cy Twombly adorned the walls, along with a photograph of Schwarzman arm in arm with his Yale classmate President George W. Bush.[11]

The Park Avenue apartment was just one of Schwarzman's many homes. In 2003 he paid $20.5 million for Four Winds, a

British-colonial-style estate in Palm Beach, Florida, which occupies a choice spit on the ocean and the Intercoastal Waterway, not far from Donald Trump's Mar-a-Lago golf club. He also owns a house in the Hamptons that was previously owned by Vanderbilt heir Carter Burden, a coastal estate in the French Riviera, and a beachfront property in Jamaica.

None of these residencies, however, was deemed opulent enough for Schwarzman's sixtieth birthday party, held in February 2007, shortly before the housing bust, when the economy had not yet crashed but the cracks were beginning to show. For that, Schwarzman reserved the Park Avenue Armory, a landmark performing arts venue that covers an entire city block. Built on public land for some of New York's wealthiest families at the height of the Gilded Age in the nineteenth century, the fortified brick edifice is held up by a massive truss system, the centerpiece of which is a thirty-one-thousand-square-foot main hall partly bathed in natural light.[12]

As New York's elite arrived, one limousine after another, more than one observer compared it to the Bradley Martin Ball, a Gilded Age extravaganza held at New York's Hotel Waldorf at the apex of the wealth gap more than a century earlier, on February 10, 1897. Back then, the party's hostess, Cornelia Martin, made a conscious effort to evoke the decadence of the Europe that America's early settlers had sought to leave behind, with its feudal lords and landless serfs. Nearly eight hundred members of America's emerging elite arrived, decked out as royalty. J. P. Morgan came as the French playwright and actor Molière; his niece, Miss Pierpont Morgan, dressed up as Queen Louise of Prussia. Among the most popular costumes was Marie Antoinette.

"The first impression on entering the room was that some fairy godmother, in a dream, had revived the glories of the past for one's special enjoyment, and that one was mingling with the dignitaries of ancient regimes," the *New York Times* reported.[13] "We are the rich," one guest wrote. "We own America. We got it. God knows how, but we intend to keep it." According to some estimates, the accumulated wealth of the families who attended the Bradley Martin Ball was as much as the other 11.6 million American families combined.[14]

This time around, the New York elite didn't dress up as European royalty, but the effect was the same. There were bankers, Jamie Dimon of JPMorgan Chase, Lloyd Blankfein of Goldman Sachs, and John Thain, the CEO of the New York Stock Exchange. They were joined by media personalities, including Barbara Walters and Tina Brown. Cardinal Edward Egan of the Archdiocese of New York attended, as did Mayor Michael Bloomberg and former US secretary of state Colin Powell. Donald Trump arrived with his third wife, Melania, on his arm.[15] Draped in a thick fur coat, the onetime *Sports Illustrated* swimsuit model puckered her lips for the waiting paparazzi, as if blowing them a kiss, before walking inside.[16]

Inside, the party continued. A huge portrait of Schwarzman, which usually hung in his living room, greeted the guests. The *New York Post* reported that in the main hall, a "huge indoor canopy" hung "with a darkened sky suspended above a grand chandelier." The design, the *Post* said, was meant to re-create the living room of Schwarzman's apartment, "even down to the grandfather clock and old masters paintings on the walls." Schwarzman paid Rod Stewart an estimated $1 million to perform. R&B star Patti LaBelle sang him "Happy Birthday."[17]

Coverage of the birthday party led to ferocious blowback. *Fortune* magazine called Schwarzman "The New King of Wall Street,"[18] but most of the attention was negative. The *Wall Street*

Journal followed up with a story that featured Schwarzman's personal chef, who said the private equity kingpin dined on $400 stone crabs and complained that one of his employees' shoes squeaked.[19] A *Financial Times* headline posited that Schwarzman, who cleared $8 billion when Blackstone went public four months later, should consider reining in his pay. *New York* magazine called him the "poster child for greed and self-indulgence of the new gilded age."[20] Even the *Wall Street Journal's* famously conservative editorial board took aim at Schwarzman's "garish" displays of wealth, blaming such showboating for prompting a proposal from a bipartisan group of senators, led by Republican Charles Grassley of Iowa, to increase taxes on private equity firms from 15 percent to 35 percent.[21] (Grassley's effort failed after Blackstone, which, to that point, had mostly avoided Washington, spent $6 million on lobbyists and successfully killed the measure.[22])

Schwarzman didn't understand why people were upset. "Obviously, I wouldn't have wanted to do that and become, you know, some kind of symbol," he explained at a conference in New York.[23] "I don't feel like a wealthy person," he told the *New Yorker* for a profile published the following February. "Other people think of me as a wealthy person, but I don't. I feel the same as when I was a fifth-year associate trying to make partner at Lehman Brothers. I haven't changed. I still think of Blackstone as a small firm. We have to prove ourselves in every deal. Every piece of paper is important. I'm always trying."[24]

STEVE SCHWARZMAN WASN'T born rich. He grew up middle class in suburban Philadelphia, attending public school, where his short stature did not keep him from athletics. He was involved in seemingly every activity the school had to offer. He played soccer and basketball, ran track, and was elected president of the student council. He joined the Key Club and the National Honor Society and volunteered to be a hall monitor.

In 1960, when he was in junior high, his parents bought a brand-new, three-bedroom, two-and-a-half-bath house with a furnished basement on Pennypack Road in the town of Huntingdon Valley, northeast of the city. It was a bucolic setting, around the corner from Lorimer Park, a 230-acre expanse of woodlands, meadows, creeks, and trails, which had been donated to the county in 1938 after the death of George H. Lorimer, the editor of the *Saturday Evening Post*. His father, Joseph, ran a dry goods store, Schwarzman's Curtains and Linens, a business founded by Steve's grandfather.

Steve Schwarzman likes to tell a story. When he was fifteen, he approached his father with a plan to open more stores and expand into a national chain, "like Sears." When his father rejected the idea, the teenager suggested expanding in Pennsylvania. Finally, he pled with him to open just one more store. "I'm very happy with my life as it is," his father said, according to the *New Yorker*. "I've got enough money to send you and your brothers to college. We've got a nice house and two cars. I don't want any more out of life." Schwarzman found this incomprehensible and complained to his mother. "That's your father," she said. "He's happy!"

Steve's parents owned that home on Pennypack Road for more than forty-four years before they sold it in 2004, two years after Joseph Schwarzman passed away. The sale price was $365,000. The buyer: an immigrant family that, according to property records, still lives in the home. This is the very definition of the American Dream: work hard, grow old, achieve your potential, and leave your children better off than you were as a child. But Steve never forgot the missed opportunity. Telling the story to an audience of business leaders at the Economic Club of Washington, DC, in 2015, Schwarzman insisted that if his father had only listened to him back in the 1960s, they could have become the first big-box bathroom store: "We would have been Bed Bath & Beyond," he said.

"But then there wouldn't be Blackstone," replied David Rubenstein, the president of the Economic Club, who was conducting the onstage interview.

"Yes, this is also true," Schwarzman said. "Then I'd be fixing up towels, which was my job at the time." Everyone laughed.[25]

STEVE SCHWARZMAN KNEW he wanted something big, but early on, it wasn't clear what. Despite attending Yale, he hardly seemed to be on the fast track. His major was Intensive Culture and Behavior, an interdisciplinary subject that combined psychology and anthropology. He studied classical music and ballet. A major undergraduate accomplishment came in 1968, when as a junior, Schwarzman arranged for female dance troupes from five women's colleges to perform at Yale, which back then enrolled only men. "A standing-room-only crowd filled the dining room," the *Yale Daily News* reported. "Most of them were eagerly awaiting a sexual extravaganza, but their hopes were dashed" when the female dancers said they "were not here to do a striptease." Instead, Schwarzman had organized the sort of event then popular in East Greenwich Village coffeehouses. One of the acts, from Connecticut College, featured four women dancers hopping around a man who slowly screwed in a light bulb as the piece began and then unscrewed it at the end. "The audience was largely bewildered," the *News* reported.[26]

As a senior, Schwarzman gained entry to the Skull and Bones

secret student society, but he still seemed aimless, so he reached out to W. Averell Harriman, the former US ambassador to Russia and governor of New York, who was then serving as President Lyndon Johnson's representative at the Paris Peace Talks—a serious though ultimately failed effort to broker a peace deal between Communist North Vietnam and our ally, South Vietnam, and bring the escalating war to an end before the 1968 presidential election. Harriman, a fellow "Bonesman," invited him to lunch at his Upper East Side townhouse. It would prove to be a pivotal moment in Schwarzman's life.

"Young man, are you independently wealthy?" the *New Yorker* quotes Harriman as saying.

"No sir, I'm not."

"Well, I am the son of a very rich man, which has made an enormous difference—that's the reason you're seeing me. If you have any interest in the political world, I advise you to become independently wealthy yourself."[27]

So, Schwarzman went to Wall Street, landing a job through a connection at the Yale admissions office with the investment bank Donaldson, Lufkin & Jenrette. But after studying psychology and anthropology in college, he was woefully unprepared, and the job did not deliver the riches he expected. (He lived in a fourth-floor walk-up on the Lower East Side, next to the precinct house featured in the opening scene of the 1970s police procedural *Kojak*.[28]) Recognizing that he needed more skills and better connections, he headed to Harvard Business School and earned an MBA.[29] That's also where he met his first wife, Ellen Philips, a course assistant. This helped his advancement, too, as she was the daughter of a wealthy Ohio industrialist.

After their nuptials in Dayton, Ohio,[30] Schwarzman headed back to Wall Street, where he joined Lehman Brothers. This time his career advanced like a rocket, as he perfected the art of the corporate merger. He worked constantly, from five in the morning until ten at night, once opening up his briefcase and working through a concert at Carnegie Hall. He made partner in 1978, just six years after arriving. Then, in the mid-1980s, there was a shake-up at Lehman, and the company's chief executive, Peter G. Peterson, was forced out. Like Averell Harriman, Peterson was fantastically well connected. He had been secretary of commerce under President Nixon and knew everyone. Schwarzman proposed they start their own firm. They called it Blackstone: a pun on Schwarzman's name (black, or *schwarz* in German) and Peterson's (stone, or *petros* in Greek).

Peterson supplied the connections, sending out personal letters to a vast network of potential clients, telling them he would provide a personal touch. Schwarzman provided the guile and extreme work ethic to get the deals done. The two spent thirty years together, buying and selling companies, making themselves fantastically wealthy, often by laying off workers and taking on vast amounts of debt before unloading the purchased assets to another investor—hopefully, at a higher price.

Steve Schwarzman's business relationship with Pete Peterson lasted longer than his marriage. In 1991 Ellen sued her husband for divorce and walked away with half his fortune. "I'm not saying that all women deserve half," she told the *New York Times*. "There are women who don't even know what their husbands do. But when the career was a joint effort, the wife is entitled to half."[31] Six years later, she married Howard Katz, a partner at Goldman Sachs.[32]

Meantime, Schwarzman just got richer. After a few years on the dating circuit, he wed a blonde lawyer named Christine Hearst. Like Steve, Christine was a social climber. The daughter of Peter

Mularchuk, who distributed appliance parts in Hicksville, a Long Island town home to polyester manufacturing, she was five years younger than Schwarzman and twice divorced. Though she was an attorney who practiced intellectual property law, Christine was known on the social circuit primarily because of her affiliation with her second husband, Austin Chilton Hearst, the grandson of the late newspaper publisher William Randolph Hearst. Though she had long abandoned her own family name, Mularchuk, Christine kept the Hearst name after marrying Schwarzman, going by the name Christine Hearst Schwarzman.[33] They are still married today.

AFTER HIS CONTROVERSIAL birthday party, Schwarzman sought to rehabilitate his image, making a $100 million gift to the New York Public Library. "The library helps lower- and middle-income people—immigrants—get their shot at the American Dream," he said, announcing the gift.[34] But like his opulent birthday party, the bequest drew derision from many and comparisons to robber barons of the Gilded Age, when the American public likewise found itself dependent on the charity of the rich. In *New York* magazine, Frank Rich compared Schwarzman to Andrew Carnegie, who had attended the library's original dedication a hundred years earlier. Like Schwarzman, Carnegie was "a ruthless tycoon second to none," Rich wrote. "But Carnegie did build a steel empire that sped the growth of the nation. Our own Gilded Age's legacy is the financial 'products' that greased the skids of America's decline."[35] In recognition of Schwarzman's donation, the century-old main branch of the New York Public Library was renamed the Stephen A. Schwarzman Building, his name chiseled into the two center columns leading to the building's main entrance, placed on a gold plaque on the marble floor just outside the front door and in the marble of the pedestals beneath the lamps at the library's Forty-Second Street entrance.[36]

The gift surely would have aroused the ire of James Truslow Adams. "I take, for the most part, but little interest in the great gifts and Foundations of men who have incomes they cannot possibly spend, and investments that roll like avalanches," he wrote in 1931. "They merely return, not seldom unwisely, a part of their wealth to that society without which they could not have made it, and which too often they have plundered in the making. . . . A system that steadily increases the gulf between ordinary man and the super-rich, that permits the resources of society to be gathered into personal fortunes that afford their owners millions of income a year, with only the chance that here and there a few may be moved to confer some of their surplus among the public in ways chosen wholly by themselves, is assuredly a wasteful and unjust system. It is, perhaps, as inimical as anything could be to the American dream."[37]

SCHWARZMAN GAVE HIS tax-deductible donation to the New York Public Library in March 2008, the same month Bear Stearns collapsed. As the crisis deepened, he looked for ways to profit off of it. At first, he had trouble identifying his best move. Unlike Tom Barrack, he had largely bypassed the opportunity to profit off the savings and loan bailout and was not practiced at this particular type of distressed buying. "No one in the world would lend us money," he told an investment conference in Boca Raton, Florida, after Blackstone was unable to buy the mortgage lender PHH for $1.7 billion. "It is the first time we haven't performed."

Schwarzman was upset, he told the conference, and he let fly what was going to be the first of a series of offensive statements he would utter during the Great Recession. "Trying to buy a mortgage bank in the midst of the subprime mortgage crisis was the equivalent of being a noodle salesman in Nagasaki when the atomic bomb went off. Not a lot of noodles left or even a person— and that's what happened to us on this deal," he said.[38]

But Schwarzman was determined to find his flip. Like Barrack, he had entered the Great Recession in a strong position. Under his leadership, Blackstone had stayed out of the complicated and toxic residential mortgage products that characterized the bubble. At first, Schwarzman loaded up on strip malls, warehouses, and suburban office buildings.[39] Then he went in with Wilbur Ross, taking a 20 percent stake in his acquisition of Florida's failed BankUnited, much as John Paulson, J. C. Flowers, and George Soros provided money for Steve Mnuchin's takeover of IndyMac. Like IndyMac, the BankUnited deal turned out terribly for the government. "The investors bought BankUnited for $945 million," Robin Sidel summarized in the *Wall Street Journal*. "They then received $2.2 billion in cash from the Federal Deposit Insurance Corporation, which also agreed to reimburse up to $10.5 billion future loan losses." Though the government took a bath, Schwarzman and Ross more than doubled their money when they took the company public in 2011.[40]

Meantime, in Washington, Blackstone fought to keep the system rigged in its favor. During President Obama's first term in office, the company spent more than $30 million on lobbying the federal government. It tried, and failed, to defeat the Dodd-Frank Wall Street Reform and Consumer Protection Act, which created the Consumer Financial Protection Bureau and financial "stress tests" for large banks that the government deemed "too big to fail." Of particular concern for Blackstone was the so-called Volcker Rule, named for former Federal Reserve chairman Paul Volcker, which restricted banks' ability to place risky financial bets on the grounds that the taxpayers might be required to bail them out again. The Volcker Rule was a huge threat to Blackstone. The company's main business was buying, and flipping, companies and properties with huge amounts of borrowed money. By safeguarding the deposits of everyday Americans, the Volcker Rule would restrict the amount of money large commercial banks such as JPMorgan Chase would have to bet on companies like Blackstone.

Those were just some of the problems Blackstone had with the law. The company also opposed provisions that required banks to disclose publicly the relationship between the amount they paid their executives and the company's performance. The idea was to catch executives who paid themselves handsomely while running their companies into the ground. Blackstone also opposed a requirement that banks reveal the ratio in pay between their average worker and the highest paid employee. When the law passed anyway, Blackstone announced it was "changing the structure of its investment" in BankUnited to avoid giving the Federal Reserve detailed information about Schwarzman's compensation.[41]

One proposal Schwarzman did defeat was President Obama's attempt to change the tax code so that companies like Blackstone paid taxes at the same rate as other businesses—the same change sought by Republican Charles Grassley before the housing bust. In the course of that battle, Schwarzman unleashed another, inconsiderate verbal missive. Paying higher taxes, he told a group of nonprofit board members, was "war . . . like when Hitler invaded Poland in 1939." Understandably, the comment sparked an immediate backlash.

"Mr. Schwarzman, shame on you—find a better way to save on

your taxes," Elan Steinberg, vice president of the American Gathering of Jewish Holocaust Survivors and Their Descendants, said in a statement.[42] Schwarzman quickly apologized, but he also got the last laugh. Like Grassley's proposal before it, Obama's plan to increase taxes on hedge fund managers also failed. Schwarzman got to keep his money.

CHAPTER 12

LOADING THE BOAT

OVER THE COURSE OF HIS career, Schwarzman rarely showed an interest in housing, beyond his own his personal accumulation of estates. But as the bust continued, it became clear that the number of vacant and foreclosed homes was piling up. The question was, How would he amass the houses? That opportunity would emerge slowly. It would come from a businessman who lived a life as simple as Schwarzman's was ostentatious, in a part of the country the Blackstone tycoon likely rarely had the occasion to visit.

MARCUS RIDGWAY GREW up on a dairy farm near an oasis in the Arizona desert. He's a fifth-generation Arizonan, dating back to the arrival of his great-great-grandfather before the state even existed. Ridgway's father was an educator, a teacher, and then a school superintendent in the tiny town of Duncan, population 665. His mother was a nurse. As a child in the 1980s, Ridgway spent most of his time outdoors among the bald eagles, great horned owls, and sandhill cranes that fly along the Gila River and the mountain peaks that surround the town. He was active in the Boy Scouts and earned the rank of Eagle. As an adult, he's served as a scoutmaster for most of the last eighteen years. "I love the outdoors and how it teaches young men to set goals and accomplish something," Ridgway told me. "It helps build character."

Ridgway's career path was never clear. He tried college, studying biophysics, then dropped out. He opened up ice cream stores, but they weren't terribly successful. So, he went back to school: first, community college in Mesa, and then Arizona State University. He graduated in 2005, at age thirty-three, with a degree in communications. Along the way, Ridgway started to dabble in real estate. He bought a fourplex in Phoenix, moved into one of the apartments with his growing family, and rented out the other three units to make money. Then he did it again.

From 2004 to 2008, Maricopa County, where Phoenix is located, grew by 500,000 people—from 3.5 million in 2004, to 4 million just five years later. During this period, many real estate speculators engaged in "land banking": buying farmland just outside the urban fringe with the hope that they would be able to flip it to developers a year or two later for construction of yet another subdivision. Ridgway saw this trend and had what he thought was even a better idea: he would buy tracts of land on the outskirts of town and turn them into trailer parks. It seemed like a win-win. He could provide "affordable workforce housing" until a developer came around to buy him out and build a subdivision. In 2006 he founded a company called the Treehouse Group with two other Phoenix-area real estate men.

One of their first trailer parks—or as Ridgway calls them, "manufactured home communities"—was in the city of Chandler, in the southeast corner of Phoenix, near the Gila River Indian Reservation. At the front of the property, near the main road, stood a farmhouse. Rather than demolish it or use it as an office for their new trailer park, Ridgway and his partners decided to rent it out.

"We weren't in residential rentals at all," Ridgway reflected, but "it sat on a very busy street," and the potential to make money by renting the house seemed obvious. So, he and his partner spray painted a For Rent sign, stapled it onto a stick, and placed the sign in front of house. Before he'd walked back to his car, his cell phone was ringing. "We had a hundred calls that weekend," Ridgway said. "We realized there was a need." So, they started buying the other houses around the trailer park that were for sale. "We fixed them up, rented them out, and then bought a few more." Then a few more. On one street near the mobile home park, they bought nine houses.

The year was 2008, and the global economy had begun to crash. Cities such as Phoenix, with their runaway sprawl and easy credit, were at the epicenter. Housing prices in Maricopa County tumbled nearly 50 percent that year, and forty thousand families lost their homes to foreclosure. The following year, there were more than fifty thousand foreclosures in the Phoenix area. In 2010, another fifty thousand.[1]

Around the mobile home park, the collapse was especially severe. Foreclosures were so common and houses so cheap that they appeared to be almost free to Ridgway and his partners. He could pay $20,000 or $30,000 for a home that just a year before had sold for $150,000. And Ridgway began to realize something important: while unemployment zoomed above 10 percent, rents weren't going down at all. No matter how bad the economy was, people still needed places to live.

The economics were incredible. If Ridgway paid $20,000 for a house and charged $1,000 per month in rent, he could make back all his money within two years. After that, it was almost pure profit. The more he bought, the more money he made. So, he kept buying. His company expanded into Mesa, closer to the center of

Phoenix, and then on the west side of the city. Then, on the other side of the country, he started to buy in Atlanta—another city hit hard by the foreclosure crisis. By the end of 2011, his company owned 1,200 homes. Ridgway said he didn't think too much about each purchase. "All the houses look pretty much the same," he told me. "They're all about the same vintage, about the same size, so we'd just buy whatever is available. We were focused on what people could pay for rent."

RIDGWAY WOULDN'T TELL me how he got hooked up with Blackstone, and other participants in the deal wouldn't grant an interview, but in April 2012, a month after Tom Barrack went on Bloomberg TV to announce he was buying houses "for infinity," Schwarzman's company signed an agreement with Ridgway's firm, Treehouse, and the Riverstone Residential Group, a Dallas-based manager of apartment complexes. Treehouse would buy the houses, and, together with Riverstone, they would find a way to manage them. Blackstone would provide the money—a lot of it. Purchases wouldn't be limited to Phoenix or Atlanta or Dallas. Blackstone wanted to buy houses anywhere a deal could be found. It called its new company Invitation Homes.

"We are loading the boat," Schwarzman said during an earnings call with investors. "This is the kind of thing that happens once every once in a while, where you see something that's a market-turning trend."[2]

Blackstone's involvement meant that Ridgway was now buying with what seemed like a nearly unlimited amount of money. By December 2012, Blackstone was spending $100 million a week on houses, Schwarzman said. It had already laid out $1.5 billion to purchase ten thousand foreclosed properties.[3] By 2014, it had spent five times that—$7.8 billion—to buy up forty-one thousand single-family homes in fourteen cities, from Seattle to Miami, with the greatest concentrations in Arizona, California, Florida, and Georgia.[4]

These purchases made a huge difference to people who lived in these cities and for the future of future of homeownership in America. But despite his "loading the boat" rhetoric, for Blackstone, the bets were comparatively small.

"Steve Schwarzman is very risk averse," said David Carey, co-author of the Schwarzman biography *King of Capital*. At the time, Blackstone had more than $200 billion in assets under management,[5] meaning the $7.8 billion it wagered buying homes represented just 4 percent of the total. In other words, as it bought up forty-one thousand homes, Blackstone was putting less of its wealth at risk than the average middle-class family does when it buys a used Toyota Corolla.

For Ridgway, though, Blackstone's involvement was life changing. He became the chief operating officer of Invitation Homes, commuting regularly from Phoenix to Dallas—or anywhere else his company might buy property. Ridgway said he didn't sleep for a year and a half, going to bed at three in the morning and starting work just four hours later. "I was getting nine hundred calls a day just from California because I was the point of contact for all the evictions," Ridgway told an Arizona talk show in 2014. The company didn't have a legal department yet. It was "stressful, really stressful," he admitted, but at the same time, he added, stress was good, because "you need the superstress to have the super-highs."[6]

COMPETITION FOR FORECLOSURES between the rival Wall Street firms was brutal. Like Barrack's housing empire, branded Colony

American Homes, and B. Wayne Hughes's American Homes 4 Rent, Blackstone's Invitation Homes concentrated its buying in the Sand Belt and Sunbelt that ran from California to Florida. The homes it bought tended to be about 1,500 square feet, with either two or three bedrooms, and two bathrooms—usually without a pool, the better to keep down maintenance costs. Though Blackstone bought homes in northern cities such as Seattle and Chicago, it bypassed struggling metros like Detroit, Cleveland, and Indianapolis, located in the nation's industrial heartland, favoring the warmer climates, where an economic turnaround seemed more likely, rents were higher, and milder winters resulted in smaller repair bills for absentee landlords. It bought both out in the suburbs and in inner-city neighborhoods that had been hard-hit by foreclosure.

The competition was particularly fierce in Atlanta, a major jobs center and the largest market for all three companies. Prices were depressed, the weather was good, foreclosures numerous, rents high. In addition, landlord-tenant law in Georgia gives nearly all the rights to the property owner. Logistically, it was also easier for national players such as Blackstone to buy in Atlanta. Unlike other parts of the country where courts auctioned off a few foreclosures every day, county courts in Georgia held one giant foreclosure auction on the first Tuesday of every month. Ridgway called it "Super Tuesday." Each month, his team would take a red-eye to Atlanta, arriving a day before the auction with cases full of cashier's checks. After the auction, they'd fly home. "It was amazing," he said, "because you'd buy a hundred-plus homes in a day, and you're just ecstatic. You're changing lives, and you're seeing a lot of crazy things."

In September 2012 the *Wall Street Journal*'s Robbie Whelan

captured what can be described only as a land rush in front of the Gwinnett County courthouse, northeast of Atlanta.[7] On a muggy Tuesday morning, more than two hundred people crowded around the courthouse steps as the auctioneer opened the bidding on nine hundred homes. Both Blackstone and Colony sent teams to the auction, carrying binders full of data on each home up for bid. In addition to basic information, like the number of square feet, bedrooms, and baths, the binders also told the corporate bidders the maximum price their company could pay and still make an immediate, substantial profit on rent. What they were interested in was maximizing "gross yield," or the amount of money they and their investors could get from rent after accounting for taxes, fees, and other expenses. If Colony eventually flipped the house years down the line when its value increased, so much the better.

"Colony had brought $3 million in checks to the courthouse," Whelan wrote. Furthermore, on that day, "52 Colony employees were bidding on homes at seven different county courthouses in Georgia, and spent a total of about $9 million."[8] Nearby, another Colony associate sat under a red canopy tent, his laptop set up on a card table, entering Colony's winning bids into a spreadsheet. In one recent day, Whelan reported, Colony had bought 133 homes in Atlanta.

RIDGWAY LEFT INVITATION Homes in May 2014. The work was too grueling, he told me, one of his children was sick, and the company had grown too large for him to manage as chief operating officer. Blackstone wanted to take the company public, and it needed an experienced Wall Street hand who could help with that. But to this day, Ridgway has nothing but great things to say about Blackstone. "They were amazing," he said, "filled with the smartest people on Wall Street." And he has no regrets about the impact the corporate buying spree has had on America's cities and our country's widening wealth gap. But the wave of purchases fundamentally changed the structure of property ownership in Atlanta's suburbs. Last year, I pulled the property rolls for Gwinnett County—a suburban area that's home to nearly a million people. The government records showed that the top fifteen landowners were all shell companies—LLCs, LPs, and other corporate creations—that focused on the single-family rental market. Most of them didn't exist before the housing bust.

When I asked Ridgway about this, he said he wasn't concerned, arguing that tenants often prefer renting from companies than from people. "Mom-and-pop landlords are either totally, totally not involved, or they are micromanaging and snooping around. People feel like their space is being invaded," he argued, going on to say that most millennials, and even Gen Xers like himself, don't want to own their own home. People move around a lot more than they used to, he said. "They know they're not going to work for Chevy or Ford for twenty or thirty years," so even if they make a good salary, they don't want to be tied down by a mortgage. "More and more people are just more comfortable with renting," he said.

But what about the decline of homeownership? I wanted to know. What about all that wealth that used to be owned by individual families, which was now controlled by Blackstone and a few other Wall Street firms? "With that logic, you're working on old assumptions that if you own a house you build wealth," he said.

Yet isn't that why you bought all these homes? I asked. To build wealth for yourself, Blackstone, and their investors? Why shouldn't that wealth be held by individual families? And what about you? Don't you own a home? Ridgway didn't want to answer that question.

CHAPTER 13

LIFE ON A LEASE

SANDY JOLLEY RENTED HER PARENTS' home from Barrack's company for eighteen months. In that short period of time, she paid Colony $42,300. Tom Barrack might argue that his firm did Sandy a favor by not forcing her to move right away, but that's not how she sees it. "Colony was dead set on getting as much money as possible. They were incredibly greedy, and they did nothing for the house that had received so much love and care from my family," she said.

In the year and a half she rented the two-story house on Benson Way, Colony put almost no money into the house. During the same period, the company constantly moved to increase Sandy's rent. After giving her a break for the first three months, Colony jacked it up to $2,400 in August 2013, as Sandy and Bruno Larrea had agreed.

Then, in September, as her first, short-term lease wound down, Sandy got a letter from another member of Strategic Property Management's team. "As you know, your lease term will soon be completed. We would like to discuss your lease options with you," the employee, Kelly Davis, wrote. "Our goal is to negotiate a reasonable rate for you to remain in your home for another year."

Kelly gave Sandy two options: a rent increase of $75 a month, to $2,475, on a yearlong lease, or $2,616 if Sandy wanted to continue month to month. Sandy pushed back, and Kelly agreed to increase the rent by $50 a month instead of $75, to $2,450. That was still more than 40 percent higher than the neighborhood average of $1,742 a month, according to the Census Bureau. But Sandy decided that, for now, at least, it was better to stay put. On November 1, 2013, she signed a new twenty-five-page lease for the increased amount. The agreement also pushed an even greater share of the obligations of property maintenance onto her. Under the terms of the lease, she was required to "keep cellar, yard, sidewalk, and driveway clean and the grass cut, bushes trimmed, and weed all flower beds; keep the front, rear, and any sidewalks clear of ice and snow, and pay the cost of exterminating insects and pests."

The document went on: "It is agreed" that Colony would "not supply, repair, replace, or install storm doors, windows, screen doors, window screens or shades, fuses, light bulbs, smoke detectors," unless they were specifically required to by law. In addition, if anything came up that was not "specifically listed in the Rental Agreement," Sandy would be responsible for those as well. Like a contract with the cable company or an Internet service provider, it was a standard agreement, and there was no room for negotiation.

Still, the lease made Colony responsible for some repairs, including "any sources of leaks." In June 2013, two months after Colony took ownership of the house, Sandy noticed her monthly water bill spike. By September, it had reached $586, almost four times the $154 she'd paid the month before. Sandy investigated and found that a pipe in the back of her yard, among the citrus trees, was leaking. She complained to the property management company over and over again, asking it to fix the leak. Nothing happened. She called Colony's corporate office. Nothing. There is "a major leaking problem in our water system," she wrote in one missive. She hired her own contractor, paying him $450 for a partial repair, but the pipe continued to drip. She no longer owned the house. She gained no equity with her monthly rent payment. All that money was going to Tom Barrack's company. At the very least, they could take care of major maintenance issues that arose. A few months later, there was break in the galvanized plumbing. Sandy filed a formal complaint.

"The landlord is in violation of the lease agreement, page 7 #19," she wrote to Colony's property management company, Strategic Property Management, in May 2014, serving a legal notice to demand it fix the leak. "As you can tell, I am frustrated," she wrote. "It has now been a year since I first notified Strategic. It is a clear violation of the lease to continue to ignore a major repair. I should not be expected to pay the highest rent in the neighborhood, pay for repair to the water system, and continually pay for excessive use of water because of your negligence." The letter prompted Colony to finally fix the leak. It also paid a portion of her inflated water bill.

But Colony's billing department had assessed extra fees, having unilaterally started charging rent at the higher $2,616 month-to-month rate, not the $2,450 due according to the lease she'd signed. The additional charges—$141 one month, compounding to $166 the next—were ultimately wiped away, but only because Sandy pushed back hard.

STILL, THAT MONEY paid to Colony did give Sandy some benefit. For one, it gave her time to get her bearings and return to work. She consulted for a local real estate agent and helped other small businesswomen with their business plans. But gradually, her side project consulting with families targeted for reverse mortgages was becoming a full-time job. And as her client list of families battling Financial Freedom foreclosure reached into the hundreds, Sandy saw a troubling pattern emerge. Steve Mnuchin's bank, she discovered, was harming not only individual families but also the federal taxpayer. At the time, Sandy didn't know about the loss-share agreement that Mnuchin had signed with the FDIC, where the government paid OneWest for the money it lost on foreclosures, but through her own case and her consulting work, she was gradually becoming aware of the legal history of the reverse mortgage that was sold to her parents and the complex web of government regulations that governed the industry. In early 2014, while she was still renting from Colony, Sandy began to think in grander terms.

Reverse mortgages, she learned, had been nearly nonexistent until 1987, when President Reagan signed a law creating a new government-insured product, the Home Equity Conversation Mortgage, or HECM. The new law extended the same government support that had been available to working-class home buyers since Franklin Roosevelt's New Deal to seniors who wanted to pull equity out of their homes. Like FHA-insured "forward mortgages" for working-class home buyers, these government-sanctioned "reverse mortgages" for seniors were to be made by private lenders, but the government promised to pay the lenders' losses if the loans went bad. The program was subsidized by insurance payments paid by the seniors who were drawing money out of their homes.

At first, the government kept the program small. For most of the 1990s, it capped the total number of reverse mortgages it would back at under thirty thousand. But in 1997 a subset of the banking industry formed a lobby group, the National Reverse Mortgage Lenders Association, NRMLA. In 1998 it got the cap raised to 150,000 homes.[1] Then, in 1999, Wall Street got involved. Lehman Brothers introduced the first mortgage-backed security for reverse mortgages.[2] That allowed reverse mortgages to be bundled and traded just like regular home loans, car loans, or any other kind of debt that was being bundled and traded on Wall Street. The majority of loans in the pool were originated by Financial Freedom.[3]

In 2000 Republican congressman James Leach of Iowa, the chairman of the House Financial Services Committee, pushed through legislation that gave HUD the authority to let reverse mortgage lenders charge higher fees—saying those higher fees would allow it to attract more lenders to provide credit to seniors. President Bill Clinton signed it into law.[4] Still, the federal government kept the number of loans small. But the industry kept pushing, and when George W. Bush was president, the reverse mortgage industry expanded its business by sneaking a few sentences into bills that financed the US military and the war in Iraq. In 2005 it added to the language to a supplemental bill funding the Global War on Terror that raised the cap on the number of reverse mortgages the taxpayers would insure to 250,000 homes. In 2006 the industry got Congress to raise the cap again to 275,000 by adding three lines to the sixty-page Department of Defense Appropriations Act.[5] The government began packaging its own fully guaranteed reverse mortgages into mortgage-backed securities—making taxpayers accountable to bondholders if the loans went bad. These mortgage-backed securities would be bought, sold, and sliced by all the same speculators who traded bundles of traditional forward mortgages. With companies such as IndyMac pushing to maximize sales, the number of reverse mortgages exploded. Though Congress never formally raised the cap above 275,000, it regularly waived the limitation in subsequent appropriations acts.[6]

The federal government, under President George W. Bush, saw very few risks and did very little to protect either homeowners who borrowed the money or the public at large. In May 2008, just two months before IndyMac collapsed and the largest reverse mortgage lender, Financial Freedom, imploded, HUD issued a glowing report declaring a "turning point in the history" of HUD's reverse mortgage program:[7] "2008 is the year in which the first members of the large and financially savvy 'baby boom' generation . . . turn 62, the minimum qualifying age for a HECM loan. . . . Not only will the new generation of senior homeowners be larger than its predecessor generation, it is likely that they will be less averse to debt and more willing to use reverse mortgages." Baby boomers, HUD said, might begin using reverse mortgages to get cash for a broad range of needs, including "home improvements, medical bills, and everyday living." Even wealthier homeowners might start turning to reverse mortgages "for asset management during retirement," the government said, tapping the wealth in their home before liquidating their stock portfolios and other assets.[8]

THE GOVERNMENT'S SUPPORT of the reverse mortgage industry was not supposed to come without strings, however. There were many, many rules designed to protect seniors. If a lender didn't follow these rules, it was not supposed to be able to collect on its government insurance policy when it foreclosed. As Sandy examined her own family's case and the stories of many of her clients, she began to think that, under Steve Mnuchin's leadership, Financial Freedom and OneWest Bank were systemically breaking these rules yet collecting government cash anyway.

For example, one of the rules mandated that before Financial Freedom seized a home—and billed taxpayers for the money it lost, including attorneys' fees and other costs—the company was first required to offer the home to the borrower's heirs. The heirs were supposed to be provided generous terms: either the outstanding balance of the loan or 95 percent of the appraised value of the home, whichever was smaller. Since many homes were worth less than the outstanding balance of the reverse mortgage during the bust years, this 95 percent formula often worked out to be a good way for families to keep the home. The problem, Sandy said, was that OneWest and Financial Freedom didn't tell families about this option and even threw up barriers when they tried to take advantage of the provision. Another trick, she said, was illegally inflating the value of the appraisals to keep the families from being able to afford the home, all in an effort to get more money out of the government insurance.

Sandy went online and searched for terms such as "federal whistleblower." She learned about the False Claims Act, a federal law passed way back in 1863 that allows private citizens to sue businesses and individuals for defrauding the taxpayer. Such lawsuits, she discovered, are filed "under seal," meaning they are kept secret from everyone but the government in order to give the Justice Department time to investigate. If the government gets its money back because of the citizen complaint, the whistleblower is entitled to keep a percentage of it as a reward. Legal professionals call this type of whistleblower case a *qui tam* lawsuit, short for the Latin phrase *"qui tam pro domino rege quam pro se ipso in hac parte sequitur,*" which means "he who brings an action for the king as well as for himself."

Further Internet research led Sandy to David Scher, a graduate of Cornell University and Fordham Law School. He was a principal at a firm called the Employment Law Group, out of Washington, DC. Scher's online biography said he had worked as in-house counsel for several major corporations, including Sony Electronics and USWeb, before focusing on whistleblower litigation.

As she looked over the Employment Law Group website, Sandy saw similarities between herself and Scher's most high-profile client, Dr. Jon Oberg. While working as a researcher at the US Department of Education, he noticed that four companies, including Nelnet Education Loan Funding, had implemented a complicated scheme to bilk taxpayers on their government-insured student loans. With Scher's help, Oberg filed suit under the False Claims Act. In 2010 the Justice Department reached a $58 million settlement with the student aid companies—$17 million of which went to Oberg. "Collaboration between the federal government and citizens with knowledge of fraud is important to the successful enforcement of the False Claims Act," Tony West, assistant attorney general for the Civil Division of the Department of Justice, said in announcing the settlement. "Whistleblowers like Dr. Oberg are critical to our efforts to recover taxpayer money lost to waste, fraud, and abuse."[9] (West left government in 2014 to work for PepsiCo and is now chief legal counsel for the rideshare company Uber.[10])

The Employment Law Group had an 800 number on its website. "Call us 24/7," it said. Sandy did.

"It was a very unusual case," Scher told me. Usually his clients were government employees or corporate insiders, but "what made

Sandy interesting was she had a personal experience and turned it into something. . . . She came in saying, 'This is my story. This happened to my parents,'" Scher said, "but she had also represented all these other people in different states in different situations, and it was always the same pattern."

After speaking with Sandy on the phone, Scher dispatched his firm's private investigator to draw up a background report; he wanted to make sure there were no skeletons in her closet. The investigator didn't find anything. "That was the basis for our starting work," Scher said. "The reality was that her documents were authentic." He asked Sandy to write him a memo detailing OneWest's alleged fraud.

On April 4, 2014, Scher sent Sandy's memo, which named five cases, including her parents', to Kyle Cohen, an assistant US attorney in Fort Myers, Florida, who'd handled some of the Employment Law Group's earlier whistleblower cases. Since Fort Myers was an epicenter of the foreclosure crisis, he'd been working on a number of mortgage fraud cases. They tended to involve relatively small players perpetrating obviously scandalous frauds. In one such instance, Cohen prosecuted a developer, Alexander Zarris, alleging he used reverse mortgages to inflate the purchase prices of the condos he was selling.[11]

In Sandy Jolley's complaint, Scher had something bigger. "I've got a surprise for you that you're not going to believe," he told Cohen. The assistant US attorney agreed to look into it.

THE WHISTLEBLOWER COMPLAINT did not solve Sandy's immediate money problems. Any settlement of her claim was likely years away. For starters, under the law, the Department of Justice and HUD had a year to decide whether to pursue the case. Unsurprisingly, the government moved slowly. Three months after submitting her claim, Sandy traveled to Washington to meet with attorneys from HUD and the DOJ. They asked for more information. She eventually sent them 116 cases of allegedly unlawful abuse of the elderly by OneWest and Financial Freedom—evidence of illegal foreclosures, servicing issues, inflated appraisals and FHA claims, and lawsuit case numbers from many of her clients.

As Sandy waited on the Justice Department, Colony notified her of yet another rent increase. "Thank you for residency with Colony American Homes. We appreciate your business and are dedicated to providing you with a place you are proud to call home," read the letter, this time from Warren Johnson, the latest property manager. Johnson urged Sandy to act quickly "to take advantage of our early-signing renewal offers"—which, in this case, would be an increase of $25 a month to $2,475 ($2,846 on a month-to-month basis). Please note, the letter said, these figures "do not include any additional items such as tax, garage rent, carport rent, pet rent, and/or detached storage rent."

By this point, her parents' belongings and the memorabilia of Sandy's childhood were nearly packed up. Sandy was tired and needed a fresh start in a new location. She was always angry. "It was so difficult," she said, "to stomach that we're paying rent because they stole the house."

WHEN FALL ARRIVED and the lease was up, Sandy and Kristin made the half hour drive to Oxnard. As they turned around the winding roads of subdivisions that bumped up against the Pacific Ocean, Sandy saw a little For Rent sign on a brown, single-story tract home. She pulled out her cell phone and dialed the number.

She was the first person to call. The rent was cheaper than her parents' home. The landlord was a person, not a company like Colony. She signed a lease.

In the three years since she moved to Oxnard, her new landlord has not raised the rent. When she calls with a problem, the landlord makes the repair. Although her family's wealth has disappeared, she's nonetheless found a measure of peace.

PART IV

THE NEW REDLINING

CHAPTER 14

A BUNGALOW IN LOS ANGELES

WE'VE GOTTEN QUITE FAR IN this book without talking about race. But you can't understand the housing bust—or the massive transfer of wealth that occurred as a result—without considering the extremely powerful role that racial discrimination played in determining the winners and losers of our recent economic disaster.

It starts with the different kinds of loans that banks made to Americans depending on their racial and ethnic backgrounds. During the boom, it didn't matter how much money African Americans and Latino home buyers made, or what their credit score was, or how much they wanted to borrow; they consistently got mortgage loans on worse terms—often, at higher interest rates—than their white counterparts did. Many financial institutions offered white borrowers standard terms, while steering people of color toward junk loans that critics said were designed to fail. One study from the National Bureau of Economic Research found that between 2004 and 2007, mortgage lenders were 105 percent more likely to grant African Americans high-cost loans than white borrowers with the same financial profile. Lending institutions were more than 78 percent more likely to charge Latinos more.[1]

Mortgage lenders' tendency to concentrate these predatory loans—usually referred to as subprime because they charge higher interest than the typical, or prime, rate—in neighborhoods where people of color were most likely to buy, led to skyrocketing numbers of foreclosures in those communities when home values fell and jobs evaporated. Although a majority of Americans who lost their homes to foreclosure were white, African Americans and Hispanics were more than twice as likely to be dispossessed.[2] White homeowners throughout the United States suffered, but entire neighborhoods that were home to people of color were destabilized by the avalanche of foreclosures.

Take Sandy's neighborhood of Thousand Oaks, California, where two-thirds of the residents are white. There, one in thirty homes were lost to foreclosure between 2008 and 2013. You could walk down any particular block—counting the houses on both sides of the street—and know that someone on this block had lost his or her home. This was way higher than historical norms, but it paled in comparison with the epidemic of foreclosure that destroyed black and Latino neighborhoods from South Florida and Atlanta, to the suburbs and inner cities of Southern California. These were the neighborhoods where IndyMac had concentrated its aggressive and predatory loans. They were the neighborhoods where Steve Mnuchin had cranked up his foreclosure machine, and they were the neighborhoods where vulture capitalists such as Tom Barrack and Steve Schwarzman did most of their buying. The result is that while the African American and Hispanic unemployment rates have fallen to historic lows in the economic recovery, the wealth gap between whites and people of color has grown to levels not seen since discrimination was legal and segregation was encouraged by the government.

This racial wealth gap is not ultimately about jobs. Yes, in America, people of different races often have different jobs and make different amounts of money. The median white family earns nearly twice as much as the average black one. But a family's wealth is about more than how much money it makes. It's about what that family owns. In the years since the housing bust, the homeownership gap between the races has widened to levels not seen in fifty years. A family that hands its paycheck over to a corporate landlord every month cannot save. A family that cannot save cannot create wealth to pass down to the next generation.

The average white family is now worth $131,000, fourteen times more than the average African American one, according to the Census Bureau. The average black family has less than $10,000 to its name. Nearly one in three black households are literally worth nothing, government statistics show, because their debts are greater than or equal to their assets. That's more than twice the rate that whites have a "zero or negative" net worth. (Hispanics fare only slightly better than African Americans. Government data show the median Hispanic family is worth $18,000, while about one in five Hispanic families are worth nothing.[3]) To understand how and why this happened, it is necessary to examine a history many whites hesitate to face even as people of color continue to feel its effects.

A TOXIC LEGACY of legalized discrimination dates back to slavery and continued when the New Deal programs of Franklin Roosevelt's administration locked out many immigrants and African

Americans, preventing them from participating in the shared prosperity that followed World War II. There are millions of examples that can be drawn upon to illuminate what happened, but let's start nearly a century ago, on March 10, 1923. That was the day M. L. Butler was born to a poor black family of sharecroppers on the J. W. Jones Cotton Farm in St. Francis County, Arkansas. The farm lay about thirty miles southwest of Memphis in the Mississippi River Delta. His father, W.M. (who, like M.L., was known only by his initials), picked cotton by hand, stooped over or crawling on his knees, his hands pierced by thorny stems until calluses formed all over. Sixty years after the legal end of slavery, W. M. Butler received no wages for his work. Instead, the owner was supposed to give him a percentage of the cotton's market value. First, though, the landowner deducted the cost of "tenant" farmers' seeds, fertilizer, clothing, and food. Their take-home pay was usually calculated down to zero.

W.M. was sixty-five years old when the enumerators from the US Census arrived at the farm in May 1930. He told them he had been born in Louisiana and that he had been eighteen at the time of his first marriage. He was on at least his second wife now. (The records aren't clear.) It was the first marriage for M.L.'s mother, Della, who at thirty-nine, was twenty-six years younger than her husband. M.L. was seven then. He had a ten-year-old sister, Eudora. Although W.M. and Della owned very little and had no formal education, they sent both of their children to school.

By 1940, W.M. was gone, and the family had relocated three hundred miles south to a farm on the other side of the river in Lincoln County, Mississippi. Della told the census taker she was a widow. She and her son, M.L., both worked as tenant farmers. The census noted that neither was paid.

Race-based degradation in the Mississippi Delta extended beyond the lack of economic opportunity or even the legally and culturally mandated segregation of Jim Crow that denied blacks the right to vote, and to attend the same schools and drink at the same water fountains as whites. Nearly every interaction with the white population reminded blacks of their lower place in the pecking order.

"In the Delta, custom forbade black drivers to overtake vehicles driven by whites on unpaved roads," historian Neil R. McMillen wrote in his book *Dark Journey: Black Mississippians in the Age of Jim Crow.* "White men, however chivalrous towards white women, neither tipped nor removed their hats for black women, and, of course, shook black hands only in exceptional circumstances. Blacks, on the other hands, were expected to show deference at every turn: to wait in nearly any line until all whites were served; to approach a white home only by the back door; to yield the right of way to whites when walking or driving." In rural areas, blacks did not smoke cigars in white company, wear dress clothes on weekdays, drive large or expensive cars, or otherwise carry on an air of prosperity, McMillen wrote, adding, "It was a breach of caste to contradict any white."[4]

In this discriminatory atmosphere, it was nearly impossible for African Americans to buy homes and build wealth. Fewer than one in five black families in Mississippi owned their homes in 1940, while almost half of white families did. But it wasn't just southern mores and state laws that kept African Americans from building wealth. The African American homeownership rate remained below 20 percent in many northern states, including Illinois, Michigan, Ohio, New York, and Pennsylvania. In each of these states, white families were more than twice as likely than black families to own their own homes.[5]

Policy decisions by a succession of US presidents fostered that gap far from the Mason-Dixon Line. In his book *The Color of Law: A Forgotten History of How Our Government Segregated America*, academic Richard Rothstein argues that, from its inception under President Woodrow Wilson, the federal government's campaign to increase homeownership had the added purpose of perpetuating racial segregation. Urban crowding and tenement conditions, Wilson thought, were leading to an unhealthy mixing of races. Though he had been president of Princeton University and governor of New Jersey, Wilson was born in Virginia before the Civil War and raised in a slaveholding family. Wilson, the same president who promoted a League of Nations following World War I, believed strongly that Anglo-Saxons were superior to other races. Shortly after his inauguration as president, he had ordered segregation in federal offices, setting up curtains to separate black and white clerical workers and forcing employees of different races to eat in different cafeterias and use separate bathrooms. When his administration launched its Own-Your-Own-Home campaign, Rothstein wrote, the promotional posters featured only pictures of white people.[6]

When Herbert Hoover became president in 1929, he strengthened the connection between theories of white superiority and the federal policies that encouraged Americans to buy homes. At a 1931 White House conference on homeownership, the president described popular songs such as "Home, Sweet Home" and "My Old Kentucky Home" as "expressions of racial longing . . . written about an individual abode." He continued: "That our people should live in their own homes is a sentiment deep in the heart of our race and of American life."[7]

The key engine powering America's modern racial homeownership divide didn't really rev up until the massive federal intervention that was Franklin Roosevelt's New Deal. The first of these racially discriminatory rules is now known as redlining. As the Home Owners' Loan Corporation was in the process of saving more than a million homes from foreclosure by issuing new, less predatory loans, it deployed an army of real estate agents across America. These agents created color-coded maps that rated the quality of neighborhoods where the HOLC might lend. The colors ranged from green ("Best") to red ("Worst"). Agents examined the physical quality of the housing stock, amenities, and business activity of each neighborhood. The surveyors' forms included sections where they could note the presence of problematic racial groups. Explicit language—such as "infiltrated by Negros" and "threatened with negro encroachment"—described neighborhoods deemed too "hazardous" for lending.[8]

This federal system institutionalized housing discrimination and segregation in every region of the country. In San Francisco, government surveyors shaded the section of the Richmond district where my grandmother lived, just north of Golden Gate Park, blue, meaning "still desirable," because there were "no adverse racial concentrations in the area." Meantime, the HOLC applied a "hazardous" red wash to the Fillmore, a neighborhood of beautiful Victorian flats immediately to the east of my grandmother's neighborhood. Although property values there were rising and the neighborhood was "well provided with schools, transportation facilities, and recreation areas," a HOLC surveyor worried the Fillmore was also a "melting pot" of "Japanese, Russians, Mexicans, and Negroes." The government described this to mortgage lenders as a "racial situation." The effect of these ratings was simple. Government-backed homeownership opportunities flowed to residents of white neighborhoods like my grandmother's and bypassed those where people of color lived.[9]

The policy became even more explicit when the Roosevelt

administration implemented the National Housing Act, which created the Federal Housing Administration, in 1934. Under FDR, that agency would back loans only to white home buyers in white neighborhoods. "If a neighborhood is to retain stability, it is necessary that properties shall continue to be occupied by the same social and racial classes," the agency's 1936 *Underwriting Manual* reads. The government instructed appraisers to guard against "adverse influences," among them "infiltration of inharmonious racial or nationality groups."[10]

Faced with patterns of discrimination from his white neighbors in the Mississippi Delta all the way to the White House, M. L. Butler searched for a way out. He looked to the military, but it was also segregated and offered few opportunities for African Americans. Indeed, when Japan bombed Pearl Harbor in December 1941, catapulting the United States into World War II, only 4,000 African Americans wore the uniform, and only 12 had become officers.[11] (This, out of 1.8 million active-duty service members.[12]) The draft was segregated, and, more often than not, African Americans were passed over by all-white draft boards.[13] As the war dragged on, Franklin Roosevelt pushed for African Americans to join the military, but only in all-black units relegated to menial or dangerous jobs.

Midway through the war, when he was twenty years old, M. L. Butler heeded the call. On May 22, 1943, he reported to Camp Shelby, a training facility just south of Hattiesburg, Mississippi, with room for about 89,000 active-duty personnel. The base also housed a prisoner of war camp that held 2,500 German soldiers. Counting civilians who came on and off the base for work, there more than 100,000 people on the post on any given day.[14] For three years, Camp Shelby was the largest city in Mississippi, and, like the rest of the state, it was segregated.

Patricia and Richard Hickerson when they married in 1946. *(Courtesy Sandy Jolley)*

Richard Hickerson photographed in 1947 while serving as a cook in the navy. *(Courtesy Sandy Jolley)*

The Hickersons purchased their first home in the San Fernando Valley, on the outskirts of Los Angeles, with the help of the GI Bill. *(Courtesy Sandy Jolley)*

Sandy Jolley at Western Airlines stewardess training graduation, 1969. *(Courtesy Sandy Jolley)*

Undated portraits of Beulah and M. L. Butler taken when they still lived in McComb, Mississippi. In 1948, the couple drove from the Jim Crow South to Los Angeles. *(Courtesy Butler family)*

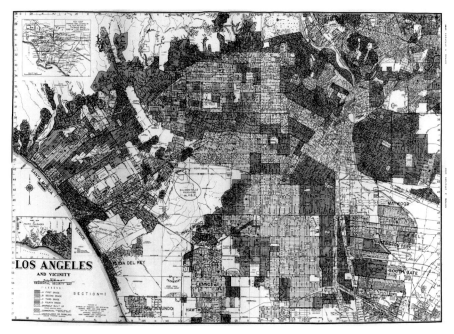

This redlining map of Los Angeles was produced by the Home Owners' Loan Corporation in 1939. Neighborhoods with large numbers of African Americans or immigrants were shaded red, too "hazardous" for lending. *(University of Richmond—Digital Scholarship Lab)*

A HOLC surveyor notes approvingly, in 1939, that deed restrictions "protect against racial hazards" in South Los Angeles. *(University of Richmond—Digital Scholarship Lab)*

In 1980, Patricia and Dick Hickerson used a VA loan to buy this home on Benson Way in suburban Thousand Oaks, where they lived for the rest of their lives. *(Courtesy Sandy Jolley)*

Beulah Butler in an undated photo in the living room of her home in South Los Angeles, which the family bought in 1963 after California governor Pat Brown signed the Rumford Act. *(Courtesy Butler family)*

In 2000, Sandy Jolley moved back home to care for her aging parents. Photographed here with her father, Dick, then seventy-seven, in her home office in 2003. *(Courtesy Sandy Jolley)*

Fred Trump, photographed in 1986. *(Adam Scull/photolink/ mediapunch/Shutterstock)*

Fred Trump launched his career building row homes in Brooklyn, which working class whites were able to buy thanks to FDR's New Deal programs. *(Brooklyn Public Library, Brooklyn Collection)*

Donald Trump attempts to stave off bankruptcy at his Taj Mahal casino in 1990. Wilbur Ross, standing behind him, represented the creditors. *(Neil Schneider/New York Post Archives)*

Donald Trump with his father, Fred Trump, July 26, 1982. *(Michael Norcia/New York Post Archives)*

Left page, bottom: An aerial view of Fred Trump's 1,860-unit Beach Haven development, which was built with $25 million in federal subsidies. The complex would later be at the center of a Senate investigation into "windfall profits" and a Department of Justice probe into racial discrimination. *(Brooklyn Public Library, Brooklyn Collection)*

740 Park Avenue, "the world's richest apartment building," where Steve Mnuchin and second wife Heather bought a 6,400-square-foot apartment for $10.5 million in 2000. Homewrecker Steve Schwarzman lives here in a 20,000-square-foot apartment once occupied by John D. Rockefeller Jr. John Thain lived in the penthouse. *(Kyle Ericksen/ Penske Media/Shutterstock)*

Heather Mnuchin was prominent in New York's society pages throughout the 2000s. Photographed here with her husband, Steve, and Donald Trump at City Harvest's twelfth annual Practical Magic ball at Cipriani 42nd Street on April 4, 2006. *(Patrick McMullan via Getty Images)*

Mike Meyers, Patricia Clarkson, George Clooney, and Steve Mnuchin attend a party for the film *Syriana* at Mnuchin's Park Avenue apartment on November 18, 2005. *(Patrick McMullan via Getty Images)*

Steve Mnuchin's Yale roommate, Eddie Lampert, oversees the merger of Sears and Kmart. Mnuchin served on the Sears board for more than ten years as it closed stores and shed workers. *(Gregory Bull/AP/Shutterstock)*

The FDIC's John Bovenzi speaks with nervous consumers outside of IndyMac's Pasadena headquarters in July 2008, after the bank collapsed and the government took it over. *(Nick Ut/AP/ Shutterstock)*

John Paulson, top right, and J. Christopher Flowers, bottom right, were the largest investors in Steve Mnuchin's acquisition of IndyMac; each purchased a 24.974 percent stake. Mnuchin's old boss, George Soros, center, was also an investor. *(top right: Matt Campbell/EPA/Shutterstock, center: Manuel Balce Ceneta/AP/Shutterstock, bottom right: AP Photo/ Osamu Honda)*

OneWest Bank executives Steve Mnuchin (chairman), left, and Joseph Otting (CEO), right. *(Ringo Chiu/Zuma Press)*

Tom Barrack, who bought the Miramax film studio for $660 million in 2010, photographed with company cofounder Harvey Weinstein at the Los Angeles premiere of *August: Osage County* in 2013. *(John Shearer/Invision/AP/Shutterstock)*

CIT Group chairman and CEO John Thain and OneWest president and CEO Joseph Otting face a skeptical public during a hearing at the Los Angeles branch of the Federal Reserve Bank of San Francisco, February 26, 2015. *(Nick Ut/AP/Shutterstock)*

Tom Barrack hosts an annual polo tournament at his Santa Barbara County ranch. Photographed here at the fifth annual Veuve Clicquot Polo Classic at Will Rogers State Historic Park on October 11, 2014, in Pacific Palisades, California. *(Jason Merritt/ Getty Images for Veuve Clicquot)*

Actor Rob Lowe, second from left, poses with his good friend Tom Barrack, actress Gwyneth Paltrow, and actor Fred Savage after receiving a star on the Hollywood Walk of Fame in Los Angeles, December 2015. *(Chris Pizzello/Invision/AP/Shutterstock)*

Chairman, CEO, and cofounder of the Blackstone Group Stephen A. Schwarzman, above, arrives for his sixtieth birthday party at the Park Avenue Armory, February 13, 2007. Donald Trump and his wife, Melania, right, were among the guests. *(Arnaldo Magnani/Getty Images)*

Jamie Dimon, left, and his mentor Sandy Weill, right, chairman of Citigroup, nicknamed "The Shatterer of Glass-Steagall" because of his successful effort to overturn Depression-era banking regulations. *(John Froschauer Mike Appleton/Bloomberg via Getty Images)*

Tom Barrack introduces Ivanka Trump at the Republican National Convention in July 2016. *(Carolyn Kaster/AP/ Shutterstock)*

Steve Mnuchin, now Treasury secretary, and his third wife, Louise Linton, hold up a sheet of new bills at the Bureau of Engraving and Printing in Washington, DC. *(AP/ Shutterstock)*

Steve Schwarzman, chairman, CEO, and cofounder of the Blackstone Group, speaks as United States president Donald Trump looks on during a strategic and policy discussion with CEOs in the State Department Library in the Eisenhower Executive Office Building in Washington, DC, on April 11, 2017. *(Shutterstock)*

Jamie Dimon, chairman and CEO of JPMorgan Chase, with Donald Trump at the White House two weeks after Trump's inauguration on February 3, 2017. *(Michael Reynolds/EPA/Shutterstock)*

Wilbur Ross, now commerce secretary, testifies before Congress on March 14, 2019. *(Jose Luis Magana/AP/Shutterstock)*

Steve Mnuchin swears in Joseph Otting as comptroller of the currency on November 27, 2017, as Otting's wife, Bonnie, looks on. *(Alex Brandon/AP/Shutterstock)*

Beulah and M. L. Butler bought this bungalow on West Sixty-Ninth Street in South Los Angeles in 1963. They paid the home off, but in 2007, Beulah took out a reverse mortgage. After she died in 2012, OneWest Bank foreclosed on the home. *(Stuart Palley)*

Beulah Butler shortly before her death at age eighty-two in 2012. *(Courtesy Butler family)*

Marcus Butler wishes his family could have kept their home. "That's what we were taught when we were younger," he said. "You get a house, you pay for it, then you pass it on to the next child or grandchild, try to keep the house in the family." *(Stuart Palley)*

Shawn Pruett, shown in April 2017, rented the Butler family home in South Los Angeles after it was sold to a company founded by Tom Barrack. Pruett died of cancer that August. *(Stuart Palley)*

Patricia and Richard Hickerson on vacation in 1997, before Patricia developed Alzheimer's disease and Dick became sick with cancer. *(Courtesy Sandy Jolley)*

Sandy Jolley goes through boxes of files from her decade-long court fight against OneWest Bank. *(Aaron Glantz)*

Sandy Jolley looks out the window of her former home in April 2019. The house on Benson Way is now part of the 80,000-house Invitation Homes empire. *(Aaron Glantz)*

Sandy with her mother, Patricia, and her sister Julie in 2010, shortly before Patricia's death. *(Courtesy Sandy Jolley)*

Through her front door in Los Angeles, a tenant displays a three-day eviction notice she received from Colony in March 2017. She owed $46.33. *(Stuart Palley)*

Sandy Jolley stands in front of the US Capitol building during a visit in May 2019. *(Courtesy Sandy Jolley)*

M. L. Butler entered the army as a private, committed to remain in the military for the duration of the war, plus six months. Enlistment records show that his civilian job was "semiskilled lumberman, raftsman, and woodchopper," and that he was single, "without dependents." Beyond that, it's not clear what M. L. Butler did during the war. He never talked about his service, and the US National Archives told me the rest of his military records likely burned in a 1973 fire that engulfed the National Personnel Records Center in Saint Louis. Whatever his experience, the young man returned home with a tough look in his eye and a chip on his shoulder.

IT WASN'T LONG until Butler, like other African American veterans, found that President Roosevelt's promise that the GI Bill would provide "emphatic notice to the men and women in our armed forces that the American people do not intend to let them down"[15] did not apply to him. The pledge included assistance with employment, education, and—crucially—homeownership. But the newly constituted US Veterans Administration relied on the Federal Housing Administration's *Underwriting Manual*. Both agencies would extend credit only to white home buyers in white neighborhoods. M. L. Butler may have fought under the same flag as my grandfather and Richard Hickerson, but after the war, the white men entered a door to homeownership that was closed to him.

In 1948 M.L. married Beulah Bates, a woman four years his junior who'd grown up in the Mississippi Delta and faced the same discrimination he did. Beulah and M.L. never told their son how they met, but you can learn a lot by studying sepia-toned portraits they posed for in a McComb, Mississippi, department store after the war. In the photos, the two of them sit individually—one following the other—on the same stretch of white bench. The studio backdrop depicts tropical flowers, ferns, and palm trees rustling in an imaginary wind. In his photo, M.L. almost glares at the photographer, his dark Stetson tilted back and resting high on his head. He's got a thin mustache and a slight paunch that obscures his belt. Though he's sitting for a formal photo, he wears a leather jacket. He looks driven and impatient, eager to move on. Beulah, by contrast, beams in her Sunday finery. Her straightened hair is pulled back to reveal modest hoop earrings. Her blouse is neatly buttoned to the top, and her jacket is closed. On the wrist of one hand crossed in her lap, her watch reflects the flash of the camera. From behind her eyeglasses, she's also looking toward the future.

BEULAH, THE ELDEST daughter of Frank and Leanna Bates, was born in 1927. When she was small, Frank labored in a sawmill, and Leanna worked as a laundress, washing other people's clothes in their home while caring for Beulah and her baby sister, Frankie B. Beulah's seventy-two-year-old grandmother, Carolina, lived with them and helped with the laundry. "Don't say we were poor," Beulah would tell her grandchildren decades later. "We had it better than most."

That didn't mean the family had an easy life. The Great Depression was unkind. By 1940, Beulah's father was out of work. Her mother, now a maid in a local hotel, made $150 a year (less than $3,000 in today's dollars). Like M. L. Butler and his mother, the Bateses were tenants—the urban, rent-paying variety. They lived in the Beartown section of McComb, then a small town of ten thousand. A couple of decades later, McComb would become a battleground between civil rights activists and violent Ku Klux Klansmen. By then, Beulah was long gone.

BEULAH AND M.L. never gave a specific reason for leaving Mississippi. "They just wanted to get out of there," their only son, Marcus, told me. It's easy to understand why. Across the South, millions of African Americans were making the same decision.

In 1940 twelve million African Americans—77 percent of the nation's black population—lived in the South. By 1970, five million had migrated north and west to cities such as Chicago, Detroit, Philadelphia, Cleveland, and San Francisco, transforming the nation. Historian Nicholas Lemann called this Great Migration "one of the largest and most rapid mass internal movements of people in history—perhaps the greatest not caused by the immediate threat of execution or starvation." In sheer numbers, he wrote, the black exodus outranked the migration of any other ethnic group—Italians or Irish or Jews or Poles—to the United States.[16] "The fever rose without warning or notice or much in the way of understanding by those outside its reach," journalist Isabel Wilkerson wrote in *The Warmth of Other Suns: The Epic Story of America's Great Migration*. "They set out for cities they had whispered of among themselves or had seen in a mail-order catalogue. Some came straight from the field with their King James Bibles and old twelve-string guitars. Still more were townspeople looking to be their fuller selves, tradesmen following their customers, pastors trailing their flocks."[17]

The Butlers drove to Los Angeles, California, in 1948, a city that virtually no African American called home before World War II. But the black population of the West was booming, as transplants traveled thousands of miles to work in the shipyards and other parts of the defense and aerospace industries that boomed with the onset of the Cold War. By the end of the 1940s, 462,000 blacks lived in California. The war, Wilkerson wrote, had "set off a virtual stampede" to the Golden State.[18]

In Los Angeles, M.L. got a job at the post office, while Beulah took the early bus every day from the home they rented near the city center to cook and clean for a woman in the luxurious coastal community of Pacific Palisades. The couple were determined to stand on their own two feet, to build wealth for their coming family, to own their own home, and to live the American Dream.

The story of the Los Angeles bungalow that M.L. and Beulah Butler eventually bought tracks neatly with the arc of American homeownership—although the Butlers waited close to two decades to attain their dream, thanks to racial discrimination baked into the New Deal.

The house was built in 1923, the same year publishing baron Harry Chandler erected the famous Hollywood sign (then reading "Hollywoodland") over a city that sprawled southward. All of 834 square feet, the house contained two bedrooms and a bathroom within its redwood frame. An apricot tree grew out back. In old photos, the house is absolutely unremarkable. If you closed your eyes and imagined a small single-family home built in Southern California between the turn of the century and the Great Depression, you wouldn't be far off. Its distinguishing feature is a nice, big living room window up behind a short porch that faces the street.

Among the home's first residents was Fred Weitzel, a World War I veteran who'd moved west from Kansas, with his wife, Grace, and fifteen-year-old daughter, Margaret, before the census taker arrived in 1930. Fred told the Census he worked in a machine shop. His wife was a homemaker. Like many of their neighbors, they rented from builder Harry C. Johnson, who lived around the corner on West Seventieth Street. New Deal programs that provided long-term mortgages with low down payments did not exist yet. But as we've seen, here, at least, Franklin Roosevelt's New Deal programs worked. In 1940 the Census Bureau reported that thirty-eight-year-old Iowa transplant Edwin Thomas had bought the home and lived there with his wife and three children. Thomas worked as a spring assembler in a bedding factory. His next-door neighbor William Conway worked as a night watchman for a lumberyard. He owned his home, too, as did his neighbor August Klein, who worked for the post office.

Everyone in the neighborhood was white, thanks in part to restrictive covenants that prevented the sale of homes to black buyers. Far from opposing such prohibitions, the government actively encouraged them. Typically, the Home Owners' Loan Corporation reserved its highest, green rating for neighborhoods where deeds forbade homes from being sold to people of color. Indeed, in its 1934 assessment of that section of South Los Angeles, the HOLC's surveyor noted approvingly that deed restrictions "providing protections against racial hazards" were still in place and accorded the neighborhood a "medial yellow" grade.[19] In the years that followed, white residents did what they could to keep black newcomers out. From 1937 to 1948, more than a hundred lawsuits enforcing racially discriminatory covenants on South Los Angeles homes were filed in county superior court.[20]

HAVING LITERALLY DRIVEN across the country to escape the segregation of Mississippi and reach for opportunity in California, M.L. and Beulah Butler were not going to let the racist policies embedded in the New Deal or their neighbors' hostility stop them from entering the middle class. Dedicating herself to self-improvement, Beulah went back to school, attending community college—even as she kept taking the crosstown bus to her job as a maid in Pacific Palisades—and used her education to land a job as an electrician for military contractor Hughes Aircraft. M.L. kept working at the post office. The couple scrimped and saved. In 1963, fifteen years after they drove west from Mississippi, California governor Pat Brown signed the Rumford Fair Housing Act. It outlawed racial discrimination in housing sales and rentals. M.L. and Beulah Butler didn't wait—that year, they finally bought their first house.

"We were one of the first black families in the neighborhood," their son, Marcus, told me. He was nine when they bought the bungalow.

THE RUMFORD ACT sparked a backlash, revealing deep racism at the heart of the Golden State, and in 1964, California voters overturned the legislature's decision to ban housing discrimination in a popular referendum. But three years later, in a 5-to-4 decision, the US Supreme Court declared the voter initiative unconstitutional. Still, there was the law and there was the practice. Observers of the time described housing integration as the brief spell between the first black family moving into a neighborhood and the last white family moving out. In South Los Angeles, blacks were buying small, sturdily built houses there just as whites were using government-backed loans to buy larger properties in the suburbs. White flight from these neighborhoods reshaped the region. Major businesses—auto dealerships, department stores, supermarkets, and movie theaters—chased customers west and north and left big gaps in the goods and services available in South LA. Between the dedication of the Angelus Funeral Home in 1968 and the opening of the West Angeles Church of God in Christ Cathedral in 2001, not a single major structure went up along South Crenshaw Boulevard, formerly one of the city's major commercial thoroughfares. Disinvestment and eroding opportunities for work helped create a chicken-and-egg conundrum. Black people moved in as whites moved out, and companies that had helped maintain a middle class began shedding workers in the 1960s because of corporate mergers and cost cutting. And fewer jobs contributed to concentrated pockets of poverty and crime in South LA neighborhoods.

Secure in their bungalow, the Butlers did their best to ignore all this. Beulah planted a rose garden in the front and a vegetable garden, including collard greens, in the back. Her outgoing personality and delicious hospitality made the Butler home a social center in the neighborhood. But ignoring the larger currents was nearly impossible. In the summer of 1965, two years after they moved in, the National Guard was called out to suppress riots that erupted in the South LA neighborhood of Watts that left thirty-four people dead and a thousand injured.[21]

Like the Butler household, South Central Los Angeles developed into a magnet for African American culture on the West Coast. Marcus Butler remembers a peaceful childhood there. His warmest memories are of playing at a park near his family's house with Los Angeles Dodgers journeyman outfielder "Sweet" Lou Johnson. "He would bring some young Cuban ballplayers with him, and I had no idea what a Cuban ballplayer was," Marcus said, "but they would teach us the fundamentals of baseball."

When he turned eighteen, Marcus followed in his father's footsteps and enlisted in the army. His service took him to Texas, where he helped coordinate logistics for the war in Vietnam. He couldn't help but notice his neighborhood's steep decline when he returned three years later. Rival gangs—Crips and Bloods—fought openly in the streets. The neighborhood kids now steered clear of the park he'd enjoyed. Relations between his neighbors and the LA Police Department, never great, deteriorated. But like his parents before him, Marcus focused on work and family. He rented an apartment and took a job loading luggage at Los Angeles International Airport that would support him, his wife, and two children over the next twenty years.

THERE WERE ALMOST innumerable instances of racist violence—institutional and individual—and urban decline during those decades, but nothing to rival what happened in Watts until 1992. The spark: a court decision from a suburban jury that acquitted four white LAPD officers for the videotaped beating of black motorist Rodney King the year before. The Butlers lived five blocks from the epicenter of the unrest at the intersection of Florence and Normandie Avenues. Through all this, the Butlers stayed in their home, made their monthly mortgage payments, increased their wealth, and purchased their piece of the American Dream.

Two years before the family paid off its mortgage and a year before the 1992 riots, Marcus's dad, M. L. Butler, died. He'd lived a rough life. M.L. had grown taciturn, and he took to sitting alone in the backyard, chewing on collard green leaves and cutting his nails with a pocketknife. He was an alcoholic, addicted to Golden Moon Gin, but he loved his family and wanted to leave the next generation with more than he'd had. Beulah kept working for Hughes Aircraft and later the Raytheon Company. She retired with a pension and a house in the clear. Then things started to go wrong.

Beulah Butler loved to play the slots. In retirement, she eagerly escaped to Las Vegas or Southern California's tribal casinos— venues that catered to seniors' hunger for attention and action. Sometimes she drove herself in her Buick Regal; other times, she boarded a chartered gambling bus that stopped in the parking lot of a Ralphs supermarket at the corner of Western and Manchester Avenues. Her favorite Vegas casino was the Horseshoe, a frontier-themed affair with low ceilings and flocked wallpaper, away from the downtown Strip.

When she won, casino workers captured the moments in Polaroids. Her frizzy, white hair framed her beaming face. The earliest of those pictures, preserved in an album, dates from the mid-1990s, after her husband's death. Small winnings ignited Beulah's smile: $800 on New Year's Eve 1994; $100 on a July afternoon in 1999. There are no photos of the many times she lost. "She had a gambling problem," Marcus told me.

But she was determined. Even as her kidneys failed, Beulah continued to travel to Las Vegas, where special dialysis centers that partner with the casinos kept her bloodstream clean. During their weekly lunches at the Red Lobster and Olive Garden, Marcus would reprimand his mother about the dangers of gambling. Beulah kept playing, though, even as her body and mind deteriorated. "She was struggling with dementia," Marcus's daughter, Jessica Butler, said. "She was so used to being independent, but she didn't remember anything. She would forget to wash. She would forget to shower."

In 2010, when Beulah Butler was eighty years old, Jessica, then twenty-seven, moved into the bungalow to take care of her grandmother full-time. She was the first in her family to go to college, graduating Humboldt State University with a degree in social work. It was then that Jessica remembers spotting mail from Financial Freedom Senior Funding. Soon she would learn that in

2007, at the height of the real estate bubble, her grandmother had taken out a reverse mortgage against the family home, with an adjustable rate that topped out at 16.6 percent. Every month, Financial Freedom gave her a $500 check that Beulah spent at the casinos. That amount, plus fees and compound interest, added to the balance she owed. Every month, Financial Freedom took away a little bit more of the Butler family home.

"I loved that house," Jessica told me. "I grew up in that house. I remember my grandma making ice cream in the back. Until the last year [of her life], we cooked together. When she passed away, I thought it would pass to my father. But that's not what happened."

Marcus said he never knew his mother had taken out the loan. "I would have told her not to," he said. "We had worked so hard to pay that home off."

BY NOW, YOU'VE probably guessed what happened next. The Butler family lost the house. After Beulah passed away at age eighty-two in 2012, OneWest Bank filed an official notice—addressed to the dead woman—at the LA County Courthouse. Its message was simple: Beulah Butler had defaulted on the reverse mortgage scheduled to come due after she passed away. The bank was calling in all the money she owed. The total came to $326,103.19—an amount, OneWest cautioned, that "will increase until the account becomes current."

When they received the notice, Beulah's survivors didn't react with the fury that Sandy Jolley did. They didn't fight back. They didn't know, for example, about the rule that required OneWest Bank to offer them the house at 95 percent of its appraised value, which, thanks to the housing bust, was a much lower amount than the big bill it had sent. Like most families caught in this kind of financial difficulty, however, they were ashamed of the financial mistakes they'd made, so they just gave up. Jessica packed up her grandmother's belongings and rented a one-bedroom apartment in the Crenshaw district. Marcus lived near his daughter, renting a small, concrete-block apartment. All those years loading luggage onto airplanes at LAX had paid well enough, but he'd never managed to save. Court records show Marcus declared bankruptcy three times to erase debt from high-interest credit cards.

The property sat empty for nearly a year. Squatters moved in. Marcus drove by, as if to keep an eye on an old love, and called the police on the intruders. "He was just heartbroken," Jessica told me.

ONEWEST FINALLY PUT the house up for bid on April 17, 2013, and sold it in front of a county government building in suburban Pomona, two weeks after it disposed of the Hickerson family home at a similar auction an hour's drive up the coast. The purchase price this time was $180,000, or about half what the bank had demanded from the Butlers. That difference didn't matter to OneWest: because the loan was insured by the government, Steve Mnuchin's bank could simply bill the taxpayers for the $148,000 difference. On top of that, the bank could have the government pay its attorneys' fees, property inspections, appraisal costs, and any other expenses related to the foreclosure process.

When the bidding was finished, the buyer of the Butler family's bungalow emerged. It was ColFin AI-CA5 LLC, the same shell company that bought Sandy's family home. The same San Diego–based foreclosure firm that dispossessed Sandy handled the transaction in South LA—after which it sent the deed to the same suburban office complex in Scottsdale, Arizona, to the attention of the same corporate vice president. Tom Barrack's company now owned the home the Butlers had sacrificed for decades to secure, just as it possessed tens of thousands of houses all over the United States.

ACROSS AMERICA, RACIAL discrimination in housing has been illegal for fifty years, since President Lyndon Johnson signed the Fair Housing Act shortly after Dr. Martin Luther King Jr.'s assassination in 1968. But all these years later, the system remains profoundly rigged against people of color. Evidence of naked prejudice is plentiful, including at the nation's largest banks. In 2009 a Wells Fargo loan officer signed a sworn affidavit telling a federal court that bank employees called African Americans "mud people" and steered even qualified borrowers of color into high-cost "ghetto loans."[22] We "rode the stagecoach from hell," a second Wells Fargo loan officer, Beth Jacobson, told the *New York Times*. "We just went right after them," targeting black families with high-cost loans. (Wells Fargo denied wrongdoing but in 2012 paid $184 million to settle discrimination claims.[23]) For their part, Homewreckers such as Mnuchin, Barrack, and Schwarzman have dismissed the notion that race played any role in their business practices, nor has anyone discovered a smoking-gun document declaring an overtly racist intent. They are emphatic, in fact, that the only color that matters to them is green. But at least one of their biggest investors has written about the systemic nature of racial bias in the industry, even as he's been happy to profit off it.

"The human suffering caused by the housing crisis will be enormous," billionaire George Soros wrote in 2008, shortly before his firm bought a stake in IndyMac. "There is significant evidence senior citizens were targeted for some of the worst predatory practices and are disproportionately defaulting on their mortgages. Communities of color are also disproportionately affected. Given that homeownership is a key factor in increasing wealth and opportunity in the United States, upwardly mobile young professionals of color will be particularly hard hit. They bought into the premise of the 'ownership society,' and their assets are concentrated in home ownership."[24]

The data tell a damning story. During the boom years, IndyMac charged high interest rates (defined by the government as more than 3 percentage points above prime) to 24 percent of its white borrowers, but 36 percent of Hispanics and 43 percent of African Americans.[25] This meant that when the recession hit, people of color, who faced higher monthly payments for the same size mortgages, were more vulnerable to foreclosure. After the crash, banks such as OneWest were supposed to address these disparities through federally sponsored loan modification programs. But instead of giving African American and Latino borrowers a chance to renegotiate on terms they could afford, Steve Mnuchin and his management team revved up their foreclosure machine.

The nonprofit California Reinvestment Coalition (CRC) analyzed thirty-six thousand foreclosures by OneWest Bank while Mnuchin was at the helm. Though roughly 40 percent of the loans IndyMac made in the Golden State before the bust were in neighborhoods where a majority of residents were people of color, the coalition found that 70 percent of OneWest foreclosures were in these majority-minority neighborhoods.[26]

After the banks foreclosed on those properties, neglect diminished their value. Another organization, Fair Housing Advocates of Northern California, investigated how well OneWest maintained and marketed homes after foreclosing on them. The group's representatives visited properties in white communities that were generally well maintained and marketed with manicured lawns, securely locked doors and windows, and attractive, professional

For Sale signs posted out front. By contrast, OneWest foreclo-sures in communities of color had descended into blight, with trash strewn around the premises, overgrown grass, shrubbery, and weeds, and boarded up or broken doors and windows. One-West properties in those areas "appear abandoned, blighted, and unappealing to potential homeowners," the group found, even where they "are located in stable neighborhoods with surround-ing homes that are well maintained."[27]

The places in which OneWest allowed its foreclosures to fall into disrepair were the same ones in which private equity firms run by Tom Barrack and Steve Schwarzman did most of their buying. In 2017 Maya Abood, a researcher from the Massachusetts Insti-tute of Technology, conducted a statistical analysis to determine which factors might best predict where these corporate landlords decided to purchase housing in California. She took into account economic factors, including the amount of money people in the neighborhood made, the typical home value, and the number of jobs nearby. Even after all that, she found corporate landlords were still more likely to buy homes in neighborhoods with large concentrations of African Americans and Latinos, as opposed to those with mostly white or Asian homeowners.[28]

"From redlining to subprime lending, US housing policy has al-ways intersected with racial justice issues," Abood wrote. "Based on the data, the rise of institutionalized and financialized single-family rental companies is no different. Because neighborhoods with a greater percentage of black (and Latino) residents are disproportion-ately impacted by large single-family rental companies, the behav-ior of these firms may constitute a violation" of fair housing laws, she said. Even if the companies weren't breaking the law, they were pressing people of color to pay higher and higher rents that ulti-mately transfer wealth from their communities to investors far away.

In the two South Central Los Angeles zip codes that surround the Butler family home, OneWest Bank foreclosed on 262 families during Mnuchin's tenure. During a similar period, federal lending data show, it refinanced just fifteen mortgages there. Blackstone and Colony then bought 219 houses in the neighborhood.

The image of a racist foreclosure king wasn't the one Steve Mnuchin wanted to project. When he bought IndyMac off the government in 2009, he pledged it would function as a "community bank." But his definition of *community* was severely limited. As it foreclosed on homeowners in suburban minority neighborhoods in desert cities such as Lancaster and Palmdale, and urban centers like South Central LA, its network of bank branches hugged the coast, from Huntington Beach to Santa Monica, where most residents are white; then branched east, in an arc through the Hollywood Hills, as if to avoid heavily black and Hispanic neighborhoods downtown; before reaching the company's corporate headquarters in Pasadena, another majority white community. Since the bank was "long on mortgages" because of IndyMac's profligate lending during the boom, OneWest Bank was generally conservative in its mortgage lending. In practice, this meant the borrowers were invariably white. From 2011 to 2015, government data show, OneWest helped just three African Americans and eleven Hispanic families buy homes nationwide. During those years, the bank did not help a single family purchase a home in South Los Angeles.

COMMUNITY GROUPS TRIED to talk to OneWest about the foreclosures and lack of community investment, but their concerns were brushed aside. Senior leaders at the bank would say, "Hey, we're working on that. Don't worry, we're working on that," recalled Orson Aguilar, then president of the Greenlining Institute, an advocacy nonprofit based in Oakland that pushes banks to increase lending in minority neighborhoods.

A soft-spoken advocate who speaks with the warmth and gentle manner of a practiced politician, Aguilar had met with hundreds of banks as head of Greenlining. Usually, he said, the best results could be found not through angry protests but in quiet meetings in boardrooms. So, he arranged for a discussion with Steve Mnuchin at OneWest's Pasadena headquarters. The bank was still located in the same sand-colored structure that Indy-Mac had been, where desperate depositors had wound around the block. Aguilar's goal was to get Mnuchin to agree to specific goals for home mortgage lending, small business investment, and antiforeclosure measures. But Mnuchin didn't want to talk about that. He wanted to see how much money Aguilar wanted personally. He seemed to think Aguilar wanted charity or a bribe.

Mnuchin "kept saying, 'How much money do you want? How much money do you want for your members?'" Aguilar recalled.

Aguilar replied that he didn't want money for himself or a donation for the groups that made up his coalition. "Mr. Mnuchin, respectfully, we're here to talk about foreclosure issues—"

Mnuchin cut him off. "Stop. Just stop. Just tell me a number," he said.

When Aguilar didn't provide one, the meeting ended. "I have never had a meeting with a banker where the banker acted the way he did," Aguilar said. The sit-down with Mnuchin "stemmed from our frustration with not getting answers from the bank on issues we care about." Now here was Mnuchin in the flesh, and he still refused to discuss them. It was the only face-to-face Aguilar had with Mnuchin—"the only time he made himself available." To Aguilar, it seemed that Mnuchin simply didn't care.

PART V

THE BIG FLIP

CHAPTER 15

TIME TO MAKE A DEAL

SO, BESIDES TAKING ADVANTAGE OF Washington's handouts, how did OneWest Bank make money? My review of government securities filings revealed that Mnuchin's bank made loans to companies that were aggressively fracking for oil and natural gas in the Bakken Formation in North Dakota, the Cherokee Basin in Oklahoma, and the Central Kansas Uplift.[1] OneWest also helped finance Corinthian Colleges, the company that owned the for-profit colleges Heald, Everest, and WyoTech.[2] All three closed their doors in 2015 amid state and federal fraud charges.[3]

The bank also made investments in Hollywood, including a $50 million loan to Relativity Media, a movie company founded by Ryan Kavanaugh, where Mnuchin served as cochairman of the board. Under Mnuchin's leadership, OneWest got paid back—with interest. But the studio's other backers didn't get the same positive return. Less than a year after Mnuchin and Kavanaugh joined forces, the company declared bankruptcy, leaving most of its creditors scrambling.[4]

As OneWest took deposits from residents of wealthier neighborhoods in Southern California, it lent to other companies that took big risks. "The loans," the *Los Angeles Times* reported, "were used to acquire companies through leveraged buyouts—deals in which private equity firms buy a company using some of their own capital plus a loan taken out on the company itself—and to fund dividend recapitalizations, a practice in which firms borrow against the value of a business and use the proceeds to pay a dividend to their investors."[5] One of those risk-taking companies was quite experienced with taking advantage of the housing crisis.

In 2013 OneWest joined a consortium of financial institutions, including Bank of America and JPMorgan Chase, that extended a line of credit to Tom Barrack's Colony Capital, and helped to fund Barrack's home-buying spree.[6] This line of credit created a financial revolving door, as Colony bought OneWest's foreclosures using a loan from OneWest. By the end of 2014, OneWest's commitment to Colony had grown to $45 million—more than all the money it made available to African American and Latino home buyers over five years.[7]

THE MAIN WAY private equity guys make money is when they eventually sell. Annual returns from running a bank are nice, but big payoffs come when you can flip your investment. That's what Mnuchin had been working toward. As IndyMac's toxic loans were liquidated, to the detriment of homeowners and the federal Treasury, the bank—now a recipient of billions of dollars in government handouts and a massive real estate portfolio bought on the cheap—increased in value. Four years in, Mnuchin started off-loading parts of OneWest that didn't fit with the vision he and his fellow board members had for the bank.

In 2013, for example, he dumped the right to collect payments on most of IndyMac's old loans to Ocwen Financial Corporation, one of the nation's largest nonbank mortgage servicer, for $2.5 billion.[8] Mnuchin and his team timed it perfectly. Ocwen was awash in consumer complaints, and, before the year was out, the Florida-based company, which counted Wilbur Ross among its board members, had agreed to pay $2 billion to settle allegations of "systemic misconduct at every stage of the mortgage servicing process."[9] As part of the agreement with the Consumer Financial Protection Bureau, Ocwen agreed to refund $125 million to nearly 185,000 borrowers who had already been foreclosed on and, in addition, promised to adopt significant new homeowner protections.[10]

Now Mnuchin wanted to sell the entire bank. He started talking to John Thain, his much richer neighbor at 740 Park Avenue. The son of a doctor from a small, nearly all-white suburb north of Chicago, Thain was an MIT graduate with an MBA from Harvard. The tall, bespectacled business leader had, like Mnuchin, gone straight from the Ivy League to Goldman Sachs, where he, like Steve, oversaw mortgage-backed securities as he worked his way up the corporate hierarchy.[11] In 1999 Thain became president of Goldman, the second most powerful person at the company, making him the boss of both Mnuchin and his mentor, Michael Mortara. Thain used the position to build his fortune. By the time he left to run the New York Stock Exchange four years later, Thain had accepted tens of millions of dollars in bonuses and amassed $300 million in Goldman stock.[12, 13] Given his vast wealth, some in the media treated his decision to go to the NYSE as an act of charity, since he would be taking a dramatic salary cut—to $4 million a year. The technocrat also received praise for bringing the august exchange into the digital age—managing, in the words of *New York* magazine's Noam Scheiber, "to persuade the traders to go along with their own extinction."[14]

It was his next career move that would make him a pariah. During the darkest days of the financial crisis, Thain's decision to use taxpayer money to line his own pocket earned him a personal rebuke from President Obama.[15] According to FDIC chairwoman Sheila Bair, in a 2008 meeting at the nadir of the crisis, Thain said he was particularly worried how the government bailout might reduce executive compensation. "I couldn't believe it," she wrote in her book *Bull by the Horns*. "Where were the guy's priorities?"[16]

Bank of America agreed to buy Merrill the same weekend Lehman Brothers collapsed. The deal came to pass thanks to the active involvement of the federal government. When it continued to hemorrhage money under Thain's leadership, Bank of America showed him the door.[17] But it wasn't long before Thain found a new employer. It didn't matter that he had run a ninety-five-year-old company into the ground and paid himself hefty bonuses while doing it—like other spectacular Wall Street failures, he landed on his feet.

In February 2010, barely a year after Bank of America fired him, Thain took the helm of CIT, a New Jersey–based business bank whose best-known borrower was Dunkin' Donuts. During the housing bubble, CIT had strayed from its core business, placing big bets on subprime mortgages and student loans. The government stepped in, saving the company by giving it a multibillion-dollar loan as the lender of last resort. Then CIT went bankrupt anyway, gaining the ignominious distinction of being one of the first banks to default on its federal bailout money—a move that cost taxpayers $2.3 billion.[18]

CIT's leaders saw a savior in Thain. "We saw tremendous upside to John," John Ryan, the company's lead director, told the *New York Times*. "We think of him as an Olympic-class athlete with a lot of potential going forward. He's the best person to position us to become profitable again."

For his part, Thain said CIT was a job creator. "CIT is a company that's very important to small and medium-sized businesses," he said. "If we're going to see the US economy continue to grow and see new jobs, we have to provide financing to those companies."[19]

Thain had another thing going for him. Because CIT's debts were wiped away in bankruptcy, he was operating with a clean slate. By 2013, he had returned the company to profitability, but taxpayers would never get back their $2.3 billion worth of bailout money.

By April 2014, officials at the Federal Reserve Board in Washington were already wondering which competitor CIT would try to take over. "There is a likelihood CIT may approach FRB in the near term to discuss an acquisition of OneWest," Michael Lippman, a financial analyst at the Federal Reserve, wrote to his superiors that month. The note set off more than 2,600 pages of correspondence that I obtained using the Freedom of Information Act. The Federal Reserve redacted most of those pages, but there were still plenty of revealing passages left uncensored.

The possible acquisition was seen as particularly sensitive. The global economic meltdown and the government bailout that followed had made regulators wary. The Dodd-Frank Act had declared that banks with more than $50 billion in assets were so important—considered "too big to fail"—that they might have to be bailed out in a crisis. A merger of OneWest and CIT Bank would create the first "systematically important financial institution" since the housing bust. It would have to be approved by federal banking regulators, including the Office of the Comptroller of the Currency (OCC) and the Board of Governors of the Federal Reserve. But Thain felt confident. On June 26 the *Wall Street Journal* ran a story that declared he was "prepared to be 'important.'"[20]

Luckily for Thain, he was supremely well connected. To grease the skids, he hired a veteran fixer, lawyer H. Rodgin Cohen, who has been variously praised as "a legendary transactional lawyer," "an icon," and "God" by the financial press. (In a single month after the collapse of Lehman Brothers in 2008, Cohen and his team advised Fannie Mae, Wachovia, Barclays, JPMorgan Chase, and Goldman Sachs.) Thain's fixer worked quietly, setting up meetings with key government officials in New York and Washington. He made no public pronouncements. If all went well, the public wouldn't know what was going on until the merger was all sewn up.

The documents I obtained show that a few days after the *Journal* article appeared, Thain began sharing a PowerPoint with government regulators about a potential acquisition of OneWest. In government documents and public presentations, he presented the merger as the best of both worlds. By buying OneWest, he would bring together New York and Los Angeles, merging a business bank with one with a network of branches. But after his first meeting with Thain on June 30, John Ricketti, a vice president of the Federal Reserve Bank of New York, offered a simpler reason the deal was being proposed: "John Thain knows OneWest chairman Steve Mnuchin," he wrote to his colleagues.[21]

A deal like this would never have been possible if Thain had been forced to pay back the $2.3 billion in bailout money CIT took from the taxpayers or if Steve Mnuchin had been asked to give back the $1 billion OneWest had received by then[22] in its loss-share agreement with the FDIC. In fact, one of the things that made the deal a "financially attractive combination" to CIT, the Federal Reserve documents show, is that nearly 90 percent of OneWest's residential mortgage loans were still covered by the agreement—meaning that payments from the federal government would continue long after the merger. Of course, no homes would have to be returned or mortgages adjusted. The government subsidies would simply keep flowing to the new owners until they finally expired in 2020, more than a decade after the bust.

A DAY AFTER his meeting with Ricketti in New York, Thain traveled to Washington to meet with staff of the Federal Reserve Board of Governors. When Rodgin Cohen first approached the Fed, the staff there thought the lawyer would kick off the process by coming in for a visit, so they planned an intimate meeting in the office of its general counsel. But Thain had his foot firmly on the gas. He showed up with Steve Mnuchin, as well as Mnuchin's number two at OneWest, Joseph Otting, and a group of ten other bankers and lawyers representing both companies. The meeting was promptly moved to a grand fourth-floor boardroom.

Then, having made their case, Thain and Mnuchin set off to meet with another set of federal banking regulators, the Office of the Comptroller of the Currency, which enforces a host of regulations, including anti-money-laundering and community lending laws, for big national banks. After that pitch meeting, Otting headed to Washington Dulles International Airport. While waiting for his flight, he picked up the phone and called an official with the Federal Reserve based in San Francisco, bringing her up to speed on their aggressive itinerary of meetings on the East Coast.

In the documents I obtained, the substance of that conversation is redacted, but there was no indication the dash toward the deal wasn't going smoothly. Indeed, in the thousands of pages of internal Federal Reserve documents, nobody raised a fuss.

When Thain announced the deal in an earnings call with investors on July 22, they were overjoyed. "My first comment was, 'Wow,'" analyst Henry Coffey said when given the chance to question Thain, "which I understood is not a very sophisticated reaction."

"That's all right," Thain replied with a smile. "We like it."

Coffey kept heaping on praise. "This is, like, excuse my"—he burst out laughing with joy—"This is incredible. . . . It's a very hot and heavy market out there for distressed assets."[23] An outsider on the line would likely have been aghast to hear these guys get so much pleasure in making money off other people's pain.

The rating agencies, which had made the mistake of giving superlative assessments to subprime mortgages before the bust, were less enthused. The day the merger was announced, Moody's placed CIT under "review for possible downgrade" because the company was financing its takeover of OneWest by adding a huge amount of debt. Standard & Poor's followed suit, giving CIT a long-term rating of "BB-," noting that the company, which had emerged from bankruptcy only recently, would be borrowing between $1.5 billion and $2 billion of the money that would be paid to Mnuchin and his partners. While OneWest's branch network was strong, and the vast majority loans were covered by the loss-share agreement, the S&P noted that CIT's takeover "will weaken the company's robust capital," posing "strategic risks and uncertainties."[24]

But Thain told his investors not to worry too much about the government. Though the FDIC would continue to pay for losses on OneWest's foreclosures, it would not be required to sign off on the takeover. The only people to worry about were the Federal Reserve, and they were being taken care of. "We're confident that we will be able to get the approvals we need," he said.[25]

THIS WAS THE deal Steve Mnuchin had been waiting for. CIT was planning to pay him, John Paulson, J. C. Flowers, George Soros, and the other investors $3.4 billion for a bank they had bought with just $1.6 billion. The government had compensated them for their losses, and now they would more than double their investment on the flip. Moreover, that didn't count the $2 billion that members of Mnuchin's ownership group had paid themselves in dividends during the time they owned the bank. Including that, the return would come to more than $5 billion. They had more than tripled their money.[26]

John Paulson, whose firm famously made $15 billion by betting against failing mortgages in the run-up to the financial crisis, had put up $400 million for its 24.9 percent stake in OneWest back in 2009. Now he would get $1.7 billion by selling that stake to Thain and CIT. In a letter to his clients, Paulson's hedge fund reported it would take in $788 million for its share of the bank—on top of having already received $511 million in dividends.[27] After accounting for the money Paulson put in, it would clear $1.3 billion. Allen Puwalski, the former FDIC bank examiner who represented Paulson on OneWest's board, updated his LinkedIn profile to reflect the accomplishment: "Money tripled, invested capital returned in less than five years."[28]

For Steve Mnuchin, the return would be even richer. Finally, he had a deal to call his own; one that would make him not just rich but truly, fantastically, gloriously wealthy. As planned, because he had assembled the group to buy IndyMac from the FDIC and served as chief of its holding company, he would get an outsized share of the return. While his own initial contribution was far less than his partners, Mnuchin would be awarded $94 million in stock[29]—an amount roughly equivalent to the combined net worth of forty thousand American families who rent, according to the Census Bureau. And the stock was only *part* of Mnuchin's compensation. Under the terms of the deal, he would serve as vice chairman of the CIT board, a part-time job that paid him $4.5 million a year.[30] Everything was coming up roses—until Mnuchin and Thain ran into a small community organization with an annual budget of $800,000.

CHAPTER 16

THE COMMUNITY FIGHTS BACK

PAULINA GONZALEZ HAD BEEN WATCHING OneWest. Short and energetic, with close-cropped hair and a smile that gave her a youthful look well into her forties, she had grown up in the city of Montebello, in east Los Angeles, in the 1980s, the daughter of Mexican immigrants. Her father worked in a garment factory. When her father got fired trying to organize a union there, he got a job as a janitor at the Biltmore Hotel, and eventually became an officer of the Hotel Employees and Restaurant Employees union (HERE).

Paulina grew up walking picket lines with her father and volunteering for political campaigns. After attending UCLA, where she earned a degree in sociology, she went to work for HERE as a researcher and then became a spokeswoman. But when the Great Recession hit, she had a revelation. "Maybe there's something else I need to be doing," she thought, "beyond the workplace, like what happens when people go home." So, Paulina stepped out on her own, becoming executive director of Strategic Actions for a Just Economy, a community empowerment nonprofit focused on helping residents of South Los Angeles. She worked with the neighborhood's most vulnerable residents, many of whom were being pushed out onto the street as their homes were lost to foreclosure. Most of her clients had been renting homes when the bank foreclosed on their landlord. She learned that after a foreclosure, the bank often turned off the water and electricity, even when tenants were still living there. "I remember one family very specifically," she told me years later. "The kids were doing homework in their car because the bank turned off the lights. That's how I saw the foreclosure crisis in South Central Los Angeles."

In 2014 Gonzalez was recruited to join the California Reinvestment Coalition (CRC), a small advocacy nonprofit in San Francisco dedicated to ensuring that banks uphold their legal obligations under the Community Reinvestment Act (CRA), a landmark law signed by President Jimmy Carter in 1977 that requires banks to lend to the poor. The law was designed specifically to deal with the legacy of redlining. It was not enough to stay clear of overt discrimination. In the language of the law, banks have "a continuing and affirmative obligation" to meet the credit needs of all communities in the cities where they operate.

These were dark days for an organization such as CRC, with foreclosure wiping up communities all over the country. Even so, it would be hard to find a bank that was doing less to fulfill its legal obligations than Mnuchin's. "There are a variety of ways for a bank to meet its CRA obligation," Gonzalez explained. It could help low-income people buy homes or refinance their debt to stave off foreclosure. It could invest in small businesses or affordable housing. "OneWest wasn't doing any of them."

The bank first came to CRC's attention through its annual survey of housing counselors, employees at government agencies and local nonprofits who advise families trying to stay in their homes.

In 2010 the counselors rated OneWest the worst offender for not offering work-arounds. Two years later, 95 percent of housing counselors rated OneWest as "terrible" or "bad," with only HSBC Bank receiving lower marks.[1] In June 2014, when John Thain and Steve Mnuchin started to meet with federal banking regulators to discuss a possible merger, data from the federal Treasury Department showed OneWest had denied three-quarters of the loan modification applications it received—a rate that was harsher than Bank of America, JPMorgan Chase, and Wells Fargo, as well as BankUnited, the Florida bank purchased by Wilbur Ross and Steve Schwarzman.[2]

Under the Community Reinvestment Act, federal banking regulators are required to assess the impact a merger might have on community lending, and they are empowered to set conditions or even block the merger if they think the law will be violated. Gonzalez decided she would confront OneWest's management and tell them they needed to present an aggressive plan to improve or else face community opposition. "From the very beginning, we decided to go all in," she told me. "Let's have a conversation with them but also make sure that they have to put together a really strong plan, given their history of harm in the state."

It was a strategy that had worked for CRC before, especially since there is money to be made by investing productively in low-income communities. After all, when people in those neighborhoods rehabilitate their homes or grow small businesses, the bank can charge interest the same as anywhere else. Earlier that same year, for example, Gonzalez had negotiated a deal with another Southern California lender, Banc of California, clearing the way for its acquisition of Popular Community Bank's twenty Southern California branches. In that deal, which was brokered by former Los Angeles mayor Antonio Villaraigosa, Banc of California agreed to invest the equivalent of 20 percent of its deposits in poor and working-class neighborhoods. Among other reforms, the bank promised to set aside a minimum amount of money for affordable-housing development and small business lending, as well as to create a low-cost checking account and lower ATM fees. It also pledged to provide an annual accounting of its goals to CRC and a host of other nonprofit organizations for the next five years.[3] CRC and its allies came to Banc of California with requests that "were realistic," Robert Braun, a partner at the law firm Jeffer Mangels Butler & Mitchell, told the *Los Angeles Business Journal.* "They asked for things that the banks can give."[4]

Gonzalez was initially optimistic that the same approach might work with OneWest. She met with Joseph Otting at the bank's Pasadena headquarters. Unlike Mnuchin and his private equity investors, Otting wasn't an Ivy-League-to-Wall-Street type. He'd grown up surrounded by corn fields in the small town of Maquoketa, Iowa, about thirty miles from the Mississippi River. His mother was a schoolteacher, and his father ran an auto dealership. The way Otting tells the story, his first exposure to lending came watching his father sell cars. Witnessing his dad shake hands and engage with customers made him want to go into banking, he told the *Las Vegas Review-Journal,* when he saw their relieved expressions after qualifying for a loan.[5]

Otting's path to bank CEO was slow and steady. He stayed close to home for school, attending the University of Northern Iowa, where he received a bachelor's degree in management in 1981. It was the darkest depths of a credit crisis that devastated small family farms and led to the consolidation of American farming into large-scale corporate agriculture. The resulting hardship sent Joseph Otting looking first east and then west for work. After Joseph briefly considered a job at Coca-Cola in Atlanta, his father prevailed on him to head to Southern California, where there might be more opportunities.

He started as a trainee at Bank of America and worked there for five years before heading to Union Bank of California for the next sixteen years, eventually rising to head its commercial banking division. Then it was on to an executive job at a larger regional bank, Minneapolis-based US Bank, where he stayed for a decade. In 2005 he became vice chairman of the company, a position he still held when the financial crisis hit.

"I always liked Joseph Otting. We'd have lunch a lot," recalled Orson Aguilar of the Greenlining Institute. "He seemed to care about the issues we cared about." But after the housing bust, a different Joseph Otting emerged, one who, like Steve Mnuchin, focused on finding ways to profit off the crisis. It started with the money that flowed following the collapse of Lehman Brothers. In November 2008 US Bank took $6.6 billion in bailout money from the federal Treasury.[6] Then, before paying back the money, it swung a massive deal with the FDIC to take over two failed Southern California banks, Downey Savings & Loan Association and PFF Bank & Trust, which had 213 branches between them. The deal featured the same kind of loss-share agreement Mnuchin had obtained for OneWest and Wilbur Ross and Steve Schwarzman had secured for BankUnited: US Bank got to keep all the money it made, but if it lost money foreclosing on homeowners, the government would pay for it. The FDIC estimated it would lose $2.1 billion on the deal.[7]

Otting was thrilled. He had recently moved back to Southern California. "The timing of this could not be better," he said in a press statement. US Bank had been trying to expand in California and Arizona. Now it would be able to do so, thanks to an assist from the government. A year later, in October 2009,

Otting swung another massive deal with the FDIC, taking over nine failed banks across Arizona, California, Illinois, and Texas. Again he got a loss-share agreement, where US Bank got to keep the money it made, but the government paid when the bank lost money on a foreclosure. The FDIC estimated it would lose another $2.5 billion on *that* deal. (Steve Mnuchin was probably jealous, for FDIC records show that OneWest bid on the banks too.[8])

But although US Bank was much bigger than OneWest, with nearly $300 billion in assets compared with $28 billion for OneWest, the private equity backers of OneWest could offer Otting something that a publicly traded company such as US Bank couldn't: the possibility of a huge payday. A leadership post at US Bank could certainly be lucrative, but it was nothing compared with a bank owned by vulture capitalists. Mnuchin's group not only paid a higher salary than most traditional banks would, but also it presented a chance for Otting to profit as a participant on a flip, versus just a salary and annual bonus.

In October 2010 Steve Mnuchin hired Otting as CEO. "Since our inception, OneWest has been committed to growing and expanding our organization as the premier regional bank focused on customer service," he said in announcing the hire. "Attracting someone with Joseph's background, knowledge of the market, client relationships, and leadership capabilities made him uniquely qualified for this position, and we are so pleased to have him join our team."[9]

Otting has never put his decision to join OneWest in the crass language of dollars and cents. In his interview with the *Las Vegas Review-Journal*, Otting echoed Mnuchin's language of community service, explaining that he saw the job as an opportunity to move up as well as to help the Los Angeles area. "We wanted to make a hometown bank," he said. "Bankers are dream makers. We all have a responsibility to help our communities."[10]

SHORTLY AFTER THE merger announcement, Paulina Gonzalez led a delegation of more than a dozen community groups to OneWest's Pasadena offices. They took the elevator up and were escorted into a conference room for a meeting with the company's top brass. Gone was the glad-handing Otting. Faced with a group of advocates with demands, he was aloof "and kind of detached," Gonzalez recalled. He laughed off the terms that her group proposed, the same ones that Banc of California had agreed to: 20 percent of deposits invested in low-income and working-class borrowers, small business lending, and a public accounting of what it had done for the community. "We also had some stuff in there around affordable housing," Gonzalez said, namely that they wanted OneWest to invest $30 million in a trust fund for nonprofit developers. "He was like, 'There's no way. We're not going to do it.'" The bank that was extending $45 million in credit to Tom Barrack's company had no interest in lending to community nonprofits.

"You have foreclosed on all these people. Part of California's housing crisis is the foreclosure crisis," Gonzalez countered. She turned to Otting. "How much do you make in a year?"

"Well, how much do *you* make in a year?" he countered.

"Joseph, that's public information," she replied. "You can look it up in our 990s"—the tax forms that nonprofits must make available to the public.

I looked up her income. It was $124,000. OneWest was a private company, so Otting's compensation was not public in 2014, but documents filed with the SEC show that CIT was promising him $12.5 million in company stock, along with an annual pay package of up to $4.5 million—meaning he stood to make $26 million over the next three years.[11]

"You know, you're sitting here. You're a millionaire," Gonzalez told him. "You know we're talking about people whose have been foreclosed upon. They lost everything, you know. And you're not engaging in that conversation."

Otting, Gonzalez decided, was "the type of person who did what he needed to get what he wanted, which was to get the merger." The community groups left empty-handed.

GONZALEZ'S NEXT STOP was a "Community Day" that CIT and OneWest organized in an auditorium near Forest Lawn cemetery, where the banks indicated they would present their Community Reinvestment plan to the public. Orson Aguilar of Greenlining also attended. He remembers it as an odd affair, not at all like the other community meetings with banks that involved dollars-and-cents discussions of investments. OneWest opened the meeting with a calisthenics performance by children from a financial education program it sponsored. It was a peculiar way of presenting its commitment to invest in communities in need.

Steve Mnuchin, John Thain, and Joseph Otting wouldn't talk about specific financial commitments to the community. Thain, he of the personal elevator, seemed somewhat uncomfortable amid the rabble and mostly kept quiet. Otting was at greater ease. He did most of the talking, holding court in his folksy, Midwestern way, but made clear his bank would not negotiate with either the California Reinvestment Coalition or the Greenlining Institute, as many of its competitors had done.

In a letter to the Federal Reserve following the meeting, Aguilar noted nearly everyone in attendance supported the advocacy organization's negotiating positions.[12] A notable exception was the Los Angeles County Museum of Art, a landmark depository of ancient and modern art that sat on a tony section of Wilshire Boulevard near Beverly Hills. LACMA, as the museum is known, had become a frequent destination for Hollywood parties. Its annual Art + Film Gala, sponsored by the Italian fashion designer Gucci, was a see-and-be-seen event where actors such as Leonardo DiCaprio, Jane Fonda, and Drew Barrymore rubbed shoulders with Italian fashion designers, producers, and musicians. Artists also attended the event, of course, as well as the museum's board of directors.[13] Among the last group was Steve Mnuchin's wife, Heather, who added the Los Angeles charity ball circuit to a society itinerary that previously had been centered on Park Avenue and the Hamptons.

The cochair of the museum's board, Terry Semel, a former longtime executive at Warner Bros. and Yahoo!, proclaimed he was "thrilled to see Heather Mnuchin join us in stewarding LACMA at such an exciting period of the museum's history."[14] He also noted the Mnuchins had given generously to the museum, donating at least $10,000 to join the "Director's Circle" and another $15,000 to take part in the "Collectors Committee." LACMA was hardly the sort of struggling community institution Jimmy Carter had in mind when he signed the Community Reinvestment Act. It had a $112 million annual budget and paid its chief executive more than $1 million a year.[15] But it was one of the few community groups to support Steve Mnuchin in his desire to cash in from CIT's takeover of OneWest Bank.

TWO DAYS AFTER the Community Day, the California Reinvestment Coalition came out against the merger, calling on the Federal

Reserve to hold hearings into how it would impact the public. The group also complained of "excessive compensation" for leaders of the two banks, which had received billions from the government and were now cashing in without paying any of it back. "The transfer of this valuable loss-share agreement from OneWest to CIT serves no public purpose, especially without clear evidence that OneWest complied with its obligations to faithfully administer loan modification programs and otherwise comply with the terms of the loss-share agreement," CRC said in its statement. "The FDIC should not rubber-stamp this proposed transfer."[16]

Again the groups asked OneWest and CIT to come to the table and negotiate a community benefits agreement with specific lending targets to low-income communities and small businesses. And again the banks refused—only this time they went further. Otting took the unusual step of embedding a form on the bank's website that generated form letters urging federal regulators to quickly approve the merger without a public hearing. "I am writing to offer my support for the pending OneWest and CIT merger," it read. "OneWest serves as a strong source of capital and banking services to the Southern California community. This merger will retain and create new jobs in California. I believe the management team and OneWest have demonstrated its commitment to our community and to serving the needs of not only their clients but the community at large, and due to this, I do not believe there is a need for a public hearing." The result was more than two thousand form letters being sent to the Federal Reserve, representing nearly all the positive comments the government received on the merger. (The Federal Reserve reported that of the 2,177 people who wrote supporting OneWest, more than 95 percent sent "substantially identical form letters."[17])

Financial analysts were puzzled by OneWest's aggressive posture and worried it would alienate the Federal Reserve, which had showed no indication that it would oppose the OneWest merger or any other corporate combination. After all, these same federal regulators had facilitated Wells Fargo's acquisition of Wachovia, and Bank of America's takeover of Merrill Lynch, and had backed JPMorgan Chase as it swallowed Bear Stearns and Washington Mutual. In most of those cases, the Federal Reserve had even provided cash or cheap credit before rubber-stamping it without insisting on specific lending commitments under the Community Reinvestment Act. Why rock the boat with a campaign of annoying, auto-generated form letters?[18]

The activists did what they could to keep up the pressure. They launched their own petition drive, garnering twenty thousand signatures, urging their supporters to write as individuals. Among the people to respond was Sandy Jolley, who, six months after filing her federal whistleblower complaint, was still waiting to hear back from the Justice Department. She also joined a protest at OneWest's Pasadena headquarters, describing herself to reporters as a "reverse mortgage suitability and abuse consultant" who had completed a standard training program offered by HUD to become a certified counselor for seniors on reverse mortgages.[19, 20]

OneWest responded to each and every critical letter, dismissing their concerns out of hand. In revised comments to the Federal Reserve, Rodgin Cohen's law firm, representing CIT and OneWest on the merger, repudiated Sandy's written concerns, claiming that OneWest had nothing to do with the foreclosure on her parents' house: "The loan in question was made prior to the existence of OWB by a former affiliate of IndyMac Bank, Financial Freedom Senior Funding Corporation, which is not, and never has been, affiliated with OneWest." The note conveniently left out that it was OneWest that foreclosed on the house, selling it for $330,000 and likely bringing in more from the government under the loss-share agreement.

ON FEBRUARY 6, 2015—almost seven months after John Thain made his first presentations in New York and Washington—the Federal Reserve and the Office of the Comptroller of the Currency rebuffed OneWest's desire for a quick decision and announced that later that month it would hold a hearing in downtown Los Angeles "to collect information relating to the convenience and needs of the communities to be served, including a review of the insured depository institutions' performance under the Community Reinvestment Act." The hearing was to start at eight in the morning and continue until everyone who wanted to speak had gotten the chance to talk.

The activists had won, but it would be a victory of no real consequence. High-ranking insiders at OneWest told me that federal regulators had assured them the hearing was merely a formality. Still, both sides fought hard to bring their supporters to the event.

The Federal Reserve's Los Angeles meeting room held about two hundred people, and on February 26, 2015, it was filled to the brim with both advocates and opponents of OneWest. The supporters came in busses arranged by nonprofits that had received grants from the bank. They wore stickers proclaiming their love for the merger. "Most of them didn't even know why they were there," Orson Aguilar told me. The room was loud, and the atmosphere was tense—totally unlike most events that take place at the Fed, which tend to involve men and women in suits monotonously deploying banking jargon. It began as scheduled at eight in the morning and lasted until well after six at night.

The first speaker, after introductory remarks from the Federal

Reserve and the Office of Comptroller of the Currency, was Thain. "This transaction will not adversely impact or reduce competition, nor will it create undue market concentration," he told the bank regulators. Otting went next. "Since inception, we have committed to building a hometown bank for the communities of Southern California," he said. "We are not closing any branches . . . [and] we're looking at new opportunities for the number of partners in ethnic communities." Mnuchin sat in the front row but did not speak. People at the hearing said he frequently put his head in his hands. He did not seem happy to be there.

Next, a parade of area nonprofits who had received grants from OneWest talked about the great work it was doing in the community. Another parade of homeowners, who were fighting foreclosure, voiced their opposition. The speakers came in groups, sitting at long tables draped in black tablecloths, opposite a panel of government officials who sat just a few feet away. Faced with raw emotion, the regulators said nothing, quietly taking notes, as one struggling homeowner compared OneWest Bank to the Ebola virus. Helen Kelly, a former criminal prosecutor in the state attorney general's office, broke out crying as she described her successful "defense of a twenty-year family home" against OneWest Bank. Kelly told the Federal Reserve she was able to get a mortgage modification only after she'd written to Steve Mnuchin's college roommate, Eddie Lampert, and Michael Dell, one of the investors in the OneWest's ownership group, "telling them of the corruption of Steve Mnuchin and how he's running OneWest Bank." The merger was "inexcusable in our nation of laws, absolutely inexcusable!" she said, pointing at the ceiling. "They are criminals. They should be in jail. As a prosecutor, I would have had all of them in jail before they spread like an evil virus and contaminated all of us in this room."

Sandy Jolley came with her sister Julie, who teared up as she told her family's story. If Sandy projected righteous indignation, her sister emanated a deep, quiet sadness. A suburban computer programmer with two grown children, it was not in her nature to stand in front of an audience. But after spending so many days in a nearly empty county courthouse, fighting desperately to keep her family home, Julie found the hearing empowering. "It was good to see that people were banding together, telling their stories, because there's a power in numbers, versus just our little family against big bad Financial Freedom," she said. "I felt energized by that, that we were not alone."

After nine hours of testimony, the exceedingly long meeting wrapped up. As the attendees headed toward their cars in the early evening darkness, Paulina Gonzalez tracked down Steve Mnuchin and made one last pitch for the bank to set aside billions of dollars for low-income communities. "Hey, Steve, let's try to work this out," she said. CIT and OneWest still had not had their merger approved. They had just been put through an exhausting public hearing. Maybe now they would be willing to make a deal. But Mnuchin pushed past her.

"No. We're done," Gonzalez recalls Mnuchin telling her. Then he turned around and walked away. Mnuchin has denied this exchange occurred,[21] but whether he actually said those words, they matched his actions. CIT and OneWest had done all they intended to do to work with regular people—which was virtually nothing.

IN THE END, Steve Mnuchin got everything he wanted. Five months after the hearing, on July 15, 2015, the Federal Reserve and OCC approved the merger, without forcing it to make any specific financial commitments to the community.[22] Mnuchin, Otting, and Thain all got paid. Mnuchin's backers, Flowers, Paulson, Soros, and Dell, flipped their investment in IndyMac and made billions. Meantime, the company struggled. CIT's accountants found OneWest's books were a mess and discovered a shortfall of more than $230 million.[23] That summer and fall, HUD's Office of Inspector General served the bank with subpoenas regarding its reverse mortgage unit,[24] likely in response to Sandy Jolley's whistleblower complaint.

CIT fired Joseph Otting in December, but he made out fine. The terms of the merger mandated he be paid $24.9 million in severance. Less than a year after the deal was finalized, John Thain announced he was stepping down as CEO. "The only thing I want is to spend time with my two-year-old granddaughter in LA," he told the *New York Times*. Securities filings show that CIT paid Thain $11.4 million in 2015 and $8.8 million the year before.[25]

Steve Mnuchin stayed on as vice chairman of CIT until the end of 2016. By then, he was busy with his new gig: campaign finance chair for a presidential candidate, Republican real estate developer, and reality TV star Donald J. Trump. Of course, Mnuchin didn't leave the company empty-handed. In addition to the vast sum of money he made on the flip, CIT gave him a severance check of $11.3 million, covering the amount Mnuchin would have made over the next two years had he stayed on the board. Like Otting, he got paid for not doing any work.

Despite its promise to build a "hometown bank for the communities of Southern California," that year, the first after CIT took over OneWest, the bank helped only one African American family buy a home in the Los Angeles area—a region where it also did not make a single home purchase loan to a Latino.

Nationally, the bank's record was just as poor. In 2016, Mnuchin's last year, it helped just four African American and four Latino families buy homes.[26]

CHAPTER 17

THE NEW DEBT BUNDLES

WHILE STEVE MNUCHIN WAS RECEIVING his windfall by flipping OneWest Bank, Tom Barrack and Steve Schwarzman were also looking to cash in by flipping their investment on tens of thousands of single-family homes. As the years passed and property values recovered, these houses were worth more and more. But Barrack and Schwarzman didn't want to cash in the same way a traditional real estate flipper does: buying a dilapidated house for cheap, fixing it up, and selling it a few years later. Instead, they wanted to find a way to flip their investment and make a killing while at the same time hold on to the properties themselves.

Barrack's and Schwarzman's publicly presented business model involved charging ever-increasing rents as they pushed most of the maintenance cost onto tenants. Collecting rent, however, is a long-term play. Even if you're able to pocket 60 cents of every dollar of rent after paying for maintenance, taxes, and other fixed expenses (as Colony was), and even if that is happening on tens of thousands of properties at a time, the returns are still gradual. They pale in comparison with the spectacularly immediate amount of money that can be made by flipping.

In short, making money on rent is boring. Schwarzman and

Barrack weren't principally in the business for the long-term re-turns of being landlords. They'd bought houses for the chance at hitting a jackpot, not a respectable annual return. The typical route for private equity is three to five years and then flip. But without selling the houses, how would they do it?

The first part of that equation was the creation of a new type of mortgage-backed securities; the same sort of complicated financial product that Steve Mnuchin pioneered at Goldman Sachs back in the 1980s and that later collapsed the entire global economy.

To understand how these worked, think back to Frank Capra's *It's a Wonderful Life*: in the nightmarish version of the movie set during the housing bust, George Bailey would have bundled all the home mortgages he made to the working families in Bedford Falls into giant, mortgage-backed securities and sold them on Wall Street. He would thus get his money right away instead of having to wait for years until the debt was repaid. (The buyers of the securities would be on the hook for that.) Then he could loan all that same money again to a whole new set of home buyers and do more bundling. The main way he would make money wouldn't be from collecting interest on loans; it would be from charging fees, and he could do that again and again.

But what about Mr. Potter, who'd used the Great Depression to hoover up (no pun intended) most of the housing in Bedford Falls? Imagine if, while already owning all the houses in town and forcing his tenants to pay high rents, he also had the ability to take out a giant loan against all of those houses and then make his tenants pay back the loan. Flush with cash, he could then buy even more property, invest the money in a completely new business, or retire far from Bedford Falls—say, in a château in the South of France. That's the product Tom Barrack and Steve Schwarzman created after they'd bought tens of thousands of single-family homes all over America.

The first one of these new securities, developed by Blackstone in October 2013, was a $479 million bundle of debt taken out against 3,207 single-family homes across five states. It was "a watershed event," *Mortgage Banking* magazine declared, saying that these types of bundles could eventually be extended to 10 million homes. "The investment and lending opportunities are immense and perhaps just beginning."[1] Blackstone celebrated by throwing a bash for three hundred at the Waldorf Astoria,[2] the stately Midtown Manhattan hotel where New York's elite had gathered for their costume ball more than a century earlier. (When I asked company insiders why Blackstone announced the deal at the Waldorf, they said it was convenient. At the time, Blackstone owned the building.)

"The execution [of the debt offering] was simply superb," crowed Richard Saltzman, president and CEO of Tom Barrack's Colony Financial, the following week. Colony was putting together a giant debt bundle on its homes, too, he said. "All in all, this is a great time for our business."[3]

EXACTLY HOW THESE transactions work is complicated and easier to explain in detail by considering a single house rather than a bundle in its entirety. Take the Butler family home in South Los Angeles, which was rolled into the first mortgage-backed security created by Colony, six months after the Blackstone deal, in April 2014.

If you go to your local county courthouse and look up any address in town, you will find the deed to that house, which is in the name of the homeowner. You can also find out how big of a mortgage the homeowner has taken out, along with details of the loan: interest rate, number of years in which to pay it off, and so on. If you look up my house in San Francisco, you will find a $338,000 thirty-year fixed-rate mortgage taken out in 2009, when we bought the house. Four years later, in 2013, you can see that, after paying down our debt slightly, we refinanced into a $324,000 fifteen-year fixed-rate mortgage, taking advantage of historically low interest rates. Taken together, the documents tell a story. If everything goes as we hope, we should own the home free and clear in 2028, the same year our oldest son goes off to college—the American Dream, as recorded at a county courthouse.

The documents recorded on the Butlers' home tell a different story, one so complicated that I had to spend weeks on the phone talking to bond traders, real estate agents, and academics to make sense of it. The first of the documents is relatively simple and represented a ghoulish counterpoint to my happily ever after. Pulled out of a drawer in a drab concrete building fifteen miles away from the house in Norwalk, was the reverse mortgage from Financial Freedom. Then there was the foreclosure from OneWest Bank and the sale of the home for $180,000 to Colfin AI-CA5 LLC. After that, there was another document that was harder to understand. Unlike my house, which was refinanced with a loan of $324,000, the Butler home (which is about the same size) had a lien recorded against it for $513,900,000. That means the owner of the house owed someone $514 million. If they didn't pay it back, the lien meant that the lender had the power to take the house.

Of course, the Butler home wasn't worth $514 million—nowhere near it. But that was the value of the lien recorded against every single house in the bundle, including the bungalow. The 144-page loan document created a business relationship between the new owner of the house, CAH Borrower 2014-1 LLC (a wholly owned subsidiary of Colony, chartered in Delaware) and JPMorgan Chase, the international banking giant. Chase was listed as the beneficiary, meaning that it provided the $514 million and could take all the houses in the bundle if Colony—or, more correctly, CAH Borrower 2014–1 LLC—didn't pay back the money. Interestingly, the loan wasn't only backed up by the houses themselves but also from the rent tenants would be paying on those homes.

After thirty-six pages of legal language and a seal from a notary, the remaining 107 pages are a list of addresses of Los Angeles County homes that were part of the deal. Similar documents were filed in courthouses the same day in Las Vegas, Phoenix, and Atlanta. Each deed of trust gives JPMorgan Chase the right to either seize the houses or simply collect and keep the rent for itself if anything goes wrong. All told, the number of homes "securitized" in the deal—in other words, that JPMorgan Chase could take if the loan went bad—was 3,399.

According to the Kroll Bond Rating Agency, Tom Barrack's company paid $540 million for the 3,399 homes ($158,000 each), buying most of them in the first six months of 2013. Now, just one year later, Colony was recouping almost all the cash it put in via JPMorgan Chase. Barrack and his investors could put that money in their pockets, use it to buy more homes, or move on to their next investment. At the same time, Colony held on to the houses and collected rent, with their tenants paying off the new mortgage-backed security.

Colony told Kroll it would be charging an average of $1,400 a month on rent, while spending just $75 per month on maintenance. Adding in its other fixed costs, including property tax, insurance, and a set-aside for future capital expenses, the ratings agency estimated Colony would clear $7,300 a year on each home in the security, or $25 million per year for the entire bundle—and that didn't count any rent increases that Colony might levee in the future. If rents went up, they would make even more money. Kroll also assumed that one out of every ten homes in the security was vacant at any given time.[4]

So, what was in it for JPMorgan Chase? After all, a back of the envelope calculation indicates that at that rate, it would take thirty years for Colony to pay back its loan—a debt it had promised to retire in five. But the $514 million loan from JPMorgan Chase is just the beginning of the story of the giant ball of debt that includes the Butler family home. After providing the half billion loan to Colony, JPMorgan Chase then divided it up into five pieces—or tranches—and profitably sold those slices of debt to investors on the bond market.

These tranches were appealing ,since Kroll declared they were a good bet for investors, in that they were likely to be paid back on time and with interest. Kroll gave the top tranche of the bundle— a $291 million slice of debt—an AAA grade, indicating "almost no risk." Three of the other four tranches were deemed to be A grade—meaning that more than 80 percent of the debt was "high quality." Other ratings agencies, including Moody's and Morningstar, gave similarly glowing assessments of the deal.

Who were those investors—the people who would be the ultimate owners of these homes should anything go wrong? For example, who bought the top, AAA tranche for $291 million? I asked Ray Pellecchia, a spokesman for the Financial Industry Regulatory Authority (FINRA), which oversees America's brokerage firms. "I'm not sure we know the answer to that question," he confessed. "All transactions that take place on the bond market are reported" on FINRA's Trade Reporting and Compliance Engine (TRACE) system, he said, but without names attached.

In any case, after their initial sale, the securities would be traded on the secondary market, where no one was keeping track. "You're not going to get any names," he said.

A spokeswoman for the Securities and Exchange Commission was also of no help. The government didn't track the transactions, she said, so maybe I should check with Colony. The company might know who owned its debt.

GIANT BUNDLES OF debt owned by largely disinterested third parties leveraged against thousands of homes—that's the twisted mess that plunged America into its worst economic downturn since the Great Depression. But we couldn't be making exactly the same mistake again, could we? Surely America's financial and political elite must have learned something from the housing bust. Those who forget history are doomed to repeat it, the saying goes. In this case, the crash was still visible in the rearview mirror. It seemed too early to forget.

To make sure I wasn't jumping the gun, I called Nobel Prize– winning economist Joseph Stiglitz, the former chair of President Bill Clinton's Council of Economic Advisers, and one of the few experts to have correctly predicted the housing bust. Sadly, Stiglitz told me that all the same problems were still in play. Because of the securitization process, the bank that lent Colony $514 million, JPMorgan Chase, had no financial stake in making sure the money was paid back. It had already sold the debt off to other investors. "It's almost identical" to the mortgage-backed securities created before the bust, he explained, "but in one way, it's worse," because now the owner of the home itself is as distant as the owner of the debt. "If the owner of the home is a thousand miles away, he doesn't know if there is a problem or not," he said.

I told Stiglitz what I'd learned about Colony's rental agreements—

that the leases put tenants in charge of most of the maintenance—and that the data Colony shared with the bond ratings agencies showed the company spent an average of just $75 a month per home on repairs. Typically, a tenant who plans to live in a house for only a year is going to make the cheapest fixes possible, he said. "What they will do is patch it for a year." Plus, Wall Street investors such as Colony and Blackstone weren't in it for the long haul. They were flippers. No party in the financial transaction was looking out for the long-term interest of the houses or the communities where they were located.

"Tenants are poor," Stiglitz said. Plus, "they move around a lot more frequently than homeowners. That's why homeownership is efficient" from a market's perspective. Colony's lease agreements, he concluded, were a recipe for the properties to decay.

That wasn't the only problem with these new mortgage-backed securities. In general, banks such as JPMorgan Chase were providing less scrutiny on the vast amounts of money they handed out to Colony and Blackstone than they were on the loans they made to individual home buyers.

When a bank helps a family buy a house, it first requires an independent appraisal. This is done to protect the bank; to make sure that the house is worth more than the amount of the mortgage. A standard appraisal form runs seven pages and includes an inspection of all aspects of the home by a trained professional, a firsthand assessment of the quality of construction, the state of the foundation, the roof, windows, staircases, heating and cooling system—anything and everything that could go wrong, down to the condition of the trim around the bathtub.[5] But when big banks such as JPMorgan Chase funded mortgage-backed securities for corporate landlords, they didn't make Colony and Blackstone hire appraisers. Instead, they relied on a cheaper tool: broker's price opinions. BPOs don't involve something as prosaic as having a maintenance professional check a hot-water heater. Instead, real estate brokers *project* a home's value based on photographs of the house and property in combination with data on recent home sales in the area. Critics call BPOs "drive-by appraisals" and the Securities and Exchange Commission has launched an investigation into Green River Capital,[6] the company that Blackstone and Colony hired[7] to value the properties in their bundles. Strangely, though, the rating agencies, whose job it is to ensure that the mortgage-backed securities are worth what the banks and corporate landlords claim, were untroubled by this system. "We felt the process was diligent," said Brian Grow, managing director at Morningstar, which, like its competitors, gave the top tranche, of $291 million, a coveted AAA rating.

From his office on the forty-eighth floor of the World Trade Center in New York, Grow argued, "There were pictures of every property." Moreover, there was a whole system of checks to keep property values from being artificially inflated like they were during the boom. "We felt there's an incentive for the brokers to provide accurate evaluations," he told me. For example, each broker was tracked with a scorecard. "If it turns out that a broker is getting the value wrong, then they'll ding that broker on the scorecard."

But what about maintenance? I asked. How could Morningstar be confident that the properties were being adequately kept up? "One of the indicators is if there's a tenant in the property," one of Brian Grow's colleagues, Brian Allen, told me. "If the property is rentable, we can make some assumption that it is in a habitable form and in good working condition."

CHAPTER 18

TOO BIG TO FAIL

IN HIS SPEECH ACCEPTING THE Democratic nomination for president in 1912, Woodrow Wilson noted the United States had grown immensely rich. But to what end? "Prosperity? Yes, if by prosperity you mean vast wealth no matter how distributed or whether distributed at all."[1] Wilson was no Socialist. He campaigned on free enterprise and limited government. But, to him, this also meant a level playing field. (Although, as we discussed earlier, Wilson's idea of a level playing field did not include providing economic opportunity for people of color, nor for that matter was he on the cutting edge of the growing movement to grant women the vote.)

Central to Wilson's assessment was a critique of large banks, which financed railroad barons and steel magnates but not the hopes and dreams of US workers. "The great monopoly in this country is the money monopoly," Wilson said:

So long as that exists, our old variety and freedom and individual energy of development are out of the question. A great industrial nation is controlled by its system of credit. Our system of credit is concentrated. The growth of the nation, therefore, and all our activities are in the hands of a few men, who, even if their actions be honest and intended for the public interest, are necessarily concentrated upon the great undertakings in which their own money is involved, and who, necessarily, by every reason of their limitations, chill and check and destroy genuine economic freedom.[2]

The architect of Wilson's economic policy was Louis Brandeis, a lawyer and social justice advocate who had spent more than a decade seeking to block J. P. Morgan & Co. from establishing a railroad monopoly in New England. Under Wilson, Brandeis helped create the Federal Reserve to regulate banks and the Federal Trade Commission, which was charged with breaking up monopolies and fighting "unfair business practices." In 1916 President Wilson appointed Brandeis to the Supreme Court, where he would serve for twenty-three years.

When Wilson was first elected, J. P. Morgan was the focus of a major congressional investigation for profiting off the economic Panic of 1907. That year, J. Pierpont Morgan himself had rallied bankers to bail out the financial system, pouring in plenty of his own money. But the congressional investigation found that Morgan had also used the crisis to expand his dominance of the American economy. By 1913, the committee discovered, officers of J. P. Morgan had created a "money trust," sitting on the boards of directors of 112 corporations with a market capitalization that rivaled the entire New York Stock Exchange.

Brandeis used the congressional report as grist for a series of blistering critiques of the banking industry published in *Harper's* magazine beginning in 1913. What galled him most was that bankers often enriched themselves at the expense of the rest of society by playing with money that wasn't even theirs. The following year, the articles were collected into a book titled *Other*

People's Money: And How the Bankers Use It. Though it was written more than a century ago, Brandeis's critique could easily have been written about the mortgage-backed securities that JPMorgan Chase created for Tom Barrack's rental empire after the housing bust.

"The dominant element in our financial oligarchy is the investment banker," Brandeis wrote. "The goose that lays golden eggs has been considered a most valuable possession. But even more profitable is the privilege of taking the golden eggs laid by somebody else's goose. The investment bankers and their associates now enjoy that privilege." Banks such as J. P. Morgan & Co., he explained, took the public's money in the form of deposits and then used that money to keep themselves at the top and everyone else at the bottom. "They control the people through the people's own money."[3]

DURING THE 2008 housing bust, Jamie Dimon, the president and CEO of JPMorgan Chase, was frequently compared with Morgan. "Dimon lives up to J. Pierpont Morgan's legacy," read a headline in the *New York Times* published on March 12, 2008, the day he bought the investment bank Bear Stearns. Like Morgan, the story said, "he is capitalizing on the fear and panic that can grip the markets to expand his storied bank empire."[4] In fact, Jamie Dimon was taking disaster profiteering to a far greater level than J. P. Morgan did a century earlier. Back then, Morgan bailed out his rivals and the government and used it to consolidate power. In 2008 the system was rigged so badly that when Dimon stepped in to provide "help," it was the government that gave him money. When Bear Stearns faltered, JPMorgan Chase emerged to save it—but only after it got a $30 billion guarantee from the Federal

Reserve. Two days later, the government gave JPMorgan Chase a $12 billion piece of that bailout.[5] In September 2008 Dimon "helped" again when the government facilitated JPMorgan Chase's takeover of America's biggest thrift, Washington Mutual. That saved the FDIC another IndyMac-style disaster, but it also gave the New York bank its first national, physical footprint, with a new network of branches across the West Coast and Florida.[6]

The acquisitions made JPMorgan Chase the biggest bank in America, leapfrogging over its competitors, with more than $2 trillion in assets. "JPMorgan Chase is a true colossus, the kind that progressives like Louis Brandeis inveighed against early in the previous century," Roger Lowenstein wrote in the *New York Times*.[7] When some of the loans inevitably went bad, JPMorgan Chase sued the FDIC, seeking indemnification against claims arising from Washington Mutual's mortgages. It dropped the suit only after the government agreed to pay it $645 million.[8]

Given JPMorgan Chase's dramatic transformation, it seemed important to ask, What kind of bank was this new behemoth? Who did it help? The headline of Lowenstein's article proclaimed Dimon to be "America's Least-Hated Banker," but the more I looked at Jamie Dimon's story, the more I saw another Home-wrecker; a vulture capitalist born into privilege who focused on the bottom line to the exclusion of his fellow man, like the others motivated by money—only money.

LIKE STEVE MNUCHIN, Jamie Dimon was raised at the center of financial elite. His father was a stockbroker. His grandfather was a stockbroker. Also, like Mnuchin, he seemed almost preternaturally focused on becoming affluent, even at an early age.

"When he was nine years old, his father asked him and his two brothers what they wanted to be when they grew up," financial journalist Patricia Crisafulli wrote in her 2009 book *The House of Dimon: How JPMorgan's Jamie Dimon Rose to the Top of the Financial World*. "Older brother Pete wanted to be a physician. Twin brother Ted said he didn't know. Jamie, however, piped up. 'I want to be rich.'"[9]

Jamie was the grandson of Greek immigrants. His grandfather Panos Papademetriou, arrived in New York in 1921, settled in Manhattan and promptly changed his name to the French-sounding Dimon. But while his grandfather worked his way slowly up the ladder at the Bank of Athens before landing a job at the brokerage[10] Shearson, Hammill & Co., the path for Jamie was much easier.

"Although he has accomplished much, Dimon's is not a Horatio Alger tale," Duff McDonald wrote in *Last Man Standing: The Ascent of Jamie Dimon and JPMorgan Chase*. "He spent the majority of his life within the same five blocks on Park Avenue, home of New York's upper class."[11] Jamie's father, Theodore "Ted" Dimon, had followed in his father's footsteps at Shearson and become close to the company's legendary chairman, Sandy Weill. The Dimons bought a country house in Greenwich, Connecticut, not far from the Weill home, and the two families often socialized together.[12]

When Dimon was in seventh grade, his father paid cash for a four-bedroom co-op at 1050 Park Avenue—a short stroll up the street from "the world's richest apartment building," where Steve Mnuchin, John Thain, and Steve Schwarzman would reside a generation later. When the housing bust shook the US economy in 2008, Dimon was living up the street in a top-floor apartment in a building with grand courtyards and gothic archways at 1185 Park Avenue.

Jamie's parents sent him to the Browning School, an all-boys private school with 189 students in converted townhouses on East Sixty-Second Street.[13] Students wore jackets and ties to class. (Notable alumni include at least three members of the Rockefeller family, as well as politician and diplomat Sargent Shriver, and Arthur Ochs Sulzberger Jr., the publisher of the *New York Times*.) Jamie's family greased the skids for him at every turn. Though he was intelligent and, by all accounts, a hard worker during his college years at Tufts University and graduate studies at Harvard Business School, it was Jamie's father's relationships that gave him a leg up.

When Jamie was in college, he and Sandy Weill had bonded in Weill's backyard going over financial statements together. After Jamie graduated from business school, his first job was special assistant to Weill, then chairman of American Express. "Most MBAs toil in obscurity before they get their shot at the big time," McDonald noted in *Last Man Standing.* "Dimon was immediately exposed to deal making at the highest levels."[14]

And Sandy Weill wasn't just any deal maker—he was the deal maker who shattered generations of federal banking regulations designed to prevent another Great Depression. The banking reforms ultimately imposed by Woodrow Wilson and Louis Brandeis had helped reduce the power of America's largest banks, but they failed to restrain rampant stock market speculation that proliferated across America in the 1920s. Millions of Americans who had never played the market before began trading "on margins," meaning they would buy stock by putting up as little as 10 percent of the purchase price and borrowing money from their stockbroker for the rest of the shares' value. This didn't matter, they were told, because the stock market would most certainly go up. It was not unlike the way salesmen at companies such as IndyMac encouraged Americans to buy houses during the bubble even when they had no money to put down and no real way to make mortgage payments.

"The celerity with which margin transactions were arranged and the absence of any scrutiny by the broker of the personal credit of the borrower encouraged persons in all walks of life to embark upon speculative ventures in which they were doomed by their lack of skill and experience to certain loss," a 1934 Senate investigation determined. "By the vision of quick profits, they assumed margin positions which they had no adequate resources to protect, and when the storm broke, they stood helplessly by while securities and savings were washed away in a flood of liquidation."[15]

When the stock market crashed in 1929, the fundamental unsoundness of this system spurred the Great Depression. Because the banks engaging in risky stock market trading were the same ones taking consumer deposits, the money Americans had placed in supposedly secure savings accounts also evaporated, and banks failed one after another. To restore trust in the banking system and make sure this didn't happen again, FDR signed legislation creating the Federal Deposit Insurance Corporation, which guaranteed almost all consumer deposits up to the then-princely sum of $2,500. But if the federal government was going to back those deposits, it didn't want them being used for the kind of speculative trading that could cause them to fail. So, Congress passed the Banking Act of 1933, also known as the Glass-Steagall Act, which said that the same bank could not be both an investment house—creating securities, buying stocks, and so on—and a commercial bank, which took government-insured consumer deposits and lent them out to help families buy homes.

The law stood for sixty-six years, until Weill orchestrated a deal that would have been illegal unless the law was changed. In

1998 Dimon was working for Weill at the Travelers Group, an insurance and investment banking giant. Weill wanted to merge with Citicorp, one of the nation's largest consumer banks, so he launched a full-fledged lobbying and public relations campaign. He personally worked the phones, calling Federal Reserve Chairman Alan Greenspan, Treasury Secretary Robert Rubin, and even President Bill Clinton, urging them to scrap the safeguards put in after the Great Depression. After the Republican-controlled House of Representatives passed repeal legislation by a narrow 214-to-213 margin, Weill called Clinton again to break a deadlock in the Senate. (A few days after the Clinton administration signaled its support for repealing the Glass-Steagall Act, Treasury Secretary Rubin raised eyebrows by accepting a top job at Citigroup as Weill's chief lieutenant.)[16]

When the global economy crashed a decade later, Citigroup collapsed. It might have disappeared completely like Lehman Brothers had the federal government not agreed to shoulder most of the losses on $306 billion of its riskiest assets.[17] At the center of Citi's failure seemed to be the repeal of Glass-Steagall, which allowed the bank to place chancy bets on mortgage-backed securities with its depositors' money. Had the Glass-Steagall Act still existed, banks that were "too big to fail" wouldn't have existed, the reasoning went, and the economic crash would have been far less severe and a massive taxpayer bailout unnecessary.

It took years, but Sandy Weill ultimately agreed with that assessment. Though he kept a four-foot hunk of wood in his office—etched with his portrait and the words "The Shatterer of Glass-Steagall,"[18] he told CNBC in 2012 that he thought it was time to reregulate the financial sector. "What we should probably do is go and split up investment banking from commercial banking," he said. The biggest banks, should "be broken up so that the taxpayer will never be at risk, the depositors won't be at risk, the leverage of the banks will be something reasonable, and the investment banks can do trading."

The TV hosts on CNBC were incredulous. Was the man known for decimating financial regulations turning into a trust buster? "Well, I think the world changes," said Weill, who was by then seventy-nine years old. "It's not the same world that it was ten years ago, and I think you have to think, 'What's this world about?'"[19]

As for Jamie Dimon, he likes to present himself as a student of history who avoided some of the worst excesses of the housing bubble by remembering the busts of the past, including the Great Depression. "Experience and judgment—I don't think they're replaceable. You go to a lot of businesses; they don't remember how bad things can get," he told journalist Patricia Crisafulli. "We will never forget the aftermath of the housing bubble, but forty years from now, believe me, someone is going to forget again somewhere." But as the head of the biggest bank in America, Dimon appears to have learned different lessons than the rest of us. He never had the change of heart of his mentor, Sandy Weill. Since JPMorgan Chase had more than five thousand deposit-taking branches[20] and a robust investment bank, it's perhaps not surprising that he doesn't want change. A new Glass-Steagall Act would mean the breakup of his company. "Glass-Steagall had nothing to do with the crisis," he gruffly told CNBC in 2016. The law, he said, was "an anachronism of the past. I know there's a lot of anger at the banks," he added, but breaking them up was not a solution.[21]

SO, WHAT DID Jamie Dimon learn from the housing bust? After the global economic meltdown, JPMorgan Chase behaved very similarly to Steve Mnuchin's OneWest Bank. Increasingly, Dimon's bank supported other people who were rich just like him. Instead of helping everyday Americans live their dreams, JPMorgan Chase exacerbated the wealth gap. Like OneWest, it was more Mr. Potter than George Bailey. Between 2010 and 2016, JPMorgan Chase's wealth management business nearly tripled in size, from $67 billion to $173 billion. But though it greatly expanded the part of its business that helped the rich invest their money, it retreated from helping Americans buy homes. As the recession turned into recovery, JPMorgan Chase's home lending shrunk by a third—from $165 billion in 2010 to $111 billion in 2016.[22] The withdrawal was particularly stark for working-class borrowers served by the Federal Housing Administration loan program, which had been created by FDR eighty years before. "The real question is, should we be in the FHA business at all?" Dimon said on a call with analysts in July 2014, three months after his bank funded Colony's first bundle.[23]

The impetus for the comment was a $614 million settlement JPMorgan Chase had been forced to pay to the government after the Justice Department declared the bank had violated the False Claims Act. In particular, the government alleged JPMorgan Chase was foreclosing on government-insured loans that should never have been made in the first place.[24] "We want to help the consumers," Dimon said, "but we can't do that at great risk to JPMorgan." If the government didn't create "some kind of safe harbor" where his bank wouldn't be fined if it broke the rules, he would stop using the program to lend to working-class homeowners.[25] True to his word, federal lending data show the number of FHA loans originated by JPMorgan Chase dropped by more than 60 percent in 2014 and fell to almost nothing the year after.

No one would deny the bank the right to screen loan applicants fairly. The problem was that JPMorgan Chase wasn't obeying the law. If he couldn't break the law, Dimon argued incredibly, he would simply bypass making loans to working-class home buyers entirely. Besides, it was faster and easier and just as lucrative to make large piles of cash available to Homewreckers such as Tom Barrack. From 2014 to 2016, JPMorgan Chase helped six thousand Americans buy homes using FHA mortgages. During the same time period, it extended almost four times as much capital to Tom Barrack's Colony, handing it $3.3 billion in cash as it created six mortgage-backed securities covering twenty-three thousand rental homes.[26]

JPMorgan Chase's transactions with Colony came quickly, one after another. After creating the $514 million debt ball that included the Butler family bungalow in April 2014, Colony and JPMorgan Chase put together a second, half-billion debt bundle covering 3,727 homes that July. Another $679 million bundle of debt followed in 2015. Then, in 2016, after Colony merged with Barry Sternlicht's Starwood Waypoint Residential Trust to create an empire of 31,000 homes that rivaled Blackstone in size and reach. JPMorgan Chase lent the new ownership group $1.1 billion in exchange for liens against 7,563 homes. Each of these giant balls of debt was carved up into tranches and sold on the bond market, with the ultimate owners of the debt unknown to the public.

TOM BARRACK ENDORSED Donald Trump in early 2016. At the time, the real estate developer and reality TV star was still a curiosity and a pariah among the GOP elite. Though he led in the polls, he was seen mostly as a sideshow who would eventually be stopped by the Republican establishment that still backed former Florida governor Jeb Bush and senator Marco Rubio.

"One of the kindest and most humble friends I've had," is how

Barrack described Trump to CNBC shortly after the Iowa caucuses. "I actually think he can win," he said. "America's ready to say, 'Why don't we approach America like you would running a business?'" Barrack seized on Trump's own campaign rhetoric, painting him as man so wealthy that he was bankrolling his own run for the White House. "So, whether you like it or don't like it, what you're getting is unfiltered and raw from a guy who's writing his own checks. I think that's novel."[27]

The truth, of course, was more complicated. It wouldn't be long before Barrack was actively reaching out to his friends seeking donations for Trump's campaign. All told, Barrack helped put at least $130 million into Trump's campaign coffers: he raised $23 million for the pro-Trump Rebuilding America Now super PAC, and, as chair of Trump's inaugural committee, he raised $107 million more.[28]

"He may have been the one peer of the president within the campaign circle," political operative Roger Stone, another longtime Trump confidant, told me. It was Barrack, Stone noted, who introduced Trump to campaign manager Paul Manafort, who would later be convicted on eight counts of bank fraud and tax evasion, and plead guilty to "conspiracy against the United States."[29] (Barrack's relationship with Manafort was long-standing, and as with Barrack's other business associates, he had profited off Manafort's distress. In 2004, for example, Barrack had given Manafort's wife a $1.8 million loan secured by their home in the Hamptons.[30] The house was later listed in an indictment the federal government sought to have forfeited as "derived from proceeds traceable in the conviction."[31])

What Barrack offered Trump was trust, Stone said. They had "maintained a very close relationship" ever since the Plaza Hotel deal in 1988, and since then Trump found Barrack to be "extremely circumspect." In addition, Stone said, Barrack brought connections which brought money into Trump's campaign coffers: "He's a smart guy and he's made a great deal of money in the real estate market."

Fund-raising also played to one of Barrack's great talents—schmoozing. The first big fund-raiser came on May 25, 2016, shortly before Barrack's company cashed in by rolling Sandy Jolley's old house into a $536 million mortgage-backed security.[32] Trump had just won the Indiana primary and become the presumptive Republican presidential nominee. Steve Mnuchin, OneWest's recently departed chairman and Trump's new campaign finance chair, sent out the fund-raiser invitations. Barrack hosted the event in a twenty-four-thousand-square-foot Santa Monica mansion that he'd bought for $25 million following his third marriage in 2014.[33] To get to the party, guests pulled their luxury cars up its long, gated, and hedge-lined drive until they reached a grand front porch held up by columns meant to evoke George Washington's Mount Vernon residence or Thomas Jefferson's Monticello.

"It was the biggest house I'd ever been in in LA," one of the donors, eighty-one-year-old retired lawyer Robert Rosenthal told me. "I've been to big houses, and I've been to castles in England where people live. This was more like a castle in England." Tickets were $25,000 a person, $100,000 to have your photo taken with Trump.

The fund-raisers' guest list was quintessentially Barrack—or perhaps quintessentially Trump. With so much of the big Hollywood money going to the probable Democratic nominee, Hillary Clinton, Barrack brought in early support from the types of people you might suspect would write a check to elect a real estate developer turned reality television star. Campaign finance disclosures show donations came in that day from Dr. Garth Fisher, a Beverly Hills plastic surgeon who goes by the nickname "the Enhancer" (his website includes a picture of him standing on a golf course in a lab coat, holding a putter, next to a twenty-foot-tall inflatable breast), and Mareva Georges, the former Miss France. Checks also flowed in from the world of real estate, including from Douglas Manchester, a combative San Diego developer whom Trump would appoint ambassador to the Bahamas. Barrack brought in a contribution from the owner of a winery next to his in Santa Barbara County. A generous check also came from another executive at Colony, and from Andy Puzder, the CEO of CKE Restaurant Holdings, the parent company of the fast-food chains Carl's Jr. and Hardee's. Puzder, who would later withdraw his nomination to be Donald Trump's labor secretary amid reports of domestic violence, was also an investor in Barrack's rental home empire.[34]

Barrack spoke briefly and then introduced Trump, who went on for an hour without notes. Rosenthal was mesmerized. At this fund-raiser full of elites, Trump didn't deviate from the populist message he was delivering at rallies on the campaign trail. In that moment, Rosenthal said, he knew Trump would win the election. "Donald Trump knows Joe Six-Pack," he explained. "I don't know how to describe it. He has a feeling for Andy Ordinary."

But Rosenthal's own path to the fund-raiser showed how substantially Trump's inner circle differed from his populist voting base. Originally from Scarsdale, an affluent suburb in Westchester County, New York, Rosenthal said he'd known Trump for years, having mingled with him on the charity circuit in Manhattan. Another connection: Rosenthal said he had once dated

Steve Mnuchin's aunt. When he heard that Mnuchin was behind a Trump fund-raiser in Los Angeles, it was an opportunity too serendipitous to pass up. He drove over from Burbank. "It's getting to be a smaller and smaller word," Rosenthal said. Within months, the Homewreckers would be going to Washington.

PART VI

ENTER THE DONALD

CHAPTER 19

AN EARLY VULTURE

THREE MONTHS BEFORE THE ELECTION, on August 5, 2016, Donald Trump released a list of fourteen economic advisors, all of whom were men, most of them bankers. We've met many of them already in this book. "I am pleased that we have such a formidable group of experienced and talented individuals,"[1] the Republican nominee for president said in a statement. The list included Barrack, Mnuchin, John Paulson, and Wilbur Ross. Another member of Trump's economic panel was Stephen Feinberg, whose private equity firm, Cerberus, ran a business similar to Barrack's, buying up single-family homes and turning them into rentals. Only two were economists. Most had no record of public service. (And five of them were named Steve.)

These Homewreckers didn't just give Trump advice. Like Barrack and Mnuchin, the rest of them had been raising money for his campaign. In June, Paulson and Ross hosted a $50,000-a-plate fund-raiser at Le Cirque, a tony French restaurant in Midtown Manhattan, raising between $5 million and $7 million. Published reports said other members of Trump's economic team, including Feinberg and Anthony Scaramucci, another former Goldman Sachs investment banker named as one of Trump's economic advisors, were also in attendance, and all agreed to pony up $250,000 each for themselves and a guest.[2]

And, yet, despite the fact that he surrounded himself with hedge fund managers and private equity kingpins, Trump savaged his opponent "Crooked Hillary" as a tool of Wall Street, often mentioning the $675,000 she'd made giving paid speeches to Goldman Sachs. "Wall Street!" he yelled to a crowd of eight thousand at the Silver Spur Arena in Kissimmee, Florida, which had recently played host to acts such as Toby Keith, Def Leppard, and Lynyrd Skynyrd. "They own her lock, stock, and barrel. She will do whatever they want her to do."[3]

TRUMP'S ANNOUNCEMENT OF his economic team, and his speech in Kissimmee, coincided with the release of new data from the Census Bureau showing that the nation's homeownership rate had fallen to its lowest level in fifty-one years. According to the Census, renters now outnumbered homeowners in nearly half of all major cities compared, with 21 percent a decade before. Many of the cities that experienced the biggest drop in homeownership were in the swing states Trump would claim to win the presidency: Florida, Ohio, Michigan, North Carolina, and Wisconsin.

Trump turned the damage to his own advantage. "What's the greatest thing that everyone wants? Homeownership, right?" he said at the Kissimmee rally, lofting a giant poster board graphic showing homeownership's decline. "That's the American Dream! The American Dream! We want the American Dream!! We want to own our home.

"Look at this chart!" Trump bellowed. "This is a disaster!" He blamed the incumbent president—"Great job, Obama!"—but, tellingly, offered no solutions. "That number is crashing," he went on. "That number is sad. That is not good." The crowd cheered. Then he changed the subject, setting off on a rambling attack on Hillary Clinton.

The tangled, forty-seven-minute speech typified the Trump campaign: economic populism for the base with little substance behind it—"We're going to win so much you're going to get tired of winning!"—punctuated by personal attacks on Barack Obama ("the founder of ISIS") and Hillary Clinton ("Lock her up!"). His few specific promises tended to double as nativist taglines, such as his promise to ban Syrian refugees or, "We're going to build a great, great wall and Mexico is going to pay for it."

Three weeks before the election, Trump unveiled a new applause line: "Drain the Swamp." At first, he said he didn't like the phrase, a promise to root out corruption in Washington. But that changed when he delivered it. "The place went crazy," he told a rally in Kinston, North Carolina, and now it was "trending all over the world." Trump exalted in another wave of cheers. "So, we like that expression."[4]

"DRAIN THE SWAMP" was the phrase that hooked Teena Colebrook, who had lost her Southern California home and two rental properties to foreclosure by Steve Mnuchin's bank. In February 2015 the fifty-eight-year-old Colebrook was among the homeowners who'd spoken at the Federal Reserve Board's hearing in Los Angeles, seeking to block the merger of OneWest and CIT. She told the Fed that she had tried six times to modify her mortgage with OneWest but had been turned down every time, even as the bank tacked on thousands of dollars in fees. "It should be jail time not sale time with bonuses for them so they can live in their $30 million mansions like Mr. Mnuchin while stealing the equity and the homes of ordinary folk like me and thousands of others," she explained.[5] In April 2015, two months after the Federal Reserve hearing, Colebrook's home was sold to Nerja Investments LLC, a shell company based in Orange County.[6]

Colebrook said she didn't learn of Steve Mnuchin's role in Trump's campaign until after the election, when he was nominated to be the Treasury Secretary. "Like many of the people I'm in touch with who were foreclosed on by Mnuchin, we voted for Trump because we're fed up—like most of America—with the politics as it is," she said. "We're fed up with the government and all those elected officials who were elected to serve the people but they're really only serving themselves." She said she believed Trump when he said, "My only special interest is to you the American people. Not major donors for party or corporations."[7]

On October 18, 2016, the same day that Trump unveiled his "Drain the Swamp" promise, Fannie Mae, the government-controlled company that FDR created to promote homeownership during the Great Depression, issued a disturbing report on the impact that companies such as Barrack's Colony and Schwarzman's Blackstone were having on the nation's housing stock. The "explosive growth of the single-family rental market has been a defining characteristic of the housing bust and recovery," wrote Patrick Simmons, Fannie Mae's director of strategic planning. But, he warned, that had come at a cost: a "starter-home shortage that now appears to be slowing the return of first-time buyers to the housing market." The swing was striking. Investor purchases had taken more than a million starter homes off the market, putting them out of reach of young families who might want to buy them. This shortage of available homes for sale, Simmons wrote, was a hallmark of the "coming of age of the large millennial generation."[8]

PERHAPS IT'S NOT surprising that Donald Trump surrounded himself with vultures who profited off pain during the housing bust and enriched themselves with the federal government's cash. Donald's own father, Fred Trump, had made his fortune in a similar fashion: gaming the system to get an inside track on foreclosures, buying distressed properties on the cheap, and then pocketing the taxpayers' money to cash in on the rebound. As the years went by, Fred would be hauled before Congress for profiteering and sued by the Justice Department for racial discrimination.

Just as Steve Mnuchin's big break was the collapse of IndyMac, so too did Fred Trump's road to riches begin with the failure of a major mortgage lender. The year was 1934. Fred was twenty-eight years old, standing six feet tall, muscular, with blue eyes, blond hair, and a thick mustache. Fred loved construction and always wanted to be a builder. "It was my dream as a boy, just as some kids want to be firemen," he said.[9] He was not easily deterred. In 1918, when Fred was twelve, his father died of the Spanish flu, a global pandemic that killed an estimated 50 million people, including 675,000 Americans. Fred, suddenly a major breadwinner for the family, took night classes in carpentry at the YMCA and studied plumbing, masonry, and electrical wiring in correspondence courses. But although he had some success in the Roaring Twenties, Trump's building business went bust in the Depression. There was no financing to build and no home buyers to buy. To stay afloat, Fred opened a grocery store near the home he shared with his widowed mother in the Woodhaven section of Queens and pined for the day that he could return to construction.

That opportunity came with the demise of one the biggest mortgage companies in Brooklyn, Lehrenkrauss & Co. The family-owned House of Lehrenkrauss, as it was called, was a fixture in the German immigrant community. Over its half century in business, it had helped more than forty thousand families buy homes. Somehow it had survived the rash of bank runs that toppled thousands of other banks, but at the end of 1933, it collapsed abruptly. As soon as that happened, it became clear that the only way Lehrenkrauss had been able to stay in business was by cooking its books.

"It was a Rock of Gibraltar institution" for the German immigrant community, Gwenda Blair, author of the family history *The Trumps: Three Generations of Builders and a President*, told me. When bankruptcy proceedings opened, she wrote, a crowd of three thousand spectators showed up at court at the Main Post Office Building in Brooklyn, overflowing the three-hundred-seat courtroom and clogging the marble-lined corridors and stairwells. Nearly everyone was angry, save a young grocer named Fred Trump, who pushed his way into the back of the courtroom seeking his chance at a fortune. Thousands of people were devastated, Blair wrote, but "Fred Trump could not have been happier."[10]

Lehrenkrauss's central conceit was similar to Michael Perry at IndyMac—although far more brazen. Unlike most banks at the time, Lehrenkrauss didn't keep mortgages on its books, but sold the debt as shares to wealthier members of the community. The company continued to service the mortgages, collecting the payments from homeowners, and then passed a portion of the profits on to its investors in the form of dividends. But the whole system was prone to fraud. In testimony before a federal bankruptcy court, the family patriarch, Julius Lehrenkrauss, testified that he sold the mortgages for amounts far above their face value and then certified the same mortgages again and again and resold them, over and over. The scheme persisted, both because members of the immigrant community trusted Lehrenkrauss and because, whenever he could, Julius would pay dividends by issuing still more stock in the company—not unlike the scheme hatched by Zero Mostel and Gene Wilder in the Mel Brooks comedy classic *The Producers.*

"Using high-pressure sales techniques that included enthusiastic testimonials from nonexistent investors and facsimiles of their dividend checks, Lehrenkrauss salesmen convinced hundreds of naïve customers to invest in worthless stock," Blair wrote. "The funds were so varied and plentiful that unraveling them was nearly impossible. . . . Julius had shuffled funds from one corporate bank account to another to give the appearance of healthy balances, and he and another senior executive had routinely extorted kickbacks."[11]

Lehrenkrauss pled guilty to grand larceny. On March 1, 1934, the balding, sixty-seven-year-old patriarch appeared in court dressed in a black suit with striped trousers and a dress shirt with a winged collar. "This day marks the termination of three generations of a proud family gone to destruction," he said.[12] Then he was carted off to Sing Sing prison to serve a sentence of five to ten years.

Fred Trump attended many of these proceedings, paying particular attention to Lehrenkrauss's mortgage servicing operation, one of the few parts of the family empire that was still making money. His interest wasn't so much in the day-to-day work of collecting mortgage payments; the amount of money to be made collecting on these loans was small, with profits that came slowly. But by owning the mortgage servicing operation, Fred would be positioned to get some extremely valuable inside information. If he knew which borrowers were falling behind on their payments, then he would know which homes were at risk of foreclosure. And by knowing that, Fred could scoop up the homes before other members of the public had the chance to bid at a public auction. It was his ticket to return to real estate.

Fred Trump wasn't the only one who wanted Lehrenkrauss's servicing operation; so did a number of other, more well-established businessmen. To best them, Trump greatly exaggerated his qualifications and assets to the court. Though his previous experience in banking was limited to occasionally extending credit to the purchasers of homes he'd built, Trump declared himself to have "been engaged for many years in the servicing of mortgages."[13] Though his only operating business was a grocery store, Fred Trump's letters were embossed on the stationary of the F. C. Trump Construction Corporation, adorned with the slogan "Permanence, Comfort," wrapped around a thumb-sized drawing of a country home. Trump also overstated his experience in real estate by five years and presented himself as a big-time builder from Queens, though he promised to relocate to Brooklyn if his bid was accepted.

According to journalist Wayne Barrett, Fred Trump made a striking impression in court. "He had an erect, almost military-like bearing, muscle bound and purposeful," with a strong German accent, Barrett wrote in the biography *Trump: The Greatest Show on Earth*. Unlike the other, more-experienced businessmen, who were represented by lawyers, Fred Trump represented himself, leading the court stenographer to mistake him for an attorney.[14]

It was a gigantic bluff, but the fantastic story seems not to have been second-guessed by the judge. In the end, Trump didn't make the highest bid for Lehrenkrauss's mortgage lists, but the court awarded them to him anyway after he talked his way into a deal with the representatives of the bank's creditors:[15] thirty-one thousand working-class German immigrants in the Bushwick section of Brooklyn and the Ridgewood neighborhood of Queens, many of whom had placed their life savings in the bank.[16]

Under the terms of the deal, the creditors were given the option of buying back the mortgage servicing rights. (Presumably they would only want to do it if the economy improved dramatically, which wasn't likely anytime soon.) In the meantime, the judge said Fred Trump could charge a fee of 0.5 percent on everything he collected from Lehrenkrauss's remaining borrowers—the rest would go to the people who actually owned the mortgages. That was enough for Trump to get out of the grocery business. Like Steve Mnuchin's IndyMac purchase seventy-five years later, Fred Trump had bought into a no-lose financial proposition. If Lehrenkrauss's homeowners made their payments, he would take his commission. If they didn't, he would foreclose and be first in line to buy their properties. "With this one favorable nod, the court had provided him with what he needed to relaunch his real estate career," Blair wrote. "It was an enormous plum, for he would be reentering the field with access to a steady cash flow, permitting him to escape the mad scramble of the small-scale builder."[17]

The Home Owners' Loan Corporation was already up and running when Fred Trump took control of the Lehrenkrauss mortgage servicing operation the following year. But like many of the Homewreckers of our current crisis, Fred Trump had no real incentive to be lenient with struggling borrowers or refer them to the HOLC, which could have helped them stay in their homes. In fact, unlike a bank, which kept loans on its books and would therefore benefit from off-loading a delinquent mortgage onto the government, a new HOLC loan for a Lehrenkrauss borrower was the worst possible outcome for Fred Trump: he would lose both his servicing commission and the chance to buy the property if it were lost to foreclosure. In fact, the easiest way for Fred Trump to make money off Lehrenkrauss's mortgage list was if the German immigrants who trusted the family company—which had already deceived them—and were now forced to do business with Trump, fell behind and lost their homes to him.

THE HOMEWRECKERS AREN'T sadists. They don't particularly enjoy inflicting pain. They are businessmen who value money first and foremost and have a special gift for seeing opportunity in the misfortune of others. If they can make the most money by hoarding houses and wrecking dreams, they will do that. But if the government changes economic incentives so that the profits come more easily when they provide homeownership opportunities to middle-class families, these same Homewreckers can be enticed to change course.

Such was the case for Fred Trump, who leveraged the federal government's support to bring the American Dream to thousands of New York families during the depths of the Great Depression. FDR signed the National Housing Act on June 27, 1934, barely three months after Fred Trump took control of Lehrenkrauss's mortgage list and began monitoring its delinquent borrowers for potential property acquisitions. The FHA was designed to extend the American Dream of homeownership to members of the working class. Under the law, the government would back loans for properties worth $16,000 and under (approximately $300,000 in today's money), but not tenement apartment buildings or mansions for the rich.

By this point, so many banks had failed that the government was the only game in town. Developers like Fred Trump could make money only if they put up buildings that served that mission. So, as he foreclosed on Lehrenkrauss's mortgage holders and bought their properties for cheap, Fred also went on a building binge, constructing row upon row of sturdy row homes with red-brick facades. Their design was almost always the same: a tiny front lawn and a short stoop with an exterior wall shared with the next-door neighbor to save space and reduce costs; inside were hardwood floors and ornamental tile around the kitchen sink, as well as furnished basements. The high quality of construction was due, in part, to the requirements the FHA placed on its insurance: Since the government would be backing the home buyer with a mortgage that lasted twenty years, the purchased home had to be built to last as well. Most of them still stand today.

Trump's biggest project was on the old Barnum & Bailey Circus grounds in the East Flatbush section of Brooklyn. On August 11, 1936, the *New York Times* reported, more than a hundred people turned out as the administrator of the FHA for the state of New York presented Fred Trump with a celebratory plaque. Forty-eight houses, already under construction, had been approved for government mortgage insurance. Trump eventually planned to erect four hundred houses there, the story said.[18]

The people who bought Trump's homes were solidly working class: skilled laborers, mechanics, clerks, and small business owners. Many were immigrants from Europe of Jewish, Irish, and Italian extractions. There were few families on government relief, and, though there was concern about the "infiltration" of Jews, a HOLC report a year later noted positively that the neighborhood was racially segregated, including the absence of Negros. As a result, the agency's color-coded redlining map shaded the area blue, for "still desirable."[19]

So tied was the success of Trump's business interests to the New Deal's homeownership programs that he became a major booster himself. In May 1939 Fred announced that he was launching a movement to put the slogan "Own a Home" on New York license plates as part of a larger "Own Your Home in New York" campaign. To kick it off, Trump said he was inviting Governor Herbert Lehman and Mayor Fiorello La Guardia to attend a luncheon on June 15 at the World's Fair grounds in Flushing. He also invited representatives of the Queens-Nassau Builders League, the Brooklyn Builders League, a variety of financial institutions, officials from the FHA and the HOLC, as well as many material manufacturers. In an interview with the *New York Times*, Fred Trump didn't shy away from his personal financial stake in the matter:

"Explaining the purpose of the drive, Mr. Trump said that the building interests he represents are particularly interested in developing extensive vacant acreage in Brooklyn, Queens, and Richmond," the *Times* reported. But this would be possible only if they could find buyers for the homes. "Despite widespread publicity issued by the FHA and the HOLC," Trump told the paper, "many persons now paying rent are unaware that they can own their own homes at a cost less than their rental payments."[20]

Looking back at the historical record, it's unclear whether the governor or the mayor attended Trump's luncheon, or if it occurred at all. Like his son Donald years later, Fred Trump was a master showman, full of bluster, often teasing major announcements in an effort to make them transpire. (His campaign to rewrite New York's license plates failed.) In any case, Fred's love of homeownership was fleeting. Two years later, in 1941, the government amended the National Housing Act, expanding the types of loans that the Federal Housing Administration could underwrite to include subsidies for large landlords. The incentives having changed, Fred Trump abandoned constructing single-family homes for purchase and became a builder of apartments for rent. He now "patriotically declared the nation needed more apartment buildings," Gwenda Blair wrote in *The Trumps*. "His turnabout on the desirability of apartments rapidly followed his discovery that building them would let him be an owner and not just a builder. After he finished a development, he would not simply visit every now and then. He would collect rent every month, and he would have equity. Duty had called, and Fred Trump had answered with alacrity."

ON DECEMBER 7, 1941, the Imperial Japanese Navy launched a surprise bombing air raid on the US naval base at Pearl Harbor, Hawaii, decimating the Pacific Fleet. Before the week was out, Congress had declared war against both Emperor Hirohito's Japan and Adolf Hitler's Nazi Germany. Millions of young men and women mobilized for the war effort, often moving across the country for economic opportunity working in shipyards and around military bases, even if they didn't join the military itself. This mass movement created housing shortages, and on May 26, 1942, Congress added section 608 to the National Housing Act, permitting the government to back mortgages of up to $5 million (or about $80 million in today's money) provided that the housing was "designed for rent for residential use by war workers."[21]

For Fred Trump, war meant money. He decamped from New York for Norfolk, Virginia, home to Norfolk Naval Base and Naval Air Station. The Pentagon had sent thirty thousand men and women to the coastal community, creating a housing shortage so acute that landlords could rent rooms to one tenant during the day and another at night. It was a builder's dream. Trump constructed thousands of units. First, he funded these projects privately and then continued with generous support from the FHA. When the war started to wind down, Fred returned to New

York to cash in on another spigot of government largesse that was opening up: to provide housing for returning veterans. While the GI Bill provided homeownership opportunities for young couples, companion programs were designed to ameliorate the housing crisis by giving returning veterans a place to rent. An especially good bit for of news for Fred Trump came in a December 1946 message from Roosevelt's successor, President Harry Truman. In a "Statement by the President Outlining the Housing Program for 1947," Truman stressed the "main point of emphasis" for his administration would be "rental housing." Returning veterans, the president told Congress, "should not be compelled to buy in order to get shelter."[22]

Two of the biggest projects Fred would ever build—Shore Haven and Beach Haven—were drawn up that year. On June 17, 1947, he filed plans for Shore Haven, a massive complex of 1,344 apartments, spread across thirty-two imposing six-story buildings spanning fourteen acres in southern Brooklyn. Though owned privately by Fred Trump, it had the look and feel of the prototypical midcentury public housing project. Legally, the government was supposed to shell out a maximum of $5 million to builders, but Fred had become close friends with the FHA's regional administrator, so the government agency divided Shore Haven into three subprojects of $3 million each and guaranteed Trump at least $9 million.[23] That same year, as Shore Haven was still going up, Trump filed plans for the even larger Beach Haven apartments in Brighton Beach, near the Coney Island amusement park. Spanning 1,860 units across fifty acres, the featureless, rectangular, Beach Haven buildings looked identical to Shore Haven. Perhaps again thanks to Trump's personal FHA connections, the federal government divided Beach Haven up into six projects for paperwork purposes and provided $25 million in taxpayer subsidies.[24]

To speed things along, Fred Trump also brought in a business partner on the Beach Haven project, bricklayer James Tomasello, whom the Organized Crime Task Force later linked to the Gambino and Genovese crime families.[25]

As the Beach Haven apartments rose, they were accompanied by a torrent of publicity that has since become the Trump family hallmark. Trump promised "a de luxe omnibus line" to transport residents to nearby Brighton Beach and a "'baby sitting' organization" to take care of the complex's children.[26] The following Mother's Day, he announced that "every prospective mother in his projects, Shore Haven and Beach Haven, will be presented with a dozen roses."[27]

Like Fred Trump's earlier single-family row houses in Brooklyn, however, these projects came with a catch. Though the Supreme Court ruled in 1948 that racial covenants were unenforceable, the government continued to throw up roadblocks to developers who were open to people of different backgrounds living side by side. While Beach Haven was under construction, another developer, the Rolling Plain Cooperative, in Chicago, was repeatedly denied FHA support on the grounds that "an interracial community was a bad risk" because in an economic depression, "it would be much more difficult to find buyers . . . than it would be in an all-Caucasian project."[28]

There is no evidence that Fred Trump ever fought the government's racist policies and plenty to suggest that housing discrimination was something he embraced enthusiastically. In 2015, when his son Donald was ramping up to run for president, an old *New York Times* report surfaced that revealed that, at age twenty-one, Fred had been arrested at a 1927 Ku Klux Klan rally in Queens that devolved into a "free-for-all battle" between a thousand Klansmen and a hundred police.[29] Though the story offered no proof that Fred took part in the rally—rather than simply being caught up in it—the article resonated. Both in those early days running Beach Haven and Shore Haven, and in the many decades since, Fred and his son Donald have been repeatedly called out for preferring white tenants to people of color, for treating the white tenants better, and charging them lower rents for better maintained accommodations.

AMONG BEACH HAVEN'S earliest residents was the legendary folk singer Woody Guthrie, the Okie troubadour who penned "This Land Is Your Land" and "Pastures of Plenty." During World War II, Guthrie joined the merchant marine. In 1943 his ship was torpedoed on the way to Tunisia. The following year, he mobilized again for the D-day invasion of Normandy, France. This time his ship was crippled by an acoustic mine off Omaha Beach.

Like many veterans, Guthrie's homecoming was difficult. He drank too much. Though he was married with three young children, he drifted, hitchhiking, freight hopping, and taking odd jobs such as writing songs for a venereal disease awareness campaign. In 1949 he accompanied Pete Seeger and Lee Hays of the popular folk quartet the Weavers to a Paul Robeson concert in Peekskill, New York, that was disrupted by a racist riot. Everywhere he turned, it seemed, life was a burden.[30]

Then, in 1950, Guthrie caught a break. His song "So Long, It's Been Good to Know You" was recorded by the Weavers and became a hit. The $10,000 advance check allowed him to get back on his feet again. His family of four moved into 49 Murdock Court, #IJ, a $120-a-month two-bedroom apartment with a large balcony facing Coney Island Hospital.[31] Their fortunes changed, he might have been happy. But Guthrie, who had joined the fight against Fascism and the racism of Hitler's Germany—and whose pre- and post-war music often focused on issues of justice and equality—was outraged to be living in an apartment complex where his friend Paul Robeson, who was black, would not be welcome. By the early 1950s, the FHA had removed racist language from its regulations and was even giving priority to interracial developments, yet Beach Haven remained segregated. Wrote Guthrie: "My worst enemy is my landlord that tries his best to make me and my family live a life of race hate just because he so sickly chose to live his own sad life that way." He also composed a song, which he never recorded, about his landlord. The lyrics were discovered by academic Will Kaufman in the archives of the Woody Guthrie Center in Tulsa, Oklahoma, in 2015, nearly a half century after Guthrie's death at the age of fifty-five.

I suppose
Old Man Trump knows
Just how much
Racial Hate
he stirred up
In the bloodpot of human hearts
When he drawed
that color line
Here at his
Eighteen-hundred-family project.[32]

When the Guthrie family moved into Beach Haven, they signed a four-year lease, but they did not stay for even two. By 1952, Woody was sick with Huntington's chorea, a degenerative neurological disease that robbed him of his musical talents and left him hospitalized for most of the rest of his life. Near the end of that year, his wife, Marjorie, alerted the Beach Haven management that they would have to break the lease.

"My husband after months of hospitalization and examination was declared incurable and is suffering from a fatal disease known as Huntington's chorea," she wrote Fred Trump's deputy. "We have three small children, and since I now know that I alone will be responsible for them, I feel it would be impossible for me to continue living in my apartment whose rental now becomes quite a hardship. . . . I believe I should be out within a week."[33]

BY 1954, FRED Trump's actions had drawn scrutiny from Washington, but it had nothing to do with either racism or high rent. In 1952 General Dwight D. Eisenhower was elected president, and his administration prioritized eliminating corruption and waste in New Deal programs. The former supreme Allied commander, who would later warn of the "military-industrial complex," was especially concerned with war profiteering. His commission targeted trade schools that tricked veterans out of their GI Bill education benefits, along with developers who kept for themselves money that was supposed to be used to house veterans.

On June 18, 1954, Fred Trump was called for a "special interview" before a US Senate panel investigating "large windfall profits" and "widespread frauds and irregularities" in the FHA. Throughout, Trump was combative and unapologetic. At the center of the investigation was Beach Haven. The committee found the project cost only $22 million—netting Trump and his partner, bricklayer James Tomasello, a $3 million windfall from the $25 million in federal subsidies.[34]

This wasn't all: under questioning from the committee's council, for example, Trump conceded that he'd paid only $180,000 for the land beneath Beach Haven, but he got the FHA to put an appraised value, without improvements, of $1.5 million—meaning that more than 80 percent of the money the government provided to buy the land went into his pocket. Then Fred turned the land over to a trust in the name of his children, including Donald, who was three years old at the time. Effectively, Fred Trump made his children his landlord, and the kids charged their father rent on his federally subsidized housing projects—first Beach Haven, then Shore Haven.[35] (In 2018 the *New York Times* would report that thanks to these and other moves, "by age 3, Donald Trump was earning $200,000 a year in today's dollars from his father's empire" and that he "was a millionaire by age 8."[36]) Under questioning from the committee in 1954, Fred Trump also conceded that he dodged gift taxes when he gave the Beach Haven property to his children—valuing the complex at the $180,000 he paid rather than the $1.5 million he got from the FHA. He also admitted to diverting $729,000 in excess proceeds from the FHA to his other companies and confessed to overcharging the government on architecture fees. The most telling moment of the hearing came when Senator Homer Capehart of Indiana asked Trump why he was not making a 10 percent capital investment as required by federal laws.

"Do you mean invest ten percent?" Trump replied. "You couldn't do it."

"You mean you wouldn't have built those buildings if you had to put any of your money in them?" Capehart asked, incredulous.

"Well, I don't say 'any.' All the money I can borrow," Trump said.[37]

Like the other Homewreckers in this book, Fred Trump preferred to play with other people's money.

THE TODDLER WHOSE name was on the Beach Haven trust documents was born on June 14, 1946, shortly before Fred Trump broke ground on the Beach Haven and Shore Haven developments that would define his career. The second youngest of five children, Donald lived a charmed childhood, growing up in a thirty-one-room mock Tudor mansion that his father built in the Jamaica Estates section of Queens. According to Wayne Barrett, the Trump family was one of the few in the neighborhood to have a live-in maid (always white) and a chauffeur (usually black). "Donald Trump had grown up apart," Barrett wrote. "His neighbors knew him by his papier-mâché Halloween mask and elaborate costume; otherwise they just watched him come and go by limo on the long, green hill. The family was very out of touch with the neighbors and grew more so as the years went on."[38]

Like so many of the other Homewreckers in this book, Donald Trump's father sent him to a private all-boys school, although Donald's was a military academy. He was an athletic achiever, batting cleanup on the school's baseball team and lettering in soccer, but he didn't have close friends. "He wasn't that tight with anyone," his roommate at the New York Military Academy, Ted Levine, told Gwenda Blair. "I think it was because he was too competitive, and with a friend, you don't always compete."[39] From there, it was two years of college at Fordham University and then a transfer to the Wharton School at the University of Pennsylvania, where he graduated in May 1968 with a bachelor's degree in economics. When Donald returned home after Wharton, he became the public face of his father's business.

DONALD TRUMP TOOK the reins of his father's company during a time of great turmoil. In April 1968, one month before he walked across the stage at Philadelphia's Civic Center to receive his diploma, riots erupted in major American cities following the assassination of Dr. Martin Luther King Jr. Amid the violence, President Lyndon Johnson pushed the Fair Housing Act through Congress. The final major piece of legislation passed during the civil rights era, it banned "discrimination in the sale, rental, or financing of housing."

"I do not exaggerate when I say the proudest moments of my presidency have been times such as this when I have signed into law the promises of a century," Johnson said at the signing ceremony. "With this bill, the voice of justice speaks again. It proclaims that fair housing for all—all human beings who live in this country—is now part of the American way of life." With the new law, the tables turned. The federal government, which had encouraged, even insisted, that developers segregate their projects, now sought to root out discrimination. Among the first targets of the Civil Rights Division of the Justice Department and the FBI would be the real estate empire of Fred—and now Donald—Trump.

On July 16, 1968, barely three months after the Fair Housing Act went into effect, an African American man saw a notice in the newspaper advertising an apartment in Sussex Hall, a six-story concrete-block apartment building Trump had constructed in the Jamaica section of Queens. When he got there, the man asked the superintendent about renting one of the advertised apartments. But according to a complaint filed with the New York Commission on Human Rights, the superintendent told him that "the apartments were not available." A few hours later, the document said, "a white friend of the complainant went to the subject premises and inquired about an apartment." The superintendent showed him one, accepted a $25 deposit, "and arranged for him to return to sign the lease."[40]

At a hearing into the complaint, the Trumps' representative argued that the experience of the two men did not represent discrimination—an apartment had simply become available during the intervening hours. But the human rights commission was not convinced. "The building in question has 190 units, and there are two Negro tenants," the commission noted. Nevertheless, the punishment was modest to the point of ridiculousness. In addition to posting future apartment openings at the offices of the local affiliate of the National Urban League, a civil rights group, Trump was asked to pay just $100 in "compensation for humiliation, outrage, and mental anguish suffered by" the man who was turned away, which the commission called "the direct result of . . . unlawful discrimination."[41]

The commission's ruling would not be the end of the matter, however. Problems persisted, and New York State's Division of Human Rights got involved, forcing Trump to sign a consent decree in 1970 that imposed ongoing government monitoring of his rental practices. "A preliminary study of Trump Village [a seven-building, 4,600-unit complex that Fred built in the mid-1960s near Coney Island] indicates a pursuit of tenant selection policies and practices which have directly or indirectly created a discriminatory restrictive pattern precluding Negros and Puerto Ricans, because of their race, color, or national origin, from obtaining apartments," the division found that October.[42] As part of the consent decree, Trump again promised to send open-apartment listings to the Urban League.

That still didn't settle the matter. By 1972, the FBI had launched an investigation. Richard Nixon's assistant attorney general for civil rights, J. Stanley Pottinger, ordered a federal probe. Pottinger was a thirty-four-year-old bulldog of a prosecutor who had provoked an inquiry into the 1970 massacre of four student antiwar protestors at Kent State University by the Ohio National Guard.[43] Later, he would become a best-selling author of legal thrillers and make headlines by dating feminist icon Gloria Steinem. But first he would lead a federal civil rights investigation into Fred and Donald Trump's real estate empire.

Thousands of pages of newly released FBI documents detail the extent of the probe. Agents fanned out across all of Trump's New York properties, interviewing tenants, building superintendents, doormen, and janitors. Many of Trump's employees told the FBI they were unaware of racist practices, but slowly a picture of systemic discrimination began to emerge. At the Briar Wyck Apartments, a massive structure with 1,200 units in Queens, a Hispanic doorman told investigators that nearly all the residents of the complex were white but that "three black girls who were renting" were "paying double rent." A white rental agent at the Sea Island Apartments on Nostrand Avenue in Brooklyn told investigators that he was advised by Trump's central office to "mark each application with certain symbols if the applicant was black." On Staten Island, a man told FBI investigators that Fred Trump had hired him to make suggestions on how the seven-hundred-unit Tysens Park apartment complex could be improved. But when he "indicated that the improvements would cost money, Trump disagreed with his suggestion and fired him."

According to the FBI documents, just 1 percent or 2 percent of the complex's apartments were rented by African American residents. Nonetheless, Fred Trump said his strategy for improving the apartments was simple: "Don't rent to blacks," the FBI records quote him as saying. The FBI records say Trump mentioned that it was against the law to discriminate, but, when pressed, told his contractor to "attempt to get black families that were in Tysens Park currently, removed."[44]

Fred Trump then offered a plan for getting his African American tenants out. "Trump stated that he knew of some cheap housing available, where a family could get a house for only $500 down," the FBI records say,[45] and told the employee he would "pay the $500 if a [black] family would move to one of those units. Trump also stated that families could be removed from Tysens Park by charging them late fees on their rent and then serving them with dispossession notices."[46]

In October 1973 the Justice Department filed suit against Fred and Donald Trump, alleging systemic discrimination. By this point, Fred had taken a step back from the limelight, and Donald had become the public face of the Trump Organization. The younger Trump furiously contested the charges. "They are absolutely ridiculous. We have never discriminated, and we never would," he told the *New York Times*, straining credulity. "There have been a number of local actions against us, and we've won them all," he declared. "We were charged with discrimination, and we proved in court that we did not discriminate."[47] To fight the charges, Donald retained attorney Roy Cohn, a ruthless attack dog who made his name as chief counsel to Senator Joe McCarthy during the anti-Communist witch hunts of the 1950s. (Widely seen as a mentor to Donald, Cohn was disbarred in 1986 for "dishonesty, fraud, deceit, and misrepresentation."[48]) In a tactic that would become familiar to Trump observers in later years, Cohn filed a $100 million countersuit alleging the government sought to turn Trump's buildings into "the Welfare Department." The judge called the gambit a "waste of time and paper" and threw out the suit.[49]

Donald was deposed in March 1974, his vintage performance described beautifully by Barrett:

He said he didn't know what the Fair Housing Act was and freely admitted that his company had done nothing to implement it. Asked when the first black had moved into one of his predominantly white projects, Donald replied, "I don't care, and I don't know." He claimed his company made decisions on who to rent to based only on the prospective tenant's ability to pay, but he couldn't resist adding a sexist comment. "We don't usually include the wife's income; we like to see it for the male member of the family," he said.[50]

The case dragged on for a year and a half, but, despite his bluster, Trump eventually settled with the federal government. Once again, there were promises. Similar to the agreement with the city of New York seven years before, Trump agreed to place advertisements in minority-owned papers and give preference to tenants suggested by the Urban League. This time, however, the agreement would be enforced by the Justice Department. It would have teeth.

IF THE TRUMPS had to be dragged kicking and screaming to integrate the company's New York apartments, they did provide housing to people of color elsewhere—in slum conditions so bad that they eventually led to Fred Trump's arrest. The elder Trump was a builder first and foremost. When it came to his white tenants, he was widely considered to produce good, solid construction. But when it came to his black tenants, his preference was to buy cheap at the courthouse and provide little in return.

Such was the case with the Gregory Estates in Prince George's County, Maryland, a sprawling 504-unit apartment complex a few blocks from the state line and Washington, DC. Seven years after he was investigated by a Senate committee for profiteering, Fred Trump was still getting great deals from the federal government. Government records show that one of Trump's companies, Bruche Realty Corporation, bought the property from the FHA for the incredibly low price of $1 in 1961. Four days later, the FHA gave him more help: a $2.3 million loan for the property, which he wouldn't have to pay in full for thirty-nine years.[51] Years later, Donald Trump told the *Washington Post* it was a distress sale.[52]

Whatever the reasons for the government giveaway, Trump didn't put much of the $2.3 million back into the project. Local building inspectors cited him for broken windows, rotted rain gutters, and the failure to install fire extinguishers. By 1976, county officials were so upset they denied Trump's application to renew the project's multifamily housing license, without which his company could not rent vacant apartments.

A flurry of telephone calls followed, the *Post* reported, and Fred Trump flew down from New York to meet with local officials. When he got there, the seventy-year-old real estate baron was handcuffed and thrown in jail. Unbeknownst to him, the county's code inspector had taken out a warrant for his arrest. Trump was "a little upset, to put it mildly," C. H. Bennett, the chief of inspection and enforcement for the county said, but the arrest was necessary because "so much money and so many inspector man-hours" were spent in an effort to have "what are everyday problems" corrected.[53]

In an interview, Irving Eskenazi, identified as vice president for "Trump concerns" in New York, blamed the tenants, who were overwhelmingly black. "We bought that property fifteen years ago," he told the *Post*. "For the first ten years, it was extremely successful. Lately, however, there has been a very serious change to the area. Low-income people started moving in."[54] But the economic class of tenants living in Trump's project hadn't changed since he bought it from the federal government. Gregory Estates had always been for low-income people. The difference was racial. When Trump bought it in 1961, the residents were poor whites. By 1976, however, they were poor blacks.

FRED TRUMP'S ARREST never made it to the New York papers. He posted $1,000 bail, left immediately for New York, and later pled no contest, paying a $3,640 fine.[55] Instead, the New York media, which had quickly moved on from allegations of racism in the family's Brooklyn and Queens projects, focused their cameras and pens on Donald, who had traded the family's mock Tudor mansion in Jamaica for a three-bedroom penthouse apartment at 160 East Sixty-Fifth Street, on the Upper East Side of Manhattan.

"He is tall, lean, and blond, with dazzling white teeth, and he looks ever so much like Robert Redford," began a fawning *New York Times* profile of Donald, published on November 1, 1976, barely a month after his father's arrest. "He rides around town in a chauffeured silver Cadillac with his initials, DJT, on the plates. He dates slinky fashion models, belongs to the most elegant clubs, and, at only 30 years of age, estimates that he is worth 'more than $200 million.'" Every sentence of the story was written in the sort of breathless prose more typical of New York's tabloids than its Grey Lady. Reporter Judy Klemesrud wrote that she met Donald at a quarter to eight in the morning outside his Upper East Side apartment as he was picked up by a chauffeur, a "husky, gun-toting, laid-off New York City policeman who doubles as a bodyguard." Trump, the article proclaimed, was a man with "flair" but was also "publicity shy." His wardrobe, it was noted approvingly, included "a white shirt with the initials *DJT* sewn in burgundy thread on the cuffs."

Most importantly, however, the article carried a message—likely the one Donald sought to send by making himself available. The Trump family would be turning its back on Fred's legacy as a provider of working-class housing in Brooklyn and Queens. Now, Donald said, the family business was all about Manhattan. "It was psychology," Donald told the *Times*. "My father knew Brooklyn very well, and he knew Queens very well. But now that psychology is ended."[56] Building and renting houses or apartment blocks for the working class would be a thing of the past. These new gleaming towers would be for the rich.

Fred Trump had ripped off the federal government and grown his business through deception and prejudice. That "psychology" would remain central to the son's life no matter the borough. In the end, it was those qualities that bonded him with Mnuchin, Ross, and the rest of the Homewreckers. And bonded they would be.

CHAPTER 20

TRUMP UNIVERSITY

WHATEVER YOU MIGHT SAY ABOUT Fred Trump, he wasn't in business for the quick fleece. A racist, a vulture capitalist, and a war profiteer, sure, but, for the most part, his buildings were solidly constructed. They stood the test of time and are still around today.

Fred didn't necessarily take this path because of a system of values and ethics. As we've seen, he was highly responsive to government incentives. After he hustled his way to Lehrenkrauss's mortgage lists and foreclosed on its borrowers during the Great Depression, he built row houses, extending the franchise of homeownership. He did this because that's how FDR's New Deal helped him to make the most money. Later, when billions of federal dollars became available to build rental housing for returning veterans, he changed his approach. Although he built segregated housing complexes (a huge *although*) and skimped on maintenance, one factor remained constant: in order for him to make money, Fred needed, fundamentally, to provide discernable value to the local community.

This is not the case today. Today's Homewreckers don't build. When they buy and sell banks or homes, Steve Mnuchin, Tom Barrack, Steve Schwarzman, and Wilbur Ross could just as easily be shorting and selling pork bellies. Their partners are bankers such as Jamie Dimon, who bundle their debt because it is lucrative. The point is that they could be bundling debt on anything—and indeed they do create custom securities on everything from delinquent credit card debt to unpaid student loans. They buy and trade bundles of debt leveraged against distressed hotels and casinos and boats and recreational vehicles at risk of repossession. Their specialty is extracting money for themselves and leaving us on the hook if things go wrong.

Donald Trump is the ultimate exponent of this moral emptiness. By 2016, he wasn't so much a builder as the brand of a builder. After taking his various businesses into bankruptcy multiple times, he was best known for hosting a reality TV show, *The Apprentice*, licensing his name on other people's buildings, and using his celebrity to sell everything from steaks to vitamin supplements.

While associates like Tom Barrack and Steve Mnuchin made big bets on banks and homes during the bust, Donald Trump traded in false hopes and dreams. Nothing typified this more than Trump University, an unaccredited real estate "school" that Trump launched to a whirl of publicity in 2005. "When I make speeches, a lot of people show up—a lot of people," Trump crowed at a Manhattan news conference announcing his new venture. "There's something out there, and I thought this would be a good time to take advantage of it."[1] As with most of Trump's initiatives back then, the news coverage was voluminous and remarkably uncritical. "Even if you're not a contestant on *The Apprentice*, you can learn from Donald Trump," National Public Radio's Steve Inskeep intoned after returning from a break on *Morning Edition* for a spot so generous it could have been an advertisement.[2]

The endeavor also got gushing, though slightly more critical, coverage from Fox News. Senior business correspondent Terry Keenan laid out the way the school would work for her host, Judge Andrew Napolitano. "It's an attempt by Trump to cash in on his *Apprentice* success," Keenan said, with no classes, no exams, no grades, and no degrees. "You know, kind of a move from the boardroom into the classroom."[3]

Most of the time, Trump didn't teach the classes, claiming he "handpicked" the instructors. But four months later, in September 2005, Trump announced he would teach a session for the school. More than two thousand people logged in, paying $249 each, to hear Trump ramble for an hour and a half about current trends in real estate. After his meandering was complete, branding consultant Jon Ward, the self-proclaimed "mastermind"[4] of Trump University's early-education programs, asked Trump about "gloomy predictions" that the real estate market was heading "for a spectacular crash in the manner of the dot-com bust. What's your take on that pessimism?"

"I don't think that'll happen," Trump responded. "There's just tremendous amounts of money pouring in, so I don't think that's going to happen. . . . I would say prices are going to go substantially higher in real estate. So, I would say you invest."[5] Donald Trump may have had a much bigger brand than Tom Barrack or Steve Schwarzman, but when it came to an actual track record in business, he was dwarfed by the other Homewreckers. So, it's hard to know if Trump was just completely wrong about the state of the economy or recognized what was happening and promoted disinformation for his own benefit.

AS THE BUBBLE built, Trump didn't let up, encouraging his students to buy. In October 2006 he published an audio recording,

Bubble-Proof Real Estate Investing: Wealth-Building Strategies for Uncertain Times. "My name is Donald Trump, and I congratulate you on owning this timely program from Trump University," Trump announced at the start. "There's been a lot of talk about a real estate bubble. That kind of talk could scare you off real estate and cut you out of some great opportunities."[6]

The rest of the "class" was a freewheeling two-hour conversation between real estate men, whom Trump called "masterful investors." These masters started by saying it was a great time to buy in Phoenix—one of the places where the bubble would soon burst the hardest. "Even though there's a risk prices will come down, I don't think it's going to happen," course leader Dolf de Roos posited. Phoenix, he said, "will continue to rise. It may not be at the rate of forty-three percent per annum, but I would be surprised if we entered a period where prices started declining." He urged anyone listening, anywhere in America, to get on an airplane and fly to Las Vegas or Phoenix, where prices were rising, to get in on the frenzy.[7] Of course, Trump University students who followed this advice were setting themselves up for disaster—the type of horrific financial decisions that sent thousands of foreclosed homes to the Homewreckers.

After the bubble finally did burst, Trump University shifted gears. No longer was it primarily an online school charging a few hundred dollars for a short course. The key to this new version of Trump University was indeed a free two-hour talk. But the free teaser served as a recruiting ground for an expensive three-day "Fast Track to Foreclosure Training" workshop that cost $1,495. During that seminar, a "Trump Gold Elite" program was pushed, with the stratospheric price tag of $34,995—more expensive than a Cadillac or an Alfa Romeo.

TRUMP UNIVERSITY FACED its first class action lawsuit in 2010, and by the time Trump had secured the Republican nomination for president in 2016, Attorney General Eric Schneiderman of New York had sued as well, alleging that Donald Trump made "false promises" to persuade at least five thousand people "to spend tens of thousands of dollars they couldn't afford for lessons they never got."[8] Trump University staff admitted in sworn statements that they had no experience in education or real estate.[9] One was a manager at Buffalo Wild Wings.[10] The Associated Press backgrounded sixty-eight of Trump University's "handpicked" staff and found that half of them had declared bankruptcy. Many had checkered pasts, including convictions for cocaine trafficking and child molestation.[11]

On May 31, 2016, less than a week after Trump held his first big fund-raiser at Tom Barrack's house in Santa Monica, a federal judge ordered Trump University's "playbooks" be revealed to the public. The documents, which ran hundreds of pages, unmasked the university not as a school in any conventional sense but as a boiler room full of marks to be exploited—not all that different from the tactic used on Dick Hickerson to lure him into the worst deal of his life.

TEN DAYS AFTER he triumphed over Hillary Clinton, Donald Trump settled three fraud complaints related to Trump University for $25 million. Schneiderman declared he'd won "a major victory" for the victims of Trump University, who had "waited years for today's result."[12] But for Trump, the settlement was small. Notably, it came with no admission of guilt and no punitive damages. The president-elect said as much in a tweet: "I settled the Trump University lawsuit for a small fraction of the potential award because as President I have to focus on our country."[13] His lawyers paid the amount on January 18, 2017.

Two days later, he was sworn in as the forty-fifth president of the United States.

PART VII

PRESIDENT TRUMP

CHAPTER 21

TRIUMPH OF THE HOMEWRECKERS

DONALD TRUMP TOOK THE OATH of office on a chilly Friday morning, delivering an inaugural address that promised an end to the corruption and impotence that had widened America's historic wealth gap. He understood that his victory had been propelled by harnessing the public's rage and envy at having been left behind in the economic recovery, and he promised that he would not forget it.

Evoking FDR's famous "forgotten man" speech from 1932 that promised to prioritize the needs of the "man at the bottom of the economic pyramid," Trump declared, "The forgotten men and women of our country will be forgotten no longer." Politicians had prospered, he said, but jobs had evaporated. Factories closed. "The establishment protected itself, but not the citizens of our country. Their victories have not been your victories; their triumphs have not been your triumphs. And while they celebrated in our nation's capital, there was little chance to celebrate for struggling families all across our land.

"That all changes—starting right here, and right now," Trump proclaimed, "because this moment is your moment. It belongs to you. . . . This is your day. This is your celebration."[1]

The moment, however, belonged not to the great mass of struggling Americans but to the new president's most ardent supporters: flamboyant businessmen who had profited off the pain of the housing bust and were now poised to steer the ship of state for at least the next four years. As Trump reached out his hand and swore "to preserve, protect, and defend the Constitution of the United States of America," his close friend and inaugural committee chair, Tom Barrack, stood behind him, smiling, in a blue scarf and black overcoat. Afterward, Barrack and Trump embraced on the US Capitol's inaugural platform. The Homewreckers had arrived.

BARRACK DIDN'T TAKE an official position in the Trump administration, reportedly turning down an offer to be White House chief of staff, treasury secretary, or ambassador to Mexico.[2] "He could have any position he wanted," Roger Stone told me, but working for the government would have meant making a lot less money. "I don't think he has the belly for public service." Stone observed.

Other Homewreckers had no such qualms. If they changed the rules of the game now, they could make more money later. Steve Mnuchin, by now dubbed the "Foreclosure King" by his critics, was confirmed as Treasury secretary. His top deputy at One-West, Joseph Otting, became the nation's chief bank regulator, the comptroller of the currency. Wilbur Ross, the bankruptcy tycoon who bought Florida's BankUnited, became the commerce secretary, charged with everything from negotiating trade deals to overseeing the US Census. Steve Schwarzman, the chairman of Blackstone, became chair of the White House's Strategic and Policy Forum, a group of business leaders who were to meet regularly with Trump; Jamie Dimon of JPMorgan Chase was named vice chair. Though the group disbanded over the summer after Trump's statement that "bigotry and violence on many sides" were responsible for a white nationalist's killing a counterprotester in Charlottesville, Virginia, Schwarzman, along with Barrack, is said to be among a small group of outsiders—including Sean Hannity (he of both Fox News and SPMK LLC's nine hundred properties)—who are put directly through to the president rather than being routed through the normal communications channels.[3] Hannity reportedly chats with Trump nightly. Schwarzman has flown on Air Force One.

ON FEBRUARY 12, 2017, less than a month into Trump's presidency, while the commander in chief was dining with Prime Minister Shinzo Abe of Japan at his Mar-a-Lago golf club, Schwarzman threw a massive seventieth birthday bash at his Four Winds estate, barely a mile and a half away. This time neither Donald nor Melania Trump could make it, but daughter Ivanka and son-in-law Jared Kushner did, along with Mnuchin, Ross, and a who's who of high finance and culture, from Henry Kravis, cofounder of the hostile takeover firm Kohlberg, Kravis, Roberts, to the fashion designer Donatella Versace. The party featured live camels, trapeze artists, fireworks, and a gondolier. Schwarzman's tennis courts were covered with Asian-themed staging. The man who'd hired Patti LaBelle to sing "Happy Birthday" for his sixtieth was serenaded by Gwen Stefani at his seventieth. After "Happy Birthday," the peroxided pop star took "a quick twirl with the birthday boy around a dance floor constructed inside a two-story tent where acrobats shimmed and jumped," the *New York Times* reported.[4]

Unlike a decade before, when Schwarzman's glorious prebust bash sparked condemnation from sources as conservative as the *Wall Street Journal*, this time the festivities sparked very little blowback. In her story, Bloomberg reporter Amanda Gordon reveled in the comparisons with Schwarzman's sixtieth. There were some differences, though, she wrote: "Remember that beautiful fur coat on Melania Trump? It was New York in February, on a weeknight. This time: no bundling required, with many folks golfing and swimming all day before a balmy night and fireworks alongside a full moon."[5]

Howard Marks, the cochairman of Oaktree Capital, a vulture firm that had bought, and flipped, three thousand foreclosures, told Gordon, "The world is an uncertain place, a lot of people are unhappy with a lot of other people, there are a lot of things that people are upset about. . . . So, it's nice to have an evening where everybody's happy, harmonious, and upbeat."[6]

THERE WAS A lot of celebrating to be had. In June the gang got together for the marriage of Steve Mnuchin and his third wife, actress Louise Linton, almost two decades younger than him. Mnuchin's new wife was a blonde B-grade actress whose biggest roles included a few minutes on-screen as a skin care consultant in the 2007 Robert Redford film *Lions for Lambs* and a single episode of *CSI: NY*.

As with Schwarzman's party, the Homewreckers showed up to lend their support. For them, flipping wives went hand in hand with flipping houses, debt, and companies. Donald Trump showed up with Melania, his third wife, twenty-four years his junior. Wilbur Ross came with his own third wife, society writer and socialite Hilary Geary Ross.[7] Tom Barrack was photographed arriving with an unidentified, much younger brunette.[8] (Barrack's third attempt at marriage, just three years before, at a wedding Donald attended, had already run aground.[9])

The wedding ceremony took place at the Andrew W. Mellon Auditorium, a limestone and granite government building that greets its guests with a grand staircase and imposing Roman Doric pillars. Erected during the Great Depression as part of a new complex for the US Department of Labor, the auditorium had been dedicated in February 1935 by Franklin Roosevelt as a gathering space for the people. This crowd, however, was not what FDR had in mind. Vice President Mike Pence officiated. A photo of a smiling Pence, with Donald and Melania alongside the newlyweds, was released to the public. America, meet your new ruling class.

MNUCHIN'S WIFE PROVED particularly tone-deaf to the way opulent displays of wealth might play, given Trump's populist message. She showed off her wedding jewelry for *Town and Country* magazine, posing half naked, in a white lace shirt with no pants, with an assortment of diamonds that included a very large engagement ring, a diamond wedding band, a diamond bracelet, two pairs of diamond earrings, a couple of diamond necklaces, another pair of diamond earrings she had turned into a cocktail ring, and a diamond brooch of two parrots kissing a pearl.[10]

Later that summer, Louise posted a photo on Instagram of her descending from a US Air Force jet on an official government day-trip to Kentucky, accompanied by an exuberant description of what she was wearing, including clothing from Hermès, Valentino, and Roland Mouret. When a commenter, later identified as a mother of three from Portland, Oregon, criticized her, Linton responded by saying that she and husband Steve had given more to their country than their haters ever could. She included a series of emojis: the curled biceps, the blowing-kisses face. "Lolol. You're adorably out of touch," Linton told her Instagram critic. "Thanks for passive aggressive nasty comment. Your kids look very cute. Your life looks cute. I know you're mad but deep down you're really nice and so am I." Amid the controversy that followed, Linton apologized and deleted the post.[11]

Mnuchin and Linton settled into a white stone mansion with nine bedrooms, 12.5 bathrooms, and 16,000 square feet of space, behind a wrought iron gate off Massachusetts Avenue. At $12.6 million, it was, *Town and Country* reported, among the most expensive homes sold in Washington that year.[12] Linton told the *New York Times* that the couple had made an easy transition to Washington. They walked their dogs in Rock Creek Park and rode their bicycles to Mount Vernon on the weekends.[13]

As they enjoyed their new mansion, they had plenty of company. Among their neighbors was Wilbur Ross, another newly arrived Homewrecker, who, together with his wife, bought a 7-bedroom, 8.5-bathroom, 10,300-square foot Beaux Arts edifice with marble floors and gold chandeliers a month before Mnuchin and Linton purchased their Rock Creek home. Property records show the couple paid $10.7 million for the home and didn't take the homestead exemption, a tax break available to families on their primary residence. Instead, they told the Washington, DC, tax collector to send the bill to their estate in Palm Beach, Florida— just a short walk from Trump's Mar-a-Lago golf club.[14]

AND THINGS WERE about to get even better for the bundlers and flippers. Their man was in the White House. Their supporters, controlling both houses of Congress, pushed through a giant tax cut for corporations and the wealthy—the sort of legislation that Hillary Clinton would never have supported. The bill, which lowered the corporate tax rate from 35 percent to 21 percent, paid off massively for the banking sector, which had its most profitable year ever in 2018. In a report the following February, the FDIC estimated that banks would have made a record $207.9 billion even without the tax cut, but the law tacked an additional $28.8 billion onto their profits.[15] In his annual letter to shareholders, Jamie Dimon said JPMorgan Chase—which made a record $32.5 billion in 2018—was able to pocket an extra $3.7 billion because of the tax bill.[16] In addition, because the bill lowered the marginal tax rate for the rich, Dimon's would be able to hold on to a greater share of his own compensation, which the bank's board increased to $31 million.[17] (And thanks to a reduction in the estate tax,[18] he would also be able to pass more of that on to his children when he died.)

If that wasn't enough, there were also special carve-outs for the Homewreckers. For starters, real estate magnates were now allowed to deduct interest expenses for property management, construction, and other real estate activities. The coup de grace, however, was a massive new tax deduction that allowed businessmen who "pass income through" LLC shell companies to pay taxes at dramatically lower rates than working people who rely on a paycheck.[19] Consider two people, both making $50,000 a year. The first, a teacher who gets paid regular wages, would face a federal income tax rate of 22 percent, meaning an $11,000 tax bill. That teacher would pay more than our second hypothetical American, a landlord who owns property through an LLC and asks her tenants to pay rent to the LLC before passing the money through the shell company to herself. At the end of the year, this landlord has made the same amount of money as the teacher:

$50,000 in profit. But the Trump tax bill entitles this landlord to a 20 percent "pass-through" deduction—meaning the IRS would assess the 22 percent income tax on just $40,000 rather than the full $50,000, for a bill of just $8,800.

Most people who pass income through an LLC make a lot more than $50,000, however, which is why independent analysts say the loophole is overwhelmingly benefitting the rich. According to Congress's Joint Committee on Taxation, approximately two hundred thousand millionaires and billionaires were expected to reap $17.8 billion because of the pass-through provision in 2018, an amount that would grow annually until it hit $31.6 billion for the year 2024.[20] Among those likely to benefit from this windfall would be Homewreckers Schwarzman, Barrack, Mnuchin, Hannity, and President Trump himself, whose financial disclosures showed that he owned or controlled more than three hundred LLCs.[21]

The tax bill was also an early Christmas present for the president's son-in-law, Jared Kushner—who had helped push the tax bill through Congress. Like much of the rest of the new president's inner circle, his son-in-law had used the housing bust to buy huge portfolios of residential real estate. Kushner's particular bet was on ten thousand fading apartment units in Rust Belt cities such as Pittsburgh, Pennsylvania, and Toledo, Ohio, which the Kushner family business held in LLC shell companies with names such as JK2 Westminster LLC. On May 23, 2017, six months before Kushner's father-in-law signed the tax bill, Alec MacGillis, a reporter at the nonprofit investigative news website ProPublica, detailed degrading conditions in Kushner's apartments in Baltimore—which he estimated were home to twenty thousand people. In the piece, headlined "The Beleaguered Tenants of 'Kushnerville,'" MacGillis painted Kushner as a classic slumlord who allowed buildings to degrade and charged tenants high fees for basic repairs.[22] With

Kushner, though, there was another cruel twist. In a bit of a rotten cherry on top of it all, Kushner took them to court when they tried to move out. The tax bill further stacked the deck in Kushner's favor. It didn't force him to be a better landlord, but now he'd be able to put more of the profit he cleared on renting these apartments into his pocket, even as the lawsuits filed by his company's attorneys marred tenants' credit reports, making it harder for them to ever buy a home—or even secure a decent apartment.

Steve Mnuchin claimed the tax bill would "pay for itself" by stimulating economic growth,[23] but in the year after Trump signed it into law, the deficit ballooned to more than $1 trillion.[24] And yet Republican lawmakers did find some ways to increase revenues—by removing tax deductions that made homeownership easier for middle-class families. They limited the mortgage interest tax deduction and capped provisions that allow families to deduct state and local property tax from their federal returns. Taken in total, the tax bill made it more expensive for middle-class families to own a home and build wealth, and easier for the Homewreckers who wanted to extract wealth from them.

THE TAX BILL is but one example of the Trump administration's preference for foreclosure kings over regular Americans. Before the newly inaugurated commander in chief had even left the National Mall, the Department of Housing and Urban Development announced it was scrapping a planned reduction in government fees associated with FHA mortgages for first-time and working-class home buyers. The Obama administration's change would have saved borrowers only $500 a year on a $200,000 mortgage, but for those on the edge of poverty, that might mean the difference between making and missing a payment. The following week, the government-controlled mortgage company Fannie Mae agreed to backstop a $1 billion debt bundle for Blackstone's Invitation Homes. Under the terms of the deal, Invitation Homes agreed to take 5 percent of the losses if anything went wrong. Taxpayers would be on the hook for the other 95 percent: $950 million.[25]

"Invitation Homes is a strong partner with deep experience managing a large volume of single-family rental properties," Fannie Mae said in a statement, adding it would use the $1 billion loan to "gather data and test the market" to make sure it was "delivering the right solutions" for families. Though it had been created during the New Deal to boost homeownership and build wealth across society, Fannie Mae now sought to "meet the increasing demand for single-family rental housing." Rather than trying to increase the availability of credit to hardworking families, the government would be throwing its weight behind corporate landlords—big time.

That was just the beginning. The Consumer Financial Protection Bureau, created after the housing bust to protect Americans from predatory lenders such as IndyMac, has been defanged. Among the changes, the agency's Trump-appointed leaders stripped the Fair Lending Unit, designed to catch racial discrimination in lending, of its enforcement powers and moved to nix an Obama-era regulation designed to prevent abuses by payday lenders.[26] Over at HUD, Secretary Ben Carson moved to remove the words "free from discrimination" from the agency's mission[27] and proposed new rules that would keep it from relying on data when making a fair housing case,[28] which advocates say would make discrimination cases far more difficult to establish.

Over at the Treasury Department, the Community Reinvestment Act, which regulators used to assess the lending practices of Steve Mnuchin's and Joseph Otting's OneWest Bank, is being gutted by the bank's former executives. Among the changes they are promoting is a proposal that federal bank inspectors inspect banks less often and reduce their focus on whether banks locate branches in low-income communities.[29] Otting's office has already issued new rules that allow banks to receive a "satisfactory" grade under the CRA even when they are found in violation of antidiscrimination or community protection laws.[30]

Passing legislation through Congress has proved more challenging, especially since the Democrats took over the House of Representatives after the 2018 midterms. But before that election ensured ongoing gridlock, the Homewreckers did secure a second signature legislative achievement. On May 24, 2018, President Trump signed an overhaul of the Dodd-Frank Act that raised the threshold of a "too-big-to-fail" bank from $50 billion to $250 billion—meaning that if OneWest and CIT sought to merge today, the Federal Reserve would not be asked to give the union additional scrutiny. The bill, passed with sixty-seven votes in the Senate, including more than a dozen Democrats, rolled back a host of consumer protections that were designed to prevent another housing bust. For example, the bill limited the number of institutions covered by the Volcker Rule, which forbid banks from placing risky bets with their depositors' money (on the grounds that the taxpayers would have to reimburse those depositors if the bank failed), and allowed smaller banks and credit unions "to forgo certain ability-to-pay requirements regarding residential mortgage loans" required by the Truth in Lending Act of 1968.[31]

Steve Mnuchin and Wilbur Ross helped push the bill through Congress. "We are unleashing the economic potential of our people," Trump said as he signed it.[32] Once again, hundreds of financial intuitions are now allowed to avoid the basic standard we are taught is at the center of prudent lending: that banks verify borrowers' ability to pay back their mortgage loans. The law also loosened the standards on the types of terms banks could offer on a mortgage—potentially bringing back toxic loan products and elevated foreclosure rates. Because those practices are now legal, predatory lenders stand to make a comeback. As the country lurches crazily from one daily scandal to the next, one thing remains constant: the Homewreckers are pulling off a grand heist—stealing America's wealth.

MEANTIME, LIFE CONTINUES. In March 2017, two months after Trump took the oath of office, I flew out to Atlanta, the largest market for corporate landlords such as Blackstone and Colony. In that city alone, the number of families who rent had increased by nearly thirty thousand between 2006 and 2016, while the number of homeowners fell. The reason for my trip was a new study from the Federal Reserve Bank of Atlanta, which tracked evictions in Fulton County, in the heart of the metro. The study's lead author, Elora Raymond, wasn't the typical government researcher. Born in Samoa, where property is held communally, Raymond was interested in the deeper questions raised by the rise of corporate ownership. What does it mean to have rights to land? How does debt interface with concepts of property?

"What we're seeing is the commodification of housing," she told me. "Do we think it's good that housing is being treated like a commodity" like copper or coffee? "Or is it more essential, like water or electricity? There's a reason that water and electricity are tightly regulated. They are treated as utilities instead of commodities because they are core to our survival."

Raymond and her colleagues looked at all of Fulton County's

single-family rentals and divided them into two buckets: big landlords that owned more than fifteen single-family homes, and mom-and-pop landlords, who owned only a few houses. They found the corporate landlords were far more likely to file eviction notices than mom-and-pops.[33] Tom Barrack's company, Colony, was the most aggressive; in 2015, the study said, it had moved to evict a third of its tenants. The impact of this was to further destabilize communities that had already been rocked by the foreclosure disaster. "It's really hard to make sure children are well fed or can read by third grade if they don't have a home," Raymond said.

What explained these numbers? Corporate landlords had the resources to use advanced metrics to screen out all but the most high-quality tenants. Colony was no different: in their reports inspecting mortgage-backed securities, rating agencies noted that Barrack's company aggressively screened potential tenants, accepting only those with verified employment and a history of paying rent on time.

"Previous evictions result in an automatic rejection," an analysis from Morningstar Credit Ratings read. Colony's tenants, it said, were "typically former homeowners who often have families and ties to the neighborhood, including a preference for the local school district."[34] In essence, Colony was taking former homeowners, who used to accrue wealth and improve their standing with every mortgage payment, and putting them in a position where their credit would be ruined—setting back for years their ability to buy a home or even secure a better house or apartment for rent.

ONE OF THE first I houses I visited after arriving in Atlanta was on Hadley Place, a winding tree-lined street in Snellville, a town of twenty thousand in Gwinnett County, in the northeastern suburbs. Like most of the homes I visited in Georgia, it looked wonderful from the outside: a split-level Colonial with a two-car garage, decorative black window shutters, and a redbrick façade. I walked up the driveway and ascended the short porch.

When I rang the doorbell, a diminutive twenty-five-year-old African American woman, Makita Edwards, came to the door in a blue college sweatshirt. When I mentioned that I was investigating her landlord, she opened up.

They were three generations living under one roof: Makita, her baby boy, Mason, and her mother, Marina Pope, who worked at a collections agency that handled medical billing. Since their family had moved in seven months earlier, life had been one disaster after another. They went without heat in the winter and dealt with persistent water leaks. Two weeks after she moved in, Makita was lying in bed with three-month-old Mason, when the ceiling fan caved in on top of them. Edwards showed me a picture of the damage. A panel of ceiling had opened up as if it were a door as the fan tumbled down. Luckily, no one was hurt.

"It's kind of insane," Makita's mother told me. Marina said she found the rental house on the Internet following her own divorce and a foreclosure. Here was another family like Sandy Jolley's, who had lost their wealth and not recovered, paying increasing amounts of money to a corporate landlord. "I was in a rushed, rushed situation. I would never recommend this company to anyone."

The maintenance problems weren't even the worst of it. Dealing with unreliable heat and the collapsed ceiling fan, they fell a few days' behind on their rent. The family was living paycheck to paycheck, and Makita's mother got paid on the fifth of the month. (Rent was due on the first.) It wasn't long before Colony's lawyer sent the family an eviction notice saying that if they wanted to stay, they needed to pay not only their past due rent of $1,580 but also a $95 late fee, $60 in court costs, and a $25 charge for the process server who delivered the eviction notice. They paid the charges, but since the family was already living on the edge, that extra $180 made them late on the next month's rent, leading to another round of additional charges. Over the next five months, Makita's family would pay more than $1,000 in fees. I told Makita that Colony, her landlord, was founded by Tom Barrack, Donald Trump's best friend. What did she think about that?

"He's at the top. He's the big guy. We're just little people in his world," she replied. "So, what can you say?"

THE REST OF my trip just went just like that. Tenants told me how they struggled without heat and coped with leaky roofs, peeling tile, and collapsing counters. One said she'd dealt with a snake infestation. Another showed me a report from a code inspector that cited ColFin AI GA LLC for a ceiling leak that channeled water through a light fixture when it rained. "Safety Hazard!!!" the code inspector wrote. A month later, the leak remained. Court records showed that many of these tenants had also been assessed late fees and been served with eviction notices, their rents weaponized by the single-minded profit motive of distant, faceless corporate landlords.

I wasn't the only one who noticed. Nationally, the Better Business Bureau reported "a pattern concerning billing or collection issues [and] repair issues" in Colony-owned homes. The litany of problems posted on the bureau's website included broken air conditioners, flooding, mold, and serious infestation. "When consumers attempt to reach the business regarding repair issues, they report that the business is unresponsive," the bureau said.

But, of course, Colony would be unresponsive—repairing cost money. It was the same logic behind the company's eviction notices, which weren't so much about kicking people out as padding profits. The company's stock filings showed it made $14 million on fees and another $12 million on tenant clawbacks, including seized security deposits, in 2016.

Still, the stock filings also showed how the company could make good money off turnover. Nationally, they showed an annual turnover rate of 34 percent—meaning one out of every three tenants would be gone by the end of the year. On the surface, an eviction rate like Colony's made no economic sense. Housing experts that I spoke to agreed. "It doesn't serve anyone well," Laurie Goodman, codirector of the Housing Finance Policy Center at the Urban Institute, told me. "If you're sitting with a vacant home for two or three months, that's going to cost you thousands of dollars. So, if you're a landlord, you basically want the tenant to stay." But Colony's stock filings also showed rents went up faster for houses that turned over than ones where the tenant remained, and vacancy rates were minimal, with just four out of every one hundred homes empty. In such an overheated rental market, where Colony and its fellow corporate landlords had dominated the housing stock of key suburban communities with good schools, tenants didn't have much leverage to fight.

Colony was a modern-day slumlord, intent on extracting as much money as possible from its tenants while shelling out as little as possible in return. This was about as far away from the American Dream as one could get. It was as if we had fallen back to the 1890s, when a wealth inequality powered by the industrial revolution led to bounded company towns and urban land barons. Then, it didn't matter how hard a family worked; there was no getting ahead—"Truly poor for having no better homes; waxing poorer in the purse as the exorbitant rents keep rising," in the words of Jacob Riis.[35] Tone-deaf to the economic impact of their rent increases on struggling families, skinflint on basic questions of habitability, their tenants were reduced to begging a distant landlord, whether in 1890 or 2019.

Despite its seemingly economic nature, the pain was not felt evenly. When Elora Raymond carried out her study on evictions in Fulton County for the Federal Reserve, she assumed they would follow a pattern that tracked with the region's development controversies. "Given the public debate, we expected to see that gentrification was a major cause of evictions," she explained. "But when we did our analysis, we couldn't find any correlation between the influx of wealthier residents and the eviction of existing, lower-income tenants." There was another factor that seemed to predict whether a tenant would receive an eviction notice, however: "the concentration of blacks in the neighborhood."

MY EXPERIENCE IN Atlanta was unsettling, so I reached out to Tom Barrack. His spokeswoman said he wasn't willing to talk. After taking equity out of the homes by creating mortgage-backed securities, Barrack was moving on. He had taken the company public by merging it with a competitor. Now he was making money on the same houses again by selling his stock.

In October 2016, less than a month before Trump's election, Barrack off-loaded three-quarters of his shares in the rental housing company, clearing $728 million. Then, in March 2017, while I was in Atlanta, he and his investment firm cashed in about half of their remaining stock. On March 7, 2017, securities filings show, Barrack made $127 million in a single day.

Clearly, he was on to other business. His investment fund's

prospectus listed caring for the elderly as a strategic area for expansion, and by the end of 2018, Colony's "consolidated health care portfolio consisted of 413 properties: 192 senior housing properties, 108 medical office properties, 99 skilled nursing facilities, and 14 hospitals."[36] But Barrack was also prospecting for other opportunities. Three weeks after he walked away from his housing company, documents show Barrack confirmed for dinner with Steve Mnuchin at Fiola Mare, a high-end Italian restaurant overlooking the Potomac River in Washington, DC. According to Mnuchin's calendar, which I obtained using the Freedom of Information Act, the two Homewreckers were to dine in the Mermaid Room with ambassadors from seven Persian Gulf states: Bahrain, Kuwait, Jordan, Qatar, Saudi Arabia, and the United Arab Emirates. Rick Gates, a Barrack deputy and Trump campaign operative who later pled guilty to conspiracy against the United States as part of the investigation into potential Russian interference in the 2016 election, was also present, along with representatives of another private equity firm. According to the calendar, Wilbur Ross, too, was invited to the dinner but not confirmed. What they were up to remains unknown.[37]

BUT WHAT ABOUT the tenants? Even as Barrack pulled away, they continued to live in the homes. What did all this mean for them? In addition to Barrack himself, I called the company, requesting an interview with anyone who might be willing to answer a few questions on the record. I was told no one was available. Eventually Colony routed me to an outside public relations consultant who provided a statement, saying the company provided an "exceptional living experience through the highest servicing standards."

It boasted that "on a scale of 1 to 5, with 5 representing highest score, our overall rating by residents was 4.6." The company claimed that evictions were rare and that nationally less than 1 percent of leases were "terminated annually as a result of service-related issues."

"We are proud of the role we have played in helping to improve our country's rental housing inventory, stabilize homes [*sic*] prices in times of distress, strengthen neighborhoods, and create jobs," the statement said. "We are honored to serve thousands of renters across the country who call our properties home."[38]

ONE SUNNY MORNING in April 2017, I drove past an expansive mansion Tom Barrack was building for a Qatari sheikh in the Hollywood Hills and continued down to the streets of bungalows that sprawled across smoggy South Los Angeles. I turned right onto Florence, passing a nightclub, a barbecue joint, and a car wash, and turned left again, parking my car on the street in front of the Butler family home. It was four years after Colony had bought the house out of foreclosure and three years after Barrack and his investors had pulled their money back out by bundling the home into a $514 million mortgage-backed security.

From the street, the bungalow looked sad. Faded photographs from years ago had showed Beulah Butler tending rows of rosebushes planted amid a lush, green lawn. But the verdant garden had long since disappeared. Instead, the front lawn was overgrown with crabgrass, the last living rose about to expire. I walked past a short metal gate in the chain-link fence that circled the yard. Inside, I could hear the incessant yapping of small dogs. I knocked on the metal mesh security door.

The man who opened it was tall and thin, with limbs barely

thicker than sticks. Gaunt and dying of cancer, he gave his name as Shawn Pruett. He was forty-six years old. It was the middle of the day, but he was dressed in just a T-shirt and boxer shorts and was so weak that he could barely restrain his seventy-pound Labrador, Wilson.

Shawn told me he used to own his own home—a small farm in Texas. "I had a wonderful garden with some beautiful flowers that I planted," he said, showing me a photo of a single-story brown farmhouse. He'd planned to take up beekeeping, he said, "but that never happened"—because he got sick: first AIDS, then lymphoma.

In 2013 Pruett sold the farm for $98,000 and headed west, hoping that treatment at UCLA Medical Center could extend his life. He told me he found the bungalow on Craigslist and rented it sight unseen. Inside, the carpet was frayed. The kitchen linoleum was peeling. Records from the Los Angeles Department of Building and Safety showed that no work permits had been taken out since Barrack's company bought it on the courthouse steps four years earlier. But it did offer Pruett one thing: Colony allowed pets, and there was a backyard where his dogs—Wilson and four dachshunds—could play.

"That's why we're here," he said, holding the screen door open for them. He said he had no idea the home had been owned by the same black family for fifty years until they lost it to a predatory reverse mortgage—although he knew the name Beulah Butler. He still got mail addressed to her, he said. He also had no idea that the house was now owned by a new breed of corporate landlord, although that explained some of his experiences. The lease agreement that Pruett signed was even more expansive than the one that Sandy had agreed to after losing her home to foreclosure. It required him to pay for and manage a host of repairs that are normally the landlord's responsibility—including sewer blockages and broken glass "regardless of cause."

But Pruett didn't have the energy or means to stay on top of repairs. After four rounds of chemotherapy, UCLA doctors had stopped his treatment. "I'm beyond help at this point," he said in his living room, surrounded by cigarette butts, with the shades drawn and the television on mute. "Basically, you're just watching me die. I know that sounds macabre, but it's true."

Outside, fronds from a neighbor's palm tree were tangled in the electrical wire leading to the house—a potential fire hazard. The lease Pruett signed made fixing that his responsibility, too. He said he didn't have the money. In the kitchen, his cupboards were filled with cans of Campbell's Soup and containers of Jif peanut butter he got from a local food bank. He said he lived on a fixed income, from federal disability insurance.

But Colony didn't see him as a human being. He was just a source of income, his house just a unit in a mortgage-backed security to be paid back or leveraged again. Pruett shared documents that showed Colony had raised his rent every year since he moved in. Another rent increase was due at the end of August. But Pruett didn't live that long. He died on August 2, 2017.

"Greed, it's just greed," Pruett told me during my visit that spring, four months before he died. "You'd think that you'd be praised and rewarded for paying your rent on time and not having any problems and all that, but instead, they raise your rent and punish you, basically, for being a good tenant."

IT SHOULDN'T HAVE been that hard to reach Tom Barrack to talk about this. How did he feel about all the evictions? About tenants, who used to be homeowners, living in houses with ceiling fans that collapsed on their babies? How did it feel to be on the top of a giant company that leveled a rent increase on a dying man? Barrack was always on TV, giving interviews as a surrogate of his good friend Donald Trump, so he obviously wasn't in hiding.

But once again his spokeswoman said he wasn't interested in talking to me. So, I asked around, got his cell phone number, and dialed him direct. After a few rings, he answered.

"Hello," he said, in that smooth Southern California voice.

I gave him my name and identified myself as a journalist who wanted to ask him about his empire of single-family homes.

"I'll have you call my associate," he said. "I'll give him your number. I'm in Mexico in the middle of lunch."

"I understand that," I said, telling him that I had already tried to work through his representatives, but I really wanted his side of the story. I started telling him about what I'd seen—"homes that are just falling apart." But he hung up on me.

ON JUNE 8, 2017, I published a story about Barrack's housing empire, detailing some of what I'd learned about his company's evictions in Atlanta and Los Angeles and featuring the Butler family, Sean Pruett, and the Los Angeles bungalow. The day after the story ran, Barrack quit the company he founded, selling all his stock and resigning his position as cochairman of its board of trustees.

Barrack signaled his resignation in an SEC filing made late on a Friday afternoon, but he wasn't walking away empty-handed. He and his investment firm, then called Colony NorthStar, both said they planned to sell all eleven million shares they together owned of company stock, which were valued at about $400 million. Add that amount to what he had off-loaded in October and March, and you get more than $1.2 billion.

But the phenomenon Tom Barrack started—where tens of thousands of single-family homes are bundled into giant mortgage-backed securities, creating new incentives to skimp on maintenance and maximize rents—outlived his ownership. His former company would still pile on onerous fees and force tenants to live with chronic leaks, mold, mites, and even the occasional snake.

One thing was refurbished, though. With Barrack gone, the corporate landlord rebranded. No longer would it be called Colony Starwood Homes—now it would be called Starwood Waypoint Homes to emphasize Barrack's lack of involvement. But that didn't last long, either. A few months later, Blackstone announced it was absorbing all thirty-one thousand of the company's homes into its Invitation Homes brand, creating what would be far and away America's largest landlord on single-family homes, with eighty thousand rentals nationwide. The merger, Invitation Homes said in a statement, would "benefit our residents and the communities and neighborhoods in which we do business."

NOT LONG AGO, I looked back at the property record to the Butler family home to see if anything had changed. It turned out that another financial transaction had been filed at the courthouse.

The bungalow had been leveraged again. The $514 million bundle of debt had been paid off by an even larger bundle of debt, Beulah Butler's former house was now part of a new mortgage-backed security funded by JPMorgan Chase that was nearly twice as large: $917 million. Property values had increased, and the corporate landlord was pulling more money out of the houses, enriching Schwarzman and the other Blackstone investors.

This bundle including the Butlers' old home was of 4,300 rental properties, which the Morningstar rating agency said Colony had bought for an average of $176,000 in 2012 and 2013. Now their estimated value (measured by broker's price opinions) was $305,000—meaning that Colony, and now Blackstone, had made $129,000 per home on top of the money they made on rent. That could have been $129,000 in wealth gained by more than 4,000 families. Like the homes in this new mortgage-backed security, the small, boxy, two-bedroom with a view of the ocean that my family bought in 2009 has nearly doubled in value. Our wealth has increased. Despite the employment uncertainty that is inherent in being a journalist, I feel secure in the knowledge that if my children are admitted to college, they will be able to afford to attend; or that if any sort of tragedy befalls our family, we can take out a loan against the increased value of the house to pay our medical bills. If the situation becomes truly dire, we can sell and make hundreds of thousands of dollars. My preferred situation, which we get closer to every month, is that we pay off the mortgage and own our home free and clear. At that point, we will have the security that comes with having no mortgage payment at all. Perhaps, if we're lucky, we'll even be able to retire.

But for the 4,300 families living in homes owned by this new mortgage-backed security controlled by Blackstone, none of this is an option. The Homewreckers have taken that opportunity from them. That is why the recovery feels so empty to so many people.

EPILOGUE

A PATH TO SHARED PROSPERITY

THE END OF THIS BOOK may seem depressing, with a small group of Homewreckers grabbing the reins of the American economy, riding off with our wealth, and leaving us in the dust. But I am not depressed. As an investigative reporter, writing this book has been an act of optimism. I have faith that when facts are brought into the sunlight, major, even systemic problems can be addressed, with benefits in the real world for the people who need them most. The act of reading this book is an act of optimism by you. You wouldn't have read this far if you thought the pursuit of equality was impossible, or that the economic problems we face are fundamentally unsolvable.

Last year, for example, my colleague Emmanuel Martinez and I took on modern-day redlining, producing an exposé that aired on our national radio show, *Reveal*, and as a two-part series on the *PBS NewsHour*, and ran in hundreds of newspapers through a collaboration with the Associated Press.

The impact started at the local level. We focused in on Philadelphia, one of more than five dozen cities where we found banks were far more likely to deny home loans to people of color than whites—even when they made the same amount of money, tried to take out the same size loan, and tried to buy in the same neighborhood. Less than a week after publication, Pennsylvania's attorney general and state treasurer announced they were launching investigations.[1] The Philadelphia City Council held hearings, passed a $100 million affordable housing measure that provides down payment assistance to underserved communities, and launched a public-private partnership to give a second look at loan applications that are denied.[2]

State attorneys general in Delaware, Iowa, Illinois, Washington state, and the District of Columbia followed suit, saying they were launching their own investigations.[3] Under pressure, some banks responded, including JPMorgan Chase, which increased lending to African Americans and Latinos and announced it would be opening new branches in neighborhoods where a majority of residents are people of color. Congress held hearings, and lawmakers in the House and Senate introduced legislation. In April, after the Democrats took over Congress, I was invited to testify before the House Financial Services Committee.

None of this is to say that lending discrimination disappeared or that the wealth gap narrowed, but it does mean that even with the Homewreckers in power it is possible to move the needle in the right direction. Making matters easier is the fact that so many good ideas for reform are already out in the public domain. In fact, we've seen many of them in this book. If those who have failed to learn from history are doomed to repeat it, then it follows that we can also learn from history to find a way out. If the wealth gap has widened to levels not seen in a century, history can show us the path to greater equality and shared prosperity.

"THE GREATEST MONOPOLY in this country is the money monopoly," Woodrow Wilson said in 1911. "So long as that exists our old variety and freedom and individual energy of development are out of the question."[4] When Wilson spoke those words the wealth gap was much as it is today—with the top 0.1 percent of Americans owning as much as the bottom 90 percent combined.[5]

After Wilson became president in 1913, he tried to fix this by creating the Federal Reserve to regulate banks and the Federal Trade Commission to break up trusts, and instituting an income tax that forced those who made the most money to pay for the functions of the government. The wealth gap did narrow for a time, but Wilson's policies—accompanied as they were by overt racism—did not provide an effective path to homeownership, and so the vast majority of Americans began losing ground again in the 1920s, during the period of rampant stock market speculation. By the time the market crashed in 1929, the bottom 90 percent of Americans owned just 15.7 percent of the country's wealth.[6]

As we've seen, this distribution only began to change after FDR's New Deal, which ushered in an unprecedented era of homeownership and wealth building, creating the white middle class. The key to this was government investment—but the sort of government investment that generates a return. Because responsible lending makes money, these monumental efforts cost the taxpayers very little. The Home Owners' Loan Corporation, which invented the long-term fixed-rate mortgage and saved a million homes from foreclosure during the Great Depression, turned a profit.[7] The GI Bill, which helped 4.3 million veterans buy homes after World War II, had, by 1956, experienced a net loss of just $30 million—less than 0.1 percent of the money lent out.[8] Accounting for inflation, that's $290 million in today's dollars, or $67 per home.

These are investments we can afford today. In fact, our government has parted with far more over the past decade bailing out banks, shelling out subsidies to corporate vultures, and inking sweetheart deals with private equity firms. Indeed, if we design the programs right, we can not only strengthen middle-class wealth, but also redress the discrimination that was baked into the New Deal. A lot of great ideas are already out there.

One such proposal, promoted by University of Georgia law professor Mehrsa Baradaran, would have the government underwrite a twenty-first-century Homestead Act. Baradaran envisions the government buying, restoring, and transferring large numbers of abandoned properties in cities like Baltimore, Detroit, Philadelphia, and St. Louis to area residents. In essence, the government would be extending to working-class Americans the same sort of revolving line of credit that OneWest Bank and JPMorgan Chase provided to Tom Barrack's Colony Capital. The difference: rather than making Barrack and his investors rich, the government would revitalize communities by turning tenants into homeowners so they could build wealth and pass it on to the next generation. "For most Americans, their home is their largest asset, and for those who do not own a home, it is their greatest expense," Baradaran wrote. "The unique success of the federal government's New Deal–era mortgage programs was that once Congress put credit mechanisms in place and made the initial federal investments, the system was able to operate successfully and without further intervention."[9]

Regardless of the program, the concept is the same. If the government invests prudently on behalf of the public, returns are likely to follow, especially if they are accompanied by restraints on the worst excesses of capital. The black-and-white footage of *It's a Wonderful Life* may be from another era, but the basic compact between banker and borrower epitomized by Jimmy Stewart's George Bailey need not be antiquated. Since the government insures more than $7 trillion in consumer deposits,[10] we have the right to insist that banks operate in a way that benefits the public. We have the right to question whether bundling, slicing, and trading debt leveraged against corporate rental homes fulfills that public trust—since we will be on the hook again when things go wrong. We have the obligation to craft policy solutions in line with our values—because these financial transactions shape our society and our relationships to each other.

Indeed, if rigged housing policies have created our wealth gap, perhaps it is time to rig them back in the other direction. Among presidential candidates, Kamala Harris and Bernie Sanders have put forward ambitious proposals, while Senator Elizabeth Warren has, as of this writing, offered the most comprehensive plan. It involves providing billions of dollars of down payment assistance to residents of formerly redlined neighborhoods, so that they can break the cycling of renting. "Housing wealth has a huge generational component to it," Warren told me. "Grandma and Grandpa buy a house. . . . House values go up over time. They take money out of the house to start a small business or if they want to send a kid to school. If they're wealthy enough to be able to live in the house until they die they pass that wealth onto the next generation, and the next generation does better, buying a nicer house."[11]

Warren would pay for her plan by increasing the estate tax on families with inheritances of more than $3.5 million to 45 percent, the same level it was when Barack Obama took office in 2009. Steve Schwarzman, age seventy-two, has a net worth of $14.4 billion.[12] A 45 percent tax on that estate would net $6.5 billion (don't worry, his heirs would still get $8 billion). That's enough, based on current median housing prices, to put a 20 percent down payment on more than 100,000 homes. Though a tax hike like that would seem to face steep odds in the era of Homewreckers, it would most certainly have drawn the approval of James Truslow Adams, who set his vision for an American Dream at odds with Old Europe, where wealth, and land, passed from one generation of dukes or duchesses to the next. What made America unique, Adams wrote, was "the dream of being able to grow to the fullest development of as man or woman, unrepressed by social orders, which had slowly been erected in older civilizations."[13]

Just "because a man is born with a particular knack for gathering in vast aggregates of money and power for himself, he may not on that account be the wisest leader to follow nor the best fitted to propound on a sane philosophy of life," he wrote, warning of "the failure of self-government . . . the failure of all that the American dream has held of hope and promise for mankind."[14]

IF WE ARE to live the American Dream, constant vigilance will be required.

On May 17, 2017, Sandy received a call from her lawyer. Twelve years had passed since her parents saw James Garner on television hawking a reverse mortgage for IndyMac's Financial Freedom, nine years since IndyMac went bankrupt, eight years since Steve Mnuchin bought it off the FDIC. It had been nine years since Sandy sued, alleging elder abuse and fraud, six years since she lost in court, and four years since she lost the home to Tom Barrack's Colony on the courthouse steps.

Now, three years after she'd filed a whistleblower complaint, Sandy Jolley was ready to get some justice. She'd been watching CIT's securities filings. She noticed when, the year before, the bank told the SEC it had taken a $163 million charge against earnings because of claims brought as a result of Financial Freedom's reverse mortgage program. "We call this a curtailment event," the company's CFO, E. Carol Hayles, told investors. In total, CIT was setting aside $500 million to settle claims related to the foreclosure process, she said, adding, "The reserve reflects our best estimate at this time."[15]

Sandy's lawyer told her the government had settled the case. But it wasn't the sort of victory she had been hoping for. Though the Justice Department issued a triumphant press release declaring it had demonstrated the government's "continued commitment to address and halt business practices that pose a serious risk"[16] to the public trust, the settlement itself was weak.

The Justice Department and Financial Freedom settlement did not cover the massive, illegal foreclosure fraud she was alleging. Instead, they settled the case on a technicality related to the timing of Financial Freedom's appraisals on foreclosures. The settlement included no admission of guilt. There was nothing there about the foreclosures themselves being wrong. In the first and last public document in the case, the government said the company erred in the dates that appraisals were carried on the homes it seized—resulting in insurance payments from the Federal Housing Administration that were higher than they should have been.

Financial Freedom agreed to pay $89 million—far less than the $163 million or $500 million figures CIT had disclosed. Worse for Sandy, the government had settled the case under a law called the Financial Institutions Reform, Recovery, and Enforcement Act (FIRREA) of 1989, rather than the False Claims Act, which is more often used to settle whistleblower complaints. Whistleblower awards under FIRREA are capped by statute; Sandy would receive the maximum allowed under the law: $1.6 million. After her lawyer took his share, Sandy would take home $978,000.

Sandy used the money to pay off her debts and pay for the long-delayed dental work and cataract surgery not covered by her health insurance. She treated herself to a new 2017 Lexus RX. She paid a lawyer to help her start a nonprofit, Consumer Advocates

Against Reverse Mortgage Abuse (CAARMA). The rest, about $600,000, she put in the bank, hoping she would not have to pay half to the tax man.

Fundamentally, Sandy says, there has still been no justice, but she continues undeterred. "I'm not a victim and I'm not a survivor," she told me. "I'm a warrior, and warriors fight." So, every day, she opens her computer and takes calls from distressed family members who are in exactly the position she was in a decade ago: desperate and scared, and trying to get out of a predatory financial product they didn't need. There have been many small victories to keep her going—among them, the marketing professional from Salt Lake City, the operating room coordinator in the Bronx, and the artist in the foothills of the Sierra Nevada mountains— all of whose homes faced imminent foreclosure until Sandy got involved. To spend time with Sandy Jolley these days is to be with a woman whose phone is always ringing—as one terrified family after another seeks her advice. Sandy says she'll keep fighting. "No matter what, no matter Trump, no matter Mnuchin, no matter Otting, in the end I feel like we will prevail," she says.

But Sandy knows that the real solution won't come from helping one person at a time. Our collective aspirations for familial wealth and shared prosperity cannot rest on the shoulders of an indefatigable gadfly. The country needs substantial, systemic change. The architecture of global finance that's been rigged dramatically in favor of the Homewreckers has to be knocked back in favor of the public. The American Dream is at stake.

ACKNOWLEDGMENTS

Any set of thank-yous for this book has to start with my parents, Stan and Marsha Glantz. They taught essential values—thrift, perseverance, passion, productivity, and generosity—that are at the heart of who I am. Thank you for imparting a thirst for justice. And thank you for contributing to help Ngoc and me live the American Dream. Thank you to my grandmother, Evelyn Kramar, and in-laws, Louis and Sophia Nguyen, for the same. Without you, we would probably still be at the mercy of the rental market. All that we have accomplished, all the risks we were able to take that paid off, were made possible by the stability and predictability of the fixed-rate mortgage. Thank you.

Thank you to my wife, Ngoc, a fantastic journalist in her own right, for being an amazing partner. Thank you for putting up with my disappearances while on assignment, and for only occasionally being annoyed when I went on and on about mortgage-backed securities. Thank you to my children, Jacob Mai and Louis Van, for your good cheer and genuine interest in the work. I love you so much.

Thank you to all the editors and managers who supported my reporting on housing and wealth over the past decade, including Sandy Close, Annette Fuentes, Steve Fainaru, Jonathan Weber, Pete Lewis, Mark Katches, Robert Rosenthal, Jim Schachter, Kevin Sullivan, Deborah George, Amanda Pike, and especially Amy Pyle, my boss for six years at Reveal from the Center for Investigative Reporting. Thank you to my new boss, Matt Thompson, and to Reveal's CEO, Christa Scharfenberg, for your support and insight.

Thank you to the Reveal colleagues who worked alongside me on these stories, including Adithya Sambamurthy, Laura Starecheski, Rachel de Leon, David Ritsher, and especially Emmanuel Martinez, my partner for more than a year on redlining reporting, and Katharine Mieszkowski, who decided this book should be called *Homewreckers*, read the manuscript as I wrote it, and is working with me to bring the journalism behind it to millions of radio and podcast listeners. Thank you to my colleagues at partner outlets, including Sara Just and Richard Coolidge at the *PBS NewsHour*, John Barth and Kerri Hoffman at PRX, Meghan Hoyer and Angeliki Kastanis at the Associated Press, and Cindy Galli and her team at ABC News for the trouble we've made together.

Thank you to all the colleagues, friends, editors, and subject matter experts who read drafts of this book and provided feedback, including Shoshana Walter, Bernice Yeung, Bruce Mirken, Jonathan Grotenstein, Maya Abood, Cheryl Devall, Sarah Alvarez, and Mehrsa Baradaran. Thank you to Antonia Juhasz and Kevin Brower for joining me for long writing days and for bearing with me when I interrupted your work to announce a new reporting discovery or turn of phrase. You have been very generous and this book is stronger because of it.

Thank you to the incomparable Beth Macy, the first person I called when I thought there might be a book to be written. "It's a great idea," you said. "Americans care about poor people, but they love to read about rich people." Thank you for your encouragement. Thanks also to Mark Schoofs, another early sounding board, who assured me in 2017 that American readers would still care about Homewreckers in 2019.

Thank you to master agent Anthony Arnove. After fifteen

years, we finally did a book together! Thank you for helping me move this project from idea to proposal, and for finding Geoff Shandler and Custom House. Geoff, I feel very lucky to be working with you. Every time you touch this book, it gets better—what every writer always wants from an editor but what we so rarely get. Thank you for making the prose sing. Thank you to the entire team at HarperCollins, including Phil Bashe, Maureen Cole, Molly Gendell, Kayleigh George, Vedika Khanna, Bonni Leon-Berman, Andrea Molitor, Shelby Peak, Ploy Siripant, Ben Steinberg, and Liate Stehlik, publisher of William Morrow. Thank you to Alan Maass for formatting my footnotes and fact-checking quotes. Without you, I would have missed my deadline.

Thank you to the staff of the John S. Knight Fellowship, which gave me a year away from journalism at Stanford University, without which I would never have had the brain space to write this book. Thank you to Cherrie Moraga and Tobias Wolff for allowing me to audit your playwriting and narrative nonfiction classes. I hope you see your teaching here. Thanks to the Stanford Law School's Policy Lab program, especially Luciana Herman, Beth Van Schaack, and Megan Karsh for introducing me to new ways of thinking. Thank you, Dawn Garcia, for guidance and counseling that has continued for years after the fellowship, and to my fellow fellows, especially Sarah Alvarez, Tonya Mosley, and Liz Gannes, for exploring the questions of real estate and home mortgage lending with me, and to Kristen Muller for being a willing coconspirator. The spark that became this book was lit in a brainstorming session in the JSK Garage.

Thank you to the San Francisco Public Library. Most of this book was written at the Main Library in Civic Center or in the library's incredible network of neighborhood branches (I wrote in at least nine of them). The physical collection is superb with even the most obscure books readily available. Thanks also for your vast digital collection which gave me immediate access to everything from complete e-books and government reports to transcripts of television interviews and earnings calls—all from the comfort of my laptop computer. Thank you for keeping access to information free.

Thank you to all writers and academics whose work I drew on while writing *Homewreckers*. All the books, articles, and reports I cite are listed in the bibliography and endnotes, but I want call out a few people whose work has been especially insightful and empowering. Thank you to Elora Raymond for your 2016 report on evictions by corporate landlords in Atlanta, and for all the conversations we've had over the last two years about concentrated property ownership. Thank you to Gwenda Blair for nerding out with me as I sought to recast your seminal research on Fred Trump's real estate empire into the twenty-first-century Homewreckers context. Thank you to Michael Kranish and Marc Fisher for creating an online library of key documents you gathered for your own book, *Trump Revealed*, which has allowed members of the public, including me, to easily read them and find other interesting passages. Thank you to Robert Nelson, LaDale Winling, and all the other scholars involved in the "Mapping Inequality" project, which has been collecting and digitizing original source documents on redlining in New Deal America. Thank you to Lance Williams for walking by my desk one day and depositing a copy of Edith Elmer Wood's 1931 book *Recent Trends in American Housing*, which you picked up at a garage sale. Reading it fundamentally reframed the way I saw the first half of this book and set me off on a whole new avenue of reporting. Thank you to Kevin Stein for teaching me about the Home Mortgage Disclosure Act, and for telling me to watch out for OneWest Bank even before Donald Trump nominated Steve Mnuchin to be his treasury secretary. Thank you, Kevin, for introducing me to Sandy Jolley.

Finally, a huge note of appreciation to all the families struggling with financial pain who agreed to share their stories. It is no fun to talk to a reporter, I know, especially when he wants you to relive and fully document the unhappiest moments of your life. Thank you to Marcus Butler, who did not hang up when I called him cold from San Francisco to ask him about a house his family no longer owned and then allowed me to visit him in his apartment. Thank you to Jessica Butler for continuing the conversation. I hope you see your family in this story. Thank you to Sandy Jolley for the many, many hours we spent together. Thank you for opening bankers boxes full of documents in your garage and for walking me through each and every beat of your story. Thank you for introducing me to your neighbors, your friends, and the other members of your family. You have been incredibly generous with your time, and I hope you see the result of all that time in this book.

A NOTE ON THE SOURCES

This book is a work of journalism, based on a combination of interviews, court documents, securities filings, and other personal and government records. Wherever possible, I have included the attribution in the text itself. In cases where I am relying on the work of others—whether a book, article, or government report—I have cited it here. Details of Sandy Jolley's whistleblower complaint and her decadelong fight to keep her family home are drawn from her personal papers, depositions in the case, and court transcripts. Because she fought so hard, there were many boxes of documents. I am grateful for her cooperation.

NOTES

Preface: The American Dream

1. *Making Home Affordable Program: Servicer Provider Report Through March 2010* (Washington, DC: US Department of the Treasury, April 14, 2010), www.treasury.gov/initiatives/financial-stability/reports/Documents/Mar%20MHA%20Public%20041410%20TO%20CLEAR.PDF.

2. Debbie Gruenstein Bocian, Wei Li, and Keith S. Ernst, *Foreclosures by Race and Ethnicity: The Demographics of a Crisis* (Durham, NC: Center for Responsible Lending, June 18, 2010), www.responsiblelending.org/mortgage-lending/research-analysis/foreclosures-by-race-and-ethnicity.pdf.

3. ProPublica, Bailout Tracker: Tracking Every Dollar and Every Recipient, s.v. "Bank of America," https://projects.propublica.org/bailout/entities/27-bank-of-america.

4. Steve King, *Who Owns Your Neighborhood? The Role of Investors in Post-Foreclosure Oakland* (Oakland: Urban Strategies Council, June 2012), www.neighborhoodindicators.org/sites/default/files/publications/whoownsyourneighborhood_report.pdf.

5. Ibid.

6. "Table 1. Median Value of Assets for Households, by Type of Asset Owned and Selected Characteristics: 2014," downloaded from the US Census Bureau website, last revised September 17, 2018, www.census.gov/data/tables/2014/demo/wealth/wealth-asset-ownership.html.

7. Diane Whitmore Schanzenbach et al., *Where Does All the Money Go: Shifts in Household Spending over the Past 30 Years* (Washington, DC: Brookings Institution, June 2, 2016), www.brookings.edu/wp-content/uploads/2016/08/where_does_all_the_money_go.pdf.

8. James Truslow Adams, *The Epic of America* (Boston: Little, Brown, 1931; Boston: Little, Brown, 1959), 404. Citations refer to 1959 edition.

9. Ibid., 416.

10. Ibid.

11. "Greeley, Waving West Past Washington," *Morning Edition*, National Public Radio online, July 13, 2005, www.npr.org/templates/story/story.php?storyId=4751791.

12. George K. Holms and John S. Lord, *Report on Farms and Homes:*

Proprietorship and Indebtedness in the United States at the Eleventh Census: 1890 (Washington, DC: Government Printing Office, 1896), available at www .census.gov/prod/www/decennial.html.

13. US Census Bureau, *Historical Statistics of the United States, Colonial Times to 1970*, 2 vols. (Washington, DC: Government Printing Office, 1975, 1976), P, 646, Series N 238-245.

14. Jacob Riis, *How the Other Half Lives: Studies Among the Tenements in New York* (New York: Penguin, 1997), 27.

15. Ibid., 22.

16. Ibid., 209.

17. Ibid., 219.

18. Holms and Lord, *Report on Farms and Homes*, table 98.

19. Eugene V. Debs, "The Majority Report," *New Times* (Minneapolis) (May 26, 1917), 4, www.marxists.org/archive/debs/works/1917/majority.htm.

20. Emmanuel Saez and Gabriel Zucman, "Wealth Inequality in the United States since 1913: Evidence from Capitalized Income Tax Data," *Quarterly Journal of Economics* 131, no. 2 (May 2016): 519–78, https://eml.berkeley .edu/~saez.

21. Richard Rothstein, *The Color of Law: A Forgotten History of How Our Government Segregated America* (New York: W. W. Norton, 2017), 60.

22. Edith Elmer Wood, *Recent Trends in American Housing* (New York: Macmillan, 1931), 185.

23. Michael A. Hiltzik, *The New Deal: A Modern History* (New York: Free Press, 2011), 70.

24. Wood, *American Housing*, 188.

25. US Census Bureau, *Historical Statistics*, Pg. 646, Series N 238-245.

26. US Census Bureau, *Quarterly Residential Vacancies and Homeownership, Fourth Quarter 2018*, February 28, 2019, www.census.gov/housing/hvs/files /currenthvspress.pdf.

27. Donald Trump, *How to Build a Fortune: Your Plan for Success from the World's Most Famous Businessman* (New York: Trump University, 2006), Audible audiobook.

28. Kyle Peterson, "Trump Entertainment Files for Bankruptcy," Reuters online, last modified February 17, 2009, www.reuters.com/article/industry-us -trumpentertainment-bankruptc-idUSTRE51G3PP20090217.

Chapter 1: The Salesman

1. Kenneth Harney, "A Reverse Mortgage Shocker: $58,000 Loan, $765,000 Payoff," *Baltimore Sun* online, January 20, 2002, www.baltimoresun.com /news/bs-xpm-2002-01-20-0201180216-story.html.

2. IndyMac Bancorp, "Form 10-K: Annual Report, 2005," filed with US

Securities and Exchange Commission, March 1, 2006, www.sec.gov/Archives /edgar/data/773468/000095012906002125/a17844e10vk.htm; IndyMac Bancorp, "Form 10-K: Annual Report, 2006," filed with US Securities and Exchange Commission, March 1, 2007, www.sec.gov/Archives/edgar/data /773468/000095013407004510/v27665e10vk.htm; "Safety and Soundness: Material Loss Review of IndyMac Bank, FSB," US Department of the Treasury, February 26, 2009, www.treasury.gov/about/organizational-structure/ig /Documents/oig09032.pdf.

3. IndyMac Bancorp, "IndyMac Completes Acquisition of Financial Freedom," press release, July 16, 2004, available on BusinessWire.com, www .businesswire.com/news/home/20040716005371/en/IndyMac-Completes -Acquisition-Financial-Freedom.

4. IndyMac Bancorp, "Form 10-K: Annual Report, 2005," filed with US Securities and Exchange Commission, March 1, 2006, www.sec.gov/Archives /edgar/data/773468/000095012906002125/a17844e10vk.htm; IndyMac Bancorp, "Form 10-K: Annual Report, 2007," filed with US Securities and Exchange Commission, February 29, 2008, www.sec.gov/Archives/edgar /data/773468/000095014808000053/v38189e10vk.htm.

5. Federal Deposit Insurance Corporation, "Fact Sheet: FDIC Sale of IndyMac FSB," press release PR-1-2009, last modified January 29, 2009, www.fdic.gov /news/news/press/2009/pr09001a.html.

6. Steve Bergsman, "Big Mac," *Mortgage Banking*, Mortgage Bankers Association, April 2001, 50–57.

7. IndyMac Bancorp, "IndyMac Signs Long-Term Contract with High-Performing CEO, Michael Perry; New Contract Structured as Pay-for-Performance Arrangement," press release, September 22, 2006, available on BusinessWire, www.businesswire.com/news/home/20060922005111/en/IndyMac-Signs-Long -Term-Contract-High-Performing-CEO-Michael.

8. *It's a Wonderful Life*, directed by Frank Capra, written by Frances Goodrich, Albert Hackett, and Capra, featuring James Stewart (1946, Liberty Films).

9. *Safety and Soundness: Material Loss Review of IndyMac Bank, FSB* (Washington, DC: Office of Inspector General, US Department of the Treasury, February 26, 2009), www.treasury.gov/about/organizational -structure/ig/Documents/oig09032.pdf.

10. Joseph E. Stiglitz, *Freefall: America's Free Markets, and the Sinking of the World Economy* (New York: W. W. Norton, 2010), 91.

11. "Moody's Rates RAST 2006-A3CB Alt-A Mortgage Deal," Moody's Investors Service, April 10, 2006, www.moodys.com/research/MOODYS-RATES -RAST-2006-A3CB-ALT-A-MORTGAGE-DEAL—PR_111316.

12. "Moody's Asia Pacific Desktop Reference," Moody's Investors Service, www .moodys.com/sites/products/ProductAttachments/AP075378_1_1408_KI.pdf.

13. Tripp et al. v. IndyMac Bancorp et al., CV 07–1635-GW (VBK) (US District Court, C.D. California, Western Division), filed March 12, 2007. Third amended complaint filed June 6, 2008.

14. IndyMac Bancorp, "Form 10-K: Annual Report, 2006," filed with US Securities and Exchange Commission, March 1, 2007, www.sec.gov/Archives /edgar/data/773468/000095013407004510/v27665e10vk.htm; IndyMac Bancorp, "Form 10-K: Annual Report, 2007," filed with US Securities and Exchange Commission, February 29, 2008, www.sec.gov/Archives/edgar /data/773468/000095014808000053/v38189e10vk.htm.

15. Sheila Bair, *Bull by the Horns: Fighting to Save Main Street from Wall Street and Wall Street from Itself* (New York: Free Press, 2012), 75.

Chapter 2: A Squandered Opportunity

1. Dean Baker, *Plunder and Blunder: The Rise and Fall of the Bubble Economy* (Sausalito, CA: PoliPointPress), 93–94.

2. Alex J. Pollock, *Crisis Intervention in Housing Finance: The Home Owners' Loan Corporation*, American Enterprise Institute, December 31, 2007, www .aei.org/publication/crisis-intervention-in-housing-finance.

3. Hiltzik, *New Deal*, 70.

4. Ibid., 71.

5. Home Loan Bank Board, Housing and Home Finance Agency, *Final Report to the Congress of the United States Relating to the Home Owners' Loan Corporation: 1933–1951* (Washington, DC: Government Printing Office, 1952), https://fraser.stlouisfed.org/files/docs/publications/holc/hlc_final _report_1952.pdf.

6. Hiltzik, *New Deal*, 71.

7. "Home Owners Hailed in Roosevelt Note: Make Nation 'Unconquerable,' He Tells Savings League," *New York Times* online, November 17, 1942, www .nytimes.com/1942/11/17/archives/home-owners-hailed-in-roosevelt-note -make-nation-unconquerable-he.html.

8. Peter J. Elmer and Steven A. Seelig, "The Rising Long-Term Trend of Single-Family Mortgage Foreclosure Rates" (working paper 98-2, Federal Deposit Insurance Corporation, October 5, 1998), www.fdic.gov/bank/analytical /working/wp98–02.pdf.

9. Alan Blinder, *After the Music Stopped: The Financial Crisis, the Response and the Work Ahead* (New York: Penguin, 2014), 326.

10. Howell E. Jackson, "Build a Better Bailout: The Paulson Plan Should Target Bad Loans, Not Burned Investors," *Christian Science Monitor* online, September 25, 2008, www.csmonitor.com/Commentary/Opinion/2008/0925 /p09s02-coop.html.

11. Alan S. Blinder, "From the New Deal, a Way out of a Mess," *New York Times*

online, February 24, 2008, www.nytimes.com/2008/02/24/business/24view
.html.

12. Blinder, *After the Music Stopped*, 326.

Chapter 3: A Run on the Bank

1. Bloomberg News, "Senator Asks Regulators to Probe the Financial Health of IndyMac," *Los Angeles Times* online, June 27, 2008, www.latimes.com /archives/la-xpm-2008-jun-27-fi-indy27-story.html.

2. Stephen Bernard, "Senator Says His IndyMac Letter Wasn't a Factor in Bank's Failure," Associated Press, July 14, 2008, www.pressrepublican.com /news/local_news/sen-schumer-defends-comments-on-indymac-collapse /article_00ab7b38-ffa9-50d2-9d53-51ee6ffda9fb.html.

3. *Safety and Soundness: Material Loss Review of IndyMac Bank, FSB* (Washington, DC: Office of Inspector General, US Department of the Treasury, March 4, 2009, www.treasury.gov/about/organizational-structure /ig/Documents/oig09032.pdf.

4. Federal Deposit Insurance Corporation, "FDIC Establishes IndyMac Federal Bank FSB as Successor to IndyMac Bank FSB," press release PR-56-2008, last modified July 14, 2008, www.fdic.gov/news/news/press/2008/pr08056.html.

5. "Unemployment in July 2008," *Economics Daily* online, Bureau of Labor Statistics, US Department of Labor, last modified August 4, 2008, www.bls .gov/opub/ted/2008/aug/wk1/art01.htm.

6. Louise Story, "Regulators Seize IndyMac After a Run on the Bank," *New York Times*, July 12, 2008, C5.

7. "FDIC Takes Over Indymac," *The Early Show*, aired July 14, 2008, on CBS, www.youtube.com/watch?v=Na5tsDaNXWs.

8. Bair, *Bull by the Horns*, 81.

9. Federal Deposit Insurance Corporation, "Failed Bank Information: Information for Miami Valley Bank, Lakeview, OH," last modified September 12, 2016, www .fdic.gov/bank/individual/failed/miamivalley.html.

10. Federal Deposit Insurance Corporation v. Perry, CV 11–5561 ODW (MRWx), (US District Court, C.D. California, Western Division), filed July 6, 2011, http://aabd.org/wp-content/uploads/2014/03/100111_FDIC-Indymac.pdf.

11. "Settlement and Release Agreement," FDIC v. Perry, www.fdic.gov/about /freedom/plsa/ca_indymacperry.pdf.

12. Max Abelson and Zachary Mider, "Trump's Top Fundraiser Eyes the Deal of a Lifetime," Bloomberg, last modified August 31, 2016, www.bloomberg.com /news/articles/2016–08–31/steven-mnuchin-businessweek.

13. Ibid.

14. Ibid.

15. Rachel Calnek-Sugin, Chris Hays, and Arya Sundaram, "Yale Men in the

Cabinet," *New Journal* online, February 2017, www.thenewjournalatyale
.com/2017/02/yale-men-cabinet.

16. Advertisement, *Yale Daily News*, October 19, 1982, 6.

17. Charlotte Libov, "Commuting by Helicopter," *New York Times* online,
August 10, 1986, www.nytimes.com/1986/08/10/nyregion/commuting-by
-helicopter.html.

18. David Zigas, "Freddie Mac Tests Foreign Waters with Securities Sale,"
American Banker, September 26, 1985, 16.

19. "Mortgages Back Eurobond Issues; Asian Loan Volume Stagnates," *Wall Street
Journal*, January 15, 1985, 1.

20. David LaGesse, "Breakthrough Seen in Resale of Car Loans: Salomon Brothers
Creates Secondary Market Product," *American Banker*, February 7, 1985, 1.

21. David Dayen, *Chain of Title: How Three Ordinary Americans Uncovered Wall
Street's Great Foreclosure Fraud* (New York: New Press, 2016), 24; John J.
McConnell and Stephen A. Buser, "The Origins and Evolution of the Market
for Mortgage-Backed Securities," *Annual Review of Financial Economics* 3
(2011): 173–92, available at https://krannert.purdue.edu/faculty/mcconnell
/publications/The-Origins-and-Evolution-of-the-Market.pdf.

Chapter 4: Life on Park Avenue

1. Robin Pogrebin, "At 80, Mnuchin Remains a Passionate Promoter of Postwar
Art," *New York Times* online, October 25, 2013, www.nytimes.com/2013
/10/27/arts/artsspecial/at-80-mnuchin-remains-a-passionate-promoter-of
-postwar-art.html.

2. Jonathan Fuerbringer, "Michael P. Mortara, 51, a Developer of Mortgage-
Backed Securities," *New York Times* online, November 16, 2000, www
.nytimes.com/2000/11/16/business/michael-p-mortara-51-a-developer-of
-mortgage-backed-securities.html.

3. Michael Gross, *740 Park: The Story of the World's Richest Apartment Building*
(New York: Broadway Books, 2005), 490.

4. Joanne Lipman, "Young Founder of ESL Partners Uses His Drive to Make
Millions," *Wall Street Journal* (Asia edition), July 4, 1991, 9.

5. Lipman, "Young Founder of ESL Partners"; Patricia Sellers, "Eddie Lampert:
The Best Investor of His Generation," CNN Money online, last modified
February 6, 2006, https://money.cnn.com/2006/02/03/news/companies
/investorsguide_lampert/index.htm.

6. Geraldine Fabrikant, "Personal Business; Big Returns, Minus the
Pleasantries," *New York Times* online, February 17, 2002, www.nytimes
.com/2002/02/17/business/personal-business-big-returns-minus-the
-pleasantries.html.

7. Mitchell Pacelle and Amy Merrick, "A Kmart Debt Holder Pushed Quick Exit

from Chapter 11," *Wall Street Journal* online, May 6, 2003, www.wsj.com /articles/SB105216829484994800.

8. Sears Holdings, "Edward S. Lampert Appointed Chairman of the Board, Kmart Holding Corporation," press release, May 6, 2003, https://searsholdings.com /press-releases/pr/1435.

9. Sears Holding Corporation, "Form 10-K: Annual Report for the Fiscal Year Ended January 28, 2006 ," filed with US Securities and Exchange Commission, March 17, 2006, www.sec.gov/Archives/edgar /data/1310067/000104746906003414/a2168332z10-k.htm; Sears Holding Company, "Form 10-K: Annual Report for the Fiscal Year Ended January 28, 2017," filed with US Securities and Exchange Commission, March 21, 2017, www.sec.gov/Archives/edgar/data/1310067/000131006717000005 /shld201610k.htm.

10. Senate Comm. on Finance, *Anticipated Nomination of Steven Terner Mnuchin* (Washington, DC: Government Publishing Office, 2017), available at www .govinfo.gov/content/pkg/CHRG-115shrg29928/html/CHRG-115shrg29928.htm.

11. Nathan Bomey, "How Sears CEO Lampert Cashes In as Stores Cash Out," *USA Today* online, March 22, 2017, www.usatoday.com/story/money/2017/03/22 /sears-holdings-ceo-eddie-lampert/99487518.

12. Sears Holdings, "Form 10-K: Annual Report, 2018," filed with US Securities and Exchange Commission, March 23, 2018, https://searsholdings.com/docs /investor/SHC_2017_Form_10-K.pdf.

13. Lauren Hirsch, "Sears Sues Former CEO Eddie Lampert, Treasury Secretary Mnuchin, and Others for Alleged 'Thefts' of Billions from Retailer," CNBC online, last modified April 18, 2019, www.cnbc.com/2019/04/18 /sears-sues-eddie-lampert-steven-mnuchin-others-for-alleged-thefts.html; Abha Bhattarai, "Sears Is Suing Steven Mnuchin and Other Former Board Members," *Washington Post* online, April 19, 2019, www.washingtonpost .com/business/2019/04/19/sears-is-suing-steven-mnuchin-other-former -board-members.

14. Laura Zumbach, "Sears Sues Former CEO Edward Lampert, Claiming He Stripped $2 billion in Assets as It Headed to Bankruptcy," *Chicago Tribune*, April 18, 2019, www.chicagotribune.com/business/ct-biz-sears-sues-lampert -esl-bankruptcy-20190418-story.html.

15. Deborah Brewster, "Soros Fund Will Provide Loans to Companies," *Financial Times* (UK edition), September 3, 2003, 1.

16. "Soros Private Equity Officials Prep Spin-off," *Alternative Investment News*, October 11, 2004, 2.

17. "Weddings: Heather Crosby, Steven Mnuchin," *New York Times* online, September 26, 1999, www.nytimes.com/1999/09/26/style/weddings-heather -crosby-steven-mnuchin.html.

18. Gross, *740 Park*, 490.

19. Ibid.

20. Greg Farrell and Henny Sender, "The Shaming of John Thain," *Financial Times* online, March 13, 2009, www.ft.com/content/c1b3ac7e-0ec1-11de -ba10-0000779fd2ac.

21. Andrew Clark, "Wall Street's SuperThain Felled by Excess in Antiques and Bank Buying," *Guardian* (US edition) online, January 23, 2009, www .theguardian.com/business/2009/jan/23/useconomy-globalrecession.

22. Vivian Marino, "A $39.5 Million Penthouse at 740 Park Avenue," *New York Times* online, April 27, 2018, www.nytimes.com/2018/04/27/realestate/a-39-5 -million-penthouse-at-740-park-avenue.html.

23. "The Blue Period," *Women's Wear Daily*, October 20, 2005, 4.

24. Patrick McMullan, "Donald Trump and Heather Mnuchin Attend City Harvest's 12th Annual Practical Magic Ball," photo, Getty Images online, April 4, 2006, www.gettyimages.com/license/605919896.

25. "Socialgenealogy," photo of Heather Mnuchin, *Women's Wear Daily*, November 14, 2005, 42.

26. "Expert Shopping Tips," *Harper's Bazaar*, April 2006, 120.

27. Nicole LaPorte and Gabriel Snyder, "Fox Kneads Dune Dough," *Variety* online, January 15, 2006, https://variety.com/2006/film/markets-festivals/fox-kneads -dune-dough-1117936184; Rachel Abrams, "Fox, Dune to Extend Prosperous Pic Partnership," *Variety* online, August 14, 2012, https://variety.com/2012 /film/news/fox-dune-to-extend-prosperous-pic-partnership-1118057787.

28. Manohla Dargis, "Norsemen of the Apocalypse," *New York Times* online, April 12, 2007, www.nytimes.com/2007/04/12/movies/13path.html; Mick LaSalle, "An Army of Giant Vikings? No Sweat. He Has a Sword," review of *Pathfinder*, directed by Marcus Nispel, *San Francisco Chronicle*, April 13, 2007, www.sfgate.com/movies/article/An-army-of-giant-Vikings-No-sweat -He-has-a-2602829.php.

29. Kerima Greene, "Warren Buffett, Mark Cuban Get 'Entourage' Movie Cameos," CNBC online, last modified June 6, 2015, www.cnbc.com/2015/06/05 /entourage-plays-buffett-cuban-for-laughs.html.

Chapter 5: The Vultures Circle

1. William D. Cohan, "Checkmate for a Wall Street Wizard?," *Fortune* online, last modified September 2, 2009, http://archive.fortune.com/2009/08/31 /magazines/fortune/chris_flowers.fortune/index.htm.

2. Martin Arnold, "J. Christopher Flowers: After the Storm, the Deals," *Financial Times* online, July 20, 2014, www.ft.com/content/770fbcc6-0cdb-11e4-90fa -00144feabdc0.

3. Eric Lipton, "As Investors Circle Ailing Banks, Fed Sets Limits," *New York Times* online, May 5, 2009, www.nytimes.com/2009/05/06/business/06equity.html.

4. "The World's Billionaires: #321, J. Christopher Flowers," *Forbes* online, March 5, 2008, www.forbes.com/lists/2008/10/billionaires08_J-Christopher -Flowers_6MBS.html.

5. Braden Keil, "Gimme Shelter," *New York Post* online, October 12, 2006, https://nypost.com/2006/10/12/gimme-shelter-90.

6. Jonathan Stempel, "Ameriquest Closes, Citigroup Buys Mortgage Assets," Reuters online, last modified August 31, 2007, www.reuters.com/article /us-citigroup-ameriquest/ameriquest-closes-citigroup-buys-mortgage-assets -idUSN3128419320070901.

7. IndyMac Bancorp, "Form 10-K: Annual Report, 2007," filed with US Securities and Exchange Commission, February 29, 2008, www.sec.gov/Archives/edgar /data/773468/000095014808000053/v38189e10vk.htm.

8. "Ameriquest Acquires Naming Rights to Ballpark in Arlington," *Dallas Business Journal* online, May 7, 2004, www.bizjournals.com/dallas/stories /2004/05/03/daily40.html.

9. "Ameriquest to Be Super Sponsor," CNN Money online, last modified October 7, 2004, https://money.cnn.com/2004/10/07/news/midcaps /ameriquest_superbowl/index.htm.

10. Mike Hudson and E. Scott Reckard, "Workers Say Lender Ran 'Boiler Rooms,'" *Los Angeles Times* online, February 4, 2005, www.latimes.com/business/la-fi -ameriquest4feb0405-story.html.

11. Ibid.

12. California Department of Justice, "Attorney General Lockyer Announces $325 Million Settlement with Ameriquest to Resolve National Predatory Lending Case," press release, January 23, 2006, https://oag.ca.gov/news/press-releases /attorney-general-lockyer-announces-325-million-settlement-ameriquest -resolve.

13. E. Scott Reckard, "Ameriquest Loan Volume Plunges," *Los Angeles Times* online, May 6, 2006, http://articles.latimes.com/2006/may/06/business/fi -ameriquest6.

14. Reuters, "Ameriquest, a Subprime Lender, Is Closing," *New York Times* online, August 31, 2007, www.nytimes.com/2007/08/31/business/reuters-citi.html.

15. Eric Lipton and David K. Kirkpatrick, "Veterans of 1990s Bailout of U.S. Thrifts Stand to Profit from Bank Crisis," *New York Times* online, November 29, 2008, www.nytimes.com/2008/12/29/business/worldbusiness/29iht -bank.4.18983479.html.

16. Federal Deposit Insurance Corporation, "Remarks by FDIC Chairman Sheila C. Bair on the IndyMac Loan Modification Announcement," August 20, 2008, www.fdic.gov/news/news/speeches/archives/2008/chairman/spaug2008.html.

17. Amy Martinez et al., "WaMu Shares Plunge 35 Percent," *Seattle Times* online, July 15, 2008, www.seattletimes.com/business/wamu-shares-plunge-35 -percent.

18. Bair, *Bull by the Horns*, 84.
19. IndyMac Bancorp, "Form 10-K: Annual Report, 2007," filed with US Securities and Exchange Commission, February 29, 2008, www.sec.gov/Archives/edgar /data/773468/000095014808000053/v38189e10vk.htm.
20. Federal Deposit Insurance Corporation, "FDIC Announces Availability of IndyMac Loan Modification Model," press release, November 20, 2008, www .fdic.gov/news/news/press/2008/pr08121.html.
21. Federal Deposit Insurance Corporation, "Fact Sheet: FDIC Sale of IndyMac FSB," press release, last modified January 29, 2009, www.fdic.gov/news/news /press/2009/pr09001a.html.
22. Gregory Zuckerman, *The Greatest Trade Ever: The Behind-the-Scenes Story of How John Paulson Defied Wall Street and Made Financial History* (New York: Broadway Books, 2009), 2.
23. Ibid., 23.
24. Lauren Schuker, "Luxury Homes of Hedge Fund Manager John Paulson," *Wall Street Journal* online, video, 3:27, October 18, 2012, www.wsj.com/video /luxury-homes-of-hedge-fund-manager-john-paulson/72EF56EB-EA99-45F7 -9C3B-A6795F3314F3.html.
25. Christina S. N. Lewis, "Hedge Funds' Paulson Trades Up in Hamptons," *Wall Street Journal* online, April 11, 2008, www.wsj.com/articles /SB120786983098906375.
26. Peter Elkind, "Rock Bottom," *Texas Monthly*, June 1989.
27. Elkind, "Rock Bottom."
28. Kathleen Day, *S&L Hell: The People and the Politics Behind the $1 Trillion Savings and Loan Scandal* (New York: W. W. Norton, 1993), 301–302.
29. Ibid.
30. Elkind, "Rock Bottom."
31. Seth Lubove, "A Hundred Horses Are Ford's Pride After Flipping Tainted Banks," Bloomberg, last modified August 7, 2012, www.bloomberg.com/news /articles/2012-08-08/a-hundred-horses-are-ford-s-pride-after-flipping -tainted-banks.
32. Ibid.

Chapter 7: Foreclosure Machine

1. OneWest Bank Group, "Investor Group Completes Acquisition of IndyMac Assets," press release, March 19, 2009, available at BusinessWire, on www .businesswire.com/news/home/20090319006355/en/Investor-Group -Completes-Acquisition-IndyMac-Assets.
2. Katherine Clarke, "Beverly Hills Home Linked to Treasury Secretary Steve Mnuchin Wants $12M," *Real Deal* online, last modified June 14, 2017, https:// therealdeal.com/la/2017/06/14/beverly-hills-home-linked-to-treasury -secretary-steve-mnuchin-wants-12m.

3. Federal Deposit Insurance Corporation, "FDIC Closes Sale of Indymac Federal Bank, Pasadena, California," press release, March 19, 2009, www.fdic .gov/news/news/press/2009/pr09042.html.
4. "Shared-Loss Agreement," Federal Deposit Insurance Corporation, www.fdic .gov/about/freedom/indymacsharedlossagrmt.pdf; "Reverse Mortgage Shared -Loss Agreement," Federal Deposit Insurance Corporation, www.fdic.gov /bank/individual/failed/indymac-reversemtg-sharedlossagreement.pdf.
5. Federal Deposit Insurance Corporation, "Bid Summary, IndyMac Federal Bank FSB, March 19, 2009," last modified May 11, 2010, www.fdic.gov/bank /individual/failed/indymac-bid-summary.html.
6. Neil Barsky, "Trump Agreement with Holders Hinges on Improving Results of Taj Mahal," *Wall Street Journal*, November 19, 1990, A3.
7. Reuters, "Chapter 11 for Taj Mahal," *New York Times* online, July 18, 1991, www.nytimes.com/1991/07/18/business/chapter-11-for-taj-mahal.html.
8. Hilary Rosenberg, *The Vulture Investors: The Winners and Losers of the Great American Bankruptcy Feeding Frenzy* (New York: Harper Business, 1992), 288.
9. Rosemary Batt and Eileen Appelbaum, "Who Is Wilbur Ross?," *American Prospect* online, last modified July 3, 2017, http://prospect.org/article/who -wilbur-ross.
10. Federal Deposit Insurance Corporation, "BankUnited Acquires the Banking Operations of BankUnited, FSB," press release PR-72-2009, last modified January 26, 2010, www.fdic.gov/news/news/press/2009/pr09072.html.
11. Ibid.
12. Financial statements for: BankUnited, FSB, May 21, 2009–December 31, 2017; First Federal Bank of California, December 18, 2009–December 31, 2017; IndyMac Federal Bank FSB, July 11, 2008–December 31, 2009; available at www.documentcloud.org/documents/5783346-BankUnited-Loss-Share.html.
13. Wilbur L. Ross Jr. to Federal Deposit Insurance Corporation, "FDIC Proposed Rules Against Private Equity," n.d., available at www.documentcloud.org /documents/5783896-Ross-Letter-FDIC.html.
14. Steven T. Mnuchin and Terrence Laughlin to Sheila Bair, "Re: Proposed Statement of Policy on Qualifications for Failed Bank Acquisitions," July 21, 2009, available at www.documentcloud.org/documents/5783897-Mnuchin -OneWest-Letter-to-Bair.html.
15. Michael Crittenden and Peter Lattman, "Rules Eased on Bank Buyouts," *Wall Street Journal* online, August 27, 2009, www.wsj.com/articles /SB125131789672261583.
16. Thomas Kupper, "La Jolla Bank Fails; OneWest Takes Over," *San Diego Union- Tribune* online, February 19, 2010, www.sandiegouniontribune.com/sdut-la -jolla-bank-seized-by-federal-regulators-2010feb19-htmlstory.html.
17. Financial statements for: IndyMac Federal Bank FSB, July 11, 2008– December 31, 2017; LaJolla Bank, FSB, February 19, 2010–December 31,

2017; www.documentcloud.org/documents/5783901-IndyMac-LJB-Loss -Share.html.

18. Robbie Whelan, "Foreclosure? Not So Fast," *Wall Street Journal*, October 4, 2010, A3.

19. Deposition of Erica A. Johnson-Seck, July 9, 2009, in IndyMac Federal Bank v. Israel A. Machado et al., 50 2008 CA 037322XXXX (15th Circuit Court, Florida), available at www.documentcloud.org/documents/5783907-Onewest -Bank-Erica-Johnson-Seck-Deposition.html.

20. Alan Johnson and Jill Riepenhoff, "Trump Treasury Pick Mnuchin Misled Senate on Foreclosures, Ohio Cases Show," *Columbus (OH) Dispatch*, January 29, 2017, www.dispatch.com/news/20170129/trump-treasury-pick -mnuchin-misled-senate-on-foreclosures-ohio-cases-show.

21. "National Mortgage Settlement," US Department of Justice, last revised January 18, 2017, www.justice.gov/ust/national-mortgage-settlement.

22. 26 U.S. Code § 121, "Exclusion of Gain from Sale of Principal Residence," rev. rul. 2014–2, www.irs.gov/pub/irs-drop/rr-14–02.pdf.

23. Laurie Goodman and Maia Woluchem, *National Mortgage Settlement: Lessons Learned* (Washington, DC: Urban Institute, April 15, 2014), www .urban.org/sites/default/files/publication/22526/413095-National-Mortgage -Settlement.PDF.

24. "Consent Order," regarding OneWest Bank, Office of Thrift Supervision, docket no. 18129, order no. WN-11–011, April 13, 2011, www.occ.gov/static /ots/misc-docs/consent-orders-97665.pdf.

25. California Department of Justice, "Attorney General Kamala D. Harris Announces Creation of Mortgage Fraud Strike Force to Protect Homeowners," press release, May 23, 2011, https://oag.ca.gov/news/press-releases/attorney -general-kamala-d-harris-announces-creation-mortgage-fraud-strike-force.

26. Nicholas G. Campins et al. to Frances T. Grunder et al., memorandum, "Executive Summary: Request for Authorization to File Action Against OneWest Bank," January 18, 2013, California Department of Justice, available at www.documentcloud.org/documents/3250383-OneWest-Package-Memo .html.

27. Joe Garofoli and Tal Kopan, "Kamala Harris' Mortgage Meltdown Record Under Scrutiny as Campaign Heats Up," *San Francisco Chronicle* online, April 1, 2019, www.sfchronicle.com/politics/article/Kamala-Harris-mortgage -meltdown-record-under-13730708.php.

28. Campins et al. to Grunder et al., January 18, 2013, "Request for Authorization."

29. David Dayen, "Treasury Nominee Steve Mnuchin's Bank Accused of 'Widespread Misconduct' in Leaked Memo," The Intercept, last modified January 3, 2017, https://theintercept.com/2017/01/03/treasury-nominee-steve -mnuchins-bank-accused-of-widespread-misconduct-in-leaked-memo.

Chapter 8: ColFin AI-CA5 LLC

1. "Statistical Brief: Who Owns the Nation's Rental Properties?," US Bureau of the Census online, March 1996, www.census.gov/prod/1/statbrief/sb96_01.pdf.

2. US Census Bureau, Rental Housing Finance Survey, s.v. "Updated 2015 Summary Tables," www.census.gov/programs-surveys/rhfs/news-and-updates/updates/update5.html, analysis by the author.

3. "Advisory to Financial Institutions and Real Estate Firms and Professionals," US Department of the Treasury, Financial Crimes Enforcement Network Advisory, August 22, 2017, www.fincen.gov/sites/default/files/advisory/2017-08-22/Risk%20in%20Real%20Estate%20Advisory_FINAL%20508%20Tuesday%20%28002%29.pdf.

4. Matthew Shaer, "How Far Will Sean Hannity Go?" *New York Times Magazine* online, November 28, 2017, www.nytimes.com/2017/11/28/magazine/how-far-will-sean-hannity-go.html.

5. Ibid.

6. Hayley Cuccinello, "Trump Bump: How Sean Hannity Earned $36 Million This Year," *Forbes* online, last modified July 16, 2018, www.forbes.com/sites/hayleycuccinello/2018/07/16/sean-hannity-celebrity-100/#1a03ad5e2d93.

7. Tina Nguyen, "Will Sean Hannity's Secret Real Estate Empire Get Him in Trouble at Fox?," *Vanity Fair* online, last modified April 23, 2018, www.vanityfair.com/news/2018/04/sean-hannitys-sketchy-real-estate-empire-get-him-in-trouble-at-fox-news.

8. Jon Swaine, "Michael Cohen Case Shines Light on Sean Hannity's Property Empire," *Guardian* (US edition) online, April 23, 2018, www.theguardian.com/media/2018/apr/22/michael-cohen-sean-hannity-property-real-estate-ben-carson-hud.

9. Ibid.

10. Ibid.

11. "Sean Hannity Responds to Latest Fake News Attack," Hannity.com, last modified April 23, 2018, www.hannity.com/media-room/sean-hannity-responds-to-latest-fake-news-attack.

12. Aaron C. Davis and Shawn Boburg, "At Hannity's Properties in Working-Class Areas, an Aggressive Approach to Rent Collection," *Washington Post* online, May 11, 2018, www.washingtonpost.com/investigations/at-hannitys-properties-in-low-income-areas-an-aggressive-approach-to-rent-collection/2018/05/10/964be4a2-4eea-11e8-84a0-458a1aa9ac0a_story.html.

13. Emily Badger, "Anonymous Owner, L.L.C.: Why It Has Become So Easy to Hide in the Housing Market," *New York Times* online, April 30, 2018, www.nytimes.com/2018/04/30/upshot/anonymous-owner-llc-why-it-has-become-so-easy-to-hide-in-the-housing-market.html.

14. Susan Pace Hamill, "The Story of LLCs: Combining the Best Features of a

Flawed Business Tax Structure," in *Business Tax Stories*, ed. Steven A. Bank and Kirk J. Stark (New York: Foundation Press, 2006), available at www .law.ua.edu/misc/hamill/Chapter%2010--Business%20Tax%20Stories%20 (Foundation).pdf.

15. Global Financial Integrity, "The Library Card Project: The Ease of Forming Anonymous Companies in the United States," March 2019, https://gfintegrity .org/wp-content/uploads/2019/03/GFI-Library-Project_2019.pdf.

Chapter 9: Polo Ponies and Wine

1. Colony Financial, "Form 10-K: Annual Report, 2011," filed with US Securities and Exchange Commission, March 9, 2012, www.sec.gov/Archives/edgar /data/1467076/000119312512105269/d268749d10k.htm.
2. Colony American Homes, "Form S-11: For Registration Under the Securities Act of 1933," filed with US Securities and Exchange Commission, May 2, 2013, www.sec.gov/Archives/edgar/data/1564515/000119312513196404 /d506077ds11.htm.
3. Colony Starwood Homes, "Colony Starwood Homes Announces Closing of $7.7 Billion Merger of Starwood Waypoint Residential Trust with Colony American Homes," press release, January 5, 2016, available at BusinessWire .com, www.businesswire.com/news/home/20160105006880/en/Colony -Starwood-Homes-Announces-Closing-7.7-Billion.
4. Thomas J. Barrack Jr., "Chicago Booth 6th Annual Real Estate Conference: Keynote Address," speech, November 6, 2012, https://vimeo.com/55244828.
5. Ibid.
6. "Tom Barrack of Happy Canyon Vineyard," advertisement, Happy Canyon Vineyard, May 31, 2015, www.youtube.com/watch?v=QyO31Oc7bI0.
7. Zack O'Malley Greenburg, *Michael Jackson, Inc.: The Rise, Fall, and Rebirth of a Billion-Dollar Empire* (New York: Atria Books, 2014), 210–13.
8. Ethan Smith, "Economic Reality Prompts a Makeover at 'Neverland,'" *Wall Street Journal* online, June 13, 2009, www.wsj.com/articles/SB124484259109711019.
9. Peter Kiefer, "Michael Jackson's Neverland Ranch Hits the Market for $67 Million," *Hollywood Reporter* online, March 2, 2017, www.hollywoodreporter .com/news/michael-jacksons-neverland-ranch-hits-market-67-million-982572.
10. Thomas J. Barrack Jr., interview by Ricardo Karam, *Wara'a Al Woojooh*, November 26, 2013, www.youtube.com/watch?v=h5mbRja3piE&vl=en.
11. "A History of the Colorado Coal Field War," Colorado Coal Field War Project, last modified December 7, 2000, www.du.edu/ludlow/cfhist3.html.
12. Barrack, interview by Karam.
13. "Thomas Barrack," obituary, *Los Angeles Times*, July 6–8, 2012, www.legacy .com/obituaries/latimes/obituary.aspx?n=thomas-barrack&pid=158400948.
14. Shawn Tully, "I'm Tom Barrack* and I'm Getting Out," *Fortune* online,

October 31, 2005, http://archive.fortune.com/magazines/fortune/fortune
_archive/2005/10/31/8359143/index.htm.

15. Ibid.

16. 131 Cong. Rec., Government Printing Office, S2977–84 (daily ed. February 21, 1985).

17. Michael Deaver, correspondence for November 1982, box no. 7620, Ronald Reagan Presidential Library, available at www.documentcloud.org /documents/5978994-Barrack-Reagan-Library.html.

18. David D. Kirkpatrick, "Who Is Behind Trump's Links to Arab Princes? A Billionaire Friend," *New York Times* online, June 13, 2018, www.nytimes .com/2018/06/13/world/middleeast/trump-tom-barrack-saudi.html.

19. Nanette Byrnes, "Tom Barrack's Search for Life After Resolution Trust," Bloomberg, last modified May 5, 1996, www.bloomberg.com/news /articles/1996–05–05/tom-barracks-search-for-life-after-resolution-trust.

20. David Henry, "Trump Finds Backer to Pump Up Casino," *USA Today*, January 21, 1997, 3B.

21. "Residential Unit Deed," agreement between Trump CPS LLC and Barrack 59th Street Partners LP, dated May 18, 1998, recorded by New York County Office of the City Register, July 30, 1998, available at www.documentcloud .org/documents/5978919-Barrack-Trump-Property.html.

22. Thomas J. Barrack Jr., speech, Republican National Convention, July 21, 2016, transcript at http://transcripts.cnn.com/TRANSCRIPTS/1607/21/se.02.html.

23. David Landis and Jon Newberry, "Donald Trump: Even His Misdeals Are Winning Hands," *USA Today*, October 4, 1988, 11B.

24. Day, *S&L Hell*, 303.

25. Tully, "I'm Tom Barrack."

26. Lee Davison, "The Resolution Trust Corporation and Congress, 1989–1993 pt. 1: 1989–1990." *FDIC Banking Review Series* 18, no. 2 (2006): 38–60, https:// ssrn.com/abstract=964489.

27. Stephen Kleege, "Bailout Proved a Bonanza for Some Early-Bird Buyers," *American Banker* online, August 9, 1994, available at Gale online, http:// link.galegroup.com/apps/doc/A15677902/ITOF?u=sfpl_main&sid= ITOF&xid=3bae26db.

28. Tully, "I'm Tom Barrack."

29. Davison, "Resolution Trust Corporation."

30. Kleege, "Bailout Proved a Bonanza."

31. "Financial Audit: Resolution Trust Corporation's 1995 and 1994 Financial Statements," US General Accounting Office, July 2, 1996, www.gao.gov /archive/1996/ai96123.pdf.

32. Tully, "I'm Tom Barrack."

33. Ibid.

Chapter 10: For Infinity

1. Foreclosure data provided to author by ATTOM Data Solutions.
2. Damien Cave, "In Florida, Despair and Foreclosures," *New York Times* online, February 7, 2009, www.nytimes.com/2009/02/08/us/08lehigh.html.
3. John Asbury, "Moreno Valley: Two Guilty in 2009 Gang Rape," *San Bernardino (CA) Sun* online, May 26, 2011, www.pe.com/2011/05/26/moreno -valley-2-guilty-in-2009-gang-rape.
4. Michael Kranish and Jonathan O'Connell, "Kushner's White House Role 'Crushed' Efforts to Woo Investors for NYC Tower," *Washington Post* online, September 13, 2017, www.washingtonpost.com/politics/kushners-white -house-role-crushed-efforts-to-woo-investors-for-nyc-tower/2017/09/13 /723a9732-82c8-11e7-ab27-1a21a8e006ab_story.html.
5. Bill Shaikin, "Tom Barrack, Leon Hindery Are Latest Players in Dodgers Bidding," *Los Angeles Times* online, January 29, 2012, www.latimes.com /sports/la-xpm-2012-jan-29-la-sp-0130-dodgers-bidders-20120130-story.html.
6. Henny Sender, "Colony Capital to Take Over Leibovitz's Loans," *Financial Times* online, March 8, 2010, www.ft.com/content/f8994112-2af0-11df-886b -00144feabdc0.
7. *United States Residential Foreclosure Crisis: Ten Years Later* (Irvine, CA: CoreLogic, March 2017), www.corelogic.com/research/foreclosure-report /national-foreclosure-report-10-year.pdf.
8. "Unemployment in November 2010," *Economics Daily* online, Bureau of Labor Statistics, US Department of Labor, last modified December 7, 2010, www.bls .gov/opub/ted/2010/ted_20101207.htm.
9. Benjamin Wallace, "Monetizing the Celebrity Meltdown," *New York* online, November 24, 2010, http://nymag.com/news/business/69782.
10. US Bureau of Labor Statistics, "Number of Civilians Unemployed for 27 Weeks and Over," last modified April 5, 2019, available at FRED, Federal Reserve Bank of St. Louis, https://fred.stlouisfed.org/series/UEMP27OV.
11. *Residential Foreclosure Crisis*, CoreLogic.
12. "Neighborhood Stabilization Program Basics," US Department of Housing and Urban Development, www.hudexchange.info/programs/nsp/nsp -eligibility-requirements.
13. Foreclosure data provided to author by ATTOM Data Solutions.
14. "Neighborhood Stabilization Program: Best Practices in Early Implementation and Course Correction," presentation, Federal Reserve Bank of Richmond, June 17, 2010, www.hudexchange.info/resources/documents/NSP _EarlyImplementation_CourseCorrection.pdf.
15. Home Loan Bank Board, *Final Report to the Congress of the United States Relating to the Home Owners' Loan Corporation: 1933–1951* (Washington, DC: Government Printing Office, 1952), https://fraser.stlouisfed.org/files /docs/publications/holc/hlc_final_report_1952.pdf.

16. Lorraine Woellert and Clea Benson, "Uncle Sam Is a Reluctant Landlord of Foreclosed Homes," Bloomberg Businessweek on NBCNews.com, last modified September 5, 2011, www.nbcnews.com/id/44375023/ns/business-us _business/t/uncle-sam-reluctant-landlord-foreclosed-homes.

17. *Vacant Properties: Growing Number Increases Communities' Costs and Challenges* (Washington, DC: US General Accounting Office, November 2011), www.gao.gov/assets/590/586089.pdf.

18. "Request for Information: Enterprise/FHA REO Asset Disposition," memorandum, Federal Housing Finance Agency, August 10, 2011, www.fhfa .gov/PolicyProgramsResearch/Policy/Documents/RFIFinal081011.pdf.

19. Barack Obama, "Remarks by the President in a Town Hall Meeting in Atkinson, Illinois," White House, Office of the Press Secretary, August 17, 2011, https://obamawhitehouse.archives.gov/the-press-office/2011/08/17 /remarks-president-town-hall-meeting-atkinson-illinois.

20. Ron Phipps to Shaun Donovan et al., September 15, 2011, available at https:// narfocus.com/billdatabase/clientfiles/172/3/1325.pdf

21. Philip Tegeler et al. to Edward DeMarco, "Re: Affirmatively Furthering Fair Housing in the Disposition of REO Properties," September 15, 2011, available at www.prrac.org/pdf/REO_civil_rights_comments_9-15-11.pdf.

22. Thomas J. Barrack Jr., "Chicago Booth 6th Annual Real Estate Conference: Keynote Address," speech, November 6, 2012, https://vimeo.com/55244828.

23. Sasha Chavkin and Martha M. Hamilton, "Commerce Secretary Wilbur Ross Benefits from Business Ties to Putin's Inner Circle," International Consortium of Investigative Journalists, November 5, 2017, www.icij.org/investigations /paradise-papers/donald-trumps-commerce-secretary-wilbur-ross-and-his -russian-business-ties.

24. Jon Swaine and Ed Pilkington, "The Wealthy Men in Trump's Inner Circle with Links to Tax Havens," *Guardian* (US edition) online, last modified November 5, 2017, www.theguardian.com/news/2017/nov/05/wealthy-men -donald-trump-inner-circle-links-tax-havens.

25. *Paradise Papers: Secrets of the Global Elite* (Washington, DC: International Consortium of Investigative Journalists). Specific Paradise Papers documents cited in this passage were provided by ICIJ to Reveal from the Center for Investigative Reporting as part of the Paradise Papers collaboration and analyzed by the author in December 2017.

26. Fannie Mae documents: "SFR 2012–1 U.S. West: Transaction Summary," n.d., www.homepath.com/content-static/pdf/structuredsales/SFR_2012-1 _USWest/SFR_2012-1_US_West_Transaction_Summary_11-01-12.pdf; "Amended and Restated Operating Agreement," October 31, 2012, www .homepath.com/content-static/pdf/structuredsales/SFR_2012-1_USWest /SFR_2012-1_US_West_LLC_Amended_and_Restated_Operating _Agreement.pdf; "Custodial and Paying Agency Agreement," October 31,

2012, www.homepath.com/content-static/pdf/structuredsales/SFR_2012-1
_USWest/SFR_2012-1_US_West_LLC_Custodial_and_Paying_Agency
_Agreement.pdf.

27. Bloomberg News, "Colony Capital Wins Foreclosed Homes in Fannie Mae
Auction," *Worcester (MA) Telegram,* last modified July 12, 2012, www
.telegram.com/article/20120712/NEWS/107129806.

28. Thomas J. Barrack Jr., interview by Betty Liu, transcript, Bloomberg TV, March 20,
2012, available at Gale online, http://go.galegroup.com/ps/i.do?p=AONE&u=sfpl
_main&id=GALE|A283624698&v=2.1&it=r&sid=AONE&asid=6b0d61ba.

Chapter 11: Son of a Linen Store Owner

1. Elaine Misonzhnik, "House Money," *National Real Estate Investor,* July 1,
2014, available at Gale online, http://link.galegroup.com/apps/doc
/A378275525/ITOF?u=sfpl_main&sid=ITOF&xid=b5500fed.

2. "The World's Billionaires: #296, Bradley Hughes," *Forbes* online, last modified
March 5, 2008, www.forbes.com/lists/2008/10/billionaires08_Bradley
-Hughes_AZEA.html.

3. Zachary Kussin, "Public Storage Founder Races to Catch Blackstone in US
Rental Acquisition Sprint," *Real Deal* online, last modified February 13, 2013,
https://therealdeal.com/2013/02/13/public-storage-founder-races-to-catch
-blackstone-in-u-s-rental-acquisition-sprint.

4. American Homes 4 Rent, "Form 10-K: Annual Report, 2013," filed with US
Securities and Exchange Commission, March 26, 2014, www.sec.gov
/Archives/edgar/data/1562401/000119312514116022/d644538d10k.htm.

5. "Real Estate Developer and 'Grave Dancer' Sam Zell: 'It's All About Supply
and Demand,'" *Knowledge@Wharton,* Wharton School of the University of
Pennsylvania, last modified September 19, 2007, http://knowledge.wharton
.upenn.edu/article/real-estate-developer-and-grave-dancer-sam-zell-its-all
-about-supply-and-demand.

6. Alan Murray, "As the Cheap-Money Party Rages, Will It Get Too Loud for the
Fed?," *Wall Street Journal* (Europe edition), February 4, 2007, 6.

7. David Carey and John E. Morris, *King of Capital: The Remarkable Rise, Fall,
and Rise Again of Steve Schwarzman and Blackstone* (New York: Crown
Business, 2010), 298.

8. Terry Pristin, "After Acquiring Equity Office, Blackstone Begins Selling It,"
New York Times online, February 10, 2007, www.nytimes.com/2007/02/10
/business/10real.html.

9. Jennifer S. Forsyth, "Deutsche Bank in Real Estate Deal," *Wall Street Journal*
(Europe edition), February 1, 2008, 6.

10. Carey and Morris, *King of Capital,* 28.

11. Andrew Clark, "The *Guardian* Profile: Stephen Schwarzman," *Guardian* (US

edition) online, last modified June 15, 2007, www.theguardian.com
/business/2007/jun/15/4.

12. Selwyn Raab and Carol Vogel, "Antique Fortress: A Special Report; Park
Avenue Armory Is Losing the Battle Within," *New York Times* online,
March 6, 1998, www.nytimes.com/1998/03/06/arts/antique-fortress-a-special
-report-park-ave-armory-is-losing-the-battle-within.html.

13. "Bradley Martin Ball: Not So Many Guests Attended the Function at the
Waldorf as Had Been Expected," *New York Times* online, February 11, 1897,
www.nytimes.com/1897/02/11/archives/bradley-martin-ball-not-so-many
-guests-attended-the-function-at-the.html?searchResultPosition=12.

14. *The Gilded Age*, directed by Sarah Colt, written by Mark Zwonitzer, aired
February 6, 2018, on PBS, www.pbs.org/wgbh/americanexperience/films
/gilded-age.

15. Michael J. de la Merced, "Inside Stephen Schwarzman's Birthday Bash," *New
York Times* online, February 14, 2007, https://dealbook.nytimes.com/2007
/02/14/inside-stephen-schwarzmans-birthday-bash.

16. Erika Harwood, "Melania Trump's Beauty Team Is Planning Its Own White
House Takeover," *Vanity Fair* online, January 13, 2017, www.vanityfair.com
/style/2017/01/melania-trump-white-house-glam-room.

17. Jacob Bernstein, "Eye Scoop," *Women's Wear Daily*, February 15, 2007, 4.

18. "The New King of Wall Street: Steve Schwarzman of Blackstone Wants to Buy
Your Company and Has a $125 Billion War Chest to Do It," *Fortune*, March 5,
2007, cover headline and subhead.

19. Henny Sender and Monica Langley, "How Blackstone's Chief Became $7
Billion Man," *Wall Street Journal* online, June 13, 2007, www.wsj.com/articles
/SB118169817142333414.

20. "On the Inside, Steve Schwarzman Is Still Just a Short Kid from Philly,"
Intelligencer, *New York* online, February 4, 2008, http://nymag.com
/intelligencer/2008/02/on_the_inside_steve_schwarzman.html.

21. "The Blackstone Tax," Review and Outlook, *Wall Street Journal*, June 20,
2007, A16.

22. Center for Responsive Politics, OpenSecrets.org, s.v. "Blackstone Group,
Lobbying" www.opensecrets.org/orgs/lobby.php?id=D000021873.

23. Mark DeCambre, "The Party's Over," *New York Post* online, October 31, 2008,
https://nypost.com/2008/10/31/the-partys-over-2.

24. James B. Stewart, "The Birthday Party: How Stephen Schwarzman Became
Private Equity's Designated Villain," *New Yorker* online, February 4, 2008,
www.newyorker.com/magazine/2008/02/11/the-birthday-party-2.

25. Stephen Schwarzman, interview by David Rubenstein, transcript, Economic
Club of Washington, September 15, 2015, www.economicclub.org/sites
/default/files/transcripts/Stephen%20Schwarzman%20Transcript1.pdf.

26. "Davenport Hosts Dancing Lovelies," *Yale Daily News*, February 29, 1968, 3.

27. Stewart, "Birthday Party."

28. Carey and Morris, *King of Capital*, 84.

29. Ibid., 85.

30. "Ohio Nuptials for Ellen J. Philips," *New York Times* online, December 30, 1971, www.nytimes.com/1971/12/30/archives/ohio-nuptials-for-ellen-j -philips.html.

31. Judith H. Dobryzynski, "A Corporate Wife Holds Out for a 50–50 Split of Assets," *New York Times* online, January 24, 1997, www.nytimes .com/1997/01/24/business/a-corporate-wife-holds-out-for-a-50–50-split-of -assets.html.

32. "Weddings: Mrs. Schwarzman and Mr. Katz," *New York Times* online, September 28, 1997, www.nytimes.com/1997/09/28/style/weddings-mrs -schwarzman-and-mr-katz.html.

33. Gross, *740 Park*, 506.

34. Robin Pogrebin, "A $100 Million Donation to the New York Public Library," *New York Times* online, March 11, 2008, www.nytimes.com/2008/03/11/arts /design/11expa.html.

35. Frank Rich, "Obama's Original Sin," *New York* online, July 1, 2011, http:// nymag.com/news/frank-rich/obama-economy/presidents-failure.

36. Marc Santora, "After Big Gift, a New Name for the Library," *New York Times* online, April 23, 2008, www.nytimes.com/2008/04/23/nyregion/23library .html.

37. Adams, *The Epic of America*, 414.

38. Zachery Kouwe, "Droppin' Bombs," *New York Post* online, May 9, 2008, https://nypost.com/2008/05/09/droppin-bombs.

39. Yu Hui-yong and John Gittelsohn, "With Latest Foray, Blackstone Could Be Your Next Landlord," *Washington Post*, July 11, 2012, A4.

40. Shira Ovide, "BankUnited IPO: Who Got Rich?" *Wall Street Journal* online, January 28, 2011, https://blogs.wsj.com/deals/2011/01/28/bankunited-ipo -who-got-rich.

41. Robin Sidel, "Schwarzman: None of Your Business," *Wall Street Journal* online, January 20, 2012, www.wsj.com/articles/SB1000142405297020375040 4577171302192177174.

42. Michael J. de la Merced, "Schwarzman's Unfortunate War Analogy," *New York Times* online, August 16, 2010, https://dealbook.nytimes.com/2010/08/16 /schwarzmans-unfortunate-war-analogy.

Chapter 12: Loading the Boat

1. Home price data from: S&P Dow Jones Indices, "S&P/Case-Shiller AZ-Phoenix Home Price Index," last revised March 26, 2019, accessed at FRED, Federal Reserve Bank of St. Louis, https://fred.stlouisfed.org/series

/PHXRNSA; foreclosure data provided to author by ATTOM Data Solutions.

2. "Blackstone Sees Two-Year Window to Buy Distressed Homes," *Mortgage Servicing News*, January 1, 2013, 23.

3. Ibid.

4. Jade Rahmani and Ryan Tomasello, "Securitization of Single-Family Rentals," *Mortgage Banking*, February 2014, available at Gale online, http://link.galegroup.com/apps/doc/A360359328/ITOF?u=sfpl_main&sid=ITOF&xid=4ce6e51c.

5. Blackstone, "Blackstone Reports Third Quarter 2012 Results," press release, October 18, 2012, https://s1.q4cdn.com/641657634/files/doc_presentations/2012/Blackstone3Q12EarningsPressRelease.pdf.

6. "The Story of Treehouse Realty," episode seven, *Arizona Real Estate Show*, November 21, 2014, on Radio Public, https://radiopublic.com/arizona-real-estate-radio-shows-p-Wl2Ngw/ep/s1!8a2ac.

7. Robbie Whelan, "Firms Flock to Foreclosure Auctions," *Wall Street Journal* online, September 12, 2012, www.wsj.com/articles/SB10000872396390443696604577644700448760254.

8. Ibid.

Chapter 13: Life on a Lease

1. "An Overview of Reverse Mortgage History," graphic, National Reverse Mortgage Lenders Association, July 9, 2018, www.nrmlaonline.org/2018/07/09/an-overview-of-reverse-mortgage-history.

2. "Rating Action: Moody's Rates the First US Reverse Mortgage Deal Aaa," Moody's Investors Service online, last modified August 24, 1999, www.moodys.com/research/MOODYS-RATES-THE-FIRST-US-REVERSE-MORTGAGE-DEAL-Aaa-PR_30694; "SASCO 1999-RM1: One for the Record Books," National Reverse Mortgage Lenders Association online, last modified June 27, 2014, www.nrmlaonline.org/2014/06/27/sasco-1999-rm1-one-for-the-record-books.

3. "Rating Action: Moody's Rates the First."

4. American Homeownership and Economic Opportunity Act of 2000, Pub. L. No. 106–569, 114 Stat. 2944 (2000).

5. Emergency Supplemental Appropriations Act for Defense, the Global War on Terror, and Tsunami Relief of 2005, Pub. L. No. 109–13, 119 Stat. 300, sec. 6074 (2005); Department of Defense Appropriations Act of 2007, Pub. L. No. 109–289, 120 Stat. 1316, sec. 131 (2006).

6. Libby Perl, *HUD's Reverse Mortgage Insurance Program: Home Equity Conversion Mortgages* (Washington, DC: Congressional Research Service, March 31, 2017), https://fas.org/sgp/crs/misc/R44128.pdf.

7. *A Turning Point in the History of HUD's Home Equity Conversion Mortgage Program* (Washington, DC: US Department of Housing and Urban

Development, Office of Policy Development and Research, Spring 2008), www
.huduser.gov/periodicals/ushmc/spring08/ch1.pdf.

8. Ibid.

9. US Department of Justice, "Four Student Aid Lenders Settle False Claims Act Suit for Total of $57.75 Million," press release, November 17, 2010, www .justice.gov/opa/pr/four-student-aid-lenders-settle-false-claims-act-suit-total -5775-million.

10. "Tony West: Chief Legal Officer," Uber website biography, www.uber.com /newsroom/leadership/tony-west.

11. US Attorney's Office, Middle District of Florida, "Middle District of Florida's Civil Division Advances Reverse Mortgage Fraud Enforcement Initiative by Resolving Civil Fraud Claims Against Tarpon Springs Condominium Complex Owner," press release, July 20, 2017, www.justice.gov/usao-mdfl/pr /middle-district-florida-s-civil-division-advances-reverse-mortgage-fraud -enforcement.

Chapter 14: A Bungalow in Los Angeles

1. Patrick Bayer, Fernando Ferreira, and Stephen L. Ross, "What Drives Racial and Ethnic Differences in High-Cost Mortgages? The Role of High-Risk Lenders" (working paper 22004, Cambridge, MA: National Bureau of Economic Research, February 2016), www.nber.org/papers/w22004.

2. Carlos Garriga, Lowell R. Ricketts, and Don E. Schlagenhauf, "The Homeownership Experience of Minorities During the Great Recession," *Federal Reserve Bank of St. Louis Review* 99, no. 1 (February 15, 2017): 139–67, https://files.stlouisfed.org/files/htdocs/publications/review/2017-02-15/the -homeownership-experience-of-minorities-during-the-great-recession.pdf.

3. "Table 1. Median Value of Assets for Households, by Type of Asset Owned and Selected Characteristics: 2014," downloaded from the US Census Bureau website, last revised September 17, 2018, www.census.gov/data/tables/2014 /demo/wealth/wealth-asset-ownership.html.

4. Neil R. McMillen, *Dark Journey: Black Mississippians in the Age of Jim Crow* (Champaign: University of Illinois Press, 1990), 24.

5. Author's analysis of 1940 census data from the IPUMS system: Steven Ruggles et al., Integrated Public Use Microdata Series, version 8.0 dataset (Minneapolis: IPUMS, 2018), last revised March 26, 2019, https://doi .org/10.18128/D010.V8.0.

6. Rothstein, *Color of Law*, 43, 60.

7. Herbert Hoover, "Address to the White House Conference on Home Building and Homeownership," speech, December 2, 1931, www.presidency.ucsb.edu /documents/address-the-white-house-conference-home-building-and-home -ownership.

8. All quotes from HOLC redlining maps from: Robert K. Nelson et al., "Mapping Inequality," in *American Panorama*, ed. Robert K. Nelson and Edward L. Ayers, accessed March 27, 2019, https://dsl.richmond.edu /panorama/redlining/#loc=4/36.71/-96.93&opacity=0.8&text=bibliograph.

9. Nelson et al., "Mapping Inequality."

10. Federal Housing Administration, *Underwriting Manual: Underwriting and Valuation Procedure Under Title II of the National Housing Act* (Washington, DC: Government Printing Office, 1936), available at https://babel.hathitrust .org/cgi/pt?id=mdp.39015018409246;view=1up;seq=1.

11. "African Americans in World War II: Fighting for a Double Victory," published in conjunction with an exhibition at the National WWII Museum, New Orleans, opened July 4, 2015, www.nationalww2museum.org/sites /default/files/2017–07/african-americans.pdf.

12. "Research Starters: U.S. Military by the Numbers," student resource, National WWII Museum, www.nationalww2museum.org/students-teachers/student -resources/research-starters/research-starters-us-military-numbers.

13. "Fighting for a Double Victory."

14. Haskel Burns, "Camp Shelby: 100 Years of History," *Hattiesburg American* online, July 8, 2017, www.hattiesburgamerican.com/story/news/local /2017/07/08/camp-shelby-100-years-history/420019001.

15. Franklin D. Roosevelt, "Statement on Signing the G.I. Bill," June 22, 1944, www.presidency.ucsb.edu/documents/statement-signing-the-gi-bill.

16. Nicholas Lemann, *The Promised Land: The Great Black Migration and How It Changed America* (New York: Knopf, 1991), 6.

17. Isabel Wilkerson, The *Warmth of Other Suns: The Epic Story of America's Great Migration* (New York: Random House, 2010), 9.

18. Ibid., 187.

19. Nelson et al., "Mapping Inequality."

20. Gerald Horne, *The Fire This Time: The Watts Uprising and the 1960s* (Charlottesville: University of Virginia Press, 1995), 27.

21. Ibid., 3.

22. Michael Powell, "Bank Accused of Pushing Mortgage Deals on Blacks," *New York Times* online, June 6, 2009, www.nytimes.com/2009/06/07/us/07 baltimore.html.

23. US Department of Justice, "Justice Department Reaches Settlement with Wells Fargo Resulting in More Than $175 Million in Relief for Homeowners to Resolve Fair-Lending Claims," press release, July 12, 2012, www.justice.gov /opa/pr/justice-department-reaches-settlement-wells-fargo-resulting-more -175-million-relief.

24. George Soros, *The New Paradigm for Financial Markets: The Credit Crisis of 2008 and What It Means* (New York: Public Affairs, 2008), 149.

25. Analysis of HMDA data by author.

26. Analysis of HMDA data by author; analysis of foreclosures by California Reinvestment Coalition.

27. California Reinvestment Coalition, "CIT Group Accused of Redlining and Violating Fair Housing Act," press release, November 18, 2016, http://calreinvest.org/press-release/cit-group-accused-of-redlining-and-violating-fair-housing-act.

28. Meredith Abood, "Securitizing Suburbia: The Financialization of Single-Family Rental Housing and the Need to Redefine 'Risk'" (master's thesis, Massachusetts Institute of Technology, 2017), 94.

Chapter 15: Time to Make a Deal

1. Examples include: Yuma Energy, "Form 10-K: Annual Report, 2015," filed with US Securities and Exchange Commission, May 23, 2016, www.sec.gov/Archives/edgar/data/81318/000135448816007616/yuma_10ka.htm; PostRock Energy, "PostRock Finalizes New Credit Facility," press release, December 20, 2012, available at www.sec.gov/Archives/edgar/data/1473061/000119312512513087/d458065dex992.htm; Sanchez Production Partners, "Form 10-K: Annual Report, 2014," filed with US Securities and Exchange Commission, March 5, 2015, www.sec.gov/Archives/edgar/data/1362705/000136270515000010/spp-20141231x10k.htm.

2. Corinthian Colleges et al., "Fourth Amended and Restated Credit Agreement," filed with US Securities and Exchange Commission, May 17, 2012, www.sec.gov/Archives/edgar/data/1066134/000110465912038883/a12-12544_1ex10d1.htm.

3. Danielle Douglas-Gabriel, "Embattled For-Profit Corinthian Colleges Closes Its Doors," *Washington Post* online, April 26, 2015, www.washingtonpost.com/news/business/wp/2015/04/26/embattled-for-profit-corinthian-colleges-closes-its-doors.

4. Gene Maddaus, "Judge Dismisses Steven Mnuchin from Relativity Lender's Fraud Suit," *Variety* online, June 28, 2017, https://variety.com/2017/film/news/steven-mnuchin-relativity-rka-dismiss-lawsuit-fraud-1202481305.

5. James Rufus Koren, "Steven Mnuchin's OneWest Favored Private Equity Firms, Did Little Small-Business Lending," *Los Angeles Times* online, January 19, 2017, www.latimes.com/business/la-fi-mnuchin-onewest-lending-20170117-story.html.

6. Colony Financial, "Lending Agreement," filed with US Securities and Exchange Commission, August 6, 2013, www.sec.gov/Archives/edgar/data/1467076/000119312513327010/d582135dex101.htm.

7. Colony Financial, "Lending Agreement"; lending figures from author's analysis of HMDA data.

8. Ocwen Financial, "Form 8-K: Current Report," filed with US Securities and

Exchange Commission, June 13, 2013, www.sec.gov/Archives/edgar/data/873860/000101905613000776/ocn_8k.htm.

9. Consumer Financial Protection Bureau, "CFPB, State Authorities Order Ocwen to Provide $2 Billion in Relief to Homeowners for Servicing Wrongs," website newsroom, December 19, 2013, last updated June 24, 2014, www.consumerfinance.gov/about-us/newsroom/cfpb-state-authorities-order-ocwen-to-provide-2-billion-in-relief-to-homeowners-for-servicing-wrongs.

10. "CFPB, State Authorities Order Ocwen."

11. Greg Farrell and Henny Sender, "The Shaming of John Thain," *Financial Times* online, March 13, 2009, www.ft.com/content/c1b3ac7e-0ec1-11de-ba10-0000779fd2ac.

12. Landon Thomas Jr., "Behind-the-Scenes Technocrat Takes Top Billing at Big Board," *New York Times* online, December 19, 2003, www.nytimes.com/2003/12/19/business/behind-the-scenes-technocrat-takes-top-billing-at-big-board.html.

13. Liz Moyer, "Timeline: The Rise and Fall and Rise of John Thain," *New York Times* online, October 21, 2015, www.nytimes.com/2015/10/22/business/dealbook/the-rise-and-fall-and-rise-of-john-thain.html.

14. Noam Scheiber, "The Brain in Thain," *New York* online, December 21, 2006, http://nymag.com/nymag/features/25991/index.html.

15. Barack Obama, "Remarks by the President Before Bipartisan Meeting on the Economy with Democratic and Republican Congressional Leadership," White House, January 23, 2009, https://obamawhitehouse.archives.gov/realitycheck/the-press-office/remarks-president-bipartisan-meeting-economy.

16. Bair, *Bull by the Horns*, 5.

17. Moyer, "Rise and Fall and Rise."

18. Tomoeh Murakami Tse, "CIT's Bankruptcy Raises New Questions About Bailout," *Washington Post* online, November 16, 2009, www.washingtonpost.com/wp-dyn/content/article/2009/11/15/AR2009111502280.html.

19. Michael J. de la Merced, "After Turmoil at Merrill, Thain Will Lead the Lender CIT," *New York Times* online, February 7, 2010, www.nytimes.com/2010/02/08/business/08thain.html.

20. Andrew R. Johnson, "Lender Is Prepared to Be 'Important,'" *Wall Street Journal*, June 26, 2014, C3.

21. Communications and documents regarding CIT acquisition of OneWest obtained from the Federal Reserve System by the author through the Freedom of Information Act, 2014, available at www.documentcloud.org/documents/5978920–2014–380-CIT-OneWest-Application-and-Related.html.

22. Financial statements for: IndyMac Federal Bank FSB, July 11, 2008–December 31, 2017; LaJolla Bank, FSB, February 19, 2010–December 31, 2017; www.documentcloud.org/documents/5783901-IndyMac-LJB-Loss-Share.html.

23. "Q2 2014 CIT Group Earnings Call," transcript, *Fair Disclosure Wire*,

July 22, 2014, available at http://go.galegroup.com/ps/i.do?p=ITOF&u=sfpl_main&id=GALE|A377533674&v=2.1&it=r&sid=ITOF&asid=31dcee2c.

24. Communications and documents from the Federal Reserve System.

25. "Q2 2014 CIT Group Earnings Call."

26. Michael J. de la Merced, "Two Banks Forged in U.S. Crisis Are Set to Merge, to Big Payoff," *New York Times*, July 23, 2014, B1.

27. Ibid., footnote 28.

28. LinkedIn, s.v. "Allen Puwalski, CFA," public profile, www.linkedin.com/in/allenpuwalski.

29. CIT Group, "Form 4: Statement of Changes in Beneficial Ownership," filed with US Securities and Exchange Commission, August 5, 2015, www.sec.gov/Archives/edgar/data/1171825/000112760215024249/xslF345/form4.xml.

30. CIT Group, "Schedule 14A: Proxy Statement," filed with US Securities and Exchange Commission, March 30, 2017, www.sec.gov/Archives/edgar/data/1171825/000089109217002703/e73548def14a.htm.

Chapter 16: The Community Fights Back

1. "Chasm Between Words and Deeds VIII: Lack of Bank Accountability Plagues California," California Reinvestment Coalition, April 2012, available at www.documentcloud.org/documents/5978998-Chasm-Between-Words-and-Deeds-VIII-Lack-of-Bank.html.

2. US Department of the Treasury, "HAMP Application Activity by Servicer, As of June 2014," accessed at FRASER, Federal Reserve Bank of St. Louis, https://fraser.stlouisfed.org/title/5156/item/519646.

3. Steven Sugarman, memorandum, August 25, 2014, available at http://calreinvest.org/wp-content/uploads/2018/08/Banc-of-California-CRA-Plan.pdf.

4. Matt Pressberg, "Activists' Protest on the Money: Coalition Scores Concessions in Lender Unions," *Los Angeles Business Journal*, October 20, 2014.

5. Wade Tyler Millward, "Man Who Oversees Country's Biggest Banks Lives in Las Vegas," *Las Vegas Review-Journal* online, May 5, 2018, www.reviewjournal.com/business/man-who-oversees-countrys-biggest-banks-lives-in-las-vegas.

6. Paul Kiel, "Bank Bailout Count: $171 Billion, 40 Banks," ProPublica, November 5, 2008, www.propublica.org/article/bank-bailout-count-171-billion-40-banks.

7. Federal Deposit Insurance Corporation, "U.S. Bank Acquires All the Deposits of Two Southern California Institutions," press release PR-124-2008, last modified November 21, 2008, www.fdic.gov/news/news/press/2008/pr08124.html.

8. Federal Deposit Insurance Corporation, "Bid Summary, California National

Bank, Los Angeles, CA, Closing Date: October 30, 2009," last modified August 15, 2011, www.fdic.gov/bank/individual/failed/calnational-bid -summary.html.

9. OneWest Bank, "OneWest Bank Names Joseph Otting President, Chief Executive Officer and a Member of the Board," press release, October 27, 2010, available on BusinessWire.com, www.businesswire.com/news /home/20101027006123/en/OneWest-Bank-Names-Joseph-Otting-President -Chief.

10. Millward, "Man Who Oversees."

11. CIT Group, "Form 8-K: Current Report," filed with US Securities and Exchange Commission, July 25, 2014, www.sec.gov/Archives/edgar /data/1171825/000089109214005596/e59749_8k.htm.

12. Orson Aguilar to Janet Yellen et al., "Strong Opposition to CIT Group Application to Acquire IMB and OneWest Bank," October 10, 2014, available at http://greenlining.org/wp-content/uploads/2014/10/Greenlining-Formal -Opposition-Letter-to-CIT-Group-Incs-Application-to-Acquire-OneWest -Bank.pdf.

13. Marshall Heyman, "Art and Film Fete Attracts New York Crowd," *Wall Street Journal* online, November 4, 2013, www.wsj.com/articles/art-and-film-fete -attracts-new-york-crowd-1383537812.

14. Los Angeles County Museum of Art, "LACMA Elects Heather Mnuchin to Board of Trustees," press release, November 14, 2012, www.lacma.org/sites /default/files/Heather-Mnuchin-Board-Appointment-11.14.12_0.pdf.

15. Museum Associates (LACMA), "Form 990: Return of Organization Exempt from Income Tax, 2014," filed with Internal Revenue Service, April 13, 2016, www.lacma.org/sites/default/files/LACMA_FORM_990_-_PUBLIC _Inspection_copy_for_website.pdf.

16. E. Scott Reckard, "Groups Urge U.S. to Reject CIT Takeover of OneWest Bank," *Los Angeles Times* online, October 14, 2014, www.latimes.com /business/la-fi-onewest-cit-protest-20141014-story.html.

17. "Orders Issued Under Section Three of the Bank Holding Company Act," *Federal Reserve Bulletin* 102, no. 1 (January 2016): 2, www.federalreserve.gov /pubs/bulletin/2015/pdf/legalq315.pdf.

18. Marshall Heyman, "Public Hearing Planned on Proposed Sale of OneWest Bank to CIT Group," *Los Angeles Times* online, February 6, 2015, www .latimes.com/business/la-fi-onewest-hearing-20150207-story.html.

19. California Reinvestment Coalition to Joseph Otting and John Thain, September 15, 2014; letters from member organizations of CRC, available at www.federalreserve.gov/bankinforeg/Comment_Letters_10-10-14_to__10-13 -14_part_2.pdf.

20. Kevin Smith, "Protesters Gather to Oppose OneWest Merger with CIT Group," *San Gabriel Valley (CA) Tribune*, December 16, 2014, www

.sgvtribune.com/2014/12/16/protesters-gather-to-oppose-onewest-merger
-with-cit-group.

21. Rachel Louise Ensign and Ryan Tracy, "Bankers vs. Activists: Battle Lines
Form Over Low Income, Lending Law," *Wall Street Journal* online, September
2, 2018, www.wsj.com/articles/mnuchins-fight-with-activists-inspired
-community-reinvestment-act-revamp-1537885753.

22. Federal Reserve System online, "Order Approving the Acquisition of a Bank
Holding Company," FRB order no. 2015–20, July 19, 2015, www
.federalreserve.gov/newsevents/pressreleases/files/orders20150721a1.pdf.

23. Zachary Mider and Saleha Mohsin, "The Mess Steven Mnuchin Left Behind,"
Bloomberg Businessweek, December 16, 2016, available at Blendle, https://
blendle.com/i/bloomberg-businessweek/the-mess-steve-mnuchin-left
-behind/bnl-bloombergbw-20161219-112801?sharer=eyJ2ZXJzaW9uIjoiMSIsI
nVpZCI6InBoaWxpcGJhc2hlIiwiaXRlbV9pZCI6ImJubC1ibG9vbWJlcmdidy0
yMDE2MTIxOS0xMTI4MDEifQ%3D%3D.

24. CIT Group, "Form 10-K: Annual Report, 2015," filed with US Securities and
Exchange Commission, March 4, 2016, www.sec.gov/Archives/edgar
/data/1171825/000089109216013044/e68394_10k.htm.

25. Michael J. de la Merced, "John Thain of CIT Group Will Step Down as Chief
Executive," *New York Times* online, October 21, 2015, www.nytimes
.com/2015/10/22/business/dealbook/john-thain-of-cit-group-will-step-down
-as-chief-executive.html; Rachel Louise Ensign, "CIT Chief John Thain Takes
9 Percent Pay Cut on His Way Out," *Wall Street Journal* online, March 21,
2016, www.wsj.com/articles/cit-chief-john-thain-takes-9-pay-cut-on-his-way
-out-1458588182.

26. Analysis of HMDA data by author.

Chapter 17: The New Debt Bundles

1. Jade Rahmani and Ryan Tomasello, "Securitization of Single-Family Rentals,"
Mortgage Banking, February 2014, 76, available at Gale online, http://link
.galegroup.com/apps/doc/A360359328/ITOF?u=sfpl_main&sid=ITOF&
xid=4ce6e51c.

2. "Blackstone's Single-Family Breakthrough Sparks 'Killer' Interest," *Total
Securitization*, October 28, 2013, available at www.globalcapital.com/article
/jjn477f80wb4/blackstones-single-family-breakthrough-sparks-killer-interest.

3. "Q3 2013 Colony Financial Earnings Conference Call," transcript, *Fair
Disclosure Wire*, November 8, 2013.

4. Kroll Bond Rating Agency, "Colony American Homes 2014–1," presale report,
March 20, 2014, available at www.housingwire.com/ext/resources/files
/Editorial/document1.pdf.

5. Fannie Mae, "Form 1004: Uniform Appraisal Report Form," March 2005,
www.fanniemae.com/content/guide_form/1004.pdf.

6. Radian Group, "Form 10-Q: Quarterly Report, First Quarter 2017," see "Item 1. Legal Proceedings," filed with US Securities and Exchange Commission, May 5, 2017, www.sec.gov/Archives/edgar/data/890926/000089092617000022 /rdn10q03312017.htm#s4438037F9C7556F5AED6F8A09F76FA0E.

7. Green River Capital, "Certification of Services Performed," filed with US Securities and Exchange Commission, May 16, 2016, www.sec.gov/Archives /edgar/data/1631651/000153949716002967/exh_99-1.htm.

Chapter 18: Too Big to Fail

1. "Wilson's Speech of Acceptance," *The Protectionist* (Boston: Home Market Club) 24, no. 5 (September 1912), 268.

2. Louis D. Brandeis, "Chapter 1: Our Financial Oligarchy," in *Other People's Money and How the Bankers Use It*, serialized in *Harper's Weekly*, November 22, 1913–January 17, 1914, available at https://louisville.edu/law/library/special -collections/the-louis-d.-brandeis-collection/other-peoples-money-chapter-i.

3. Ibid.

4. Eric Dash, "Dimon Lives Up to J. Pierpont Morgan's Legacy," *New York Times* online, March 18, 2008, www.nytimes.com/2008/03/18/business /worldbusiness/18iht-dimon.1.11211648.html.

5. Steven M. Davidoff, "JPMorgan's $12 Billion Bailout," *New York Times* online, March 18, 2008, https://dealbook.nytimes.com/2008/03/18/jpmorgans-12 -billion-bailout.

6. JPMorgan Chase, "Acquisition of Assets, Deposits and Certain Liabilities of Washington Mutual's Banks," investor presentation, September 25, 2008, www.sec.gov/Archives/edgar/data/19617/000119312508201638/dex992.htm.

7. Roger Lowenstein, "Jamie Dimon: America's Least-Hated Banker," *New York Times Magazine* online, December 1, 2010, www.nytimes.com/2010/12/05 /magazine/05Dimon-t.html.

8. Jonathan Stempel, "JPMorgan Ends WaMu Disputes with FDIC, to Receive $645 Million," Reuters online, last modified August 19, 2016, www.reuters .com/article/us-jpmorgan-settlement-washing-mut-bk-idUSKCN10U28M.

9. Patricia Crisafulli, *The House of Dimon: How JPMorgan's Jamie Dimon Rose to the Top of the Financial World* (Hoboken, NJ: John Wiley & Sons, 2009), 53.

10. Duff McDonald, *Last Man Standing: The Ascent of Jamie Dimon and JPMorgan Chase* (New York: Simon & Schuster, 2009), 1.

11. Ibid., 3.

12. Crisafulli, *House of Dimon*, 54.

13. McDonald, *Last Man Standing*, 3.

14. Ibid., 21.

15. Senate Comm. on Banking and Currency, *The Pecora Investigation: Stock Exchange Practices and the Causes of the 1929 Crash* (New York: Cosimo Reports, 2010), 6.

16. "The Long Demise of Glass-Steagall," published in conjunction with *The Wall Street Fix*, written and produced by Hedrick Smith and Rick Young, directed by Young, on PBS, aired on May 8, 2003, www.pbs.org/wgbh/pages/frontline /shows/wallstreet/weill/demise.html.

17. Dan Wilchins and Jonathan Stempel, "Citigroup Gets Massive Government Bailout," Reuters, November 23, 2008, www.reuters.com/article/us-citigroup /citigroup-gets-massive-government-bailout-idUSTRE4AJ45G20081124.

18. Katrina Brooker, "Citi's Creator, Alone with His Regrets," *New York Times* online, January 2, 2010, www.nytimes.com/2010/01/03/business /economy/03weill.html.

19. "Sandy Weill: Time to Change Glass-Steagall," interview, CNBC, July 25, 2012, www.cnbc.com/video/2012/07/25/sandy-weill-time-to-change-glass -steagall-act.html.

20. JPMorgan Chase, "2018 Annual Report," April 2019, www.jpmorganchase .com/corporate/investor-relations/document/annualreport-2018.pdf.

21. "Dimon full interview," CNBC, August 1, 2016, www.cnbc.com/video/2016 /08/01/dimon-full-interview.html.

22. JPMorgan Chase, "Annual Report."

23. "Q2 2014 JPMorgan Chase Earnings Conference Call," transcript, *Fair Disclosure Wire*, July 15, 2014.

24. United States Department of Justice, "JPMorgan Chase to Pay $514 Million for Submitting False Claims for FHA-insured and VA-guaranteed Mortgage Loans," press release 14-120, last modified September 15, 2014, www.justice .gov/opa/pr/jpmorgan-chase-pay-614-million-submitting-false-claims-fha -insured-and-va-guaranteed-mortgage.

25. "Q2 2014 JPMorgan Chase."

26. The six mortgage-backed securities are: CAH 2014–1 Borrower LLC, CAH 2014–2 Borrower LLC, SWAY 2014–1 Borrower LLC, CAH 2015–1 Borrower LLC, CSH 2016–1 Borrower LLC, CSH 2016–1 Borrower LLC.

27. Patricia Martell, "The 'Kind' and 'Humble' Side of Trump," CNBC online, last modified February 1, 2016, www.cnbc.com/2016/02/01/the-kind-and-humble -side-of-donald-trump-countdown-to-iowa-caucus.html.

28. Federal Election Commission, Campaign Finance Data, s.v. "Rebuilding America Now," financial summary, April 1–December 31, 2016, www.fec .gov/data/committee/C00618876/?cycle=2016; 58th Presidential Inauguration Committee, "Form 13, Report of Donations Accepted," filed with Federal Election Commission, April 18, 2017, http://docquery.fec.gov/pdf/286/2017041 80300150286/201704180300150286.pdf.

29. Dylan Matthews, "Why Paul Manafort Pleaded Guilty to 'Conspiracy Against the United States,'" Vox.com, March 13, 2019, www.vox .com/2018/9/14/17860410/conspiracy-against-the-united-states-paul -manafort-plea.

30. Michael Rothfeld, "Manafort Got Loans Throgh Ex-Trump Aide," *Wall Street Journal* (Eastern Edition), New York, NY, March 31, 2017, A.6.
31. Indictment. United States of America v. Paul J. Manafort Jr. and Richard W. Gates III, Case 1:17-cr-00201-ABJ Document 13, filed December 30, 2017, www.justice.gov/file/1007271/download.
32. CSH 2016–1 Borrower LLC.
33. Mark David, "Colony Capital's Thomas J. Barrack Jr. Hangs High Price on Santa Monica Mansion," *Variety* online, August 8, 2016, https://variety.com/2016/dirt/real-estalker/thomas-barrack-colony-capital-santa-monica-mansion-1201832827.
34. "Executive Branch Personnel: Public Financial Disclosure Report (OGE Form 278e): Puzder, Andrew F, Secretary, Department of Labor," US Office of Government Ethics, February 8, 2017, available at www.documentcloud.org/documents/6167252-Puzder-Andrew-F-final278.html; Marianne Levine and Timothy Noah, "Exclusive: Puzder's ex-wife told Oprah he threatened 'you will pay for this,'" February 15, 2017, www.politico.com/story/2017/02/puzder-oprah-winfrey-labor-235030.

Chapter 19: An Early Vulture

1. Jana Kasperkevic, "Trump's Band of Economic Advisers: Six Steves and Few Former Enemies," *Guardian* (US edition) online, last modified August 5, 2016, www.theguardian.com/us-news/2016/aug/05/donald-trump-economic-advisers.
2. Michelle Celarier, "Meet the Wall Street Titans Who Back Trump," Intelligencer, *New York* online, June 22, 2016, http://nymag.com/intelligencer/2016/06/meet-the-wall-street-titans-who-back-trump.html; Alexandra Stevenson, "A Who's Who of Financiers is Expected at Trump's New York Fund-Raiser," *New York Times* online, June 16, 2016, www.nytimes.com/2016/06/17/business/dealbook/a-whos-who-of-financiers-is-expected-at-trumps-new-york-fund-raiser.html.
3. Donald Trump, campaign rally speech, Kissimmee, Florida, August 11, 2016, on Right Side Broadcasting Network, www.youtube.com/watch?v=EVkFnc3Msbk.
4. "Trump Explains Why He 'Didn't Like' the Phrase 'Drain the Swamp' but Now Does," video, *Washington Post*, October 26, 2016, www.washingtonpost.com/video/politics/trump-explains-why-he-didnt-like-the-expression-drain-the-swamp-but-now-does/2016/10/26/4a2f257a-9be0-11e6-b552-b1f85e484086_video.html.
5. Federal Reserve Board, public meeting transcript, Los Angeles, February 26, 2015, www.federalreserve.gov/bankinforeg/citgroup-onewest-meeting-transcript-20150226_Part1.pdf.
6. Nerja Investments, "Form LLC-12: Statement of Information (Limited Liability Company)," filed with California Secretary of State, September 24,

2018, https://businesssearch.sos.ca.gov/Document/RetrievePDF?Id =200919610015-24890153.

7. "Trump Voter Lost Her Home, Blames Trump's Pick for Treasury Secretary," MSNBC online, last modified December 2, 2016, www.msnbc.com/all-in /watch/trump-voter-lost-her-home-blames-trump-s-pick-for-treasury -secretary-823502403634.

8. "Many Starter Homes Have Shifted from Owner-Occupancy to Rentals," Fannie Mae, Economic and Strategic Research, October 17, 2016, www .fanniemae.com/resources/file/research/datanotes/pdf/housing -insights-101816.pdf.

9. Alden Whitman, "A Builder Looks Back—and Moves Forward," *New York Times* online, January 28, 1973, www.nytimes.com/1973/01/28/archives/a -builder-looks-backand-moves-forward-builder-looks-back-but-moves.html.

10. Gwenda Blair, *The Trumps: Three Generations of Builders and a President* (New York: Simon & Schuster, 2015), 109.

11. Ibid., 128.

12. Wayne Barrett, *Trump: The Greatest Show on Earth: The Deals, the Downfall, the Reinvention* (New York: Regan Books, 2016), 32.

13. Blair, *The Trumps*, 130.

14. Barrett, *Greatest Show*, 33.

15. Blair, *The Trumps*, 136.

16. "Act to Force Lehrenkrauss Creditor List," *Brooklyn (NY) Daily Eagle*, February 9, 1934, 1; "150 Lehrenkrauss Creditors Form Protection Group," *Brooklyn (NY) Daily Eagle*, February 22, 1934, 1.

17. Blair, *The Trumps*, 136.

18. "Builders Get Plaque FHA: Officials Attend Opening of Brooklyn Model Home," *New York Times*, August 12, 1936, 36.

19. Brooklyn Section B6 at: Robert K. Nelson et al., "Mapping Inequality," in *American Panorama*, ed. Robert K. Nelson and Edward L. Ayers, accessed March 27, 2019, https://dsl.richmond.edu/panorama /redlining/#loc=13/40.6480/-73.9310&opacity=0.8&sort=99&adview=full&city =brooklyn-ny&area=B6&adimage=3/75/-111.

20. "Seek 'Home' Slogan for Motor Plates: Builders Ask Aid of Governor and Mayor in Ownership Drive," *New York Times*, May 14, 1939, 4.

21. Senate Comm. on Banking and Currency, *FHA Investigation: Report Pursuant to S. Res. 229* (Washington, DC: Government Printing Office, 1954), 8, available at www.washingtonpost.com/wp-stat/graphics/politics/trump -archive/docs/fha-investigation-report-by-senate-banking-comm-earlier -version.pdf.

22. Harry S. Truman, "263. Statement by the President Outlining the Housing Program for 1947," letter, December 14, 1946, available at www.trumanlibrary .org/publicpapers/index.php?pid=1833&st=&st1=.

23. Senate Comm. on Banking and Currency, *FHA Investigation: Hearings Pursuant to S. Res. 229*, vol. 4 (Washington, DC: Government Printing Office, 1954), 882, available at www.washingtonpost.com/wp-stat/graphics/politics/trump-archive/docs/fha-investigation-1954-part-4.pdf.

24. Senate Comm. on Banking and Currency, *FHA Investigation: Hearings*, vol. 2, 123, available at www.washingtonpost.com/wp-stat/graphics/politics/trump-archive/docs/fha-investigation-1954-part-2.pdf.

25. Bair, *Bull by the Horns*, 171.

26. "1,600 Car Garage for Trump Houses," *Brooklyn (NY) Daily Eagle*, December 11, 1949, 37.

27. "Happenings of Interest Around and About the Borough," *Brooklyn (NY) Daily Eagle*, May 13, 1950, 3.

28. Eunice Grier, George W. Grier, and the Commission on Race and Housing, *Privately Developed Interracial Housing: An Analysis of Experience* (Berkeley: University of California Press, 1960), 123–24.

29. "Warren Criticizes 'Class' Parades: Police Head Declares Neither Facisti nor Klan Had Any Place in Memorial March," *New York Times* online, June 1, 1927, 16, www.nytimes.com/1927/06/01/archives/warren-criticizes-class-parades-police-head-declares-neither.html.

30. Will Kaufman, *Woody Guthrie's Modern World Blues* (Norman: University of Oklahoma Press, 2017), 27–28.

31. Nora Guthrie, *My Name Is New York: Ramblin' Around Woody Guthrie's Town* (New York: powerHouse Books, 2012), 70.

32. Kaufman, *Modern World Blues*, 218–20.

33. Will Kaufman, "In Another Newly Discovered Song, Woody Guthrie Continues His Assault on 'Old Man Trump,'" The Conversation, last modified September 5, 2016, http://theconversation.com/in-another-newly-discovered-song-woody-guthrie-continues-his-assault-on-old-man-trump-64221.

34. Senate Comm., *FHA Investigation: Hearings*, vol. 2, 123.

35. Senate Comm., *FHA Investigation: Hearings*, vol. 1, 395–417, available at www.washingtonpost.com/wp-stat/graphics/politics/trump-archive/docs/fha-investigation-1954-part-1.pdf.

36. David Barstow, Suzanne Craig, and Russ Buettner, "Trump Engaged in Suspect Tax Schemes as He Reaped Riches from His Father," *New York Times* online, October 2, 2018, 36, www.nytimes.com/interactive/2018/10/02/us/politics/donald-trump-tax-schemes-fred-trump.html.

37. Senate Comm. on Banking and Currency, "Special Interview to Investigate Federal Housing Administration," executive session transcript, Washington, DC, June 18, 1954, available at www.washingtonpost.com/wp-stat/graphics/politics/trump-archive/docs/fred-trump-fha-special-interview.pdf.

38. Barrett, *Greatest Show*, 73.

39. Blair, *The Trumps*, 237.

40. Materials from an FBI investigation (1972–74) of the Trump Management Company, obtained through the Freedom of Information Act, vol. 1, 37–38, 54–57, available at https://vault.fbi.gov/trump-management-company /Trump%20Management%20Company%20Part%2001%20of%2008/view.

41. Materials from an FBI investigation, 37–38, 54–57.

42. Ibid., 60–64.

43. "Civil Rights Protector: John Stanley Pottinger," *New York Times* online, March 30, 1974, www.nytimes.com/1974/03/30/archives/civil-rights -protector-john-stanley-pottinger-an-early-job.html.

44. Materials from an FBI investigation, 37–38.

45. Ibid.

46. Materials from an FBI investigation (1972–74) of the Trump Management Company, obtained through the Freedom of Information Act, vol. 3, 53, available at www.documentcloud.org/documents/6143968-Trump -Management-Company-Part-03-of-03.html.

47. Morris Kaplan, "Major Landlord Accused of Antiblack Bias in City," *New York Times* online, October 16, 1973, www.nytimes.com/1973/10/16 /archives/major-landlord-accused-of-antiblack-bias-in-city-us-accuses -major.html.

48. Margot Hornblower et al., "Roy Cohn Is Disbarred by New York Court," *Washington Post* online, June 24, 1986, www.washingtonpost.com/archive /politics/1986/06/24/roy-cohn-is-disbarred-by-new-york-court/c5ca9112 -3245-48f0-ab01-c2c0f3c3fc2e.

49. Barrett, *Greatest Show*, 83.

50. Ibid.

51. Prince George's County property records, obtained by the author. Deed: www .documentcloud.org/documents/5980356-PG-Record.html, FHA Loan: www .documentcloud.org/documents/5980354-PG-Loan-1961.html.

52. Michael E. Miller and Michael Kranish, "Donald Trump First Swept into the Nation's Capital 40 Years Ago. It Didn't Go Well," *Washington Post* online, October 21, 2016, www.washingtonpost.com/local/donald-trump-first-swept -into-the-nations-capital-40-years-ago-it-didnt-go-well/2016/10/21 /934b07b8-8f08-11e6-9c52-0b10449e33c4_story.html.

53. Karen DeYoung, "NY Owner of PG Units Seized in Code Violations," *Washington Post*, September 30, 1976, C1.

54. Ibid.

55. Miller and Kranish, "Donald Trump First Swept."

56. Judy Klemesrud, "Donald Trump, Real Estate Promoter, Builds Image as He Buys Buildings," *New York Times* online, November 1, 1976, www.nytimes .com/1976/11/01/archives/donald-trump-real-estate-promoter-builds-image -as-he-buys-buildings.html.

Chapter 20: Trump University

1. Patrick Cole, "Trump Unveils Online University: Venture Bearing His Name Will Start Offering Classes This Week," *Orlando (FL) Sentinel*, May 24, 2005, C3.
2. "Trump Leaps into Higher Education," *Morning Edition*, National Public Radio, February 21, 2006.
3. "Interview with Former FBI Agent Greg Esslinger," *International Wire*, Fox News, May 23, 2005.
4. Jon Ward, "Meet Jon Ward," website biography, www.jonward.net/more-about-jon.
5. Donald Trump, *How to Build a Fortune: Your Plan for Success from the World's Most Famous Businessman* (New York: Trump University, 2006), Audible audiobook.
6. Dolf de Roos et al., *Bubble-Proof Real Estate Investing: Wealth-Building Strategies for Uncertain Times* (New York: Trump University, 2006), Audible audiobook.
7. De Roos, *Bubble-Proof Real Estate Investing*.
8. Eyder Peralta, "New York AG Sues Donald Trump over 'Unlicensed' University," *The Two-Way*, National Public Radio, August 24, 2013, www.npr.org/sections/thetwo-way/2013/08/25/215454970/new-york-a-g-sues-donald-trump-over-unlicensed-university.
9. Chris Isidore, "Ex-employees on Trump University: 'A Fraudulent Scheme' and 'a Total Lie,'" CNN Money online, last modified June 1, 2016, https://money.cnn.com/2016/06/01/news/trump-university-employees/index.html.
10. Stephanie Saul, "Trump University's Checkered Past Haunting Candidate," *New York Times* online, February 26, 2016, www.nytimes.com/2016/02/27/us/donald-trump-marco-rubio-trump-university.html.
11. Michael Biesecker, "Trump U Staff Included Drug Trafficker, Child Molester," Associated Press online, October 27, 2016, www.apnews.com/1566b9e1ca44464db34de22e09aa5ea9.
12. New York State Office of the Attorney General, "Statement by AG Schneiderman on $25 Million Settlement Agreement Reached in Trump University Case," press release, November 18, 2016, https://ag.ny.gov/press-release/statement-ag-schneiderman-25-million-settlement-agreement-reached-trump-university.
13. Donald Trump (@realDonaldTrump), Twitter, November 19, 2016, 5:34 am., https://twitter.com/realdonaldtrump/status/799969130237542400.

Chapter 21: Triumph of the Homewreckers

1. Donald Trump, "The Inaugural Address," White House, January 20, 2017, www.whitehouse.gov/briefings-statements/the-inaugural-address.

2. David D. Kirkpatrick, "Who Is Behind Trump's Links to Arab Princes? A Billionaire Friend," *New York Times* online, June 13, 2018, www.nytimes.com/2018/06/13/world/middleeast/trump-tom-barrack-saudi.html; David Graham, "Why Trump Can't Find Anyone to Be His Chief of Staff," *Atlantic* online, December 10, 2018, www.theatlantic.com/politics/archive/2018/12/trump-chief-staff-nick-ayers/577762.

3. Olivia Nuzzi, "Donald Trump and Sean Hannity Like to Talk Before Bedtime," Intelligencer, *New York* online, May 14, 2018, http://nymag.com/intelligencer/2018/05/sean-hannity-donald-trump-late-night-calls.html.

4. Laura M. Holson, "Camels, Acrobats and Team Trump at a Billionaire's Gala," *New York Times* online, February 14, 2017, www.nytimes.com/2017/02/14/fashion/stephen-schwarzman-billionaires-birthday-draws-team-trump.html.

5. Amanda L. Gordon, "Schwarzman Parties at 70 with Camels, Cake and Trump's Entourage," Bloomberg, last modified February 13, 2017, www.bloomberg.com/news/articles/2017-02-13/schwarzman-parties-at-70-with-camels-cake-and-trump-s-entourage.

6. Ibid.

7. Laura M. Holson, "A Palm Beach Power Hostess Prepares for Trump's Washington," *New York Times* online, February 11, 2017, www.nytimes.com/2017/02/11/style/hilary-geary-ross-wilbur-ross-donald-trump-washington-society.html.

8. Rebecca Harrington, "Inside the Extravagant Wedding of Treasury Secretary Steve Mnuchin and 36-Year-Old Actress Louise Linton," *Business Insider* online, last modified June 25, 2017, www.businessinsider.com/steve-mnuchin-louise-linton-wedding-dress-trump-pence-photos-2017-6; Katie Rogers, "A Weekend Wedding for the Treasury Secretary," *New York Times*, June 25, 2017, ST12.

9. Rachelle Barrack vs. Thomas J. Barrack Jr., Los Angeles Superior Court Case #BD644726, filed August 16, 2016.

10. Leena Kim, "All the Jewels Louise Linton Wore to Her Wedding," *Town and Country* online, June 19, 2017, www.townandcountrymag.com/the-scene/weddings/a9933935/louise-linton-wedding-jewelry.

11. Robin Givhan, "Louise Linton Just Spelled Out Her Value System for You Common Folk," *Washington Post* online, August 22, 2017, www.washingtonpost.com/news/arts-and-entertainment/wp/2017/08/22/louise-linton-just-spelled-out-her-value-system-for-you-common-folk; Yashar Ali (@yashar), Twitter, August 21, 2017, 6:25 P.M., https://twitter.com/yashar/status/899804610256351233/photo/1.

12. Sam Dangremond, "See Inside Treasury Secretary Steven Mnuchin's $12.6 Million Washington Home," *Town and Country* online, July 18, 2017, www.townandcountrymag.com/leisure/real-estate/g10325252/steven-mnuchin-washington-house; Redfin, s.v. "2600 Rock Creek Drive NW, Washington, DC

20008," accessed April 25, 2019, www.redfin.com/DC/Washington/2600
-Rock-Creek-Dr-NW-20008/home/10174286.

13. Rogers, "Weekend Wedding."

14. Washington, DC, Office of Tax and Revenue, Real Property Assessment, available at www.documentcloud.org/documents/6144321-Wilbur-Ross -Assessment.html.

15. Federal Deposit Insurance Corporation, "FDIC Quarterly Banking Profile – Fourth Quarter 2018," February 21, 2019, www.fdic.gov/news/news/speeches /spfeb2119.html.

16. Jamie Dimon, "Chairman and CEO Jamie Dimon's Letter to Shareholders," JPMorgan Chase, April 4, 2019, https://reports.jpmorganchase.com/investor -relations/2018/ar-ceo-letters.htm?a=1#.

17. JPMorgan Chase, "Form 8-L: Current Report," filed with the US Securities and Exchange Commission, January 15, 2019, www.sec.gov/Archives/edgar /data/19617/000001961719000006/form8-kcompensation2019.htm.

18. Robert McClelland, "Fixing the TCJA: Restoring the Estate Tax's Exemption Levels," Tax Policy Center, March 20, 2019, www.taxpolicycenter.org/taxvox /fixing-tcja-restoring-estate-taxs-exemption-levels.

19. Drew Harwell and Jonathan O'Connell, "The Many Ways President Trump Would Benefit from the GOP's Tax Plan," *Washington Post* online, November 10, 2017, www.washingtonpost.com/business/economy/the-many-ways -president-trump-would-benefit-from-the-gops-tax-plan/2017/11/10 /d82c8116-c4ba-11e7-aae0-cb18a8c29c65_story.html.

20. Congress of the United States, Joint Committee on Taxation, Tables Related to the Federal Tax System as in Effect 2017 through 2026, April 23, 2018, page 6, table 3A, www.jct.gov/publications.html?func=startdown&id=5091.

21. Donald Trump, "Form 278e: Executive Branch Personnel Public Financial Disclosure Report," filed with US Office of Government Ethics, May 16, 2016, available at https://assets.documentcloud.org/documents/2838665/5-18-16 -Report.pdf.

22. Alec MacGillis, "The Beleaguered Tenants of 'Kushnerville,'" ProPublica, last modified May 23, 2017, www.propublica.org/article/the-beleaguered-tenants -of-kushnerville.

23. Kate Davidson, "Treasury Secretary Steve Mnuchin: GOP Tax Plan Would More Than Offset Its Cost," *Wall Street Journal* online, September 28, 2017, www.wsj.com/articles/treasury-secretary-steven-mnuchin-gop-tax-plan -would-more-than-offset-its-cost-1506626980.

24. Katia Dmetrieva, "Trump Budget Sees $1 Trillion Deficits for Next Four Years," Bloomberg, last modified March 11, 2019, www.bloomberg.com/news /articles/2019-03-11/trump-2020-budget-sees-1-trillion-deficits-for-next-four -years.

25. Diana Olick, "Government's Fannie Mae Will Back PE Giant Blackstone's

Rental Homes Debt," CNBC online, last modified January 25, 2017, www.cnbc
.com/2017/01/25/governments-fannie-mae-will-back-pe-giant-blackstones
-rental-business-debt.html.

26. Kate Berry, "CFPB's Mulvaney Strips His Fair Lending Office of Enforcement
Powers," *American Banker* online, February 1, 2018, www.americanbanker
.com/news/cfpbs-mulvaney-strips-his-fair-lending-office-of-enforcement
-powers; Kate Berry, "CFPB Takes Big Step Toward Unwinding Payday Lending
Rule," *American Banker* online, February 6, 2019, www.americanbanker.com
/news/cfpb-takes-big-step-toward-unwinding-payday-lending-rule.

27. Erin McCormick, "Ben Carson's Housing Agency Drops Pledge to End
Housing Discrimination," *Guardian* (US edition) online, March 7, 2018, www
.theguardian.com/us-news/2018/mar/07/ben-carson-housing-department
-mission-statement-discrimination-inclusion.

28. Office of the Assistant Secretary for Fair Housing and Equal Opportunity,
HUD, "Reconsideration of HUD's Implementation of the Fair Housing Act's
Disparate Impact Standard," June 20, 2018 www.federalregister.gov
/documents/2018/06/20/2018-13340/reconsideration-of-huds-implementation
-of-the-fair-housing-acts-disparate-impact-standard.

29. Department of the Treasury, Office of Comptroller of the Currency,
"Reforming the Community Reinvestment Act Regulatory Framework,"
September 9, 2018, www.federalregister.gov/documents/2018/09/05
/2018–19169/reforming-the-community-reinvestment-act-regulatory-
framework.

30. Office of Comptroller of the Currency, OCC Bulletin 2018-23, "Revisions to
Impact of Evidence of Discriminatory or Other Illegal Credit Practices on
Community Reinvestment Act Ratings," August 15, 2018, www.occ.gov/news
-issuances/bulletins/2018/bulletin-2018-23.html.

31. Economic Growth, Regulatory Relief and Consumer Protection Act, Public
Law No: 115–174, www.congress.gov/bill/115th-congress/senate-bill/2155
/actions.

32. Donald Trump, "Remarks by the President Trump at Signing of S.2155,
Economic Growth, Regulatory Relief and Consumer Protection Act," White
House, May 24, 2018, www.whitehouse.gov/briefings-statements
/remarks-president-trump-signing-s-2155-economic-growth-regulatory
-relief-consumer-protection-act.

33. Elora Raymond et al., "Corporate Landlords, Institutional Investors, and
Displacement: Eviction Rates in Single-Family Rentals," Federal Reserve Bank
of Atlanta, Community and Economic Development Discussion Paper Series,
December 2016, www.frbatlanta.org/-/media/documents/community
-development/publications/discussion-papers/2016/04-corporate-landlords
-institutional-investors-and-displacement-2016-12-21.pdf.

34. "Colony Starwood Homes 2016-1 Trust," presale analysis, Morningstar

Credit Ratings, May 19, 2016, available at www.documentcloud.org
/documents/3762492-Colony-Starwood-Homes-CSH-2016-1-Borrower-LLC
.html.

35. Riis, *How the Other Half Lives*, 22.

36. Colony Capital, "Colony Capital Announces Fourth Quarter and Full Year
2018 Financial Results," Exhibit 99.1, filed with US Securities and Exchange
Commission, March 1, 2019, www.sec.gov/Archives/edgar/data/1679688
/000167968819000011/exhibit9912018q4pressrelea.htm.

37. Calendar of Treasury Secretary Steve Mnuchin obtained using the Freedom of
Information Act by the author, page 127, www.documentcloud.org
/documents/5980353-Secretary-Steven-Mnuchin-Calendar.html.

38. Charles D. Young, statement, on behalf of Colony Starwood Homes, n.d.,
available at www.documentcloud.org/documents/3859853-Colony-Starwood
-Homes-Statement-for-the-Center.html.

Epilogue: A Path to Shared Prosperity

1. Aaron Glantz, "3 Investigations Opened after Reveal Uncovers Redlining in
Philly," Reveal, February 22, 2019, www.revealnews.org/blog/3-investigations
-opened-after-reveal-uncovers-redlining-in-philly.

2. Aaron Glantz, "We Exposed Modern-Day Redlining in 61 Cities. Find Out
What's Happened Since," Reveal, October 25, 2019, www.revealnews.org
/blog/we-exposed-modern-day-redlining-in-61-cities-find-out-whats
-happened-since.

3. Aaron Glantz and Emmanuel Martinez, "State Attorneys General Probe
Lending Disparities," Reveal, March 13, 2018, www.revealnews.org/blog/state
-attorneys-general-probe-lending-disparities.

4. Brandeis, "Our Financial Oligarchy."

5. Emmanuel Saez and Gabriel Zucman, "Wealth Inequality in the United States
since 1913: Evidence from Capitalized Income Tax Data," *Quarterly Journal of
Economics* 131, no. 2 (May 2016): 519–78, https://eml.berkeley.edu/~saez/.

6. Ibid.

7. Home Loan Bank Board, "Final Report to the Congress of the United States
Relating to the Home Owners' Loan Corporation: 1933–1951" (Washington,
DC: Government Printing Office, 1952), available at https://fraser.stlouisfed
.org/files/docs/publications/holc/hlc_final_report_1952.pdf.

8. The President's Commission on Veterans Pensions, "Findings and
Recommendations: Veterans Benefits in the United States" (Washington, DC:
April 1956), 301, www.va.gov/vetdata/docs/Bradley_Report.pdf.

9. Mehrsa Baradaran, "A Homestead Act for the 21st Century," May 2019 (The
Great Democracy Initiative), https://greatdemocracyinitiative.org/wp
-content/uploads/2019/05/Homestead-Act-050719.pdf.

10. FDIC, "FDIC 2018 Annual Report" (Washington, DC: Government Printing

Office) 86, www.fdic.gov/about/strategic/report/2018annualreport/2018ar
-final.pdf.

11. Aaron Glantz and Emmanuel Martinez, "Sen. Warren's Bill Is Designed to
    Combat Modern-Day Redlining," Reveal News, September 26, 2018, www
    .revealnews.org/blog/sen-warren-offers-bill-overhauling-bank-laws
    -combating-racial-discrimination.

12. "The World's Billionaires: #100, Steve Schwarzman" *Forbes* online, May 13,
    2019, www.forbes.com/profile/stephen-schwarzman/#5094d76b234a.

13. Adams, *The Epic of America*, 404.

14. Ibid., 416.

15. "Q2 2016 CIT Group Earnings Conference Call," transcript, *Fair Disclosure
    Wire*, July 28, 2016, available at http://ir.cit.com/Cache/1500089036.
    PDF?O=PDF&T=&Y=&D=&FID=1500089036&iid=102820.

16. US Department of Justice, "Financial Freedom Settles Alleged Liability for
    Servicing of Federally Insured Reverse Mortgage Loans for $89 Million," press
    release, May 16, 2017, www.justice.gov/opa/pr/financial-freedom-settles
    -alleged-liability-servicing-federally-insured-reverse-mortgage.

BIBLIOGRAPHY

Adams, James Truslow. *The Epic of America*. Boston: Little, Brown, 1959. First published 1931 by Little, Brown (Boston).

Bair, Sheila. *Bull by the Horns: Fighting to Save Main Street from Wall Street and Wall Street from Itself*. New York: Free Press, 2012.

Baker, Dean. *Plunder and Blunder: The Rise and Fall of the Bubble Economy*. Sausalito, CA: PoliPoint Press, 2009.

Baradaran, Mehrsa. *The Color of Money: Black Banks and the Racial Wealth Gap*. Cambridge, MA: Belknap Press of Harvard University Press, 2017.

Barrett, Wayne. *Trump: The Greatest Show on Earth: The Deals, the Downfall, the Reinvention*. New York: Regan Books, 2016.

Blair, Gwenda. *The Trumps: Three Generations of Builders and a President*. New York: Simon & Schuster, 2015.

Blinder, Alan. *After the Music Stopped: The Financial Crisis, the Response and the Work Ahead*. New York: Penguin, 2014.

Bovenzi, John F. *Inside the FDIC: Thirty Years of Bank Failures, Bailouts, and Regulatory Battles*. Hoboken, NJ: John Wiley & Sons, 2015.

Brandeis, Louis D. *Other People's Money: And How the Bankers Use It*. New York: Frederick A. Stokes, 1914. Reprinted online by the Louis D. Brandeis School of Law Library, University of Louisville, https://louisville.edu/law/library/special-collections/the-louis-d.-brandeis-collection/other-peoples-money-by-louis-d.-brandeis.

Carey, David, and John E. Morris. *King of Capital: The Remarkable Rise, Fall, and Rise Again of Steve Schwarzman and Blackstone*. New York: Crown Business, 2010.

Chernow, Robert. *House of Morgan: An American Banking Dynasty and the Rise of Modern Finance*. New York: Grove Press, 2010 (20th anniversary ed.).

Crisafulli, Patricia. *The House of Dimon: How JPMorgan's Jamie Dimon Rose to the Top of the Financial World*. Hoboken, NJ: John Wiley & Sons, 2009.

D'Antonio, Michael. *The Truth About Trump*. New York: St. Martin's Press, 2016.

Day, Kathleen. *S&L Hell: The People and the Politics Behind the $1 Trillion Savings and Loan Scandal.* New York: W. W. Norton, 1993.

Dayen, David. *Chain of Title: How Three Ordinary Americans Uncovered Wall Street's Great Foreclosure Fraud.* New York: New Press, 2016.

Desmond, Matthew. *Evicted: Poverty and Profit in an American City.* New York: Crown, 2016.

Freeland, Chrystia. *Plutocrats: The Rise of the New Super Rich and the Fall of Everyone Else.* New York: Penguin Press, 2012.

Greenburg, Zack O'Malley. *Michael Jackson, Inc.: The Rise, Fall, and Rebirth of a Billion Dollar Empire.* New York: Atria Books, 2014.

Gross, Michael. *740 Park: The Story of the World's Richest Apartment Building.* New York: Broadway Books, 2005.

Hiltzik, Michael A. *The New Deal: A Modern History.* New York: Free Press, 2011.

Horne, Gerald. *The Fire This Time: The Watts Uprising and the 1960s.* Charlottesville: University of Virginia Press, 1995.

Kaufman, Will. *Woody Guthrie's Modern World Blues.* Norman: University of Oklahoma Press, 2017.

Kranish, Michael, and Marc Fisher. *Trump Revealed: An American Journey of Ambition, Ego, Money, and Power.* New York: Scribner, 2016.

Lewis, Michael. *Liars Poker: Rising Through the Wreckage of Wall Street.* New York: W. W. Norton, 2010. First published 1989 by W. W. Norton (New York).

McDonald, Duff. *Last Man Standing: The Ascent of Jamie Dimon and JPMorgan Chase.* New York: Simon & Schuster, 2009.

O'Toole, Patricia. *The Moralist: Woodrow Wilson and the World He Made.* New York: Simon & Schuster, 2018.

Riis, Jacob. *How the Other Half Lives: Studies Among the Tenements in New York.* New York: Penguin, 1997. First published 1890 by Charles Scribner's Sons (New York).

Rosenberg, Hilary. *The Vulture Investors: The Winners and Losers of the Great American Bankruptcy Feeding Frenzy.* New York: Harper Business, 1992.

Rothstein, Richard. *The Color of Law: A Forgotten History of How Our Government Segregated America.* New York: W. W. Norton, 2017.

Soros, George. *The New Paradigm for Financial Markets: The Credit Crisis of 2008 and What It Means.* New York: Public Affairs, 2008.

Stiglitz, Joseph E. *Freefall: America's Free Markets, and the Sinking of the World Economy.* New York: W. W. Norton, 2010.

Wilkerson, Isabel. *The Warmth of Other Suns: The Epic Story of America's Great Migration.* New York: Random House, 2010.

Wood, Edith Elmer. *Recent Trends in American Housing.* New York: Macmillan, 1931.

Zuckerman, Gregory. *The Greatest Trade Ever: The Behind-the-Scenes Story of How John Paulson Defied Wall Street and Made Financial History.* New York: Broadway Books, 2009.

INDEX